Personal Destinies

Personal Destinies

A Philosophy of Ethical Individualism

By David L. Norton

PRINCETON UNIVERSITY PRESS

Copyright © 1976 by Princeton University Press

Published by Princeton University Press, Princeton, New Jersey
In the United Kingdom: Princeton University Press,
Chichester, West Sussex

Library of Congress Cataloging in Publication Data
will be found on the last printed page of this book

Publication of this book has been aided by
The Andrew W. Mellon Foundation

Princeton University Press books are printed on acid-free paper
and meet the guidelines for permanence and durability of the
Committee on Production Guidelines for Book Longevity of the
Council on Library Resources

Printed in the United States of America

ISBN 0-691-07215-9
ISBN 0-691-01975-4 (pbk.)

5   7   9   10   8   6   4

Contents

Beloved Pan, and all ye other
gods who haunt this place, give
me beauty in the inward soul;
and may the outward and
inward man be at one.
Socrates, *Phaedrus* 279

Preface

Responding (we may suppose) to admirers who ascribed his achievements to his genius, Thomas Edison dryly observed that genius is "ninety-nine percent perspiration and one percent inspiration." Similarly, when Isaac Newton was asked how he had been able to discover the mechanical principles of the universe, he answered, *Nocte dieque incubando*—"By thinking about it day and night."

What is most significant about these statements is that they abolish the fixed distance commonly thought to separate the "genius" from the ordinary human being. For although sustained attention may be rare, given life's multifarious distractions, it is not occult. And no person can be thought to be incapable of what Edison termed "perspiration," nor indeed of "inspiration" in the minimal amount cited.

This implied proximity of genius to ordinary personhood is true to the etymology of the word "genius." In classical Roman belief, *genii* were the tutelary gods or attendant spirits allotted to all persons at birth, determining the character and governing the fortune of each individual. The Greek equivalent of *genius* is *daimon*, and "eudaimonism" is the term for the ethical doctrine (which achieved its first systematic formulation in the words of Socrates and the writings of Plato and Aristotle) that each person is obliged to know and live in truth to his *daimon*, thereby progressively actualizing an excellence that is his innately and potentially. Our aim in the present study is to present eudaimonism* in a form that, while preserving fidelity to

---

* In chapters to follow the term *eudaimonism* is sometimes replaced by *perfectionism* or *self-actualization ethics* according to

ix

the spirit and profound principles of the classical formulation, extends and in certain respects modifies it for service
to contemporary life.

Beneath the accretions of contravening epochs and cultures a vestige of the original eudaimonistic intuition endures today, I believe, in the individual's residual conviction
of his own irreplaceable worth. But this small conviction
is wholly unequipped to withstand the drubbing it takes
from the world, and from which all too often it never
recovers. At its first appearance it is buffeted by alarms and
commotion, and trampled beneath the scurrying crowd.
Propped upright it is conscripted to this cause or that
where roll call is "by the numbers," truth is prescribed, and
responsibility is collective, the individual's share being determined by arithmetic apportionment. What remains is a
merely numerical individuation, deriving its fugitive worth
from the collective whole of which it is a replaceable part.

The individual's small intuition of his own irreplaceable
worth, however, is the intimation of an individuation of an
altogether different sort from the merely numerical, namely
qualitative individuation that renders each person unique
in his (in the Greek term) *arete*, or personal excellence.
Qualitative individuation is held by eudaimonism to be the
foundation of norms of social life that are self-supporting
because they are the expression of the meaningful living of
individuals, which in turn is the expression of love. In the
Socratic meaning, love (*eros*) is the aspiration to higher
value. It connects every actual individual to his *daimon*, or
innate excellence, constituting his self-enlistment in the service of that value for which he is uniquely responsible and
which, as a variety of goodness, subsists in the relationship
of complementarity with all other human excellences.

The treachery is that as a potential awaiting progressive

context. The terms are used as synonymous basically, differing only
in emphasis and feeling. Formally and inclusively I employ the
term *normative individualism.*

actualization, qualitative individuality, though it may be a powerful force in the end, is weak and tentative in the beginning. Through long exercise of self-discipline the integrity of the mature person possesses the tensile strength of moral necessity, the inner imperative "I must." But at its first expression it is timorous and untested, and in this condition it is no match for the juggernaut that is the world. From this recognition it follows that the meaningful living that is conditioned upon self-truth and self-responsibility will seldom occur in the world until it receives nurture in its earliest intimations by supportive cultural institutions. Today, on the contrary, our cultural institutions—predominant among them that of public education—work directly to stifle individuation in its early stages. Partly this approach results from our need to educate and otherwise manage our young *en masse* (although in due course we shall argue that this need does not preclude the nurture of individuation). But active opposition also exists and is firmly rooted—for example, in the supposition that the stability of social relations demands priority for the respects in which persons replicate one another and are thus indistinguishable. (Against this we shall argue for the superiority of social relations founded in the complementarity of diverse excellences.) The approach is likewise firmly rooted in the supposition that "natural endowments" are conferred by birth only upon a privileged few, leaving the majority empty-handed, and rendering an education predicated upon the universality of natural endowments a waste of time and effort, or a subterfuge of elitism. This belief is sufficiently widespread to qualify as "common sense." Noteworthy personal excellence appears to be uncommon in the world. But we must notice that this incontrovertible truth is equally compatible with the supposition that "natural endowments" are universally distributed, yet often are unactualized. Not only is widespread waste of natural endowments a predictable consequence of cultural neglect, but it is transparently true that beneath our general sophistication today lingers an ingrained parochialism in our inability to recognize and to affirm the bountiful variety of human values. Unlike the botanist's enthusiasm for floral diversity, or the appreciation for the diversification of the aviary by the ornithologist, whatever axiological diversity that by happenstance may be manifested in the human sphere is greeted for the most part by suspicion and disparagement. This, we shall argue, is parochialism, calling for the direct intervention of skillfully designed educational programs. But such programs require foundation in determinate conceptions of personhood, of the world, of life, of good growth—in short, they require philosophy. And that is what it is the business of our study to provide, namely the philosophical foundation for the patterns of education and the types of cultural institutions that can effectively nurture the full variety and complementarity of individual human destinies.

Eudaimonism is this foundation, for by its conception of the essential nature of the person, "natural endowments" (innate potential excellences, daimons) are universalized. Potentials are dispositional properties, constituting the "hidden side" of personhood that is its metaphysical distinction; personhood is not a thing. As Abraham Maslow says, personhood has its future within it, active at the present moment. As a dispositional property, this potentiality cannot be shown empirically to exist, and can be ascribed to a person only retrospectively, by inferring from its present to its past existence: by his manifest ability at mathematics today, for example, an individual is inferred to have possessed the potentiality for good mathematics in childhood. But although there can be no empirical demonstration of the universality of innate potential excellences, it is a priori certain that where such universality is established as a presupposition founding cultural programs, the manifestations of personal excellences in the world will be dramatically increased.

Meanwhile there are isolated individuals in whom the intuition of their own unique potential worth has in some measure proved formative. For them the world's din has not stilled the inner voice, and they are quietly and decisively living their lives according to their own inner imperative. What unfolds in following pages will have served its purpose if a few such persons will find in it what they themselves would wish to say, had the writing of philosophical books been their destiny. As it is my destiny, it is what I can offer to such of these persons as may read my work, in partial repayment for the immeasurable enrichment I have myself received from those persons of this sort that I have known.

A few of the themes I develop have received tentative and provisional treatment in certain of my previously published essays. Germinal ideas of Chapter 1 first appeared in an essay entitled "Daimons and Human Destiny," published in *Centennial Review*, vol. 13, no. 2 (Spring 1969); some of the educational recommendations of Chapter 10 were sketched in "Does God Have a Ph.D.?" *School Review*, vol. 80, no. 1 (Nov. 1971); Chapters 9 and 10 owe a minor debt to my piece (written with Mary K. Norton), "From Law to Love: Social Order as Self-Realization," *Journal of Value Inquiry*, vol. 6, no. 2 (Summer 1972); two or three pages of Chapter 9 are together taken from my pieces, "Social Entailments of the Theory of Self-Actualization," *Journal of Value Inquiry*, vol. 7, no. 2 (Summer 1973), and "Toward an Epistemology of Romantic Love," *Centennial Review*, vol. 14, no. 4 (Fall 1970); and portions of the criticism of Rawls in Chapter 10 appeared in my essay, "Rawls's Theory of Justice: A 'Perfectionist' Rejoinder," in *Ethics*, vol. 85, no. 1 (Oct. 1974). I wish to thank the editors of the respective journals for permission to make use of material published under their auspices.
During the summer of 1972 I was freed of summer teaching by a University of Delaware General Faculty Research

Summer Grant, enabling me to complete preliminary drafts of Chapters 6 and 7. I here express gratitude for the opportunity afforded me by the grant.

What measure of cogency the book possesses must be credited in good part to the skill, the judgment, and the patience of Princeton University Press's Philosophy and Social Science Editor, Sanford G. Thatcher. The book's basic theme is somewhat out of the mainstream of current Anglo-American philosophizing, yet he unerringly perceived its objective and has immeasurably improved its means of getting there. His falcon's eye for proper development, for weak or missing argumentation, and for errata, have straightened and strengthened its course. Likewise he has extended the book's range, most notably by directing me to current work by Thomas Nagel and Robert Nozick. I wish to record my great good fortune at our alliance.

The book has also benefited extensively from the insight and critical acumen of Burleigh T. Wilkins, Professor of Philosophy at the University of California, Santa Barbara, and Professor Paul G. Kuntz, Philosophy, Emory University. By what must have been heroic effort, both men saw virtues in an early draft and were generous enough to give me detailed suggestions, nearly all of which have been incorporated. Professor Wilkins prodded me to greater scrupulosity in argumentation and extricated me from several stylistic mannerisms. Professor Kuntz read a later version of the book as well, and it is largely due to his organizational acumen that my early fits and starts have been worked into something approaching sustained movement.

To my wife, Mary, I owe the profoundest debt, in this endeavor as in every other. I have been sustained throughout by her love, her confidence, and her indomitable spirit. All of the ideas and principles in pages to follow have been continuously refined in discussion with her and in our conjoined work at teaching and writing. Chapter 4, especially, intermingles our ideas, for as it was written, Mary was coincidentally at work upon Sartre for her own purposes.

Personal Destinies

1

The Ethical Priority of
Self-Actualization

I have had much trouble getting along with my ideas. There was a daimon in me, and in the end its presence proved decisive. It overpowered me, and if I was at times ruthless it was because I was in the grip of the daimon. I could never stop at anything once attained. I had to hasten on, to catch up with my vision. Since my contemporaries, understandably, could not perceive my vision, they saw only a fool rushing ahead.

These words by Carl Jung have a twofold significance. They signal a deep human dilemma in the present, and they echo an ancient understanding of life that was the heart of classical humanism but has been lost to recent times. We will examine the classical understanding for what it can offer to present living.

Writing in his late years (the passage is from the autobiographical *Memories, Dreams, Reflections*), Jung speaks of something like an "inner voice" that has constituted the necessity in his life and determined its direction. While it has made him sometimes "ruthless" and cost him friends, it is clear that he nonetheless cannot dispute it and attributes to it responsibility for his achievements.

Strangest to our ears is Jung's very conviction of the presence of the inner voice itself, for most of us today have no sense of an oracle within. Indeed, I offer it as our ranking malaise that that about which we instinctively believe we can be most certain—ourselves—is in fact our sorest bewil-

3

derment. We are apprehensive that an ear turned to our inwardness will detect at most only meaningless murmurings, that a resort to the inner self will be a dizzying tumble into a bottomless pit. Fearing this, we anchor ourselves upon external things, we cast our lot with the fortunes of objects and events that appear to be untainted by the disease of selfhood—if necessary, cleansing them of fingerprints, depersonalizing them in order that they may better bear our weight. Turning our backs to the void, we become infinitely distractable by outward things, prizing those that "demand" our attention. We secretly treasure the atmosphere of world crises, for the mental ambulance-chasing it affords. Meanwhile we armor ourselves with mirrors to deflect the inquiring eyes of others. Asked what I think about something— the movie last night, the painting in the gallery—I borrow words from the newspaper review or desperately scrape the walls of memory for some fragment from a course I took in college.

In short, what Jung seems most confident of, his oracle within, is just that about which most of us altogether lack assurance. We do not know what Jung was talking about, and we rather wish to believe that neither does he.

The other feature that makes the citation interesting is that it chooses for the inner voice the word *daimon*, a word both Greek and pagan. For when I used the term *inner voice*, readers will have thought first of "conscience." But in truth to Jung and our own need, the idea of conscience must be put aside. In the first place, in our cultural setting the idea of conscience carries either a Judeo-Christian or a predominantly Freudian meaning. In both cases it means a voice within the individual that belongs to an authority outside him. Stark as the difference in other respects may be between the voice of God and the voice of the individual's parents and community, for our purposes both are alike in serving to deflect inquiry away from the individual himself, redirecting it to an external authority. And second, "conscience" conveys the meaning of a voice of prohibition, whereas what Jung speaks of and what current life most urgently requires is a voice of constructive determination.

The word *daimon* is at home in classical antiquity, its meaning constituting the nucleus of the Hellenic sensibility to which critical exposition was ultimately given by Socrates, Plato, and Aristotle. The formal and systematic ethics it generates is rightly named eudaimonism. But when we translate *eudaimonia* as "happiness," as we invariably do, we turn the original meaning upside down. For happiness, as we use the word, means extended pleasure, while pleasure is the feeling that attends the gratification of desire; and as extended gratification of long-term desires, happiness is taken to be the supreme aim of living. By the eudaimonist, however, such pleasure and happiness are adjudged useless for the purpose they claim to serve. What the eudaimonist demands to know first is whether the gratified desire is right desire or wrong desire. Because pleasure attends the gratification of right and wrong desires indiscriminately, it offers no guidance to worthwhile living, and, as "pleasure in the long run," happiness is in the same condition. The mistranslation of eudaimonia as "happiness" is therefore fatal to the guidance that true eudaimonia offers. Eudaimonia is both a feeling and a condition. As a feeling it distinguishes right from wrong desire. Moreover it attends right desire, not only upon its gratification, but from its first appearance. Because eudaimonia is fully present to right living at every stage of development, it cannot constitute the aim of such living, but serves instead as merely a mark, a sign. It signals that the present activity of the individual is in harmony with the daimon that is his true self.

In pre-Hellenic Greece, sculptors made busts of the semideity Silenus that had a trick to them. Inside the hollow clay likeness was hidden a golden figurine, to be revealed when the bust was broken open. Toward the conclusion of Plato's *Symposium*, Alcibiades says that Socrates is akin to a bust of Silenus. On the outside he is bald and pot-bellied, and he clothes his thoughts in earthy language; but he who can

5

perceive the Socrates within the clay will cast his eyes on "the most divine." This episode means much more than would a testimonial to the uniqueness of Socrates, made by a drunken Alcibiades. It is a testimonial to the exceptionality of Socrates that makes use of the fundamental Greek conception of personhood. To the Greek understanding not Socrates alone, but every person is a bust of Silenus, inevitably in some degree flawed and misshapen in appearance, but containing inside a golden figurine—one's daimon. (Whether slaves were excluded, as most scholars suppose, is a question to which we shall address ourselves in due course. At present it is sufficient to say that such exclusion would represent the Greek belief that slaves are not persons.)

The exemplariness of Socrates has only begun to serve our theme. As readers of the *Dialogues* know, Socrates had a very disconcerting way about him. In the midst of the most rational, meticulous, definition-centered inquiry, he would sometimes abruptly absent himself to consult his daimon. The more urgent the issue at hand, the more apt he was to do this. In the *Symposium*, where the inquiry is into the nature of love—the sole subject on which Socrates professes himself to have knowledge—he leaves before the discussion begins. Sent to find him, a servant reports that he is fixedly standing in the portico of a neighboring house, "And when I call to him he will not stir."[1] Knowing that this is Socrates's way, his friends agree not to disturb him but to await his arrival. Characteristically Socrates returns to a discussion bearing the word of his daimon as if it were authoritative.

This Socratic tactic can be keenly annoying to modern readers. Some commentators have looked upon these Socratic retreats as outcroppings within him of archaic Greek irrationalism.[2] This supposition is careless and mistaken.

Socrates's action was perfectly rational and endlessly instructive, with special relevance to the central malaise of living today. By example, he was offering a neglected cri-

terion of truth, one he believed to be ultimate and which today we overlook or depreciate to our peril. To show what
he was after I shall first use modern terms, for they will be
clearer. There most certainly are two distinguishable kinds
of truths, "truths of reason" (that two plus two equals four)
and "truths of fact" (that the sky appears blue). By his resort to his daimon Socrates added the class of "truths of
self," personal truths.

For illustration, just now I am seated at my desk in my
office, which is situated within a large university campus.
Spread about the campus are a great many departments of
the various colleges of the university, each of which is cus-
todian of a collection of truths and prospective truths.
Many of these truths do not figure directly in the workings
of my own purposes—truths in the care of the chemistry
department, for example, and the department of physics,
and the schools of nursing and of agriculture. But there is
a collection of truths that are actively working and being
worked within me, or are in my path—philosophical truths,
and within this compass, truths of philosophy of the kind
at which I specialize. In this picture, then, some truths are
within me, but many are outside. I do not for a moment
deny that the truths outside me are truths.* But I say to
others, "These truths are yours; give them your best care,
and from time to time I shall want you to tell me about
them." On the other hand I cannot relegate the tending of
my truths to others, nor can I allow them to go untended,
for they belong to my being. To neglect or mishandle them
is to diminish my being.

Neither bad modern commentary nor Socratic irony itself should divert us from this lesson, his greatest. When
Socrates turned to his daimon he was turning to himself.
Concerning the truth at hand he was saying, yes, surely, it
is a truth of reason or a truth of fact, but before I offer it I

* In eudaimonism's conception, the truths that are the individual's
own to explicate are within him implicitly, and self-actualization
consists in rendering explicit what one implicitly is.

7

must discover whether it is a personal truth and a part of myself, for otherwise I must leave its enunciation to others. (Recall that to deliver others of their truths by *maieutic*, or "midwifery," was the requirement of Socrates's own daimon, it was his personal truth.) To speak a truth that belongs to another is untruth, for speaking belongs to living, hence to speak another's truth is to live a life that is not one's own. So loath are persons to seek out and speak their own truths that, as pedagogue, Socrates must equip himself with the bag of canny tricks that he draws upon endlessly in the *Dialogues*. The most overt and relentless of these devices is the preclusion of hearsay. In the *Meno*, for but one example, the question for consideration is the nature of virtue, and Meno begins confidently to repeat what he has heard about virtue from the great sophist Gorgias; but Socrates interrupts to say that, since Gorgias himself is not present, never mind him, and speak instead what Meno thinks.[3] The preclusion of hearsay represents the profound common intent of all the Socratic tricks. They work to turn the seeker after truth to the truth within himself, and they do so because of the epistemological and metaphysical priority of personal truth. Self-knowledge is the precondition of knowledge of other things, and truth to oneself is the precondition of truthfulness to others. The source of truth and reality in the world is the reality individuals give to their lives by each living the truth that is his own.

Living one's own truth constitutes integrity, the consummate virtue. The word means wholeness, oneness, as against partiality and multiplicity. Eudaimonistic "integrity" exhibits a marked kinship to the "identity" that contemporary men and women are said to be searching for, provided we recognize that integrity characterizes the *process* ("integration") by which a diversity is made into a singular thing—in the epigram of the great eudaimonist G. W. Leibniz: "The wiser a man is, the less detached intentions he has, and the more the views and intentions he does have are comprehensive and interconnected."[4] Integrity manifests

8

truth, reality, and identity in the living being. Its principle is singular and right aim. Its vehicle is love in the meaning of the Greek *eros*, love of the ideal.

Our consideration of "personal truth" reveals that the great enemy of integrity is not falsehood as such but—ironically—the attractiveness of foreign truths, truths that belong to others. For example, if in the next moment I should be interrupted at my work by a phone call from an individual asking me to stand for president of the regional branch of a certain national organization, I shall not be much enticed if I do not know the caller, have no respect for the work of the organization, and take no pride in my administrative abilities. But the case is quite different if the caller is an esteemed friend, the organization does work I admire, and my administrative abilities are such as to contribute to the success of the regional chapter. Here I am forcibly tugged from my work. If I happen to be uncertain just what my true work is, I shall be tractable to depictions of it by well-meaning others.

When an individual allows himself to be deflected from his own true course, he fails in that first responsibility from which all other genuine responsibilities follow, and whose fulfillment is the precondition of the least fulfillment of other responsibilities. This intractability of integrity will at first sight seem harsh, and it will therefore be well to introduce here the distinctive conception of liberality contained in eudaimonism.

What is commonly called liberality (or "liberalism") is the condition of being open, available to all truths. But this is precisely eclecticism, confusion, the absence of integrity understood as singularity of personhood. And because truths of different kinds exhibit the characteristics of incommensurability (their difference is such that they cannot be measured by a single standard or reduced to members of one series) and incompossibility (their difference is such that they cannot co-exist within the same system), such openness introduces both multiplicity and contradiction, and the creature in question stands "divided against himself."

Against this notion, the liberality that eudaimonism nurtures and prizes lies in the recognition that outside the individual's constellation of personal truths lie countless other truths belonging to other persons, relying upon others for actualization and ordering. By his obligation to truth per se, then, each individual must recognize and encourage lives different from his own. Philosophically this is formulated as the principle of ultimate varieties of value, which we discuss in Chapter 5. The vital practical question is, can an individual (or culture, or historical epoch) respond affirmatively to and even encourage values alternative to his own? Everyday life affords abundant evidence of the quickness of persons to disparage the interests of others; it affords plentiful evidence that the common response to one man's advantage is resentment and envy by others. But it will be apparent that such lessons do not answer the question if we distinguish what people do from what it is possible for people to do. Amid the contingencies of the world the true case is obscured by ignorance and error. What the world acclaims is often unworthy and deserving of scorn. The common belief that one man's gain means others' loss is amply supported by appearances. Nevertheless, as a philosophical undertaking, eudaimonism cannot capitulate to appearances, but must plumb for the buried truth. And the truth that eudaimonism finds is rich with implications, promising a better way. In formal expression this truth is the principle of the complementarity of excellences. It affirms that every genuine excellence benefits by every other genuine excellence. It means that the best within every person calls upon and requires the best within every other person.

The principle is rational and a priori, for it follows from the definition of excellence. It is a true principle if the definition of excellence from which it follows is the true definition of excellence, but its truth in this sense does nothing to establish it as a possibility for actualization in the world. That possibility will be established if the workings of the principle are exemplified in the existing world, and eudaimonism has discovered and put to use two such workings, the first of which is psychological while the second is pedagogical.

It is an empirical, psychological truth that the individual who is confident of his own worth does not feel threatened by the worthiness of others but, on the contrary, acutely perceives such worthiness and generously acknowledges it. Nor does this apply exclusively or primarily in cases where excellences are commensurable or qualitatively alike—recognition by one baseball player of another, for example, or between two philosophers (indeed, proximity here often affords the severest test). For personal excellence presupposes accurate self-knowledge, and the self thus known is a determinate individual under the meaning of Spinoza's dictum, "*omnis determinatio est negatio.*"[5] The perfect fulfillment of a determinate individual is a limited fulfillment, containing what Leibniz called "the imperfection of finitude."[6] The worthy man's most avid aspiration to greater excellence of personhood does not overstep the boundaries of his finitude but ever more clearly affirms these very boundaries, and by so doing it becomes the call of this finite excellence for supplementation by the qualitatively different excellences of others.

The psychological truth can be stated more formally as the proposition that the condition of the individual's acknowledgment of the worth of others is his confident sense of his own self worth. This truth, to repeat, is not empirical merely, but a manifestation in the existing world of the principle of the complementarity of excellences. The full disclosure of the importance of both truth and principle must await our investigation of the social philosophy of eudaimonism in Chapters 8, 9, and 10. There, it will be proposed that the condition of justice in the world is the presupposition of the equivalent unique potential worth of every individual. This presupposition alone can afford ground to that confident sense of self worth by the individual that enables him generously to affirm the manifest worth of others when and where it appears.

The empirical pedagogical exemplification of the principle of the complementarity of excellences lies in the emulation of example. Here is the great principle of Greek pedagogy from the Homeric code, through the Golden Age, to the teachings of Socrates. In the cardinal matter of attaining to his excellence the individual amid his fellows is positioned in a hierarchy, his level of attainment surpassing that of some persons but being surpassed by that of others. In this situation his task is twofold: he is to learn from the example of those above him, and at the same time he is by his own example to teach those beneath. What of the very best men of the *polis*? Their situation is critical, for, finding none who surpasses them, they will be in danger of succumbing to pride or complacency. This danger is corrosive, threatening the entire *polis*. For should aspiration to excellence lapse among the best, then they—the consummate teachers—no longer exemplify this aspiration, and the echo of their lapse reverberates downward.

This sets the pedagogical function of the moral heroes of myth and legend, first in the oral tradition and finally upon the tragic stage. Each exemplifies a measure of aspiration and integrity that surpasses the best men of the *polis*, but only just (for it was already an established psychological fact that if the disparity be too great, not emulation but discouragement, or something else again—worship—results). Thus the functioning of the hierarchy is preserved by extending it at the upper end to a different modality of being from the actual, namely the possible that is not yet actual but can become such.

Integrity requires careful distinction between imitation and emulation. Imitation is replication of particulars, emulation is adoption of an exemplified universal or principle. But for purposes of illustration let us begin by forgetting this distinction. Now suppose that I am asked to "imitate" a man who is at this moment walking down the corridor outside my office door. Interpreting "imitate" here to mean "doing as he does," and "doing as he does" to mean "walking as he walks," I arise from my chair at my desk and begin to walk in the corridor, trying to replicate the man's gait, which, let us say, has a slight hitch in it. But what shortly occurs to me is the great discrepancy between my walking, which is as someone else walks, and the other's walking, which is in his own way. Mindful of this I try again, and this time I walk the corridor in my own walking fashion. Now, however, I realize that, while I walk because he does, he walks to his own purpose. At this point I return to my desk and resume my pondering and typing, offering this as a nearer resemblance to the man's action because, as the other man was active in his way, so I am active in mine. But for this resemblance the word "imitation" will not work, and a different word is needed. Hereby we see that, were the word *emulation* unknown, we should shortly be required to invent a term to distinguish what emulation means from what we mean by imitation. To emulate a worthy man is not to re-live his individual life, but to utilize the principle of worthy living, exemplified by him, toward the qualitative improvement of our individual life.

Of the two empirical exemplications of the principle of the complementarity of excellences here considered—the psychological and the pedagogical—the psychological instance shows that it is possible for an individual to recognize and affirm values different from his own. What the pedagogical instance additionally offers is confirmation of the possibility for an individual to actively encourage and nurture the manifestation of values different from his own. For the great pedagogical principle of the emulation of example is rooted in the fact that the manifestation of worth by any individual activates like inclinations (albeit of very different strengths) in those individuals who witness the manifestation and recognize the worth. The life of the worthy individual does in fact support the manifestation of alternative values. We must notice that it does so, not by actively taking a hand in the affairs of the other, not by so to speak "crossing over," but strictly by being what it is. The importance of this point is that it commensurates integrity with social value. It thereby joins personal ethics and social ethics as domains of one coherent system—no small gain when we reflect that disparity between the two is the rock upon which most of our great ethical systems lie broken. Were the worthy man's support to others to require his actively taking a hand in their affairs, then it would be purchased at the cost of his own integrity and on condition of his default at his own first responsibility, for the life of the other is incommensurate with his own and can only be lived by him through relinquishment of his own. But such "help" is a tragic contradiction. It is a contradiction because the only help that can be truly such must be grounded in the integrity and moral responsibility of the helper. It is tragic because it is just this contradiction that is perpetually lived under the names of altruism and social service, availing nothing.

Eudaimonism teaches that the supreme help a man gives to others subsists *in* his integrity and self-responsibility, and cannot be predicated upon the ruin of these. Thus our preliminary social excursion returns us to stand once again before an intractable personal integrity that constitutes the core of prescriptive eudaimonism. To understand it, we must painstakingly take it apart and reconstruct it.

Each person is a bust of Silenus containing a golden figurine, his daimon. The person's daimon is an ideal of perfection—unique, individual, and self-identical. It is neither the actual person nor a product of the actual person, yet it is fully real, affording to the actual person his supreme aim and establishing the principle by which the actual person can grow in identity, worth, and being. Prior to the appearance of the person in the world this ideal of perfection is not nothing, for his appearance in the world cannot be a presentation *ex nihilo*. Instead, its aboriginal status is pure, unactualized possibility. The appearance of the person in the world then constitutes the actualization of that unique possibility. As thus actualized, the possibility exhibits new characteristics (namely, that what of it is as yet not actual is entailed by what is actual); it has become what is termed a potentiality. But the actualization of a possibility is not negation of it as a possibility or the substitution for it of some other thing—the necessary, for instance. As a possibility it is eternal. An actualized possibility, as we say, "exists," but it may at any time cease to exist, in which case it has lapsed from actuality to the status once again of pure possibility.

In philosophical literature as well as in ordinary discourse the actualization of a possibility is often termed *realization*, and eudaimonists themselves employ the term *self-realization* to name their ethics. But as thus used, *realization* is a misnomer, and seriously misleading. To say that a possibility that assumes a working place in the existing world is thereby "realized" is to imply that it was unreal before. But pure possibilities are in and of themselves fully real—indeed, in respect of essence and identity they are supremely so. They are only nonexistent. And the belief that whatever is nonexistent is nothing is what George Santayana calls "a stupid positivism, like that of saying that the past is nothing, or the future nothing, or everything nothing of which I happen to be ignorant."[7] For historical reasons that cannot be assessed here, the propensity to this belief is today widespread. As its sworn enemy, eudaimonism can extend it no comfort, and therefore must shun the careless use of "realization." At the same time the name "eudaimonism" is today archaic and cryptic and calls for a more descriptive substitute. The term "self-actualization" has a bit of currency[8] and is descriptively accurate. Hereafter we shall often use it as the name for the ethics of eudaimonism.

To conclude, our analysis of the person comprises three fundamental elements. Two of these elements are the distinct modalities of being—actuality and possibility—while the third is a relation between the two that gives rise to an existential process, namely the relation of potentiality. Every person is both his empirical actuality and his ideal possibility, or daimon. Connecting the two is a path of implications, whose progressive explication constitutes what the Greeks termed the person's "destiny" (*eimarmene*, deriving from the archaic *moira*, or "fate," and representing the interiorization within man of what had earlier been thought to be imposed upon him from the heavens). According to self-actualization ethics it is every person's primary responsibility first to discover the daimon within him and thereafter to live in accordance with it. Because perfection is incompatible with the conditions of existence, one's daimon can never be fully actualized in the world, but by living in truth to it one's unique perfection can be progressively approached, and such endeavor manifests in the world one's excellence or *arete*—an objective value. Each person is free to adhere to his destiny or deviate from it but he cannot change it. And because (metaphysically) it is possibility that is the normative mode of being, he can manifest worth in the world only by living in accordance with his destiny.*

The meaning of two great Greek imperatives will now be clear. *Gnothi seauton*, "know thyself," was inscribed on the temple of Apollo at Delphi. The second had many phrasings: "choose yourself," "accept your destiny," in the words of Pindar, "become what you are" (Pythian Ode II, line 72). The self that one is required to discover and know is not his empirical person but his daimon (and his empirical person thereafter as the imperfect reflection of the daimon). "Become what you are" recognizes man's freedom to deviate from his own true course and advises that self-discovery is but the beginning of self-responsibility. Together these

---

* The question whether a life can be well-lived which is not innately the individual's own will be taken up in Ch. 6, under "Maturation."

two admonitions point to the supreme moral achievement of integrity—singular, right selfhood. It is expressed in the quality of *pistis*—the self-trust of an individual who has made himself trustworthy. It is this achievement that was personified upon the stage of the fifth century B.C. in the life of the tragic hero.

From Homer and Hesiod through the poets of the sixth century culminating in the great tragedies of the fifth runs an unbroken preoccupation with the life of the hero. Meantime the meaning of heroism underwent gradual but profound humanization. Military virtues gave way to civil ones, the arena for significant conquest was established within the person himself, preoccupation with deeds led to concern for character.[9] As the upshot of this development the tragic stage took its place as a public scientific laboratory for the rapt study of human nature. The basic question examined was ethico-metaphysical. What the Greek demanded to know above all else was whether, amid alien and powerful forces at work in the world, man is to be counted a real and powerful force or whether, instead, his being is derivative, dependent, mere appearance. The answer hammered out upon the tragic stage was clear to the Greeks, however it may puzzle us: Man counts if he chooses to count.

To the insatiable curiosity of the Hellenes the tragic stage produced the continuing reenactment of a single encounter. The drama was the impending collision of two mighty forces, one of them blind and impersonal, the other intelligent, purposive, and personal. The impersonal force is variously represented, appearing sometimes as archaic Fate (e.g. the curse upon the house of Agamemnon), sometimes as a nature–mechanism (*automaton*), sometimes as capricious chance (*tyche*), or again as the imponderable will of certain gods. But always that which is set against the inhuman force is the same—it is the force of human character as personified in the tragic hero.

What the conditions of tragedy require of the hero is undeviating consistency of behavior deriving from unity of self. The hero must be true to himself, for then we know what he will do. If only this is ensured, then the tragedian has but to set these two juggernauts, Fate and moral character, on a collision course.

A hundred times we want to cry to the hero, "Don't do what you are about to do—do something else, do anything else." But we know that he cannot do anything else, for to do something else would be to be someone other than he is, hence to destroy the unity of character that is a condition of tragedy.

Most of us are not moral heroes, which is to say we cannot be depended upon to be what we are. Our aims shift, our loyalties flicker, our loves wink on and off like fireflies. We are one person one minute and someone else the next, we are no one unalterably. Borne down upon by the engine of Fate we will sidestep and wave it goodby, easily abandoning our claim to the track. But in this case the Greek question—Does man count?—is answered in the negative, and tragedy itself is impossible. Can we imagine Oedipus mumbling, "But I really didn't mean it"?

The force that lends consistency, power, and predictability to personhood is moral necessity. The term has almost lapsed from use in recent decades. Logical and metaphysical necessities are necessities antecedent to human will and regulative of it. Moral necessity is consequent upon human will and expressive of it. It is the necessity that the worthy man gives to his life, thereby rectifying that greatest oversight of Epimetheus in his distribution of advantages to the creatures.

Ordinary experience teaches that many people are largely unreliable at doing what they ought; a few are generally reliable; and there are some truly worthy individuals who are unfailingly scrupulous both at doing what they believe they ought and at seeing to it that the ought that appears to them is the true ought. Here is intractable integrity. It is apparent that the life of this rarer sort of individual possesses a cogency, a determinateness, and a predictability (provided one troubles to seek out the true principle of the life in question) lacking in other lives. The fact of human freedom has a telling effect upon predictability. Accurate prediction springs from knowledge, and true knowledge of a person is knowledge of his daimon and destiny. By means of it one can know in advance what the person ought to do, but not what he will do. Greek tragedy works because it is certain that what the moral hero ought to do is what he will do.

In virtue of the regulatory (normative) function of ideal possibilities, a person's every act entails acts to follow. This is expressed by the distinction between the explicit and implicit sides of the act. For example, if I were to take paint brushes in hand to daub on canvas the first touch of what is to be a portrait, my taking up the brushes is at that moment the explicit act; but implicit within it is the finishing of the portrait. In just this way every human act contains implications that, in strictness, represent the fulfillment of the act. We thus uncover the inherently *promissory* nature of human activity, a nature that follows from the participation of possibility in actuality. Strictly, any act entails the entire succession of acts that leads from it up to that daimon, or perfect possibility, of which the act in question is the imperfect expression. Responsibility originates in the promissory nature of human activity and is to be understood as the obligation to fulfill one's promises. But as acts can be right or wrong, so for promises. An act is wrong when it is contrary to one's destiny, and such an act promises wrongly by forecasting an excellence that is not this individual's own. Each right promise, then, will be at the same time the fulfillment of a prior promise, and the life of integrity thus reveals itself to be a single, temporally extended act, which is both the making and fulfilling of a single promise. Accordingly the determination of rightness reverts to an original promissory act, from whose rightness follows the rightness of the succession of this act's entailments. Because rightness means "in accordance with one's daimon," the individual's first right act presupposes self-discovery. But the admonition "Know thyself" is improperly addressed to childhood, becoming meaningful, as the Greeks were fond of saying, "when the young man's beard begins to grow." This fact alone demonstrates that eudaimonism is and must be a developmental ethics and epistemology, incorporating in its very foundations a conception of the stages of personal life. Moreover since (as shall appear) the rightfulness of acts can only be known a posteriori, mistakes are inevitable, requiring a period prior to the demand for integrity when mistakes can be made with impunity—a period of exploration and experiment. This time is adolescence, when the individual is not to be held to his promises. The first right promissory act, from which the integral life follows, marks the inauguration of that stage of life called adulthood or maturity.

The certainty with which the worthy individual can be counted upon to fulfill his promises is what we have termed *moral necessity*, and it is in virtue of moral necessity that a man "counts." To the great question, Greek tragedy answers, "A man counts if he chooses to count," thereby affirming moral necessity as a necessity that a man himself gives to his life.

As term and concept, *moral necessity* has for some time lain neglected. Its disrepute in philosophy reflects the conclusion that it is at best a loose metaphor that spreads confusion and very likely hides contradiction in that to which it refers, namely acts of free choice. But this conclusion is itself the product of confusion and error. Moral necessity is genuine necessity and not a figure of speech. Empirical demonstration of this is to be found in the life of the truly worthy individual, of which only one is needed to serve as demonstration (thus it is that one worthy man is the bad conscience of the world). Theoretical confirmation appears in the recognition that the concept applies not to the physical world as such, or to the domains of logic or mathematics as such. Moral necessity applies to the conduct and meaning of life, and in this domain choice is strictly determinative. For while it is unalterably the case that two plus two is four, that mechanical gravity obtains, that unanticipatable events befall the individual, and that one day he will die, what meaning each of these facts shall have for him and what line of future conduct they shall serve are for him to choose. We must not be deterred from this truth by the fact that much of what passes for choice is not in the least determinative, for neither is it real choice, being instead but half-choice and equivocation. The circulation of false coin may indeed weaken an economy, but it cannot invalidate the science of economics.

Thus a man is free to choose his life, and by truly free choice he confers upon his life that special kind of necessity by which his life must be counted among the world's realities. Given that his choice is not only genuine but right, his living actualizes an objective and unique value in the world. He thereby contributes an affirmative answer to the generic question, "Does humanity count?," but he speaks for himself alone, and to his answer must be added that of every other individual. To the generic question, human history to the present time answers equivocally, and the operative response remains the hypothetical, "Man counts if he chooses to count."

By now it will be clear that self-actualization ethics is a form of innatism, and further clarification can be gained by considering certain immediate objections to it on this ground. One's daimon is a normative potential to individuated character and is inborn, subsisting from birth as innate potentiality. The quickest objection to this position comes from "environmentalism," the doctrine spawned several decades ago by rigorously empirical psychology and sociology, which is now sufficiently widespread to qualify as "common sense." According to it, "personality" in any differentiated sense is the product of cultural factors, coming into being in the growing person's progressive interiorization of contents—likings, aversions, norms, beliefs—prev-

alent in the life of his culture and family. The overriding
objection to this view is that it ascribes to personhood a
radical duality that is both theoretically unintelligible and
practically unworkable. For the environmentalist is compelled to acknowledge that each person's basic physical
characteristics—blue or brown eyes, yellow or black hair,
height, bone structure—are innate, subsisting within him
at birth as part of his genetic inheritance. Moreover he must
also admit that such characteristics are present at birth implicitly rather than explicitly—that is, as potentials for subsequent actualization (as an infant you were not your
present height; as a baby I did not have my long, pointed
nose). For the environmentalist to then ascribe responsibility for traits of character to an entirely different source is
to bisect the individual on the line of the old mind–body
dualism. The cleft is essential, which is to say that the "individual" comprises two different substances, thereby constituting not an individual but a pair. This irremediable
two-ness not only discredits the aim of integrity but renders
all relations between body and mind—for example knowledge, or purpose—unintelligible. In times past, philosophers could be excused for countenancing this nest of
imponderables by their leave to resort to a God whose ways
shall ever be mysterious to men. But today such a move is
forbidden by the requirement upon philosophy to make
what it says intelligible in its own terms.

In light of the above it becomes apparent that whatever
the currency of the environmentalist doctrine it remains a
dark saying, and prima facie credibility lies not with it, but
with innatism's contention that alike, potentials of physi-
ognomy and of character are inborn contributions of genetic inheritance that may be fostered or impeded in their
actualization by environmental factors, but remain un-
altered as potentials. The difference is that physical potentials are actualized by processes that are independent of the
individual will, while choice and volition play an essential
part in the actualization of potentials of character.

A second objection presupposes that innate potentialities for excellence in individuals are distributed unequally by the "natural lottery." Hence while innatism has some claim to truth descriptively, it cannot be allowed to spawn an ethics, for such an ethics would be founded in injustice, constituting a contradiction in terms. I say that the unequal distribution of potentialities for excellence is presupposed, rather than observed or shown, and it is important to notice that this must be so. It cannot be otherwise because we are here speaking of potentials as such, which are inaccessible to observation. No aptitude test can *show* anything but performance—the rest is inference. The inaccessibility of potentials to observation means that all that we can indubitably know is that some individuals in the course of their lifetimes achieve surpassing excellence at what they do, while many do not rise above mediocrity. But this can imply either an original inequality in the distribution of talents or an unequal actualization of original talents. Which is in fact the case remains indemonstrable. On the other hand we can say with assurance that the talents and capacities that men and women actualize are unequally recognized by a given culture, resulting in neglect or even suppression of certain excellences (e.g. Plato's curtailment of poetic inspiration within the Republic). But this is enough to suggest that recognition of a wider spectrum of diverse excellences will elicit excellences in quarters where heretofore the potentialities for them have gone unsuspected. In the words of Pericles, "What is honored in a country will be cultivated there" (Thucydides, *History of the Peloponnesian War*, Book II, 46).

By presupposing an equivalent potential worth in every individual, self-actualization takes the road less traveled. (But as was indicated in the Preface, "genius" did not have our restricted applicability in its original meaning.) Justification for this move cannot be sought in the proposition's empirical truth, for potentials are empirically unverifiable. Instead, eudaimonism justifies it by the superiority of the sort of personhood, the sort of justice, and the sort of love that this presupposition can be counted on to foster in the world. To provide this justification will be the task of Chapters 6 through 10.

A third prima facie objection to innatism is the belief that the conception of an innate destiny eliminates meaningful human freedom. More serious still, the contention is that it does this in a way that convicts eudaimonism of self-contradiction. For it is evident that the kind of freedom that can be endorsed by eudaimonism is not caprice but strictly freedom of and for self-determination.* But self-determination is autonomy (it is argued), while the conception of an innate daimon constitutes the opposite of autonomy, namely heteronomy. This is so because, just as no one asks to be born, so no one can possibly ask to be born as that which (according to eudaimonism) he is. His daimon befalls him, so to speak; it comes to him from a source other than himself. Thereby his autonomy is destroyed, for what is other than the individual constitutes him, and this is the meaning of heteronomy.

Eudaimonism responds to these objections with an invitation to look more closely to the source of the daimon. Were the daimon to be rightfully ascribed to a source that is a being of a strictly (categorially) different kind from the being of the individual whose innate daimon it is, then heteronomy would indeed obtain. But such is not here the case. In genetic inheritance the immediate source is the individual's parents, and as human beings they represent the same category of being as the individual himself. But by genetic inheritance the individual is heir not to his parents

---

* Roughly, caprice is freedom to do whatever one freely wills, self-determination is freedom to do as one rightfully must. Caprice is unregulated and, as such, is predicated upon the mere absence of restraints, i.e. upon lack, nullity, or void, while self-determination is a freedom that is ever answerable to determinations of right and wrong and is thus predicated upon this presence. In self-determination, "freedom for" takes logical precedence over "freedom from."

24

alone, but also to their parents, the parents of those parents, and so on. Ultimately every dividing line by which the individual's inheritance might be restricted proves to be no more than a convenience. The conclusion to be drawn is that each individual is the heir of the unrestricted humanity of which his parents are in his particular case the agents. Heteronomy does not obtain here because the individual *is* humanity, in a particular instance. And genetic inheritance is fully capable of accounting for the individuation of daimons, for, in the words of Theodosius Dobzhansky, "biology not only recognizes the absolute individuality and uniqueness of every person . . . but in fact supplies evidence for a rational explanation of this uniqueness."[10]

Heteronomy is set aside by recognition of a dimension of personhood that has not thus far been identified in our study—generic humanity. Our mapping of the triad of aspects of personhood—possibility, actuality, and destiny—discloses each person to be a unique particular. But our work is unfinished, for what each person truly is is a universal–particular, and something must now be said of the universal humanity that subsists within each individual.

A first-order truth appears in the maxim of Terence, *Nihil humani a me alienum puto*—"Nothing human is alien to me" (*Heauton Timoroumenos*, Act 1, Scene 1, line 25). Each person is both a unique, irreplaceable individual and an instance of generic humankind. But generic humanness subsists within him, not as an amorphous and undifferentiated universal, but rather as the complete constellation of discrete, individual potentials. It is thus that he finds himself capable of responding to excellences different from his own—enjoying to the full the music of Beethoven or Stravinsky, for example, or the paintings of Raphael, of Turner, of Franz Kline. And by "enjoy" we speak here of the capacity to be fulfilled by these experiences. For here lies the essential interdependence of human beings, that in each individual are countless potentials that he himself cannot fulfill in virtue of his own singular destiny. There is no one, I think, who has not at some time felt himself ennobled by the noblest work of another. Nor will anyone have altogether failed to recognize that the grandeur of the great man or woman is also the grandeur of the race of which all persons are members. What occupies us just now is the work of uncovering the objective ground of such feelings. At the same time the feelings just described are self-evidently incomplete and experienced by us as such. They cannot be made to stand by themselves, but instead they resolutely point to our own responsibility. To enjoy the achievement of a Beethoven in default of one's own responsibility is vicarious living, the antithesis of autonomy and thus of integrity. But to enjoy it together with self-responsibility is to correlate the two requisite aspects of self-fulfillment.

The presence within each individual of the constellation of discrete human potentialities affords the implicit condition of freedom understood as self-determination. To live freely the life that is one's own requires perennial knowledge of alternatives, and knowledge of these alternatives as live options such that the free man can at any moment choose to do, not what he will do, but one of several different things. Now the principle of such a man's life derives from his daimon and works in such a way that what he will do follows from what he has previously done and leads to what he must ultimately do. But what of the other acts that at any moment he can do—are they to be regarded as devoid of principle? Not so, for as a human act each of them implies its own past and entails its own future. And as before, principle derives from daimon, from which it follows that the capacity to perform at any given time different acts requires the subsistence within the individual of different daimons. In the man who is living in truth to himself these alternative daimons subsist as unactualized possibilities that, as such, are not potentials. As possibles they are possible actuals, which is to say they are not unactualizable. But to act upon any one of them is to transform it into a potential, while at the same time necessarily allowing one's true potential to lapse to the status of a pure possibility; and this constitutes the lapse of one's fundamental (self-) responsibility.

In sum, the ever-present opportunity in every person to act in disaccord with his destiny attests to the presence within every individual of possibilities that are not his own. These possibilities are human possibilities, which is to say each is the daimon of another person, actual or possible.* So much our ordinary experience invites us to recognize. Eudaimonism urges, against the casual supposition that one's options are few, that in truth the common humanity of each individual comprises the totality of human possibilities.[11]

Albeit in barest outline, we now have eudaimonism's conception of personhood in our hands, and it will be useful to begin to see what light it casts into shadowed regions of practical life. Deep within the antagonisms, frustrations, cruelties, and thwartings that taint life's unfolding in the world, the keenly focused investigative eye detects a common denominator in one hallmark of human nature—its duplicity.

Perhaps the oldest and profoundest philosophical distinction is that between appearance and reality. Its *locus classicus* (though by no means its first expression) is the famous allegory of the cave in Book VII of Plato's *Republic*, whence it infuses the subsequent metaphysical tradition. Its deep place in philosophy reflects its enduring place in everyday experience. Set oneself to seek out the locus of this problem and the answer will not be long in coming. For of things in the world it will be apparent that all are irremediably what they are but for the single exception of man, who alone can become what he is not, and thereby introduce disparity be-

---

* Genetic evidence suggests that not all possibles will achieve eventual actualization. According to Dobzhansky, "possible gene combinations [are] far more numerous than can ever be realized in people now living or those to be born in the future" (*Mankind Evolving*, p. 31).

tween his seeming and his being. Do appearances deceive in the case of the stone, perhaps, or the river, or the lily? In all such instances it is true that innermost reality does not divulge itself to the passing glance. Nevertheless surface and depth are fixedly connected together as levels of a continuum. In such cases appearances do not deceive, they simply do not without prodding tell the whole truth.

But in man's case, experience soon teaches that appearance often belies reality—bravado masks a coward, seeming friendship hides enmity, the saying is belied by the doing and the doing by the being. Only the human wolf wears sheep's clothing, and conversely. That duplicity is exclusively a human trait is owing to the presence in human beings of a slip plane between surface and depth. Its name is freedom.

If the case were merely that a given individual performed an act that was "unlike him," the most we should want to say is that So-and-so, while remaining the person he is, performed an incongruous act. But such is never the case, for by performing an incongruous act (when it genuinely is such, rather than merely appearing as such thanks to our ignorance of the person) person So-and-so activates a principle that entails other acts, and that creates antecedents to itself by altering the meanings of preceding acts. This principle is the principle of organization of a person incommensurably different from person So-and-so. Because of this difference of principle (and the account of it given by eudaimonism's structure of the person, as set forth in this chapter) we are entitled to say of So-and-so, "he is a different person." Strictly in such cases the judgment must be that he both is and is not a different person. He is a different person in that the principle of his existence is a different principle; but he remains the same person in respect of his innate destiny.

For the *locus classicus* of the duplicity in human being our source must once again be Plato—this time the famous image in the *Phaedrus* of the human soul as a charioteer with two horses, a white one, which struggles to rise aloft, and a black one, which tries to plunge below. Here the soul of man is represented as a radical equivocation in being, a relentless argument with itself. Here, too, appears the true form of the much misunderstood priority ascribed to man by classical humanism. Under humanism man appears, not as the supreme being metaphysically or morally, but rather as his own first problem, upon his solution to which rests all hope of his success with other problems.

Plato's opposing horses symbolize the double-mindedness of the person who is not "becoming what he is" and hence in whom discrepancy exists between appearance and reality. He is in the situation of an individual perpetually confronting a fork in the road and perpetually obstructed from taking either branch by his insistence on taking the other. In this condition he can only dither on the same spot, or else he treads one branch with ever-mounting regret at not being afoot upon the other. Thus half-hearted, he does not know that feeling of "being where one wants to be, doing what one wants to do," which signifies effectiveness in the actualization of value. In the acute words of Kierkegaard, "Purity of Heart is to Will One Thing."[12] Strikingly, the "will to one thing" is capable of subsuming all things whatever according to its singular principle, hence intractable integrity does not entail the sacrifice of scope. Nothing that experience can possibly bring is forbidden to it, for the reason that the "given" in experience does not come bearing its own meaning but acquires its meaning by the selection (from the possible meanings of the thing or event) performed by the individual's personal principle. What alone is precluded to integrity is the exchange of its true principle for another.

(As we again touch upon the intractability of integrity—a theme readily susceptible of misunderstanding—it will be worthwhile to notice that it, like eudaimonism as a whole, is entirely devoid of asceticism. The term *asceticism* refers to renunciation or abstention that is regarded as virtuous as such. But for eudaimonism all virtue is inseparably attached to the actualization of value, being instrumental to such actualization. In this condition, all "not doing" is strictly subservient to doing, and cannot constitute for so much as a moment a rightful aim. It only happens that the doing of what is to be done entails the not doing of everything else that might have been done instead. For eudaimonism, then, an ethics of prohibition is a contradiction in terms, just as there can be no psychology of negative content. Ethics is inherently affirmation. It is because the ascetic Antisthenes inverted the priorities of negation and affirmation, thereby trying to substantialize nothingness, that Plato termed him a "Socrates gone mad.")

Such is the tension of the life that is lived athwart itself that many of our most persistent strategies for living are aimed at its alleviation. In opposition to eudaimonism certain prevalent strategies try to resolve the tension by denying the reality of choice and the meaningfulness of self-responsibility. The self, it is said, is unreal; or else it is real, but a sort of reality to which "choice" is precluded, and of which responsibility cannot be predicated—most certainly responsibility cannot be predicated of itself. These are the strategies of dependence and depersonalization. In this interest distraught individuals do their utmost to transform themselves into objects, automata, abstractions, derivations, denying that their lives might be otherwise than they factually are. "I had to . . . !" "It was necessary that I . . . !" "Conditions required of me . . . !" "Custom dictated . . . !" "God willed . . . !" "The cosmos decreed . . . !"

We protest overmuch. And by our very protestations we preclude the surcease of tension the strategy was intended to achieve. For in the nature of the case the disclaimer cannot be made once and for all, but must be remade perpetually and moment by moment. And this felt requirement for an incessant *apologia pro vita sua* betrays, not the nature of a thing, which inexorably is what it is, but a nature that

30

is engaged at a perpetual remaking of itself. In sum, the strategy highlights the very obligation it anxiously denies.

To the equivocation that is the actual person eudaimonism offers the way of the two great Greek imperatives, *Know thyself* and *Become what you are*. The resolution of inner contradiction lies in discovering one's daimon and living in truth to it, thereby achieving identity, being, and objective value. Such a person is one who both possesses and does not possess perfect goodness (*kalôn*—the beautiful, perfection). He does not possess it in actuality, yet he possesses it in aspiration. He is thus conceived as the lover of perfection, his love (*eros*) consisting in "desire for generation and birth in beauty" (*tiktein en tô kalô*—Plato, *Symposium*, 206). Moreover he loves first of all that perfection among the host of perfections that is innately his own—in the words of Socrates, "Every one chooses his love from the ranks of beauty according to his own character" (*Phaedrus*, 252)—and thus by love and aspiration his own determinate individuality is perfected. In the world he manifests *arete*, excellence of unique personhood; he actualizes unique and irreplaceable value that is true value for all persons, and value that others cannot themselves actualize.

Throughout this opening statement of eudaimonist principles our acknowledged debt has been to the Athenians of the fifth century, to the implicit coherent sensibility of that astonishing culture, and to its leading spokesmen. But this classical sensibility can be thought to differ from the eudaimonism of our present account in two important respects.* In the first place good evidence suggests that the Hellenes did not believe all human beings to be invested with potential excellences in the form of daimons, but instead exempted several major classes, namely slaves, *barbaroi* (non-Hellenes, "babblers"), possibly women, and perhaps artisans and tradesmen. Second, there is reason to believe

---

* Detailed analysis of the metaphysical roots of these divergences is reserved to Ch. 5.

that in the Hellenic conception all men's daimons were not of equivalent worth, but were instead arranged in a hierarchy such that, in their final perfection (were such attainment possible), some persons would be superior to others.

To begin with the first question as it concerns tradesmen and artisans, passages are to be found in Plato and Aristotle the gist of which, in the words of A. W. H. Adkins, "seems to deny to the artisan any *arete* at all."[13] But the judiciousness in Adkins's use of the qualification "seems" will be evident if we consider the frequency with which Socrates, Plato, and Aristotle offer artisans and tradesmen as models of self-actualization. Indeed, Socrates persists in using such examples, sometimes in the face of criticism for doing so by his aristocratic pupils,[14] in order to elicit recognition by just such pupils of the truth that is now before us. This teaching is perpetuated by Aristotle, for example in Book II of the *Nichomachean Ethics*, where the good housebuilder and the good lyre player are chosen to illustrate that the *aretai* are achieved by continuous exercise. As so for Plato, who for example in the *Republic* (597) asserts the superiority of the good housebuilder over the imitative artist because the former is guided in his work by vision of a determinate perfection.

Concerning women much advice is to be found in Plato and Aristotle that appears to insist upon their subservient position, and to derive this position from woman's subservient nature. Typical of this is Aristotle's approving citation of the line by Sophocles, "A modest silence is a woman's crown" (*Politics*).[15] Yet at the same place in the *Politics* Aristotle devotes himself to the discussion of the special feminine virtues. Nor can we afford to forget that for fifth-century Hellenes the deep truth of the relationship between the sexes was contained in a great myth, the myth of the soul-mate (preserved for us by Aristophanes in the *Symposium*), according to which the male and female souls are ideally equal and complementary, together constituting a true whole. Finally we are confronted by the overriding consideration that Greek polytheism gave mighty testimony to virtues that were personified by feminine deities. Dike, goddess of justice, and daughter of Zeus, is unquestionably in the top rank of Greek deities, as is Athene, symbol of the honor and glory of Athens—likewise Demeter, goddess of human fruitfulness and of the fruitful soil, and Hera, queen of the heavens, and Artemis, soul-mate of Apollo and goddess of the moon and the hunt.

This apparent contradiction can be resolved by distinguishing, especially in the *Republic* of Plato and the *Politics* and *Rhetoric* of Aristotle, between philosophy, which pursues universal, abiding truth, and practical counsel, which possesses only just enough truth to be useful for a given time and condition. (In the *Politics* Aristotle himself marks this distinction, justifying his own lengthy preoccupation with "the practical part" by insisting that, while it is not philosophy, yet it is "not unworthy of philosophy.")[16] With this distinction made, reconciliation occurs by the affirmation of women's *aretai* as an absolute (philosophical) truth, together with an allowance for contingent factors that prompt maxims advocating the treatment of women as dependent creatures. What this amounts to, in my belief, is that the best and wisest Hellenes, spoken for by Aristotle, recognized that women possessed potential *aretai* (and hence daimons) not in the least inferior to men's, but that they were—thanks to contingent conditions—considerably less advanced in development toward self-responsibility, and hence in a condition akin to that (to employ an analogue often used by Aristotle and Plato) of precocious and talented children. If this is so, then the treatment of women as dependents, advised by Plato and Aristotle, should be regarded strictly as a provisional measure, awaiting woman's self-discovery and *autarkia* (autonomy).

What has been said of women is applicable as well to slaves and *barbaroi* who, compared to women, are less developed and more childlike still. Here, however, we are yet further thrust upon our own inferences from Greek princi-

33

ples, for our chosen spokesmen become equivocal if not self-contradictory. For example Aristotle in one place says that, like the freeman, the slave possesses a complete soul.[17] This prompts the following comment from Ernest Barker: "A difficulty here arises in Aristotle's argument. If the slave has in him *both* of the different parts of the soul, the rational as well as the irrational, why should he be treated as if he had only the irrational part?"[18] The difficulty can be resolved by the consideration advanced above in the case of women, namely that, although the slave possesses the faculty of reason, his capacity to exercise it is undeveloped, thereby precluding to him *autarkia*. This is not at odds with the answer Aristotle himself gives, which is that the rational faculty of the slave, while inadequate for his own deliberation about alternative courses of action (and therefore for *autarkia*), enables him to understand the reason in his master's commands and follow the ordered course of action.[19] Explicitly, nothing here suggests that the slave possesses potentiality for improvement at reasoning leading to eventual *autarkia*. But this potentiality for improvement at reasoning *is* implied when Aristotle says that every slave must be given hope of one day achieving his freedom.[20] For freedom *is autarkia*, which in turn presupposes independent reasoning. It is true enough that the freedom that the master gives the slave can be "external" freedom only, i.e. freedom from external controls over him. But such a gift can only be appropriate when the recipient is capable of self-control.

The meaning of slavery to the Hellenes is complicated by certain factors. In the first place it was a fact of Hellenic life that a free man might at any time be transformed into a slave by being taken captive in war, perhaps even by another Greek. The transformation could also be brought about by such other personal misfortune as might destroy a man's economic independence, in which case slavery sometimes waylaid wives and children as well. Indeed, great attainment is vulnerable to the *hubris* that incurs

34

nemesis, and thus "The mightiest have most cause to fear a fall."[21] Slavery was a possible fate for anyone, even a Solon or a Sophocles. In the words of Aeschylus, "None, neither great nor young, might outleap the gigantic toils of enslavement and final disaster."[22] But in such cases the individual's essential nature remains what it was, and the daimon and destiny that were his as a free man are within him no less as a slave. Second, by eudaimonism's conception of the person, every individual is in himself partly slave, partly free man. For the slavery with which we are here dealing means simply dependence, whether by nature (i.e. in the person's essence) or by circumstance (e.g. by conquest). But the free man's *autarkia* is confined to the course of his personal destiny, while he remains everlastingly (by nature, "essentially") dependent upon others for those excellences that are not his own. A cardinal expression of this truth appears in Plato's *Lysis*, where Lysis is disclosed to possess *autarkia* in the directions of reading, writing, and lyre-playing, but not elsewhere (the examples used by Socrates are weaving, chariot driving, and mule training).

Alike, these two considerations prod us still further in the direction of erasing a hard and fast distinction between slave and free man, if we would understand the Greeks. Especially, the absolute distinction between beings possessed of a daimon and a destiny, and other beings who are devoid of these, must be abandoned.

In the matter of a hierarchical arrangement of daimons, the paradigmatic formulation appears in Book iii of Plato's *Republic*, where persons are held to divide naturally into three classes according to whether the material of their souls is gold (rational nature), silver (spirited nature), or brass or iron (appetitive nature). But the apparent strictness of this class distinction is first of all mitigated by the consideration (*Laws*, 644d) that every soul contains each of these elements, while its distinctive nature is decided according to which element leads and serves as the organizing principle. Second, there is indeed a hierarchy of value among the respective *elements* of the soul, as the symbolism of gold, silver, brass, and iron suggests. Only the rational soul—the soul led and organized by reason—can fully possess self-knowledge and fully manifest self-responsibility. But we can see that this condition is precluded to no person whomever, if we remember that in the very marrow of the Republic is Plato's mythologized doctrine of reincarnation (his account of innatism), which affords to every person an infinitude of lifetimes to manifest his full potential. In this light the apparently rigid social classes of the Republic are revealed to be, not philosophical truth, but heuristic practical maxim. In truth, every person's daimon is a qualitatively unique perfection to be progressively actualized. As a perfection it is not susceptible of qualification by degree, hence it is identical in amount of value to every other daimon. But the *Republic* is a utopian blueprint that, as such, is responsible not only for depicting the social ideal but also for connecting this ideal to actual existence. And in the existing world, from which the ideal must arise, some individuals are advanced at self-actualization, some have barely begun, and some live at cross-purposes with themselves and are thus at a great remove from their rightful work. The apparently strict classes are merely Plato's concession to the practical fact, given the arduousness of eudaimonist requirements, that many persons will not achieve their rightful *arete* within the course of a lifetime. In principle everyone can; but in fact everyone won't. In this light, Plato's strict classes are revealed to be provisional only, and instrumental to something quite different, namely the ideal of a society of equivalent and complementary individual excellences.

The golden supremacy of reason need not mean that as persons achieve rationality and *autarkia* they lose their individuality and become all alike.* Rather, reason is that

---

* This is meant as a summary statement. The difficult question of the status of individuation in both Plato and Aristotle is treated in detail in Ch. 5, pp. 144-151.

unique instrument by which identity and reality can be achieved by the person. It is also true that each individual's daimon, for Plato, *is* an Idea; but the Idea that the individual is is an individual Idea and unique to himself, hence individuality is not lost in the final outcome, but perfected.

I therefore submit that the true aristocracy of the Hellenes rests in the distinction between persons who know themselves and are living in truth to themselves, and those who do not. Fundamentally the hierarchical distinction is not between statesman and carpenter, but between the right and good (eudaimonic) and the wrong and bad (dysdaimonic) practice of either. But as this distinction is tractable, so the aristocracy founded upon it is merely provisional and instrumental.

The fact remains that, for Plato, what it means to be a person is to have perceived the Forms between prior incarnations, and presently to be able to "recollect" and be guided by one of them—hence to be infused by a daimon. And for Aristotle, to be a person is to be one who "partakes not only of living but of living well" (*De Partibus Animalium*, 656a), hence likewise to be able to avail oneself of the guidance of one's daimon. If Hellenic culture of the fifth century was not in fact a social democracy, its ethical eudaimonism implied an ideal equality of fulfilled persons, and its leading minds were not far from recognizing these implications.

But our evocation of Hellenic eudaimonism cannot end without a word about Nietzsche's famous distinction between the Apollonian and the Dionysian tendencies in Hellenic life. The distinction was drawn by Nietzsche as a youthful philologist in *The Birth of Tragedy*, a work which F. M. Cornford says left a generation of scholars toiling in the rear.[23] Against the cold, clear air of Greek rationalism, Nietzsche counterpoised Greek Dionysianism—enthusiastic, orgiastic, mystical, distinction-dissolving—in a profound dialectic. The lasting effect on subsequent Greek scholarship was its awakening to the deep-lying nonrational factors in the constitution of the culture of ancient Greece. Today these factors have been brilliantly revived in such seminal works of scholarship as E. R. Dodds's *The Greeks and the Irrational*, Martin Nilsson's *Greek Piety*, and F. M. Cornford's *From Religion to Philosophy*,[24] such that nothing can responsibly be said about the Greeks without taking account of them. My purpose here is to indicate that by our previous exposition this accounting receives full measure, for in the conceptions of daimon and eudaimonism, the Apollonian and the Dionysian patterns achieve consummate synthesis.

For our spokesmen we have called upon the learned men of Greece—her philosophers, her playwrights, her poets. Shall it be supposed, therefore, that what has been spoken for is exclusively Apollonian—the aristocratic, leisured, rational sensibility of the *polis*? But to do so would be to perpetuate the mistake of compartmentalizing Greece on the basis of the Apollonian–Dionysian distinction. And indeed, scholars have effected such compartmentalization, ascribing Dionysianism to the uneducated populace in the backward parts of Greece, ascribing Apollonianism to the educated aristocracy of the *polis*, and debating whether Apollonianism or Dionysianism came first historically.[25] The truth is that each factor entails the other, and together they subsist in the Greek sensibility as a whole, and in all persons to whom we refer as "the Greeks." Nowhere is the coalescence better demonstrated than in the concept *daimon* and in eudaimonism, as the latter is exemplified and the former explicated in the writings of such spokesmen as Homer, Pindar, Sophocles, Aeschylus, Plato, and Aristotle. By no means are these writings to be regarded as *de novo* dreaming and theorizing, but rather as the unified Greek sensibility rising to expression. No one who is familiar with the writings of Aristotle, for example, will have failed to recognize his perpetual reliance on the common understandings of his time.*

* Transparently the case in the *Poetics* and *Nichomachean Ethics*, but no less true of the highly abstract works. Collingwood shows,

For Aristotle, "doing philosophy" consists in subjecting common beliefs to analysis for the purpose of unveiling their implications and presuppositions. For Plato, doing philosophy is something very different, but the difference is such that "the Dionysian" is in no way sacrificed to "the Apollonian," but synthesized with it.

The mistake of regarding Plato as the consummate Apollonian takes foothold in his reverence for mathematics, as epitomized in the inscription that, according to tradition, appeared over the door of his Academy—*Let Only Those Who Know Geometry Enter Here.* But we do well to notice that it is this characteristic that constitutes Plato's "Pythagoreanism" (Aristotle, *Metaphysics* 1.6), and Pythagoreanism is mathematical mysticism. As Alvin Gouldner observes, it is false to suppose "that mysticism and a strong commitment to mathematics are necessarily incompatible."[27] That Plato is not the consummate Apollonian but the consummate synthesizer of Apollonian and Dionysian strands in the Greek sensibility will be apparent if serious attention is given to his treatments of "inspiration," "divination," and "divine madness," notably in the *Ion*, the *Phaedrus*, and the *Timaeus*.[28] As this is not the place for an extended exegesis, we confine ourselves to the following paradigmatic citation. "That divination is the gift of heaven to human unwisdom we have good reason to believe, in that no man in his normal senses deals in true and inspired divination, but only when the power of understanding is fettered in sleep or he is distraught by some disorder or, it may be, by divine possession. It is for the man in his ordinary senses to recall and construe the utterances, in dream or in waking life, of divination or possession, and by reflection to make out in what manner and to whom all the visions of the seer betoken some good or ill, past, present, or to come."[29]

---

tellingly, that the *Metaphysics* is the description and analysis of the presuppositions of the science of Aristotle's time.[26]

Here we are told that inspiration occurs to an individual when he is out of his ordinary senses, but that he must recover his ordinary understanding if he is to comprehend what has appeared to him and how to turn it to use. But the point lies still deeper, to be uncovered in the recognition that love, devotion, and enthusiasm are intrinsic to Plato's *nous* and to his dialectic. Among recent commentators, John Herman Randall captures it best. "In Plato," Randall says, "the realm of *nous*, of 'mind,' is not the realm of science, but what since the Romantic revolution we have called the realm of the 'imagination'—that realm in which we can see life perfected and clarified, made whole and complete, a perfected work of art. . . . Hence Platonic dialectic is not, as Taylor supposes, symbolic logic, nor yet the religious quest for the Divine, as Plotinus saw it. It is rather the imaginative experience of the artist, his flight of soul as his vision enlarges to embrace all truth and beauty."[30]

For our purposes it is of central importance that in Plato the centrality of love, devotion, and enthusiasm does not herald a retrogressive movement to an undifferentiated and aboriginal Dionysian unity, but points instead to a prospective reunion based in perfected individuation. It is in the individual that the reconciliation of Dionysian and Apollonian themes occurs. The individuation, clarity, and rationality that Apollonianism wins out of the aboriginal Dionysian unity is not sacrificed but brought to perfection, and henceforth integration of individuals is to be progressively realized by the perfection of differences, on the principle termed by Plato the "congeniality of excellences."[31] This higher integration shall be our theme in Chapters 8, 9, and 10, which are intended to set forth the social entailments of eudaimonism.

Let me add that to the historical questions we have examined in the late pages of this chapter no conclusive answers are possible, nor for our purposes are they required. Conclusiveness is impossible because the best evidence remains indirect, and the sought-for historical "facts" are of the nature of beliefs. In these conditions the best results remain interpretive, and admit alternative interpretations. The principle of our own interpretation is that of coherence. Where the Greeks themselves were undecided, or our evidence is of itself unclear, we have sought the entailments of the basic Greek principles. By coherence we can make a limited claim to have uncovered what the Greeks ought to have believed about a given matter, whatever in fact they may have said or failed to say.

Finality of interpretation is not required, because our objective is not slavish reproduction of the spirit of Hellas, but the presentation of a eudaimonism serviceable for today. This endeavor finds its parentage in ancient Greece, where eudaimonism first rose to systematic expression. If our account must go further than theirs, if moreover we find ourselves obliged to rectify what we believe to be certain ancient errors, we may do these things in full confidence that the Greeks, with their esteem of emulation and their scorn of mere imitation, would not have wished it otherwise.

2

Critique of Recent Eudaimonisms: British Absolute Idealism

From its wellspring in ancient Greece, eudaimonism courses through Western history like a subterranean stream, outcropping at intervals to become the explicit philosophy of a time and people, then turning underground again, ever-present beneath the surface and available to persons who can break through the crust of a contravening culture.

In recent Western philosophy, two quite different schools have given forceful expression to eudaimonistic principles, and it will be useful to see what advances over classical eudaimonism they may afford. These schools are British Absolute Idealism of the late nineteenth century and continental Existentialism. Together with the advantage of historical proximity to us, each holds special doctrinal interest for our study—Existentialism because it is so resolutely individualistic; and British Absolute Idealism because it issues in part from traditional British individualism, to which all modern individualisms must acknowledge a debt.

In the words of E. Ehrhardt, "As regards the general welfare of individuals, Great Britain was for a long time the only country where serious precautions were taken to ensure imprescriptible liberties for the individual. British traditions, the Anglo-Saxon temperament, and the Calvinist education all tended to the enfranchisement of the individual."[1] Arguing that British individualism was first economic and thereafter political and social, Tawney ascribes its origin to the ruin of the feudal nobility by the Tudors, which, by democratizing the ownership of land, prepared the way for the *bourgeois* republic.[2] Tawney describes the liberation of the individual as an economic entity, first from subservience to the church, and thereafter from subservience to the state. The church, burdened by the obsolescence of its teachings, was in the end forced to acquiesce to the eighteenth-century doctrine that "trade is one thing and religion another." Meanwhile the state, reflecting a secularization that found formal expression in the political philosophy of John Locke, desacralized the "natural law" that was its own foundation. "Nature," says Tawney, "had come to connote, not divine ordinance, but human appetites, and natural rights were invoked by the individualism of the age as a reason why self-interest should be given full play."[3] It remained only for Locke to prove that the state that interferes with property and business destroys its own title to exist.

That the individualism thus unleashed moved quickly to flagrant excesses will occasion no surprise if we consider the sort of individualism it was—mechanical, egoistic, and smug. It was smug in the sense that it regarded individuation as a fait accompli, rather than as a task and a responsibility. It could regard individuation thus because its conception of individuation reached no deeper than the merely numerical, as befitted its philosophical mechanism. Tawney offers a statement of this mechanism by the seventeenth-century writer G. Malynes as epitomizing the spirit of the time. " 'We see,' wrote Malynes, 'how one thing driveth or enforceth another, like as in a clock where there are many wheels, the first wheel being stirred driveth the next and that the third and so forth, till the last that moveth the instrument striketh the clock.' "[4]

Finally this mechanistic individualism could be unabashedly egoistic on the strength of its doctrine that all relations are purely external and can have no essential effect upon the entities related. By such a doctrine egoism is endorsed, for nothing else is possible. Persons are self-enclosed, atomic particulars; what is to be done for each must be done by each, and devil take the hindmost.

With respect to this traditional British individualism, the "self-realization" ethics of nineteenth-century British Absolute Idealism arises primarily as a corrective, seeking to sustain individualism by rendering it sound. Against mechanism and egoism it espouses a comprehensive organicism that emphasizes the whole while at the same time insisting upon the unique character of every particular element of the whole. Its doctrine of internal relations defeats atomic particularism and its attendant egoism. Against the merely numerical individuation that is a fait accompli, British Absolute Idealism reaffirms the ancient truth that individuation is an arduous task, and a moral one. For it is individuation of character that holds moral value; and the valuable elements of character do not combine spontaneously to form an organized and directed whole, but must be organized and directed by a conjunction of aim and discipline.

Prior British individualism had remained grotesquely simplistic, reducing individuation to what could be seen, felt, smelled, and chewed-upon—namely, to physical and denumerable individuation. It proved ultimately devastating by fostering rampant egoism. British Absolute Idealism works within this tradition to wrench it to the truth by means of a conception of the individual as a whole within a larger whole, both wholes being ideal and, as such, tasks of actualization. Its untarnishable contribution centers in the emphasis it gives to the place of coherence in a truth and a reality to be achieved.

We shall concern ourselves with the three major texts of British Absolute Idealism in the "ethics of self-realization."*

---

* *Self-realization* is the term employed by Bradley, Green, and Bosanquet, and will be used here despite the imprecision noted in Chapter 1. Strictly, what is meant by "self" is ideal, but nonetheless fully real, hence not to be "realized" but, rather, actualized.

In order of publication they are F. H. Bradley's *Ethical Studies* (1876), T. H. Green's *Prolegomena to Ethics* (1883), and the two-volume study by Bernard Bosanquet, *The Principle of Individuality and Value* (1912), and *The Value and Destiny of the Individual* (1913).

The primary intention of Bradley's *Ethical Studies* is to establish the nature of the self that seeks "realization." According to Bradley, analysis of ordinary experience shows that what we mean by the self can be neither a mere collection of states (a bare multiplicity) nor an abstract universal (a bare unity), but must rather and in some sense be a unity of diversity and a diversity within unity. In formal terms it must be a "concrete universal," a universal that "not only is above but is within and throughout its details."[5] Yet this conjoined unity and diversity is contradictory. As such it identifies the inescapable task of the self as that of attaining to self-consistency. To perform this work the self must perpetually go beyond the contradiction it is, constituting itself as a more inclusive whole—a process of self-transcendence that is at the same time (in terms yet to be made clear) progressive self-realization.

Accordingly the immediate task of ethics is to identify "the true whole, realizing which will practically realize the true self."[6] Already, however, Bradley encounters a formidable difficulty, for by his lights there can be but one true whole, namely the Absolute, the self-same, all-inclusive, super-individual reality that contains all finite things brought to their fulfillment and released from their finitude. The difficulty is that such a whole is both so far beyond ordinary conception and so contrary to our ordinary grasp of ourselves and our circumstances as to be incapable of guiding daily life.

Recognizing this, Bradley sponsors instead as the whole in which the person is to realize himself the more proximate whole that consists of the person's social community. This community, Bradley argues, is both factually within the individual and normatively above him, determining his

rightful role or "station." It is necessarily within him because as infant and child he was socially dependent, inte-
riorizing family and community patterns of feeling, belief,
and behavior, and "if you make an abstraction of all this,
which is the same in him and in others, what you have left
is not an Englishman, nor a man, but some I know not what
residuum, which has never existed by itself and does not so
exist."[7] It is "above" him both in the sense that as a wider
whole it is superior to him in respect of reality, and because
factually it antedates him and holds a place for him. Regarding the individual, then, his social community is the
"real moral idea" that he must realize in himself. To the
question, How do I know what course of action is right for
me?, Bradley says we must start from the "obvious fact that
in my station my particular duties are prescribed to me, and
I have them whether I wish to or not."[8] As noted above, for
its assignment of my station and its duties the community
possesses both de facto and de jure authority. To be moral
I must myself will my performance of my duties within my
station. For refinements of discrimination within one's station, Bradley relies upon the intuitive judgments of rightness by the worthy man (the man who wills his station and
its duties). He carefully distinguishes the faculty of such
judgments from "conscience," and what he offers as its hallmark is a good approximation of the feeling associated by
the Greeks with eudaimonia, though Bradley does not employ the term.[9]

The doctrine of "My Station and Its Duties" is open to the
immediate objections that it awards undue moral authority
to the community (and, beyond, to state or nation) in any
case and that it disregards the evident fact that communities, states, and nations can be bad as well as good.

Bradley belatedly (in *Ethical Studies*) seeks to blunt
these charges by acknowledging that beyond every actual
community is a "higher whole" to which actual communities
are responsible. This means that no actual community is an
absolute moral authority, and the authority possessed by

actual communities is no more than relative and derivative. Indeed, I believe we are entitled to infer that a given community possesses moral authority only on condition that it likewise is growing in reality and self-consistency, for otherwise it is not a community. In this case even the bad community is growing better, and it exhibits relative moral authority in virtue of the identity of proportion between it and its constituent individuals, as against the better community and its constituent (better) individuals.

If we object that the community can have no moral authority over its individuals because it just *is* its individuals, Bradley sympathetically undertakes to tutor us in the cardinal truth of idealism, that the whole is always greater than the sum of its parts. In the present case this means that the community possesses more reality and goodness than the individual, and hence it represents his proximate moral authority.

But it remains the case that the moral authority of the community is derivative and remains unintelligible until its source is laid bare. This means that Bradley's ethics is not self-standing, but leads inexorably to the metaphysics it presupposes—in short, the negotiable terrain of *Ethical Studies* leads to the catacombs of *Appearance and Reality*.

In *Appearance and Reality* the fulcrum of Absolute Idealism is expressed thus by Bradley: "Ultimate reality is such that it does not contradict itself; here is an absolute criterion. And it is proved absolute by the fact that, either in endeavoring to deny it, or even in attempting to doubt it, we tacitly assume its validity."[10] Whatever contains contradiction cannot be real, yet also cannot be wholly unreal insofar as it "appears" (in experience). It is incomplete reality (termed "appearances"), and all such incomplete reality strives to overcome internal contradiction and attain reality.

We shall skirt the "ontologizing of logic" embodied in the criterion. It would be convenient to invoke the current separation of "truths of reason" from "truths of fact," charging

Bradley with the hypostatization of a principle applicable only to reason (and perhaps ignoring his formidable rejoinder, namely that the analytic-synthetic distinction of judgments, and ultimately the subject-object distinction in epistemology, contain relentless and self-defeating contradictions). We are forbidden this resort by our own conviction that identity and noncontradiction are in any case principles of philosophy, subsumable under the rubric of "sufficient reason" to which philosophy must adhere. Whether or not reality can contradict itself we will leave an open question. But our *conception* of reality cannot contradict itself if it is to be intelligible, and to render intelligible accounts is the unremitting obligation of philosophy and philosophers. We therefore accept the stricture that Bradley's "absolute criterion" lays upon our statements, albeit for reasons different from his.

But what Bradley does next is to define noncontradiction ("internal harmony") in an extraordinary way. He says that it means all-inclusiveness and is incompatible with restriction and finitude.

> For that which is not all-inclusive must by virtue of its essence internally disagree; and, if we reflect, the reason of this becomes plain. That which exists in a whole has external relations. Whatever it fails to include within its own nature, must be related to it by the whole, and related externally. Now these extrinsic relations, on the one hand, fall outside of itself, but, on the other hand, cannot do so. For a relation must at both ends affect, and pass into, the being of its terms. And hence the inner essence of what is finite itself both is, and is not, the relations which limit it. Its nature is hence incurably relative, passing, that is, beyond itself, and importing, again, into its own core a mass of foreign connexions. Thus to be defined from without is, in principle, to be distracted from within.[11]

It follows that reality is devoid of relations. It is without relations to anything external to itself because it is all-inclusive. It is without internal relations because everything that it contains is brought to fullness of reality and is therefore likewise all-inclusive. Reality is, so to speak, a summation of all-inclusives that, because they are identical with one another, are in fact one and not many. In sum, reality is the undifferentiated One that "somehow" (the *how* is said by Bradley to be inexplicable)[12] includes all diversity while transforming its character. And Bradley argues that this One must be individual, that it is experience, that it has positive rather than negative character (presumably as against the connotations of the Hindu description of Atman-Brahman as "neti, neti"—"nothing of that sort, nothing of that sort"), and that it possesses "a balance of pleasure over pain."[13]

From this supplementation by citations from *Appearance and Reality* it is clear that Bradley's *Ethical Essays* offers nothing final, but strictly an "interim ethic." Indeed, the very notion of ethics proves to be merely provisional, for "it is an endless process and therefore a self-contradiction, to be transcended in the Absolute"[14] (where what ought to be, is, changelessly). And as ethics itself is provisional, so the self-realization that constitutes the content of ethics is doubly so. Where "self" refers to a determinate individuality amid others of its kind, it is a mere appearance, which in the process of realizing itself becomes something that is not a self as just defined. We can, if we wish, speak of the Absolute as an individual self which, in the process of realizing itself (through the realization of all appearances) retains its selfhood and its individuality. But we are here speaking of a single individual without others, and thereby we overturn the meaning of "individuality" given above.

For our purposes the inescapable conclusion is that Bradley's self-realization is at most an apparent eudaimonism that is not really such. Against Bradley's ethics and metaphysics, eudaimonism is an individualism (in the above sense of a one among others of its kind) not merely in the beginning, but in the end. Against Bradley's metaphysical and axiological monism, eudaimonism is resolutely pluralistic on both counts, affirming the principle of the ultimate varieties of human value. Indeed, the argument that each individual should aspire to become the whole of reality and value was known well by the Greeks. They branded it ignorant, overweening pride. The propensities to it evoked from the classical world the counsel of *sophrosune*—moderation or proportion—according to which the individual must aim neither too high nor too low, but instead must seek himself.

A further conclusion is that, even as a provisional ethic, Bradley's is unworkable. It asks for moral discrimination and determination from an authority that is itself undifferentiated and indeterminate and, in consequence, cannot provide what is required (or can do so only arbitrarily). The Absolute must be undifferentiated, as we have seen, because differentiation is internal contradiction. The Absolute is indeterminate (or "infinite") because determination is negation, constituting "qualification by the rejected."[15] Since in this condition the Absolute is the final authority for affairs beneath, there can be no authority for discrimination and determination. But for men as finite creatures, to do *this* means *not* to do everything that might have been done instead, hence to be workable an ethics must contain principles by which to distinguish better from worse among particular acts. This the Absolute cannot do. It does establish as better the act that is more inclusive, but the more inclusive act is less determinate, and as such it is not merely more difficult to act upon, but impossible to act upon. The hidden truth that the Absolute can say nothing concerning determinate acting is kept hidden by Bradley's resort to the social community, which as a differentiated whole does not exhibit the incapacity just noted. But the source of the differentiation within the community cannot be the Absolute for the reason just noted, and in fact differentiation can have no authority in Bradley's metaphysics and ethics.

In sum, loss of ultimate individuation (each a one among others) leaves Bradley not with an ethics alternative to eudaimonism, but with no ethics at all. In this light we are entitled to regard Bradley's intended ethics as a backward step from eudaimonism, which, as such, instructs us in what to avoid. A workable ethics for finite creatures cannot offer a conception of the good that represents it as an undifferentiated universal. Instead, either the good must be conceived as self-differentiated, or else a principle of differentiation must be added that is itself good. And an unworkable ethics is a contradiction in terms.

Because T. H. Green recognizes this, his work appears more promising for our purposes than Bradley's. The ultimate reality that serves as the moral absolute is conceived by Green not as an undifferentiated oneness, but as an ideal community of perfected individuals. Speaking directly against Bradley, he says that the moral ideal is emptied of any real meaning "if we suppose the end of the development to be one in the attainment of which persons—agents who are ends to themselves—are extinguished. . . ."[16] To stand upon the ultimate reality of individuals, each of whom is a one among others, Green, who accepts the principle of the noncontradictoriness of the real, must deny Bradley's contention that all relations introduce contradiction into their terms. For Green, relations "eternally exist," and reality is an "unchanging order" that "is an order of relations."[17] Moreover those relations that eternally exist are the very relations among things and terms in the actual, temporally changing world. For although such things and relations are elements of changing nature, the fact of the existence at any given time of a particular relation is an eternal fact, in the sense that the proposition asserting the existence of the relation at that time is tenselessly true. But changing relations are thus eternal only in the total system of all relations that ever have been or ever shall be actual. This system is itself eternal; and because relations require a consciousness in which to appear (for they can only be what they are to a consciousness that embraces both of the terms related), the eternal system of relations presupposes an eternal consciousness for which it is an eternal object.[18]

Within this system the finite person is, to begin with, a creature of wants, impulses, and desires. Desires are distinguished from wants and impulses in that they alone contain a distinction between the self and its object. Desire is therefore confined to self-conscious beings, for only such beings are capable of distinguishing themselves from the objects of desire.[19]

Such a being cannot be made up of its desires, for it can distinguish itself not merely from the objects of its desire but also from its very desires. A man does not attempt to satisfy all of his desires for he recognizes that they often conflict. Among conflicting desires he must choose those to be gratified. His choices are acts of will, and they are free in the sense of not being determined by antecedent natural conditions. In particular, acts of will are not determined by desires. They are not the result of the stronger desire canceling weaker ones, nor are they strands woven out of combined desires. In order to account for the regulation of desire by will "we must suppose the action of a principle wholly different from desire. . . . [W]e must suppose a determination of desire by the conception of self, its direction to self-satisfaction."[20] Thus the conception of the realized self serves as the principle of desires, affording the distinction between right and wrong desires, desires that are better and desires that are worse. And the agent's motive in moral action is his idea of a personal good that, insofar as it is realized, constitutes an objective good in the realized community of which the realized agent is a member.

Individuality therefore lodges in the principle of desires and the idea of a personal good from which the principle derives, and we must discover the nature of such individuality, together with the source of the idea of a personal good. Specifically we must know whether the individuality dwelled upon by Green consists in qualitative distinctions or distinctions that are merely numerical. In a significant passage Green supplies his answer.

> It does not follow from this that all persons must be developed in the same way. The very existence of mankind presupposes the distinction between the sexes; and as there is a necessary difference between their functions, there must be a corresponding difference between the modes in which the personality of men and women is developed. Again, though we must avoid following the example of philosophers who have shown an *a priori* necessity for those class-distinctions of their time which after ages have dispensed with, it would certainly seem as if distinctions of social position and power were necessarily incidental to the development of human personality. There cannot be this development without a recognized power of appropriating material things. The appropriation must vary in its effects according to talent and opportunity, and from that variation again must result differences in the form which personality takes in different men. Nor does it appear how those reciprocal services which elicit the feeling of mutual dependence, and thus promote the recognition by one man of another as an "alter ego," would be possible without different limitations of function and ability, which determine the range within which each man's personality develops, in other words, the scope of his personal interests.
>
> Thus, under any conditions possible, so far as can be seen, for human society, one man who was the best that his position allowed, would be very different from another who was the best that *his* position allowed.[21]

Green's references to diversity of excellences, talents, and paths of development carry the prima facie suggestion that the individuality he endorses centers in qualitative distinctions. But when we look more carefully we notice, first, that he appears to reject the innatist account of the origin of individual differences. I say *appears* because Green is equivocal here. He wants to "avoid following the example of philosophers who have shown an *a priori* necessity for those class-distinctions of their time which after ages have dispensed with." This leaves untouched the question of individual distinctions which after-ages have not dispensed with. But this is only careless—or cautious—wording by Green. As the full text of the *Prolegomena* makes clear, he rejects innatism altogether as an account of individuality. What is innate and variable consists only of the "solicitations"—needs and impulses—of the animal organism, and these are in no way normative but require regulation from a source outside themselves.[22]

Next we must give our attention to the term *necessarily incidental*, by which Green characterizes the status of the individual differences of which he speaks. I think we remain truest to Green if we invert the words and ponder an *incidental necessity*. Clearly an incidental necessity is different from a strict (metaphysical or logical) necessity, and just as clearly it is different from a moral necessity. It is a necessity that is imposed by "incidents," or contingent conditions. Individuals are born and reared, and are bound to live, amid differing circumstances, and this is necessarily so, for it is impossible* that everyone be born in the same place, at the same time, to the same parents. Likewise it is impossible* within a given community that there be no "distinctions of social position and power," and no distinctions among the material goods "appropriated" by individuals. Here, then, is incidental necessity. But it can be responsible for *only an incidental individuation*, and if morality itself is not incidental, such an individuation cannot be a

---

* The impossibility here is epistemological and nomological, rather than logical or metaphysical. In the second case (above) it may be arguably such; but we are here concerned only to adhere to Green, not to examine the question independently.

moral one. When Green says "It does not follow . . . that all persons must be developed in the same way," we shall perhaps recall the opening of the constructive part of the *Republic* by Socrates, "I am myself reminded that we are not all alike; there are diversities of natures among us which are adapted to different occupations" (*Republic* 370). But any resemblance is merely verbal, for what Green means to say is only that it is fortunate that all persons need not be developed in the same way, for incidental necessity does not permit identical development.

Therefore we concur in Sidgwick's conclusion that Green's "individual" is "essentially a self-distinguishing, self-objectifying, combining, unifying consciousness. Nothing more, if we consider it apart from the 'solicitations' it receives from the animal organism, which are supposed to mislead it into the pursuit of pleasure."[23] In criticism, Sidgwick simply calls attention to the fact that such self-consciousness is common to all men and identical formally, hence differences among individuals can only be difference in content, the only sources of which are "data and environment"(afforded by Green's "incidental necessity"). Thus differences are merely circumstantial and are morally irrelevant.

Indeed, the source of the consciousness of men, according to Green, is none other than that eternal consciousness for which the relations of the actual world are, in the manner previously described, the eternal object. This eternal consciousness is "the abiding self," in which "the idea of the human spirit, or all that it has in itself to become, is completely realized."[24] Moreover Green says it necessarily exists, for "if there were no consciousness for which it [abiding satisfaction, perfection] existed, there would be no sense in saying that *in possibility it is*, for it would simply be nothing at all."[25]

Among the lesser conundrums here is the annulment of moral meaning that the existence of such a consciousness effects. As Sidgwick says, "For God, or the eternal con-

55

sciousness . . . is necessarily conceived as unalterable; it is eternally in reality all that the human spirit is in possibility, and there are no conceivable perfections that could be added to it; and the process of man's moral effort is surely futile if it is to end in nothing but the existence of that which exists already."[26]

When Green bases the possibility of human perfection upon the antecedent *existence* of such perfection (in an existing eternal consciousness) he gravely confuses the relationship of the modalities of the real. For a thing to be possible it is not first of all necessary that it be actual; but conversely, for a thing to be actual it is first of all necessary that it be possible. Only thus can contingent existence appear; for if existence is the condition of possibility, what does not exist cannot possibly exist, and all that exists does so necessarily.

But for our purposes the fatal defect in Green's *Prolegomena* is that individual consciousness derives from an "eternal consciousness" that is one and undifferentiated, and therefore incapable of affording differentiated moral guidance to individuals. Indeed, Green repeatedly urges the individual to guide himself by the generic ideal, e.g. "the perfection of man," or the "ideal of humanity." But no finite individual can act according to "humanity," because his finitude dictates that his every act be determinate, while "humanity" is an indeterminate concept. At each fork in the road "humanity" goes both left and right, and also backward, while at the same time remaining fixed upon the spot.

No less than Bradley's, Green's "individuals" prove to be merely provisional, called upon in the end to sacrifice their individuality, and expected from the beginning to commence to do so by adopting a generic ideal. At bottom Green's individuals differ only numerically, representing the same consciousness in a multiplicity of spatio-temporal positions. And this puts an end to the ideal community that inspired our hopes at the outset, for among merely numerical individuals there can be no complementarity, for none can be or do what each of the others cannot be or do for himself. The sufficient reason for community is abolished, and philosophically it subsides into the singular "abiding self." In the end Green's "self-realization ethics" is realization of but the One Self which, unaccountably, has got itself scattered in a great many places.

The story as told by Bosanquet is a slight variation on the themes of Bradley and Green, and our treatment shall accordingly be brief.

Promisingly, Bosanquet disputes Green's conception of individuality on the ground that, insofar as the conception admits of qualitative distinctions, the distinctions derive from contingent circumstances and are morally irrelevant.[27] On the other hand Bosanquet condemns as empty abstraction any conception of individuality that entirely rejects contingent circumstances. His own offering makes use of the creative artist as an analogue of the self-realizing individual and "the type of the characteristic logic or movement of the self." Like the artist, the self-realizing individual internalizes the content his environment contingently affords, and subsequently he re-expresses it in the form of works and acts, but between his reception of contents and his re-expression, the contents are transformed by the principle of his individuality. Bosanquet says, "I do not see how an initiative or originality more complete than this can be conceived or desired, or can be consistent with a self that is anything at all."[28]

Well and good—until we begin to see in what this initiative and originality consists. Concerning the source of the personal principle that accomplishes the transforming, Bosanquet first argues that it cannot be circumstantial nor can it be innate, for "the antecedent character thus brought down from heaven would itself be mere circumstance."[29] (We saw this contention laid to rest in the previous chapter, pp. 24-25.) Nor can it consist in desire or purpose because, he says, these are only negative, while a real individuality must subsist positively.*[30]

To shorten the story, the source to which Bosanquet ascribes principles of individuality is the "unity of a harmonious cosmos," which is the "completed system of an eternal self."[31] It is in fact Green's "abiding self" all over again. Moreover the distinction Bosanquet is anxious to make between his conception of the individual and Green's is based entirely upon Bosanquet's misreading of Green, for as we have seen previously, Green's *moral* individual is not circumstantially determined, but derives from the "abiding self." For Bosanquet the only real self is the "eternal self," and self-realization consists in the "remoulding" of this self "by its own yearning for totality."[32]

In the end I find it hard to clear Bosanquet of a trace of duplicity in his treatment of qualitative individuality. By his celebration of the "initiative" and "originality" of the creative artist, qualitative individuality is certainly brought to mind. But it is rudely banished by the sequel where we learn that all that qualitatively distinguishes one person from another is " 'personality' in the worst sense, what we try to avoid." And Bosanquet proceeds to the claim that "The most real personal feeling is the most universal, like tragic emotion. When we come to consider the material, so to speak, of persons, the objects of their attention and achievements, we see how much they have in common, and how little, from the point of view of what is great in the world, their distinctness seems to matter." He goes on to say that what is real in persons is common to all, and what is

---

* Here Bosanquet ought to have hearkened to astute psychology of Socrates in the *Symposium*. Love, Socrates says (*Symposium* 200), is a form of desire, and desire presupposes the desirer's lack of what he desires. But by no means is it therefore pure lack, for by his love the lover also, though in a different sense, possesses what he loves. Given the nature of the person as both actuality and possibility, there is no paradox here. What he lacks in actuality he possesses in possibility, in virtue of his love. Love is therefore the relation between possibility and actuality in the integral life.

distinct is "external and superficial."[33] This passage comes close to marking a turn-about. Did we only misunderstand the earlier citation? Undoubtedly. But ought not Bosanquet to have forestalled so likely a misunderstanding?

We conclude with some summary observations on nine-teenth-century British Absolute Idealism: the final citation from Bosanquet epitomizes its one-eyed view of the finite human person. In him Absolute Idealism sees only common humanity, dismissing his distinctiveness. But metaphysics aside, fidelity to experience forbids such a move. In his presence to us, each human being is both like all others and distinctive, and neither aspect can be allowed to blind us to the other. One or the other may be given precedence "for certain purposes," but the truth shall not be displaced by this convenience.

Eudaimonism preserves both commonality and excep-tionality in its conception of the person as a "universal-particular." His commonality consists in the subsistence within him, not of an undifferentiated universal, but of the constellation of discrete human possibilities, while his ex-ceptionality rests in the qualitative uniqueness of the possi-bility that is his personal destiny. It remains to test this conception against Bradley's claim that every notion of finite selfhood fails by self-contradiction.

We begin by endorsing two of Bradley's theses, namely that demonstrably the individual is in some way inclusive of others and that relations always penetrate their terms (formulated by Leibniz as the principle that "every extrin-sic denomination has an intrinsic one for its foundation").[34] With this much granted to Bradley, we can narrow our at-tention to his argument against the conception of a self that is determined by its interests, needs, or purposes. Bradley says, "This general view may serve to lead us to a fresh way of taking self; but it obviously promises very little for meta-physics. For the contents of self are most variable from one time to another, and are largely conflicting; and they are drawn from many heterogeneous sources. In fact, if the self means merely what interests us personally, then at any one time it is likely to be too wide, and perhaps also too narrow; and at different times it seems quite at variance with itself."[35]

It is true that interests are of themselves contingent, variable, and often circumstantially inspired. But these characteristics do not qualify a self that is determined by a *principle* of interests. According to eudaimonism the principle of interests is itself an interest, but an enduring, dominant interest, not circumstantially produced but innate. It subsists within the individual as a potential to be actualized, and its actualization produces organization and unification of other interests, transforming the native heterogeneity of experience through its singularity. It is capable of assimilating any experience whatever, in the respect that whatever the experience, it is experienced as distinctively one's own in the qualitative sense. Because it is thus extensively unlimited it cannot be found "too narrow." But neither is it "too wide," for by remaining just what it is, the unification it achieves is preserved against diversity and multiplicity, against "double-mindedness" and reduction to the mindless numerical. In fact, the individual is thus a "concrete universal" in a sense similar to Bradley's, in which "nothing can be lost," but everything is "made good, so as to minister to harmony."[36] But in the true meaning of "individual" he is a concrete universal among others of his kind.

There need be no contradiction in the interrelationship of a multiplicity of such individuals. The doctrine of the internality of all relations introduces contradiction only on condition that the foreign terms of the relation appear within each other as foreign. If B is substantively different in kind from A, and by relationship to A appears within A as B, then indeed A stands in self-contradiction as being both itself and what it is not. But if B appears in A under an aspect that is determined by the principle of A, then no contradiction is involved. Moreover interpenetration only produces contradiction when A and B as originally constituted are mutually exclusive. But by the conception of the self as set forth by eudaimonism, A and B cannot be so understood, for each of itself contains the possibility of the other as part of its "common humanity."

The theory of relations presented here is termed "perspectivism" or "monadism."[37] Its unity lies in the preservation by each subject of its singular "point of view" upon all things.* Inner discord results from combination or exchange of "points of view," and within the undisciplined consciousness such combinations and exchanges will be sure to occur, and to occur randomly. "Know thyself" and "Become what you are" are precisely the calls to the discipline that diminishes and aims ultimately to abolish this source of inner discord.

To take the case a step further, internal contradiction will be eliminated only if the principle of the individual's interests is unique to him, for otherwise the principle itself is infected with the diversity Bradley notes with respect to content. Hence the system here conceived is predicated upon the ultimate uniqueness of every individual, and the Greek intuition of ultimate individuation is vindicated.

To summarize our findings: Absolute Idealism affords no advance over classical eudaimonism, and in fact can make no ethical contribution whatever. Nor is its critique of finite individuality effective against eudaimonism's conception of the person as a "universal-particular." Rather, eudaimonism's ideal of a community of perfected, unique, and complementary individuals remains viable ethically, while the "self-realization" of Absolute Idealism cannot provide normative principles for determinate action. There remains an ultimate discrepancy in Absolute Idealism, whose treatment must await its place in the progress of our inquiry (in Chapter 5, on the metaphysics of individualism). According

* Leibniz's phrase, "point of view," is employed here for its simplicity and vividness. It has the defect of connoting visual perspectives, while the perspectives of which we speak are systems of meanings.

to Absolute Idealism all development in the world is the self-realization of the Absolute, the real, singular, and solitary individual. But by the ordinary meaning there cannot be but one individual, for the word "individual" refers to a one among others of its kind. And we shall see that such is necessarily the case, for that there are others of the same kind is a necessary condition of the "completeness, coherence, and self-containedness" by which Absolute Idealism (correctly) defines individuality. To be an individual, a concrete universal must be one among others of its kind, and the exemplification of this principle appears not only in the necessary multiplicity of persons in the world but likewise in the necessary multiplicity of "worlds," or "universes," or "absolutes," or "abiding selves." The condition for any concrete individual is other individuals of his kind, and this condition is first of all logical and a priori, and only thereafter empirical. Therefore we agree with Max Scheler's contention that a hypothetical Robinson Crusoe who has lived always on his desert island and never seen another human being, will recognize himself as a social being—a one among others of his kind—insofar as he recognizes himself to be an individual.[38] Correspondingly we shall propose that from the recognizable individuality of our world must be inferred the necessary subsistence of alternative worlds.

In fairness, British Absolute Idealism has been judged harshly here because it has been abstracted from its historical setting and judged in the conceptual context of ethical eudaimonism. If we restore it to the context of traditional British individualism we immediately elevate it, for there it stands as a corrective to the narrowest and most untenable conception of the individual—numerical, mechanical, egoistic. By its conception of the individual as an ideal whole within a larger ideal whole, and as a moral task, British Absolute Idealism unquestionably moved toward the truth. But it fatally overstepped, and by losing the individual in the whole it proved itself to be but one more over-reaction in the historical dialectic of extremisms. As Rudolph Eucken says, "The historical process of human society exhibits a rhythmical tendency; we perceive in it a movement from a general order to the individual, as also a movement from the individual to the general order, and the culmination of either seems to lead inevitably to the other."[39]

The pendulum-swing of excess to contrary excess is unproductive, and should be wrenched into a development. Individualism—even of the soulless sort—is an advance over pre-individual collectivism, for it multiplies the possibilities available for actualization. In its initial phases it is inevitably crude and brutal, indulging in excesses of egoism, competition, strife, and alienation. But at this stage a reversion to anti-individualistic absolutisms is not inevitable, but only a resort of desperation arising from poverty of imagination, i.e. from inability to visualize what has not heretofore happened in history. The corrective constituting development is the refinement of crude individuation toward a profound individuation that discovers the inherent sociality of true individuals. This sociality is a whole that is to be won, not by suppression of its parts, but by their fulfillment *as parts*. Under the term "consequent sociality" it furnishes the theme of Chapters, 8, 9, and 10.

In the meantime our historical assessment must take account of the pendulum-swing that constitutes modernity's most uncompromising expression of ethical individualism—continental Existentialism.

3

Critique of Recent Eudaimonisms:
Kierkegaard and Nietzsche

By all odds the most daring and vigorous proponent of self-actualization ethics since the Hellenes has been twentieth-century continental Existentialism and its two flaming precursors, Søren Kierkegaard and Friedrich Nietzsche. Of twentieth-century existentialists we shall concentrate upon Sartre, whose *Being and Nothingness* constitutes the apex of the movement insofar as it does not merely repeat but seeks to surpass Greek eudaimonism. For while all existentialists affirm qualitative individuality as the normative determinant in human behavior, Sartre alone denies innatism, contending that each self is its own groundless and spontaneous construct or "fundamental project." By this contention *Being and Nothingness* achieves profound originality.

The way to Sartre, however, was laid by Kierkegaard and Nietzsche, and we shall begin by giving careful attention to these two philosophical daredevils, each of whom undertook entirely alone to lay waste every opponent of the moral sovereignty of the solitary individual—the person who, finding himself amidst a throng, nevertheless assumes sole self-responsibility and thereby introduces into his life its moral necessity.

To confront these two figures full-face we must at the outset shun the perennial mistake of regarding one or both as essentially nihilistic destroyers. Each was a relentless ethical constructivist who was obliged to lay to rest the swarming misconceptions of his time in order to prepare the way for warranted affirmations. Doubtless, misconceptions swarm in every time, and the constructive thinker may

64

be thought to have a responsibility to handle them gently—amending, eliciting, guiding. But such a pedagogical procedure presupposes that the misconceptions stand on a continuum with the truth: common belief, so to speak, is on the path to truth but has sat down with itself prematurely. But suppose common opinion is not merely short of the truth but is entirely contrary to the truth; then gentleness is only complicity in error, and what is required is common belief's complete undoing, root and branch. Such was the situation according to the assessments of Kierkegaard and Nietzsche. Common belief sat down with itself—on the wrong path. Reigning philosophy sat down with itself—on its head. And Christianity was for Nietzsche retrograde and immoral in its marrow, while to Kierkegaard it had become institutional and thereby "numerical," which for Kierkegaard meant closed to the truth.

In Kierkegaard's famous dictum, "Subjectivity is the truth."[1] Subjectivity comprises everything that each individual experiences immediately as his own. It is identical with "thought" in the broad Cartesian sense of "doubting, understanding, conceiving, affirming, denying, willing, refusing, imagining, feeling."[2] Credit for recognizing the arena of subjectivity as the ground of truth must go to Descartes, who pointed out that one's thought, feeling, or fantasy, whatever else it might be, is indubitably one's thought, feeling, or fantasy. Unfortunately Descartes dashed past this seminal insight to proclaim the indubitable existence of something else entirely, namely *res cogitans*, thinking substance. *Res cogitans* is not one's own thought (or subjectivity) but all thought. Moreover it is no longer even subjectivity (as defined above), for it has been made over into an object for thought and thereby expelled outside of thought, subsisting as a cosmic substance.

The analogous mistake by Hegel is the antipode against which Kierkegaard develops a profound individualism. In the words of the consummate philosopher of the Absolute: "By the term 'I' I mean myself, a single and altogether determinate person. And yet I really utter nothing peculiar to myself, for everyone else is an 'I' or 'Ego,' and when I call myself 'I,' although I indubitably mean the single person myself, I express a thorough universal. 'I,' therefore, is mere being-for-itself, in which everything peculiar or marked is renounced and buried out of sight; it is as it were the ultimate and unanalyzable point of consciousness. We may say [that] 'I' and thought are the same, or, more definitely [that] 'I' is thought as thinker."[3]

Terming it the "evaporation" of the individual in the undifferentiated universal of thought, Kierkegaard strenuously opposes Hegel's thesis. The thesis is blind to the absolute categorial distinction that marks off one's own subjectivity from that of others, namely that only one's own is immediately available to him, while others' must be inferred. To mark this absolute distinction Kierkegaard reserves the term "subjectivity" for that which is immediate exclusively to each person. Subjectivity is what distinguishes one "I" from every other, from its own standpoint. Hegel can obliterate this distinction only by pretending to speak from every standpoint at once, a feat that is identical to speaking from no standpoint, and that convicts itself of empty abstractionism.

Hegel's universal "being-for-itself" is not "for itself" (self-conscious) except to a hypothetical Absolute, which no person is, and if one person lacks immediate access to others like himself, much less does he have immediate access to universal being-for-itself. From subjectivity such being can be inferred without contradiction, but the inference is not necessary. And the being thus inferred is devoid (as we saw in the cases of Bradley, Green, and Bosanquet) of normative power. An undifferentiated Absolute is normatively impotent because it can offer no principle for the apportionment of responsibility—it is undifferentiated, and that is that. The responsibility that goes with consciousness is undifferentiated if consciousness itself is both undifferentiated and the ground of normativity. Such responsibility would

66

be everyone's and no one's in particular. But every finite person is "this one and no other." As such it is impc ssible for him to act for everyone, and a "responsibility" for him to do so is a contradiction in terms (for responsibility presupposes possibility). To be what it is, responsibility must be apportionable such that it can be fulfilled by acts that are exclusive of other acts. Such apportionment is afforded by subjectivity (in Kierkegaard's meaning) in virtue of the distinction it establishes between one self and every other. The ubiquitous synthesizing of Hegel's "both-and" is exchanged by Kierkegaard for the determinateness of the disjunctive "either/or." One is not both himself and other persons, nor can such a synthesis afford a regulative ideal, for as such it obliterates the ground of morality. As for the Greeks, so for Kierkegaard, each person is in the exclusive sense his own first problem.

Kierkegaard is also at one with classical eudaimonism in affirming that the self that the individual is to actualize progressively is a priori and innate. Thus he says, "I do not know whether it is true that at each man's birth two angels are born, his good angel and his bad angel. But this I do believe (and I will gladly listen to any objection, although I will not believe it) that at each man's birth there comes into being an eternal vocation for him, expressly for him. To be true to himself in relation to this eternal vocation is the highest thing a man can practice, and, as that most profound poet has said: 'Self-love is not so vile a sin as self-neglecting.' Then there is but one fault, one offense: disloyalty to his own self or the denial of his own better self."[4]

In this passage Kierkegaard's debt to the Greeks is conspicuous. What he adds to their general conception is first of all a developed conception of the stages of life by which self-actualization must proceed* and, second, a theory of

---

* Greek conceptions of the stages of life are not lacking—e.g. Solon's ten stages (Solon, Bergk, *Poetae Lyrici Graeci*, II, 27), the three stages noted by Plutarch (*Lycurgus* 21.11-15), the six stages of

individuation according to which each person's individuality derives from an ineffable God and is humanly unintelligible, to be discovered not by reason but by faith. We shall consider each of these Kierkegaardian offerings in turn.

Much has been written about Kierkegaard's three stages of personal development, therefore we shall offer here only such a summary as will divulge those points that bear directly on our purpose. The three stages are termed by Kierkegaard the aesthetic, the ethical, and the stage of faith. While the person cannot discover his "vocation" (or unique destiny) until the final stage, the logic of the stages is such that no stage can be circumvented, for the complete fulfillment of the requirements of each stage is the prerequisite to entrance upon the next. Only by exhausting the demands of a given stage does one exhaust its promise, thereby reaping the *despair* by which the stage is relinquished. Moreover each stage is a wholistic perspective upon all things, including other stages. Consequently from within a given stage nothing can be learned about other stages, for whatever information about them an individual may receive is converted by him into the terms of the stage in which he presently finds himself. Finally, because the stages are incommensurable perspectives, the movement from one to another cannot be accomplished by gradual transition, but only by abrupt exchange (hence the celebrated "leap of faith" by which the third stage is attained has been preceded by a structurally identical "leap" between stages one and two).

The first, or aesthetic stage is thoroughly youthful and replete with those qualities that constitute virtues in youth—energy, vivacity, directness, daring, restlessness. It is the stage of the "sensuous immediate," dominated by spontane-

---

Plato's "ladder of love" (*Symposium* 210), or Aristotle's three stages (*Rhetoric* 1388b–1390a)—but they were not systematically integrated with eudaimonism. The *Nichomachean Ethics*, for example, treats moral life as but a single stage.

ous likings and aversions, and able to indulge these to the full due to its thoughtlessness, for the aesthetic stage is pre-rational. The stage is personified in two archetypes, Johannes the Seducer and the "musical" Don Juan[5] (of Mozart; for according to Kierkegaard music is uniquely the medium of the sensuous-immediate).

Don Juan is pure immediacy, for him "to see is to love," and not to see is to love no longer. Incapable of anticipation or recollection, he precludes the anticipations and recollections of the women he seduces by the tactic epitomized in his motto, "To horse and to spur, in this extremity"—the tactic of haste. To understand how he seduces 1003 women in Spain alone, we must recognize that he is entirely indiscriminate. Whether the woman before him be rich or poor, noble or peasant, fat or lean, beautiful or ugly—these are matters of no moment to him; she is a woman, and that is all that matters.

On the side of the women we must recognize that at bottom they are not fooled by Don Juan, nor does Don Juan deceive them. Deception on Don Juan's part is impossible, for deception is misrepresentation, which requires duplicity, two-sidedness, while Don Juan is pure immediacy and therefore incapable of deception. Shall we suppose that 1003 women (in Spain alone) are deceived by a being who is incapable of deception? To do so would be to suppose that they deceive themselves—a supposition as untenable as it is unproductive, for women are not such colossal fools as this in the very affairs (of the heart) at which they are rightly credited with expertise. No, we must seek Don Juan's secret in a positive benefit he confers upon the women he seduces (and by this orientation Kierkegaard directs us to look for the specific virtues of the aesthetic stage, for only when its virtues are fully recognized—and embodied —can the necessity for the stage's transcendence be perceived). Kierkegaard finds it in Don Juan's very indiscrimination. By disregarding differences among women, Don Juan reveals his aim to be the essential feminine, the generic womanness in every individual woman, and his interest elicits and valorizes this essence in every woman. Don Juan does this precisely because, as pre-rational and unreflective, he is unable to compare and contrast. Therefore not only is he confined to pure presence, but amid pure presence he perceives the generic essence, shorn of transitory adornment (for essences present themselves; they only seem hidden, requiring to be laboriously uncovered or circuitously inferred, because transitory qualities dance and dazzle us). In its own way, then, simplicity is not falsehood but truth— truth in the mode of pure immediacy, which can grasp essences in their qualitative vividness, yet cannot know that they endure (hence cannot know them *as* essences) because by immediacy time is contracted to point-instants, and appearances are shorn of past and future. Accordingly the woman in Don Juan's arms is shorn of her past and her future, thereby gaining her freedom. ("Hurrah for Freedom," exclaims Don Giovanni as the three avenging masks advance upon him in the last act of Mozart's opera, and "*Viva la Libertà*" is picked up by twelve different voices, ringing forth to the final *tutti*.) The past of which she is shorn was also her servitude, for her future had been extrapolated from it by expectation and habit. But in Don Juan's arms she discovers the freedom to choose whatever future she wishes, and thereby to choose herself.

In short, Don Juan offers vividness, liveliness, immediacy, freedom—qualities of life that are spoiled by promises and duties, recollections and anticipations. For memory detains us from advancing with the present, while many are the prospective joys that are worn out by anticipation.

The annihilation of the present by anticipation and recollection is effectively represented in the figure of Johannes the Seducer. So committed is he to his plotting and scheming that the moment, when it arrives, is nothing, and afterward he has only his plotting and scheming to remember. And wholly unlike Don Juan, Johannes longs for possession, yet can possess nothing because he is forever an absentee, having projected himself forward and backward in time. In truth, the woman in his arms finds herself utterly alone.

Johannes is the malevolent ruin of the aesthetic, yet even Don Juan, as the purity and attractive innocence of the sensuous immediate, is doomed to despair. For without duration he has no identity at all. "Who am I?" asks Don Juan in the original play by Tirso de Molina, and he answers, "A man without a name." He has been only a catalyst of a reaction in the women he seduces, leaving no trace in the result.* Yet his despair at his own nothingness takes the form, according to Kierkegaard, of an "aesthetic spiritlessness"[6] that does not recognize itself as despair. The truth of the matter is that Don Juan succumbs to boredom (and the episodic repetitousness of Casanova's extensive *Memoirs* defies the reader to follow them more than halfway without lapsing into this same condition). Lacking reflective capacity, Don Juan can neither compare nor contrast, and is thus enmeshed in a relentless and unrelieved sameness in which he succumbs finally to boredom. Thus overcome, we may suppose that he no longer dashes about but sits down with himself, and thereby he unwittingly assumes the posture of readiness for—an idea.

In Kierkegaard's format the first and second stages of self-actualization are incommensurable because what immediacy requires is precisely that which it is not and cannot be, namely mediation. Mediation is the province of the idea, and the second or "ethical" stage is the stage of rationality, epitomized in the second volume of *Either/Or* by Judge William. To overcome the transitoriness of spontaneous preference and distaste (the aesthetic stage), life must acquire the unity, coherence, and duration that is afforded by the universal but singular idea. What must be won here is

---

* Here again, Casanova may instruct us concerning Don Juan: for the former was a scrupulous user of male contraceptives—fashioned from the intestines of livestock—and is not to be supposed to have left behind him a trail of progeny nursed by resentful mothers.

symbolized, as against the ephemeral serial seductions of Don Juan, by Judge William's strict fidelity in marriage to a single woman. Yet rationality is destined to inevitable failure because its universality, far from connecting particulars, is purchased at the cost of particulars. It therefore (and Hegel's ethics is for Kierkegaard the prime example) transforms life into an abstract universal that is empty of all finite historical content—of the content that shone in the aesthetic stage, for example—and thus it abandons that which it promised to preserve. Instead of providing a principle by which life can be ordered, it hands down principles for the sacrifice of living.

The despair marking the demise of the ethical stage is not alone the despairing emptiness of rationality but a summarizing despair that encompasses and annihilates both the first and second stages. It is despair of attaining salvation by one's own efforts, despair of helping oneself, and thereby it is the despair that opens to faith. To be open to faith a man must "die to the world, and hate himself,"[7] for self-centeredness and world-centeredness are irreconcilable with God-centeredness. So long as he retains the slightest hope in his own efforts a man will cling to himself and thereby preclude that salvation that requires his "becoming nothing in the hand of the Helper for whom all things are possible."[8]

Faith is the stage in which finite and infinite meet as witnessed in the Incarnation of God in Jesus Christ. Kierkegaard emphasizes the rational ineffability of faith by characterizing it as the absurd. It calls for the relinquishment of rationality in the "teleological suspension of the ethical" as personified in Abraham, who acts to fulfill a commandment he can in no way understand and one requiring that he violently sacrifice that which among earthly things he most loves, his son Isaac. Thus Abraham demonstrates that faith is "expressed in him whose life is not merely the most paradoxical that can be thought, but so paradoxical that it cannot be thought at all."[9] But to relinquish oneself as Abraham does is thereby to gain oneself. Kierkegaard describes the transformation in deliberately circumlocuted terms. "Faith," he says, "is precisely this paradox, that the individual as the particular is higher than the universal, is justified over against it, is not subordinate but superior—yet in such a way, be it observed, that it is the particular individual who, after he has been subordinated as the particular to the universal, now through the universal becomes the individual who as the particular is superior to the universal, for the fact that the individual as the particular stands in an absolute relation to the absolute. This position cannot be mediated, for all mediation comes about precisely by virtue of the universal; it is and remains to all eternity a paradox, inaccessible to thought."[10]

For our purposes the principal point to be wrested from the passage is that the determinant of "higher" individuality rests with God (The Absolute) and is strictly unintelligible to persons themselves. But before turning to this we must take care to follow Kierkegaard's delineation of the very subtle relationship of this superior individuality to human understanding. In the first place, while it is in faith that one discovers his unique and eternal vocation, faith itself is only possible "after he has been subordinated as the particular to the universal," or in other words only after the absolute limit of his own rational endeavor has been reached. Thus, while faith in a definite sense annihilates reason, it thereby presupposes it, and the antithesis between the two is not absolute but dialectical.

Second, the haste of many commentators to give full weight to Kierkegaard's call for a leap into the absurd has tended to obscure the large place reserved by him within faith for services that only discursive reason can provide. In short, our investigation of faith according to Kierkegaard must not be diverted by *Fear and Trembling* from his other treatments such as, most notably, *Works of Love* and *Purity of Heart Is To Will One Thing*,[11] in which it is disclosed that faith, while contrary to prudence and common sense, has a fine internal logic of its own. In particular *Purity of Heart* is unsurpassed as a short guide to self-actualization, and it demands on every page that an individual have his wits about him. With stunning psychological acuity Kierkegaard unearths every seduction and self-deception lying in wait for him who seeks to live in truth to himself. But the canniness and rational acumen that *Purity of Heart* calls upon is strictly put to the service of faith.

Of all opponents of eudaimonism, Kierkegaard must surely be the most welcome to eudaimonists themselves, just as he is the most dangerous. He is the most welcome because he sets out to win converts to eudaimonism, presenting eudaimonist truths in striking form and contributing countless invaluable insights in the course of his presentation. But eudaimonism is fostered by Kierkegaard in order that its failure may be complete and its abandonment final.

For to Kierkegaard the solitary individual must be alone with God to find himself in the truth; he must acknowledge his utter dependence upon God. This acknowledgment is the "fundamental condition" for salvation, and because this alone is lacking in the eudaimonist, he is deepest in sin and "infinitely remote" from the truth, while at the same time being nearest to the truth save only for the "knight of faith" himself. To will to become an individual without reliance upon God is the sin of defiance, "which really is despair by the aid of the eternal, the despairing abuse of the eternal in the self to the point of being despairingly determined to be oneself."[12]

Against "defiance" (more strictly, anthropocentric self-actualization), Kierkegaard offers two pointed contentions, neither of which is more than contingently effective. The first is the claim that such self-actualization necessarily *is* defiance of God, presupposing Him in order to deny Him. But this argument is plainly question-begging, presupposing both the reality of the Christian God and His universal recognition among men. It paraphrases the once common belief that atheism consists in the active denial of God, which thereby presupposes Him, even constituting a proof of His existence. The contention is indefensible logically, for to generalize it would be to transform all denial into affirmation, thereby peopling the world with every sort of fantastic creature (my denial of the fiery dragon presupposes and thereby affirms its existence). It performs this trick by simply confusing conceptions of things with the existences of the same things. What is required to deny God is not His existence, but only a conception of Him. Apart from this logical fallacy, an empirical one is also involved, for historically the immense diversity of human beliefs and principles renders it implausible that all who live without the Christian God must live expressly against Him. For example those religions, philosophies, and moral systems that antedate the appearance of Christianity in the world—Hinduism, Buddhism, and eudaimonism, to name but three—can have had no such instigation in the minds of their founders and early adherents. On the other hand if Kierkegaard means to allege that ignorance of God is nonetheless defiance of him, then the claim succumbs to the generalization principle, for we cannot seriously be thought to defy everything of which we may be ignorant—Atman-Brahman, for instance, or Hegel's Absolute, or the cosmic principles of astrology.

Against Godless self-actualization Kierkegaard's second pointed charge is that it cannot be successful at what it undertakes, which is the constituting of itself as an individual. This is so, he says, because self-actualization is "really related to itself only as experimenting with whatsoever it be that it undertakes." For it "lacks seriousness and is able only to conjure up a show of seriousness when the self bestows upon its experiments its utmost attention."[13]

But this contention breaks upon an historical wall whose every stone is the committed life of a scientist, artist, craftsman, humanitarian, for whom the natural order was more than sufficient for exacting "seriousness." Doubtless it would be folly to deny that the great majority of lives are unsteady in their aim and less than conclusive in their integrity, but, to disprove the indispensability of Christian faith to "seriousness," majorities are not needed—a single instance will suffice. Not only does history disclose many instances, but it exhibits a "saint" of eudaimonism in the person of Socrates. A thoroughgoing humanist, Socrates advised that if there be gods, then by all accounts of their superior powers they can safely be left to manage their own affairs, leaving men free to devote themselves to human problems. And the integrity manifested by Socrates in his single-minded demonstration of the power of personal truth in human life stands as the consummate example, capable of sustaining emulation by every person.

At the same time the example of Socrates discloses a crucial flaw in Kierkegaard's case against anthropocentric self-actualization. If we allow Kierkegaard to define "unseriousness" as episodic experimentation without commitment, then the life of Socrates betrays no trace of it. In the face of patent failure and, at last, under sentence of death, Socrates remained irrevocably what he was. The tenacity of Socrates demonstrates that in human affairs no failure can be final; toward a given end there will always, in the nature of the case, be recourses as yet untried. And the case of Socrates further demonstrates that neither circumstances nor other persons can pronounce failure upon the man who does not pronounce it upon himself.

This means that a man's self-acknowledged failure to attain salvation by his own efforts—the acknowledgment that in Kierkegaard's scheme of the stages is the necessary prerequisite to the theocentric faith of the final stage—can never in truth be final. Never can it constitute the recognition of the ultimate failure of anthropocentrism, but always must it be a mere giving up out of weariness, a conditional and unnecessary giving in. Accordingly, Kierkegaard's "knight of faith" is not him who has resolutely and courageously tested human nature and found it wanting, he is and must be one who has simply given up on himself. His resort

76

to faith attests to his faint-heartedness, and the immense strength ascribed to him by Kierkegaard as the individual who "wills one thing" is revealed to have a foundation of sand. For there can be no testimony to the final failure of the human enterprise short of human extinction, nor can there be testimony to the final failure of an individual life short of the end of—not that life alone (as the case of Socrates shows)—but of all human life. It is this recognition that undergirds a resolute humanism and by which it spurns the seduction of self-relinquishment in faith.

Our task has been to evaluate the philosophy of Kierkegaard as it bears upon classical eudaimonism, and the following conclusions are now in order. Kierkegaard advances eudaimonism significantly by his recognition that an account of self-actualization must be genetic, in terms of stages of development and readiness, and that the stages are in significant respects incommensurable, each affording values and imposing obligations exclusive to itself. Further, by his keen psychological insight and his deep understanding of the dynamics of personal destiny and self-responsibility, Kierkegaard repeatedly casts new light upon the course of self-actualization.

But it must not be forgotten that Kierkegaard sought to perfect eudaimonism in order to destroy it, and this intention permeates his account of the human enterprise in its entirety. To become an individual is each person's highest task, but he can do this only before God, for God is the source of his individuating principle; and he can do this only in faith, for as a finite existent he can in no way comprehend the Infinite. The upshot is that individuation is humanly unintelligible, and the nature of each person's individuality is and will ever be unintelligible to him. In sum, each person's enterprise of individuation is a matter for blind obedience alone, to which he can in no way contribute out of his own resources. It follows that nothing in the way of a method for self-discovery can be offered, since delineation of a method requires knowledge of the end that the method is intended to serve. Here we see why not one word about a method for self-discovery appears in the otherwise splendid eudaimonist treatise, *Purity of Heart Is To Will One Thing*, nor anywhere else in Kierkegaard's writings. For it must be remembered that the aesthetic and ethical stages—themselves replete with methods, and together constituting a method—are wholly prior to the person's discovery of his true individuality. This discovery marks the onset of the third stage, occurring in faith and before God. And as individuation is "so paradoxical that it cannot be thought at all," it is not amenable to the ministrations of method. One can but act, and trust in God. But here the responsibility for man is lifted from his shoulders and transferred to God, and in this situation ethics—as Kierkegaard fully recognized, terming faith the "suspension of the ethical"—is impossible. It is impossible, not because there are no principles of normative judgments (each person's principle of individuation is such), but because such principles cannot be humanly known or subjected to test.

Kierkegaard thus resolves the paradox of human existence, as the relation of the infinite in the finite and the eternal in the temporal, by assigning all authority and power to the eternal. But eudaimonism stands by a different resolution, and one that preserves the integrity of individuals, not merely in the beginning and derivatively, but in the end and finally. For Kierkegaard is right in insisting that individuality requires the presence of the eternal in the temporal. It is only by its reflection of something eternal that a principle of individuation can achieve identity amid the disparateness and transitoriness of human wants and desires. By the touch of the eternal the principle affords continuity to personal life, changelessness amid change. But eudaimonism finds the eternal in the metaphysical category of possibility, whereas by Kierkegaard the eternal is deified. The difference is monumental. For under eudaimonism the eternal, as the merely possible, is impotent, requiring human agency for its actualization. But for Kierkegaard the eternal is a God whose omnipotence renders human agency gratuitous. Under eudaimonism each person is responsible for making himself an individual by means of the eternal. For Kierkegaard it is the Eternal that makes individuals and is responsible for them.

The consequence is that Kierkegaard's doctrine of the stages is no innocent offering, to be accepted gratefully by eudaimonism as a contribution toward its own completion. The sting in its tail consists in the tenets that individuation comes from an omnipotent God and is humanly unintelligible—doctrines that are fatal to eudaimonism and, indeed, to ethics. At most, eudaimonism learns from Kierkegaard of the indispensability to itself of a conception of stages of personal growth, each with values and obligations of its own. To develop such a conception, however, eudaimonism must not follow Kierkegaard but rather must begin afresh, looking at life with its own eyes.

"Higher than 'Thou shalt' is 'I will;' higher than 'I will' stands 'I am.' "[14] These words by Nietzsche cast cold light upon the inner being of the "knight of faith," disclosing hollowness there. For the "I am" is the *Übermensch* or "higher man" within the human person, the powerful, creative, unique identity to be attained by self-actualization. The means of self-actualization is the "I will," the will to power or *vis creativa*, which, released from the fetters of convention, reason, sentiment, and guilt, becomes the "long will" of self-founding and integral personhood. But this priority of will was not even ventured upon by Kierkegaard's "knight of faith" in the anthropocentric portion of his quest. In relation to that quest it represents an altogether untried modality and a further stage. Thereby it demonstrates what we have previously noted concerning anthropocentrism, namely that its recourses can never be exhausted, that untrod paths will ever lie before it. Not only has the "knight of faith" prematurely abandoned both the aesthetic and the ethical stages, but he leaves untouched entire modalities and stages—witness the stage that is affirmed by Nietzsche to hold life's consummation. To him who chooses it "seriously," anthropocentrism can never be depleted or discredited, and herein appears the "unseriousness" of the knight of faith, who first chooses himself and then—unchooses; and then repeats this process; and finally chooses to represent himself as God's choice. He thereby places himself among those who, in Nietzsche's words, "dare to fulfill their task only as the command of a god; only as an 'inspiration' is their value legislation a *bearable* burden under which their conscience is not crushed."[15]

Against such vacillations Zarathustra's charge rings out: "Let your spirit and your virtue serve the sense of the earth, my brothers; and let the value of all things be posited newly by you."[16] His call to "Choose yourself" does not mean for an hour or so, or until trouble arises, but first and finally, for only by such an unequivocal choice is one's own being founded.

Solitude as the true situation of the moral individual is insisted upon no less by Kierkegaard than by Nietzsche, but for Kierkegaard it means the aloneness of the individual in his relationship to God. For Nietzsche such pseudo-solitude begets only pseudo-individuality, and against it he inveighs: "Are we never to have the right of remaining alone with ourselves? Are we always to be watched, guarded, surrounded by leading-strings and gifts? If there is always someone round about us, the best part of courage and kindness will ever remain impossible of attainment in this world. Are we not tempted to fly to hell before this continual obtrusiveness of heaven, this inevitable supernatural neighbor?"[17] (For myself, I am glad that at this moment Nietzsche has forgotten the Biblical advice that God is the companion even of the residents of hell.)

Loyalty to life, according to Nietzsche, begins in the resolve to seek life's principle within itself and not in something outside it—not, for example, in a God or supernature that, by being conceived as all that life is not—infinite, eternal, changeless, perfect goodness, perfect plenitude—stands as antithetical to life. Life's fundamental character is perpetual process, whose nature is a "self-surpassing," and whose internal agency is will. Will affords self-surpassing by apprehending possibilities and transforming them into actualities. It cannot be conceived as will to life or will to existence, for thus it would be in the contradictory position of striving to become what it already is. Nor can it be conceived as the will to what is other than itself, for thereby it is self-alienating and self-contradictory. The famous conclusion offered by Nietzsche is that the principle of life is will to power, understood as life's perpetual will to its own increase and perfection.[18]

Much of the aversion this doctrine has produced will be allayed by noticing its striking resemblance to Aristotle's dictum that the aim of life is first to live well, and next to live still better. To be sure, the difference remains that for Aristotle the aim is given to life by reason, while for Nietzsche the aim is pre-rational and vital. But this difference cannot account for the disparity of responses to the two doctrines. For Aristotle's offering is generally taken for a benign truism, while Nietzsche's regularly provokes indignation and outrage. Such exaggeration results because the hearer jumps to conclusions on the basis of mere words. The hearer thinks that what Aristotle is talking about everyone already knows, and what Nietzsche is talking about no right-minded person wants to hear. But he misconceives what is being spoken about in each case.

Far from nihilistic, Nietzsche's ambition is to "transvaluate all values" according to the normative standard of life's own self-surpassing. To this end he calls for the replacement of "good" and "evil" by "health" and "sickness" as evaluative concepts. By the concepts "good" and "evil," conventional morality has sought to obstruct and suppress will to power in the name of purported authorities outside of life itself, but "health" and "sickness" are evaluative concepts that find their authority in life as will to power. Health denotes all that contributes to ascendent vitality, while sickness characterizes whatever contributes to life's degeneration and demise (and includes, in Nietzsche's judgment, both the "good" and the "evil" of conventional morality).

But sickness and health are hereby tied to life as will to power, while the latter remains as yet abstract, for "There is no such thing as 'willing,' but only a willing *something*."[19] On this intentionalist principle Nietzsche identifies the ultimate aim of will to power (and likewise the "ideal" that is required if the concepts of health and morbidity are to "make sense") as the *Übermensch*—the "higher man" who constitutes the consummation of life and the complete manifestation of human virtue.

If we would understand Nietzsche aright the first supposition to be discarded is that the concept of the *Übermensch* will designate a cadre of "blond beasts"[20] who will dominate and suppress the masses of humanity. It is precisely against the suppression of humanity that Nietzsche strove lifelong. His "Yea-saying" is the affirmation of life itself by means of every individual life. But each individual must in the first instance affirm his own life—no other can do it for him; and in the absence of such self-affirmation the individual remains a dependent creature. "He who cannot obey himself is commanded."[21] Like the child he is commanded —until he can obey himself.

Nietzsche's *Übermensch* is the higher being in every person. We know this to be necessarily the case because, as life itself, every person is will to power, and by the intentionality of will (affirmed by Nietzsche in the citation above), the object of will to power—the *Übermensch*—must likewise subsist within every person. In Zarathustra's words, it is "the phantom that runneth on before thee [and] is fairer than thou."[22] This ineluctable logic receives practical endorsement when we find Zarathustra preaching the same message to the sick, the weak, and the convention-bound ("you virtuous ones") as to his followers, namely "That your virtue is yourself and not something foreign, a skin, or cloak; that is your truth from the foundation of your souls."[23]

Likewise the servant and "the herd" are not persons distinct from "the noble ones" but components of personhood within every person. Indeed, these components supply the foundation and scaffolding of the *Übermensch*, and Nietzsche's diatribes against them must not be thought to be aimed at their eradication.* What Nietzsche attacks is the relegation of leadership in the formation of personality or social structure to the essentially subservient components.

The servant within every individual comprises the merely instrumental components—sensation, affection, imagination, and, yes, reason—which, because they are incapable of apprehending the *telos* of life, must accept the organizing authority of the teleological faculty, the intentional will, and lend themselves to its self-surpassing. "The herd" (undifferentiated common humanity) is assuredly within every person because what Nietzsche means by individuality is an emergent property. "First, peoples were creators; and only in later times, individuals. Verily, the individual himself is still the most recent creation."[24] Every person begins as common humanity and ever thereafter bears common humanity within him; therefore Zarathustra warns his followers, "And you have long belonged to the herd. The voice of the herd will still be audible in you."[25] They are to seek within themselves the singular principle that can organize and give direction to "the herd" within.

In sum, within each person are "master" and "slave," *telos* and means, a "higher man" and "herd." Health consists in the sovereignty of what is highest, sickness in disarray, and

---

* Nietzsche says it is "fortunate" to "have only one virtue and no more" (*Zarathustra*, Part I, "On Enjoying and Suffering the Passions"). It follows that fulfilled individuals are not devoid of dependence. The fulfilled individual is dependent upon others because of their expression of virtues that he does not possess.

degeneracy in the usurpation of authority by what is lowest. Likewise for society. Nietzsche's social and political philosophy does not posit the necessity of persons of the "herd" type, but only the inevitability of their presence and the likelihood that at any given time such persons will constitute the majority. His true social ideal is a "higher society" analogous to the "higher man" and composed exclusively of such. The "phantom that runneth on before thee" is within every person, but in practical fact most persons will not undertake the hard self-demands and relentless endeavor required to keep pace with their "phantom." This fact draws from Nietzsche neither abuse nor despair, he merely affirms it. What he vigorously castigates is the leadership of the human endeavor by persons who "cannot obey themselves" through sheer weight of numbers (with the help of conventional morality and the "bad conscience" of exceptional persons). No one will have failed to observe that small children issue commands by dozens; and, in general, demands upon others come quickest from those who ask least of themselves. But in the interest of the qualitative improvement of human life, commands from these sources are not to be obeyed.

Concerning the form of the *Übermensch* as it subsists in each person, Nietzsche sets forth the following features. It appears within each person in a form unique to him. It is innate and strictly unalterable by the individual, who can choose only to fulfill or neglect it. It subsists not as a fait accompli but as a potentiality and a task. It is discovered not by reason but by will—i.e. by action—and is conceived and clarified by reason only a posteriori. And to the degree to which it is actualized it ennobles not only the individual but all humanity. We will say a few words about each of these traits as Nietzsche offers them.

Nietzsche will allow no foothold to the idealist fallacy that the universal is prior to and higher than particulars. Thus "There is no will: there are only treaty drafts (*Willens-Punktationen*) of will that are constantly increas-

84

ing or losing their power."[26] Conceived singularly, the
Übermensch is an abstraction and will remain such until
that time (perhaps never to arrive) when every individual
human being is engaged in self-actualization, in which case
the *Übermensch* becomes concrete as the unifying principle
of the community of such individuals. Meanwhile within
each person subsists "your virtue, [which] you have in common with nobody."[27] To live in accordance with it is one's
"most individual responsibility,"[28] and such is the diversity
that health in one person "could look like its opposite in
another."[29] The consummate pluralism here can best be
indicated by drawing upon Nietzsche's epistemology. By
Nietzsche's meaning of "virtue" (integrity, self-identity), it
determines truth and not conversely. Thus "the *valuation* 'I
believe that this and that is so' [is] the essence of 'truth.' "[30]
As each man's virtue is unique, his truth constitutes a coherent, qualitatively unique perspective upon all things, and abstract "truth" (as in "the truth," rather than "Socrates's
truth," or "So-and-so's truth") is not singular, but consists
in the sum of complementary fulfilled perspectives upon all
things. Correspondingly "the truth" about any particular
thing consists in the sum of fulfilled perspectives upon that
thing, and the thing itself is the limit of the series of all possible fulfilled perspectives upon it. This perspectivism is
sufficient testimony that Nietzsche's pluralistic individualism is not provisional but final, "For many who are noble
are needed, and noble men of many kinds, that there may
be a nobility. Or as I once said in a parable: 'Precisely this is
godlike that there are gods, but no God.' "[31]

Concerning innateness, Nietzsche contends that the "hidden masterful something" is within each person at his birth,
where it expresses life's "self-surpassing" no less than does
the moral growth of a single life. Startlingly, perhaps,
Nietzsche insists that it resides in the body, advising that
"There is more reason in your body than in your best wisdom."[32] This is not "materialism" in the ordinary sense, for
the body is not inert or opaque matter but active and pur-

posive substance that rumors consciousness as its further extension. By assigning the "higher self" to body, Nietzsche forestalls the introduction into human personality of the dualism implied by "spirit" and which, once introduced, can never be overcome. For "spirit" is perceived by Nietzsche to be an essentially reactive concept, being initially conceived as everything that natural life is not, and thereafter undermining life from within (and the ordinary meaning of "mind" is a domestication of "spirit" that preserves the reactiveness of the latter). Nietzsche's assignment of the *telos* of life to body is the assignment of valuation to will. He thus may be said to have anticipated the present philosophical conclusion that valuation is "noncognitive," but without today's professional prejudice that the noncognitive is the frivolous. It is not the thesis but the prejudice that is responsible for axiological skepticism and nihilism.

Accordingly, to Nietzsche's understanding the first commandment of moral life is not the Greek "Know thyself," but, in Zarathustra's words, "Choose thyself." Knowledge cannot serve for self-discovery, either a priori or introspectively, for one's potentiality is not what it is by logical necessity, nor can pure possibilities be apprehended by reason other than abstractly, and therefore not as one's own. To be apprehended by reason, possibilities must first be actualized, which is to say one must first act and then assess the result—in short, introspection is retrospection (though it can indeed infer the future course of lines of action already taken).

To choose oneself is to acknowledge and abide by one's own inclinations and aversions, yet this apparently straightforward task is immensely complicated by the fact that before one is ready to assume it one is (in childhood and youth) the receptor of "culture" consisting in valuations of others. To choose oneself requires therefore that "the weights of all things must be determined anew,"[33] and it is for this kind of learning that Nietzsche stresses the pedagogical indispensability of forgetting, defining man as uniquely "this animal which needs to be forgetful, in which forgetting represents a force, a form of *robust* health."[34]

Self-discovery, then, occurs in a choosing that analysis reveals to consist in forgetting, acting afresh, and reflecting upon the result, and the sign that distinguishes the choice of self is that "joy" that is to "feel stronger," not by comparison with others, "but with oneself in the midst of a state of growth."[35] Given self-discovery, what follows in moral life is the *amor fati*, which Nietzsche terms "my formula." It is not for the individual to alter his innate truth, but rather "You should think through your own senses to their consequences."[36] By so doing, one progressively actualizes what he innately is and has been from birth, a unique excellence and a "higher man" *in potentia*. Thus "Choose Thyself" is followed by the second imperative, "You shall become the person you are."[37]

It is the failing of précis of the philosophies of others that the substance of the person's thought is stripped of the style by which he expressed it, becoming thereby always in some measure diminished. If the discrepancy cannot be rectified, in the case of so vivid a stylist as Nietzsche its presence must at least be highlighted by allowing the original to speak for himself for a time without interruption. The following passage on integrity is unsurpassable as description, and it exhibits the intensely personal style by which Nietzsche cannily individuated his readers, speaking to each alone.

How is it at all possible to keep to one's own way? Constantly, some clamor or other calls us aside; rarely does our eye behold anything that does not require us to drop our own preoccupation instantly to help. I know, there are a hundred decent and praiseworthy ways of losing *my own way*, and they are truly highly "moral"! Indeed, those who now preach the morality of pity even take the view that precisely this and only this is moral—to lose one's *own* way in order to come to the assistance of a neighbor. I know just as certainly that I only need to expose myself to the sight of some genuine distress and I am lost. And if a suffering friend said to me, "Look, I am about to die; please promise me to die with me," I should promise it; and the sight of a small mountain tribe fighting for its liberty would persuade me to offer it my hand and my life—if for good reasons I may choose for once two bad examples. All such arousing of pity and calling for help is secretly seductive, for our "own way" is too hard and demanding and too remote from the love and gratitude of others, and we do not really mind escaping from it— and from our very own conscience—to flee into the conscience of the others and into the lovely temple of the "religion of pity."

As soon as any war breaks out anywhere, there also breaks out precisely among the noblest people a pleasure that, to be sure, is kept secret: Rapturously, they throw themselves into the new danger of *death* because the sacrifice for the fatherland seems to them to offer the long desired permission—*to dodge their goal;* war offers them a detour to suicide, but a detour with a good conscience.[38]

The passage contains suggestions of the evidence upon which Nietzsche's reputation for uncharitableness and even cruelty is built. But one should note the intensely personal style, and bear in mind that the foremost adversaries to the "higher man" within each person are likewise within each person. Does it now become evident that Nietzsche's spleen and sometimes fury are directed first of all against the recalcitrant and wayward inclinations in himself? Indeed he often says as much, citing the "excessive hardness" of his books as a "sort of revenge" taken against his own vulnerability.[39] Moreover his firmest principles forbid cruelty to others, and castigation of others is counterproductive—this latter because self-responsibility is sought, while an individual who responds to another's castigation of him behaves dependently. What Nietzsche does—as the personal style effectively indicates—is to live what he writes and write as he lives, offering himself as an example to others. Even when we have recognized that his animosity is directed against the enemies within himself, the question remains, are such violent means necessary to self-conquest? What of gentle persuasion, love, and self-forgiveness? At this early point in our study of self-actualization we must shun facile answers. I wish only to point out that in Nietzsche himself the divisive forces were at their strongest; the "black horse" (of Plato's image) was a fearsome stallion, hence the resort to hammer blows in the interest of unification. Within Nietzsche, "the peddler," "the spider," and the "last man" strove against one another and against the higher man with exceptional vigor. Nor was the incarnate son of God absent within the greatest adversary of Christianity. The notes of his final madness he signed alternately as "Dionysus" and "The Crucified." Shall we conclude from this that the life-long battle for self-unification was in Nietzsche's case lost? But so much the more may we then gain from an example that is no middling one, but life's hardest case.

To refer again to the passage cited above, "keeping to one's own path" means refusing the continual cries for assistance by others. But this "ideal selfishness" does not in fact withhold from others, for it is the condition, instead, of the worth of the individual's contribution to others. He who allows others to determine his responsibilities leaves his own living undone, for he is perceived by others, not as an end in himself, but as instrumental to their ends. He therefore exemplifies the mere instrumentality of human worth. But he who "keeps to his own way" manifests intrinsic worth and at the same time demonstrates the accessibility of intrinsic worth to every human being. It is thus that each man's integrity is a "bestowing virtue." Not only is personal excellence an objective value in the world, but it is the harbinger of that excellence within every other person of which those others may themselves have been unaware. It is in these respects that "man becomes the transfigurer of existence when he learns to transfigure himself,"[40] and it is thus also that "a single individual can under certain circumstances justify the existence of whole millennia."[41] However, the reminder to all persons of the "higher man" within themselves will not inevitably be received with gratitude. In particular it will anger those who defend their lying, cheating, and stealing by contending that all men do the same, or would if they could. It is with respect to this argument that so much as a single worthy individual is the bad conscience of the world, and will be pulled down by the many if only they can lay hold of him.

We have seen that "joy" (the feeling of increasing strength of personhood) is the mark of the integrity of one's will to power. Normally short-term and episodic, joy becomes extended by the rightness of the "long will" to become a durable "Yea-saying" or affirmation of existence. Concerning this Yea-saying, two definitive marks remain to be considered, one of them retrospective while the other is prospective. As against all shrinking from reminder of one's past and all "wishing it had been otherwise," the life of integrity enjoys a memory that is completely without regret in virtue of the *necessity* that integrity confers. Concerning every past episode recalled in memory, it can truthfully say, "I could not have done otherwise except by becoming someone other than I am." In the other direction, the prospective test of the integral life is its ability to will the endless future re-enactment of itself without the least alteration. Here is Nietzsche's startling doctrine of the Eternal Return, according to which all that happens will be endlessly repeated just as it was. Preposterous cosmology! Ridiculous history! Disreputable physics! But as a test of the life of integrity it is a masterstroke, for who but the individual who has done his utmost and best can face the prospect of the Eternal Return with equanimity? That Nietzsche's world recoiled in horror at the thought, that ours of today does likewise, speaks tellingly. Moreover Nietzsche's genius is measured when we recognize that the touch of the eternal, necessary to true individuality, appears here for the first time in the history of philosophy and religion in a conception that is not antithetical to life itself—not nonliving eternal being, but an eternity of the becoming of life itself as self-surpassing. With incredible tenacity Nietzsche "remains true to the earth." I can think of no more apt tribute than the line by Holderlin, "He who has thought most deeply loves that which is most alive."[42]

With the modern eudaimonists we have followed the outline of each system by making out a balance sheet, indicating gains and deficits as against classical eudaimonism. Here we shall depart from that practice, for the major respect in which Nietzsche differs from classical eudaimonism is shared by and brought to culmination in the work of the most forceful of twentieth-century existentialists, Jean-Paul Sartre. For the present we shall therefore content ourselves with an indication of this common vector as it makes its first appearance in Nietzsche, postponing a critique until Sartre has been considered.

We have identified Nietzsche's epistemology as perspectivism, and it now becomes necessary to notice that each perspective has a double reference, indicating on one side things and on the other side the person whose perspective it is. For Nietzsche the determination of truth is confined to the latter referent; a perspective is true if it expresses the self-identity of the individual whose perspective it is, and an element of a perspective is true if it coheres to every other element through relations of mutual implication. But what of the relationship of the perspective to the things—trees, mountains, tables, persons, events of the past, "facts of life" such as birth and death? For Nietzsche the priority of subjective integrity precludes any regulation by the objects of knowledge and inevitably falsifies the objects. Thus "Truth is the kind of error without which a certain species of life could not live. The value for *life* is ultimately decisive."[43] How do we know that it is error with respect to its objects? Because knowledge is necessarily abstractive, simplifying, inventive; and the abstracting and simplifying are our own work, proceeding according to one's own principle or "long will." Nor can it be otherwise, for life does not require truths (in the objective sense) but "regulative articles of belief."[44] Indeed, Nietzsche insists that objective truth is detrimental to life:

> This perspective world, this world for the eye, tongue, and ear, is very false, even if compared [with] a very much more subtle sense-apparatus. But its intelligibility, comprehensibility, practicability, and beauty begin to cease if we refine our senses; just as beauty ceases when we think about historical processes; the order of purpose is already an illusion. It suffices that the more superficially and coarsely it is conceived, the more valuable, definite, beautiful, and significant the world appears. The deeper one looks, the more our valuations disappear—meaninglessness approaches! We have *created* the world that possesses values! Knowing this, we know, too, that reverence for truth is already the consequence of an illusion—and that one should value more than truth the force that forms, simplifies, shapes, invents.[45]

To allow the object to determine our percept, concept, intention, or action is to relinquish self-responsibility. As values derive from self-responsibility (by means of valuation), this "objectifying tendency" is a movement toward a valueless world and valueless human existence. On the contrary, man's fundamental task is to instill values in the world, a task that is to be accomplished by the valuations of individuals, each of whom must live in accordance with his own truth. In sum, according to Nietzsche the sole source of value and truth in the world is the autonomous individual—all rests with the rectitude of his will. At bottom epistemological criteria are vital criteria. There is "no limit to the ways in which the world can be interpreted; [and] every interpretation [is] a symptom of growth or decline."[46]

But what are the vital criteria? "Health" is integration according to principle when such integration is progressively increasing in power and thereby in scope and in coherence. "Sickness" is progressive disintegration marked by diminishing scope and coherence. The instrument of integration is the will to power or "long will," but the object of the "long will"—the *Übermensch*—is nothing more nor less than this will itself in perfected form. But this will not do, for will, in order to be a surpassing of self, must lack that which constitutes its object and at which it aims. This means that the perfected will, if it is truly to be will, must be a lack no less than ordinary will (a perfected lack, if you choose). Here, however, will to power appears in the guise of a lack struggling to become a lack, and this is nonsensical. To be such, will requires an object that takes the form of its own completion or fulfillment, and it must be in this form that the individuated *Übermensch* appears in each individual. What is the source of this form? It can be neither God, nor "spirit" (as an independent principle), nor the Platonic Forms, for alike, these sources are conceived in reaction against life, and the will thus directed is aimed at the destruction of life. For Nietzsche there can be only one source for the objects of a life-affirming will, namely that will itself. Finally, because will to power is *vis creativa*, it is invention, we are led to the recognition that the *Übermensch*, as it appears in each person, is his own invention, which, as such, is subject to but one criterion—that it be what it is.

Thus in Nietzsche are the roots of the Sartrean doctrine that each man is his own arbitrary creation. The doctrine is properly termed "Sartrean" for only in the work of Sartre does it attain unequivocal expression. In Nietzsche's vitalism lingers a vestige of innatism that draws withering fire from Sartre. The originality in Sartre's theory of self-actualization centers in a phenomenological analysis of personal choice that discloses it to be utterly groundless, free, and self-constitutive. In the long philosophical stream of self-actualization ethics, this conclusion marks Existentialism's distinctive contribution.

4

Critique of Recent Eudaimonisms: The Existentialism of Sartre

For Sartre, "Being is an individual venture."[1] Each self constitutes itself as a "fundamental project"—a supreme, enduring, and unique aim that infuses and organizes the secondary and tertiary structures of personality. "Fundamental project" is the product of a choice that is absolutely free, for it is entirely without antecedents to which it can refer itself. ("Bad faith" in its countless forms is the attempt by choice to claim antecedent determining ground for itself, but bad faith inevitably fails, for as a lie told to itself it knows itself to be a lie.) The sole restriction upon free choice is that it cannot choose to be incapable of choice, which is to say that human being cannot choose to be being of another kind—for example material being, inhuman being. In Sartre's words, "No limits to my freedom can be found except freedom itself or, if you prefer . . . we are not free to cease to be free."[2]

To avoid the more prevalent misunderstandings of Sartre and to see the forcefulness of his demonstration, it is useful at the outset to lay bare the single principle upon which his case depends. In the first place, human being is a distinctive kind of being (termed by Sartre "being-for-itself" or simply "for-itself"); it is consciousness. The principle is that whatever appears in consciousness appears *as* consciousness. Now consciousness is a nexus of meanings. Accordingly whatever may be given to consciousness can appear in consciousness only as a meaning, and meanings are the product of consciousness itself—therefore consciousness is strictly self-constitutive and self-responsible. Just now, let us say, you open your eyes and see before you a table. You are not responsible for the presence of the table nor in this situation can you avoid seeing it, for there it is. But what appears within you is not the material table itself but a meaning that is necessarily your meaning, namely what the table means to you. You can adopt the conventional meaning, which as conventional is "everyone's" prior to being yours, but its adoption by you is your choice. The table cannot be responsible for its meaning to you because its being is not the being of meaning but something altogether different, material being, nonconscious being and therefore nonmeaning being (termed by Sartre "being-in-itself"). The only possible source of the meaning in question is the being of meaning, namely conscious being, being-for-itself; and because being-for-itself is always "an individual venture," it is you alone who are responsible for the meaning of the table—and every other "given"—in your consciousness.

To this point we perhaps follow Sartre willingly enough save for a certain discomfort created by the "alone" of the last sentence. It seems to us that partly, indeed, we are responsible for our own meanings, yet we want to insist at the same time that this responsibility must be shared, for are there not a variety of external factors to which our meaning is required to conform? We offer one or two such determinants—and watch wide-eyed as they succumb to Sartre's critical analysis. Anxiously we hunt up others and offer them—to the same result; we cast our net to the furthest corners, to no avail. Naked, we stand alone with our responsibility; the sole determinant of our meanings is we ourselves, each of us as a solitary individual, constituted as such by his ultimate intention, his fundamental project. It is this meaning—fundamental project—that is the sole condition upon the secondary meanings ("*petites projets*") and tertiary meanings (e.g. the apprehension of the table) of the individual consciousness, and it is the product exclusively of the individual's free choice.

More than to any other man, credit must be given to

Sartre for uprooting false limits to human freedom. Self-responsibility admits of no compromise and no partnership. By his relentless pursuit of bad faith in its every refuge, he discloses that every melioristic attempt to shift just a little of the burden of responsibility for choice is at bottom the attempt to disclaim self-responsibility totally. Man is "condemned to be free"[3] and must not anticipate intermittent parole, for freedom is an absolute, and not susceptible of qualification by degree. To support this tenet Sartre hounds down every rumor of determinism, and it will be worth our while just now to follow him for a time.

Let us consider the past, whether in the form of our personal past or as the previous history of the human race: are we presently not its involuntary product in significant respects? But what is the past? For the question of its influence upon us to make sense, we cannot mean the past *as* past, for that past is dead and gone. We must refer to the past that is active in the present, in our present, and therefore in us. But within us the past appears as a meaning that it cannot have given itself, but that on the contrary can only have come from ourselves. Specifically, the past in us is so as a meaning that is conferred by our fundamental project, and our fundamental project is our choice of our future. Therefore the future determines the past, and not conversely. But once more, the past that is determined by the future is not the past *as* past, for as past it is not present and therefore not within us in any sense. What is present within us must be a meaning of the past, and it is this meaning that is determined by—again—not the future, *as* future, but the future that is within our present as our chosen future.

For example, we may consider the notion of "my tradition" in the usual sense of the historical continuum that includes the individual and that he perpetuates. In my own case I was born a St. Louisan, a Missourian, and an American, of predominantly English ancestry. Now "St. Louis" evokes a proud tradition sprung from French-Canadian trappers and fur traders, featuring the Mississippi River as

97

its corporeal and spiritual artery, annexing beer and shoes, and commemorating itself as "Gateway to the West" in a mighty arch of stainless steel designed by Eero Saarinen and lately erected on the riverfront. There is, resoundingly, a "St. Louis tradition." But I myself left St. Louis at the first chance, leaving behind its tradition as well. Nor is it the tradition of Missouri to which my waking life expresses allegiance. Toward my country I feel pride and gratitude, which I hope is expressed in all I do, but the expression is indirect. Concerning England, her past and her people, my knowledge is spotty and my feelings are mixed and somewhat distant. My vital tradition is none of these, but is instead the grand tradition of Western philosophical thought. From it I daily draw inspiration, and daily I strive to conserve and carry forward its precious but precarious values. But how did the history of Western philosophy come to be "my tradition"? It came to be such by my choice of philosophy as my life work. Thus my chosen future has chosen my past, and such is inevitably the case, for living time is an unbroken continuum of which past, present, and future are but modalities. Were I the living exponent of "St. Louisism," no less would "my tradition" be the product of my choice.

And so for the traditions of nations and peoples, for,

> . . . this decision with respect to the value, the order, and the nature of our past is simply the *historical choice* in general. If human societies are historical this does not stem simply from the fact that they have a past but from the fact that they reassume the past by making it a *memorial*. When American capitalism decides to enter the European war of 1914–1918 because it sees there the opportunity for profitable transactions, it is not *historical*; it is only utilitarian. But when in the light of its utilitarian projects, it recovers the previous relations of the United States with France and gives to them the *meaning* of the paying of a debt of honor by Americans to France, then it becomes historical. In

particular it makes itself historical by the famous sentence: "Lafayette, we are here!" It goes without saying that if a different view of her real interests had led the United States to place itself on the side of Germany, she would not have lacked past elements to recover on the memorial level.[4]

Like the enterprising woodchuck she is, determinism has countless burrows prepared against the coming of the fox. She has just been flushed from her refuge in the past, where will she run next? Let us suppose she is now holed up in "the situation." Surely she is secure here, for it is an unalterable truth that life forever finds itself amid alien things that exhibit "coefficients of adversity" to life's intentions, and thereby prove coercive. But the fox pursues and already is at his digging—listen!: "In particular the coefficient of adversity in things can not be an argument against our freedom, for it is *by us*—i.e., by the preliminary positing of an end—that this coefficient of adversity arises. A particular crag, which manifests a profound resistance if I wish to displace it, will be on the contrary a valuable aid if I want to climb upon it in order to look over the countryside. In itself—if one can even imagine what the crag can be in itself —it is neutral; that is, it waits to be illuminated by an end in order to manifest itself as adverse or helpful."[5]

Nearer to current sociological thinking is the example of the person whose childhood took place in the situation of an urban ghetto. Now the facts of his situation—having been reared in a ghetto—are unalterable, but they cannot appear in him for what they are in themselves ("pure facticity") but only as meanings, and as meanings they are freely chosen. By general agreement today the meaning of these particular facts is "disadvantage" and "deprivation." But where this meaning is the individual's own it is such because he has chosen it freely from among countless alternatives. An anecdote will help to make this clear. Some time ago I found myself addressing a political conference as one of four speakers. By far the best address was given by a state senator, a twenty-eight-year-old black man who was just then being groomed by his party for national office. At dinner afterward I put to him the obvious question: as young, black, and politically prominent, how did he account for his success? "Quite simply," he said: "I was reared in a ghetto and graduated to the streets at an early age. Consequently in my twenty-eight years I have had the experience which it takes over-protected, middle-class, suburban whites twice my years to acquire. I have only sought to use it well." His argument was that an over-protected childhood and youth, and not a ghetto upbringing, constitutes deprivation. I did not think to ask whether he chose politics consciously to effect this transvaluation, but Sartre's case for the freedom of meanings finds confirmation in this man, regardless.

Situational determinists are fond of examples *in extremis*, but fare no better with them. Think of the Nazi concentration camps and one must at the same time think of two men who used their experience of the death camps to construct affirmative theories of human psychology from which to derive therapeutic techniques. I refer to Viktor Frankl and Bruno Bettelheim.

Nor is the fox thwarted by the stimulus-response mechanism of behavioristic technique. No less than with rats and pigeons, human behavior can be altered by the systematic administration of simple rewards and punishments (the latter lately termed "negative reinforcements"). The case is readily commensurated with freedom by the recognition that "conditioned" individuals choose to work for the proffered rewards, while likewise choosing to avoid the "negative reinforcements." The fact that some persons are insusceptible to conditioning is currently taken by behaviorists to reflect merely the imperfection of their techniques, whereas instead it demonstrates the erroneousness of behaviorism's mechanistic conception of the person. In sum, behaviorism simply nurtures and capitalizes on the ambition of bad faith to be relieved of self-responsibility. It is hardly the first program that has sought to prosper by human weakness.

Shifting ground once more, some "facts of life" are indeed inescapable, but what is inescapable about them is not a shape or character they impose upon life, but only their demand that every individual confer upon them one meaning or another. The foremost example is death. Death comes to every man but can do nothing to insinuate the meaning it shall have for any man. Together, poetry and philosophy furnish all the evidence that could be desired of the countless alternative meanings that have been imputed to death —the *carpe diem* motif, the death-defiance of romanticism, death as creator of love in Tristanism and the early Hegel (for examples). Death cannot determine life, though it may forcefully prompt life to determine itself. The contention by Heidegger that death is the condition of life's meaningfulness is opposed by Sartre, but our consideration of the issue must await a subsequent chapter (Ch. 7).

Eventually determinism turns away from the world outside and postulates the determination of personality from within. Here the handiest resorts are to emotions, "the unconscious," innate "gifts" from the "natural lottery," or innate "character." Of course there are other possibilities, but remarks on these four will establish the Sartrean pattern of response and enable ready extrapolation.

Common sense is prone to regard the individual as the victim of his emotions, but Sartre's extended analysis[6] discloses emotion to be a type of intentional behavior, specifically the endeavor to constitute the world as "magical" and to control it by "magical" means.* From Sartre's theory of

---

* By "magical" means, Sartre refers to means that handle a situation by altering our states of consciousness exclusively—thus fainting "magically" alleviates a danger by erasing our consciousness of it. A "magical" world is one where "magical" means are appropriate. Sartre's theory bears striking resemblance to Freud's account of primitive magic as "omnipotence of thought."[7] Primitives, by

emotions as voluntary projects, existential psychotherapy has evolved a convincing therapeutic technique that the reader can try upon himself. The angered individual—to take the most difficult case—must be made to describe the situation that has angered him. His description is then demonstrated to be an interpretation (which it inevitably is), and alternative interpretations are constructed, each of which prompts a different emotional response. He is now obliged to acknowledge that he constructs his emotions if he constructs his interpretations, and the latter is demonstrated empirically, for example, each time he confronts a puzzling situation and must "sort through" a number of possible interpretations.

For concrete illustration of the recognitions involved, suppose that just now I, as the father of an infant son, am feeding the little fellow his first "solid" food (actually a kind of cereal soup) from a spoon. I have prepared this wretched stuff carefully and lovingly because the pediatrician's memo says my son needs it and will like it. And I have used up the better part of an hour doing so, thanks to my ineptitude in the kitchen. I seat myself and begin the feeding, but as fast as I spoon the gruel in, my infant spits it out again by a deft movement of his tongue. I am hurt by the rejection of my loving preparation, annoyed at the pediatrician, and enraged by what appears to be the calculated effrontery of my infant. At this moment my wife enters the scene. Sizing it up, she explains to me that the boy presently knows only how to suck, and that his sucking is produced by the rhythmic movement of his tongue, outward and inward, beneath the nipple. Therefore if I will only continue to hold the spoon in place when he pushes the cereal out of his mouth, in the next moment he will suck it in again, then out, then in, and out and in until finally it is swallowed. I

---

energetic dancing, exhaust their hatred for a member of another tribe (for example), and infer the extinction of the object of their anger from the extinction of the anger.

now see that I have misinterpreted the situation. There is no "cause" for anger here, and immediately my anger vanishes, being replaced by loving patience with a touch of contrition. (By the same token, however, the individual who so chooses can persist in his anger come what may, and supply himself by way of his interpretations with abundant "cause" for so doing.)

It is but a short step from particular emotions to "temperament" as predisposition to a fixed pattern of emotions and to "character" as predisposition to a distinct pattern of subjective activity in general. In Sartre's words, character, like temperament, is "a vow." For example, "When a man says, 'I am not easy to please,' he is entering into a free engagement with his ill-temper, and by the same token his words are a free interpretation of certain ambiguous details of his past. In this sense there is no character; there is only a project of oneself. But we must not, however, misunderstand the *given* aspect of the character. It is true that for the Other who apprehends me as the Other-as-object, I *am* ill-tempered, hypocritical or frank, cowardly or courageous."[8]

We have noticed the sense in which emotion is "magical" response to a world that is constituted in its magical aspect. In contrast to it, rational conduct "will consider the situation scientifically, will reject the magical, and will apply itself to realizing determined series and instrumental complexes which will enable us to resolve the problems."[9] Rational conduct causes the world to arise in its technical aspect. "But what will make me decide to choose the magical aspect or the technical aspect of the world? It can not be the world itself, for this in order to be manifested waits to be discovered. Therefore it is necessary that the for-itself in its project must choose being the one by whom the world is revealed as magical or rational; that is, the for-itself must as a free project of itself give to itself magical or rational existence."[10]

As is the case for "emotional" and "rational" persons, so

too for persons of every other character-type—for example, the "aesthetic type" whose pattern is spectatorial and appreciative, and constitutes the world in its aspect as art or spectacle, or the "phlegmatic" or "melancholic" types. Character is not the product of innate disposition but of a choice of responsive pattern that is persisted in by re-choosings.

If common sense supposes "talents" to be inborn gifts awarded by the "natural lottery," a more resolute inquiry discloses them to be nothing antecedent to their exercise, but only skills accumulated in the wake of their exercise. The notion of a "born painter" who does not paint is pure mythology. In being-for-itself, existence precedes essence. It is solely by painting that a man constitutes himself as "a painter."[11] Talent is nothing other than acquired ability deriving from activity that is engaged in by choice.

The same applies to our incapacities—for despite our cherished convictions, we have no innate, "constitutional" incapacities, and what we offer as such proves under scrutiny to be the product of choice. It is quite true that a person may engage in a given activity for a considerable time and show no improvement in his ability. But to account for this requires only that we recognize, in such phenomena as ambivalence, distraction, half-heartedness, and *dysdaimonia*, that one can choose not to give himself fully to what he does. Consider a common and sharply defined incapacity, the inability to think mathematically. As a teacher I know of no stricter divide among students than that separating those who are good at mathematics from those who are inept. Indeed, the great cleft between science and the humanities is largely its product. Those who are inept at mathematics invariably account for their ineptitude by claiming constitutional incapacity—they "just haven't the head for it." But we must ask them to consider the following line of thought.

Mathematics (and likewise formal logic) is distinguished from non-mathematical studies by the certitude of its results. In all other studies the principle of degrees of truth and falsity applies: the worst answer to a problem contains at least a grain of truth, however minute, and the best answer falls short of perfect certitude, while the majority of answers contain both considerable truth and considerable falsity. But in mathematics a proffered answer will be either perfectly correct or wholly incorrect. It is because of the "excluded middle" between truth and falsity (strictly, validity and invalidity) that studies of the processes of high-level mathematical discovery show it to be punctuated by dark nights of despair and sudden illuminations resembling religious revelations. Because there are no intermediate positions between truth and falsity (validity and invalidity), "discovery" can only be the instantaneous jump from ignorance to knowledge, and this accounts for the relative frequency, in the diaries, letters, and journals of the great mathematicians, of statements of the type: "It came to me like a flash of lightning in a dark sky."

But what has just been said about the process of high-level mathematical discovery is equally true of mathematical learning at the most elementary levels. Unlike students of other subjects, the student of mathematics who does not know the solution to a given problem is with respect to it in no middling way—he is totally and abysmally ignorant. This "you-have-it-or-you-don't" characteristic makes mathematical learning a humiliating experience, and especially is this so in the beginning, where one's experience does not yet assure that with persistence "the light will come."*

By any estimate of human nature it follows that many persons will (for a variety of reasons, e.g. pride, insecurity, etc.) choose to avoid humiliation by avoiding mathematics.

* What I say about the "you-have-it-or-you-don't" character of mathematical knowledge applies to problem-solving within a given mathematical system, i.e. strictly speaking to "validity" and "invalidity." Concerning the systems themselves it is uncertain today whether the question of their truth or falsity can logically arise; and the matter of criteria by which, if it arises, it might be resolved is shrouded in even darker obscurity. But these questions are philosophical, not mathematical.

This voluntary avoidance, not constitutional incapacity, accounts for mathematical ineptitude. I find that most students who at first invoke their constitutional incapacity will readily recognize themselves in this description. It is a case of Platonic "recollection"—recognition of what one already knew, but didn't know that one knew.

What we "know without knowing that we know" is today commonly ascribed to "the unconscious," and a few words must be said about Sartre's opposition to this concept. That there neither is nor can possibly be such an entity as an unconscious mind or self is one of the fundamental tenets upon which Sartre founds existential psychoanalysis. Human being (for-itself) is pre-reflexive consciousness, a "pure transparence" that is devoid of hidden chambers or opaque lumps. That an "unconscious consciousness" cannot be is driven home by Sartre's interrogation of Freud's paradigmatic formulation. In the Freudian trinity of Id, Ego, and Super-ego, "unconscious" contents subsist in the Id, and are prevented from entering the Ego by the censoring activity of the Super-ego. But if the "censor" (Super-ego) is to be effective, it cannot act blindly, but must "know what it is repressing. In fact, if we abandon all the metaphors representing the repression as the impact of blind forces, we are compelled to admit that the censor must choose and in order to choose must be aware of so doing."[12] Because the censor must know what the Ego does not know, the locus of bad faith (pretending not to know) is merely shifted from the self as a whole to the portion of it termed the Super-ego. In sum, the effort to establish "the unconscious" as a part of ourselves which is not ourselves and which determines ourself from outside itself, is a failure. We are not the instruments of unconscious forces for which we cannot be held responsible; we only find it convenient sometimes to represent ourselves as such.

Rather than track the fox further we shall refer the reader to *Being and Nothingness* with the assurance that wherever he thinks the woodchuck may have gone next, there the fox will be found, digging him out. Sartre's philosophy admits no exception to the principle that "human reality cannot receive its ends . . . either from outside or from a so-called inner 'nature.' "[13] "Existence before essence" obtains because prior to choice for-itself is nothing, and therefore absolutely free.

The grinding logical problems inherent in the concepts "nothing" and "nothingness"* will be obviated if we take their meaning to be, not absolute, but relative and modal, and a certain amount of evidence suggests that Sartre sometimes, at least, has such a meaning in mind.[14] The distinction between an absolute nothingness and an efficacious nothingess has ancient roots, appearing in the Greek contrast between two kinds of nonbeing, *ouk on* and *mē on*— the nonbeing that is pure lack and can have no commerce with being, and the nonbeing that is creative becoming. The nonbeing that is creative becoming is not absolute nothing but relative and modal; it is possibility that, as such, is *nothing actual*. Accordingly for Sartre nothingness is not merely "what is not," but instead "is what it is not, and is not what it is."[15] The apparent paradox can be resolved if the *is* and *is not* refer to different modalities, such that human being is not (in actuality) what it is (in possibility), and conversely. Thus the nothingness that the for-itself is before choice is a nothingness in fact, which is at the same time all (human) possibilities. This rendering of Sartre does not undermine the distinction on which he insists between his system and Aristotelian potentialities.[16] The Aristotelian con-

---

* Suggested famously, for example, by Parmenides, who announced that it is impossible to speak of nothing, and thereby broke his rule in the act of stating it; or by the dictum, *Ex nihilo, nihil fit*; or by Lewis Carroll's play on the systematic ambiguity of the term "nothing" in *Alice through the Looking-Glass*. A useful bibliography on the logical perplexities of the concepts "nothing," "nothingness," and "negation" is provided by P. L. Heath in his "Nothing" entry in *The Encyclopaedia of Philosophy*, Paul Edwards, Editor in Chief (New York: Macmillan and The Free Press, 1967) vol. 5. The entry itself is a delight.

ception is termed "magical" by Sartre because it ascribes potentialities to all existing things, while Sartrean possibilities are confined to for-itself. And Aristotelian potentialities constitute teleological determinism in the sense that each existing thing possesses but one, and therefore contains a predetermined future. Against this, the possibilities to which we have just resorted as an interpretation of Sartre are, as Sartre himself insists, exclusively human possibilities. They entail no teleological determinism because *all* subsist within the individual, and which one is to be actualized rests with his choice. His freedom is in this situation indeed fearful because it can find for itself no foundation; it is entirely unlimited and unconditioned except by its own being as freedom. Because in possibility it is not this or that but everything, its choice to become this or that can only be self-founding.

Nor does this interpretation wrestle a trussed-up Sartre into the eudaimonist camp, for in the eudaimonist conception each person comprises the totality of human possibilities, only one of which is actual as his unique potentiality or destiny. The interpretation is offered here both for its intrinsic interest, and because it highlights the rift between Sartre and eudaimonism.

Sartre confutes both classical eudaimonism and Nietzsche on the same point. He sees in each the attempt to furnish man with an end drawn from a source outside himself and antecedent to his choice. In Nietzsche's formulation the will to power furnishes the individual with his end. We have seen that Nietzsche does not conceive the will to power as a universal that constitutes the reality of individuals, as did Schopenhauer. But within each individual, will to power is conceived by Nietzsche as originally an unconscious force responsible for consciousness and individuation, and as such (for Sartre) it perpetrates the same subterfuge as does the unconscious of Freud. Likewise it falls to the recognition that consciousness is "pure transparence." As with emotions, so too the for-itself is the "free foundation of . . . its volitions."[17] Indeed, "In relation to freedom there is no privileged psychic phenomenon. All my 'modes of being' manifest freedom equally since they are all ways of being my own nothingness."[18] Will is not constitutive of choice, but, conversely, choice is constitutive of will. As the term *voluntary* implies, will is inherently reflective (conscious and self-aware), and its goal "is not so much to decide what end is to be attained since in any case the chips are down; the profound intention of the will bears rather on the *method* of attaining this end already posited."[19]

Concerning eudaimonism, Sartre says "it is a matter of envisaging the self as a little God which inhabits me and which possesses my freedom as a metaphysical virtue."[20] According to this doctrine, the act of the individual is free when it "exactly reflects" his essence, but true freedom is precluded by the tenet that the individual *is* his essence "in the mode of being of the in-itself."[21] Sartre's charges here are somewhat tangled and require careful combing. By the last statement he accuses eudaimonism of mispresenting human being (for-itself) as that kind of being that for Sartre it categorically is not and cannot be, namely being-in-itself (nonconscious being, the being of objects). Being-in-itself "is what is is"; being-for-itself "is what it is not and is not what it is." But it is Sartre who misrepresents eudaimonism here. To be sure, according to eudaimonism the individual is irremediably his daimon or essence, but he is so not in actuality but in possibility; hence we can say of him that "he is his possibility." This perfectly accords with Sartre's distinction between for-itself, which contains possibilities—hence "is" (in possibility) what it "is not" (in actuality)—and in-itself, which is devoid of possibilities. Further, for eudaimonism the individual's being is not his possibility exclusively, but also his actuality, and in virtue of these two modalities of being within him he is, without contradiction, and as Sartre says, the being that "is what it is not and is not what it is." In short, Sartre's allegation that eudaimonism mistakes man for a thing cannot be made to stick.

The real difference is that for eudaimonism freedom appears on the foundation of human being (as a combination of actuality and possibility), while for Sartre freedom *is itself* the foundation of actuality and possibility in human being. Sartre thus accords full metaphysical status to freedom as one of two kinds of being, namely nothingness. His supportive argument occupies Part One of *Being and Nothingness*. It consists, first, in the demonstration of the presence in the world of negation (in *"negatités"* such as destruction, fragility, adversity; in questioning, imagination, intentionality, self-transcendence, anguish, and bad faith), and second in the argument that the source of negation in the world must be a being that is its own nothingness, and that this being is for-itself, human being.

In behalf of classical eudaimonism, our rejoinder to Sartre must center upon his hypostatizations of freedom and nothingness, but this teminus shall be approached through the concrete testimony of ordinary experience. Specifically, it follows from Sartre's position that the individual creates himself (by choice of his fundamental project, literally *ex nihilo*), while the phenomenology of adolescence attests that autonomous self-awareness first appears, not as creation, but as discovery.

Those who have thought seriously about the question— notably developmental psychologists and certain philosophers, including all eudaimonists—generally agree that autonomous self-awareness in the individual is preceded by a stage in which it is not to be expected.[22] This prior stage is what we term childhood, and its essential meaning is dependence, including identity-dependence. Child-identity is autonomous in no respect, but necessarily derives from such agencies external to the child as parents and community. To be sure, identity-conflict can occur even in childhood, but in this case its real source is two or more conflicting external agencies and it remains to be settled there, for the child lacks autonomous agency.

Correspondingly, if first self-awareness cannot be sought

in childhood, neither will it be found in mature adulthood, for adulthood consists in courses of action predicated upon self-awareness and related to it as consequents to antecedent. Accordingly the search for the first occasion of self-awareness centers in a segment of development preceding adulthood and following childhood, the stage of life termed adolescence.

In adolescence, autonomous self-awareness first occurs in the form of one's awareness of being *misidentified* by *the other*. The form bears stressing because it establishes the distinctive coloration of adolescence in its feeling of being fated to be perpetually "misunderstood." Throughout childhood the individual has unquestioningly accepted adult identification of himself, usually that of his parents. Where a third party misidentified him, the third party was referred to the parentally constructed identity. Now, however, it is in the parental identification that the adolescent recognizes misidentification, which is to say misidentification now appears in the identification of him by the heretofore privileged other, and hence in his identification by any other. Beneath this sense of misidentification and responsible for it is the adolescent's new-found awareness of something within him for which *only he can speak*. The moment is portentous and felt to be such. By its tone of "from this moment and forever-more," it signals a future very different from the past, it marks a disruption of the personal continuum. At the same time misidentification by others cannot be corrected because the new found "inner self" of the adolescent as yet has no voice with which to speak to the world, it is but a murmur within, audible to one person alone, and this helplessness projects itself as "fated to be misunderstood."

That self-awareness occurs suddenly not only is confirmed by introspection but is insured deductively by the fact that what appears in it is a genuine novelty that, as such, must have its moment of first appearing. Moreover its appearance transforms the world of the individual into the *world of its appearance*, and this world is unlike that in which the individual heretofore (as a child) had his being. The event is sudden, unexpected, and astonishing. There is nothing of the feeling of intention in it, as would certainly be the case if, as Sartre contends, the event were an act of creation. (And we must remember that Sartre himself forbids any resort to "unconscious" creation.) On the contrary it is frequently touched with pain, and resisted or suppressed for a time by the adolescent, whose desires all run the other way. He wants familiarity; he wants to fulfill his parents' expectations of him as he has always done, yet he cannot. Through none of his own doing he is by this moment projected from the world he knows into a strange new landscape that will exact of him the utmost canniness if it is to be successfully navigated. Not only does the first moment of autonomous self-awareness exhibit the marks of unintentional discovery to the exclusion of the marks of intentional creation, but through a good three-quarters of its course adolescence typically offers a convincing portrayal of itself as having been thrown into deep water without benefit of swimming lessons, where it develops the rudiments of buoyancy only after extended flounderings and thrashings about. Such behavior does not suggest Sartrean self-creation, which by its choice of fundamental project arms itself at the same stroke with its principle of self-regulation. On the other hand the adventure of autonomy that adolescence is can be resisted persistently, producing developmental arrest. In such cases the dependence of childhood is prolonged, sometimes throughout a lifetime. But where this occurs it is the result of choice (though the fact may be concealed in self-deception), for the new voice within has been heard.

Not only does the immediate quality of the first moment of self-awareness disconfirm Sartre's theory, but in Sartrean terms the very tenor of adolescence as fated to be misunderstood by others is impossible. In the first place, early adolescence precedes the alleged choice of one's fundamental project. This is necessarily so because for choice to be genuinely such requires knowledge of alternatives, and this knowledge is by no means contained in the first moment of self-awareness that inaugurates adolescence. Therefore what must follow the first moment of self-awareness is the discovery of alternative possible life-styles through exploration, and this exploration is the very essence of adolescence that, as such, comes to a close with decision. This means that on the Sartrean model misidentification by others cannot occur in adolescence, for prior to the choice of one's fundamental project, one is nothingness, and as such can offer no resistance to any identification whatever. (In Sartre's words, prior to choice the individual "is nothing. He will not be anything until later, and then he will be what he makes of himself."*) Alternatively, we have seen that this nothingness is perhaps not pure void but rather everything in possibility. But precisely as everything possible, no possible identification can fail to apply. Thus in Sartrean terms the adolescent can neither be misidentified nor find any ground for feeling himself to be such. But the fact remains that the fundamental tonality of adolescence is the feeling of being fated to be misidentified ("misunderstood"), and to account for it as a groundless, universal illusion is logically absurd. (It is a serious question whether an illusion unique to the individual can be groundless, but a shared illusion logically cannot be.) Surely the sound course here lies in taking adolescence seriously, which means that we must take its feeling of being perpetually misunderstood as something to be intelligibly accounted for. If Sartre's theory of self-creation renders it unaccountable, this result speaks forcefully against Sartre's theory. The tenor of adolescence becomes accountable when self-creation is dismissed in favor of self-discovery. In the first moment of self-awareness, and therefore at the onset of adolescence, one *discovers* the autonomous self within, a self that is innate and was therefore present during the incubation of childhood, but

* See note 22.

unavailable until this moment. It remains to be tested, drawn out, lived, and in the full sense known, but its first appearance is enough to account for the tenor of adolescence as being fated to be misunderstood.

Accordingly, human being is by no means the nothingness Sartre says it is prior to its choosing. From birth each human being is a unique and determinate something in the mode of a potential. To this potential an identity must at first (in childhood) be supplied heteronomously, after which this furnished identity must be exchanged for an actuality that derives from living in accordance with one's potentiality.

Sartre's case (in Part One of *Being and Nothingness*) for the nothingness of being-for-itself rests upon the recognition that whatever for-itself is, it might be otherwise. Because the "might be otherwise" is no illusion but a constitutive characteristic of for-itself (indeed, it is freedom; but Sartre does not hereby ascribe an essence to for-itself, for "freedom has no essence"[23]), the "otherwise" is *in* the for-itself, and for-itself is the being that "is what it is not, and is not what it is."

At first sight the condition of anything's being something other than it is would appear to be the possibility of its not being what it is. It is here, according to Sartre, that nothingness enters the world "like a worm" which "lies coiled in the heart of being."[24] Just as, in the case of for-itself, what it is not must be within it as what it is, so this negation of what it is must likewise be within it as its own nothingness. At this point it will be recognized that to define for-itself as nothingness is to regard negation as the condition of affirmation in human consciousness (i.e. of free affirmation), and this is what Sartre does.

We may notice that here the logical fallacy in Nietzsche appears, for in Nietzsche's philosophy (unlike that of Heraclitus, which inspired him), negation can find no ground. Life is but the singular force of will to power, whose every manifestation can be nothing other than the expression of itself. Therefore Nietzsche's call for "Yea-saying" is gratuitous, for nothing that life may do can be anything other than its Yea-saying. And this recognition pinpoints the inadequacy in Nietzsche's philosophy, for negation is present in his description of the world—degeneration is the negation of life, sickness is the negation of health—but his theoretical apparatus can offer no account of it. By what means might negation arise? The readiest is through a conflict of positive forces, but this requires the introduction of a second principle alongside that of life as will to power—for example, spirit—and this move was resolutely refused by Nietzsche, who leaves negation inexplicable. Into the breach steps Sartre, who accounts for negation, however, not as a by-product of the conflict of affirmative forces, but as the activity of the being that is nothingness, i.e. human being.

Sartre's enthronement of nothingness is instigated by his supposition that negation is the condition of affirmation, and the supposition is false. Man is an identity problem due not to deficit in his being, but to surplus. The being that "is what it is not, and is not what it is" is a problem, not of impoverishment, but of superabundance. The original apprehension by the for-itself of its freedom arises, not on its annihilation of what it is, but on its apprehension of itself as *not only* what it is, but also as something else—and something else again.* It is as impossible to posit an original negation as it is to think of nothing, or feel nothing. Sartre appears to recognize this when he says that whereas for-itself is pure negation, and negation presupposes something to negate, therefore for-itself presupposes being-in-itself as pure positivity and is "logically subsequent to it."[25] But he fails to see that the same logic applies with equal force to the for-itself considered alone. Indeed, negations in the world appear not as primary phenomena, but as by-

---

* The "else" requires stress, for what we speak of here are alternative possible actualities, and not mere continuous additions to the self's present actuality.

products of the being that is the negation of itself, and self-negation presupposes positivity in the self. It is therefore a logical mistake to conceive of the self as an original nothing-ness. This finds empirical confirmation in the recognition that personal consciousness contains no lacunae; it is a plenum concerning which our use of the word "nothing" always denotes but the absence of what we seek, which is at the same time the presence of something else. Aboriginal consciousness is therefore a *something*. Moreover its aborig-inal activity consists not in the negation of its something, but in the recognition of itself as also "something else be-sides." No negation as yet appears, but rather multiplicity. What instigates negation is the requirement for determina-tion that is imposed by action. Negation never attacks the solitary outpost of self—it must first be assured of another outpost for its base. Negation is neither original nor a be-ing; it is the product of conflict between two or more posi-tivities. This conclusion overturns Sartre's ontological thesis that human being is Nothingness Absolute.* Not his empti-ness but his multiplicity gives occasion in the individual for his self-negation, which cannot be absolute. It follows that human freedom is not the groundless freedom of self-manu-facture, but freedom for self-discovery and self-adherence. Because this latter freedom is much more complete than we agree to suppose, Sartre's relentless advocacy of absolute freedom works partly to good purpose. But at a deeper level it constitutes a danger to true human freedom, for it expresses nothing less than a capitulation to the powerful forces of alienation at work in contemporary life. The man who has no authentic feelings, and must on every occasion manufacture his feelings, is no exemplar of freedom, but rather the self-alienated product of special conditions of life today. What is true here with regard to particular feelings

* But is compatible with our interpretation, pp. 107-108, of human being prior to choice as "nothing actual, everything possible," and argues for this interpretation as the way to save the best of *Being and Nothingness* from sinking in consequence of the ontological leaks.

is no less true concerning the self as a whole. The individual who perpetually engages in arbitrary self-manufacture requires therapy, not canonization.

Our assessment of Sartre's contribution to the theory of self-actualization has been confined to *Being and Nothingness*. His subsequent thought on these themes stands to *Being and Nothingness* neither as extension nor as refinement, but as contradiction. Second, his subsequent thought abandons self-actualization for a different stance, a stance, moreover, that is hollow and falls of its own weight. Finally, Sartre himself refuses to notice or at any rate to acknowledge that these alterations have occurred. Together, these considerations pronounce Sartre's later thought about man's being to be markedly inferior to *Being and Nothingness*, which stands as the apex of Sartreanism.

Briefly, in his essay (originally a lecture given in 1946) "Existentialism is a Humanism," Sartre places as a condition upon the individual's choice that he must recognize that by his choice he chooses, not for himself alone, but "for all men."[26] This would be consistent with the principles of *Being and Nothingness* if it meant simply that by his choice the individual activates a possibility that thereby stands revealed to other men as a possibility. But this is not what Sartre means. He means that by his choice the individual actualizes a possibility for all men as their actuality. He also means that the individual must consciously choose for humanity, and not for himself alone. Moreover the value chosen (and the object of any choice is necessarily conceived to be a value by the chooser[27]) is affirmed by the choice to be a value for all humanity, and therefore a proper object of choice by every person.

To begin with the aim of one's choice—that it can consciously be a value for humanity, as Sartre now insists, is contradicted by the statement in *Being and Nothingness* that "the for-itself never aims at ends which are fundamentally abstract and universal."[28] According to the fundamental principles of *Being and Nothingness*, there is no universal for-itself except as a conceptual abstraction. In the realm of for-itself, "Being is an individual venture."[29] An individual for-itself can choose only for itself, although it is true that the "profound meaning" of the choice is universal[30] in the sense described above, that it exhibits a universal possibility. But this is a universal consequence of a particular choice, and not a universal choice. Furthermore in the terms of *Being and Nothingness* universality of the chosen value follows from choice, but in a narrowly restricted form. What is actualized by one's choice is a value for all (a good piece of scientific research, for example, or a good work of art), but it is such strictly as *one's* choice, not as a universal value that should be chosen by all. To assert that the individual's choice is of a universal value that deserves therefore to be the choice of all is to destroy the qualitative individualism of *Being and Nothingness* with the dictum that all persons shall choose alike.

In "Existentialism is a Humanism" we are also told that, by choosing, the individual *acts* for all. In the first place this violates the cardinal tenet of *Being and Nothingness* that no man can act for another, but each can act only for himself. Moreover it is only *as* humanity that the individual can act *for* humanity, therefore Sartre's claim requires that each individual be within himself common humanity. In "Existentialism is a Humanism" Sartre affirms this to be the case. He says that the subjectivity of the self "is not a strictly individual subjectivity, for we have demonstrated that one discovers in the *cogito* not only himself, but others as well,"[31] and he names what is discovered "intersubjectivity." It follows that when the individual acts he does so not as an individual but as universal humanity. Hence his "anguish," for "choosing all mankind as well as himself, [he] can not escape the feeling of his total and deep responsibility."[32]

The disparity will be evident if we recall that in *Being and Nothingness* intersubjectivity can never be experienced. Sartre's analysis of the prime social phenomenon, "the Look," demonstrates that others can appear to us only as objects of our look, or as our experience of our own objectness under their look—never in their freedom and their subjectivity. For this reason love—the profoundest endeavor at an interpenetration of subjectivities—must fail. "The problem of my being-for-others remains therefore without solution. The lovers remain each one for himself in a total subjectivity; nothing comes to relieve them of their duty to make themselves exist each one for himself; nothing comes to relieve their contingency nor to save them from facticity."[33]

"Existentialism is a Humanism" reflects Sartre's sensitivity to the charge that his previous work valorizes arbitrary choice. But Sartre's new stance destroys the foundations of individualism while doing nothing to remove the arbitrariness of choice. Ironically he makes himself a target for Kierkegaard's deadliest arrow: "Being an individual man is a thing that has been abolished, and every speculative philosopher confuses himself with humanity at large; whereby he becomes something infinitely great, and at the same time nothing at all."[34]

Arbitrariness remains because the "universality of man" that we discover within us cannot be antecedent to our choice, serving as its foundation (as which it would constitute prior essence). Instead it arises with our choice, by which we participate in creating this universal.[35] But a "humanity" that arises in our act affords no regulation of the act; it is simply the case that what we do becomes predicable of humanity. The notion that the fact of such predication produces forebearance in the individual agent has no basis. The moral simpleton readily generalizes his worst behavior, insisting that everyone else does likewise, or would if he could.

If "Existentialism is a Humanism" compromises the principles of *Being and Nothingness*, Sartre's subsequent *Critique of Dialectical Reason* (his attempted reconciliation of existentialism and Marxism) does so doubly and trebly. It is, therefore, by *Being and Nothingness* alone that

Sartre's contribution to self-actualization ethics is to be judged, and the pertinent question is, can his services counterbalance his disservice?

Unquestionably Sartre advances self-actualization ethics by offering a most ingenious, relentless, and concrete demonstration of the primacy of the virtue of self-truth ("integrity," or in Sartre's term "authenticity"). Nevertheless the advance here is but the addition of a voice, albeit an eloquent one, for the concept is as old as self-actualization ethics itself. Where Sartre makes a constitutive contribution is by his recognition that, with regard to the ultimate ends of individual lives, "there is no privileged psychic phenomenon." Previous self-actualization theory had elevated one human faculty or another—reason by the Greeks, will by Nietzsche, faith by Kierkegaard—to the position of privilege, both as the exclusive means to self-fulfillment and as the exclusive end. Under Sartre's tutelage it becomes necessary to recognize that, without exception, every mode or faculty of subjectivity is a reservoir of ends and a contributor to means—there are manual, technical, sensual, voluntarist, and visionary destinies no less than "rational" ones, subsisting in ideal complementarity. Indeed (as shall be determined in Chapter 5), all destinies are alike rational, not in virtue of the inherent rationality of their ends, but because they employ possibilities as ends of activity and thereby transform mere flux into patterns of development.

In the words of George Santayana, "Every impulse in man or beast bears its little flame of spirit."[36] The abandonment by self-actualization ethics of its biases with respect to privileged faculties means recognition of excellences of craftsmanship, commerce, athletics, conservation, etc., which are fully equivalent in amount of worth to the privileged or "status" endeavors upon which a given culture prides itself. This in turn conduces toward relinquishment of the age-old superstition that by the "natural lottery" of birth, a handful of persons are "gifted" beyond the rest. This notion instills injustice in the natural order, and warps conceptions of subsequent justice by rendering it remedial and selective from the outset. From this initial impress justice cannot recover. Against it we shall argue that justice finds its necessary presupposition in the innate, equivalent, qualitatively unique, potential worth of every person. Sartre's banishment of the bias of privileged faculties removes the primary obstacle to the establishment of this presupposition. But it does so only if innatism can be maintained against Sartre's doctrine of the nothingness of for-itself. Our case against Sartre is stated. Prior to choice, the individual human being is not void but superabundance. He lacks, not content, but selective principle; yet he contains this principle implicitly, and the function of choice is to render the principle explicit as the enduring theme of personal development.

Being and Nothingness is a showcase for Sartre's genius at applied phenomenology, and invaluable as such. But it is built upon an ontological mistake that is corrosive and disastrous. By misconceiving possibility as absolute nothingness, Sartre at the outset builds in the inexorable conclusion that "man is a useless passion."[37] *Ex nihilo, nihil fit.* By identifying possibilities as absolute nothingness Sartre precludes all actualization of possibilities whatever. But the intractable meaning of "possibility" is "possible actuality," and on this meaning the viability of the human enterprise is restored. This meaning of "possibility" issues from a metaphysics very different from Sartre's.

5

The Metaphysics of Individualism

Self-actualization ethics arises from two distinctive presuppositions whose status calls for investigation. Because investigation of the status of ultimate presuppositions is the province of metaphysics, and metaphysics has lately fallen into disrepute at the hands of philosophy herself (Anglo-American "analytic" variety), a few words shall be said concerning its place in our inquiry.

Metaphysics is the terminus of a chain of regressive justification that begins with acts, pursues the principles of those acts, then the presuppositions of those principles, and finally the ultimate presuppositions of those (relative) presuppositions. Our focus is ethics, and the principles in question are therefore normative principles (of self-actualization), while the presuppositions are the presuppositions of those principles. This arrangement is dictated by the levels of generality of the subject-matter itself, and it occasions a hierarchy of distinguishable enterprises. The task of morality is not to examine its principles but to act upon them. But as such practical morality is not self-justifying. Instead it looks for support to ethics, the theoretical discipline whose task is to investigate and compare the principles of normative judgments. Ethics renders such principles explicit both intensively and extensively. It divulges their essential meaning, and it displays their entailments, implications, and correlations. Concerning any moral act, then, ethics shows what the principle of the act is, what the principle presupposes, what other principles follow from this presupposition, and what other acts are entailed by the act in question. But the presuppositions that constitute the subject-matter of ethics are relative presuppositions that derive from logically prior ones. These prior presuppositions are ultimate in the sense that there are no presuppositions prior to themselves from which they derive, and the work of disclosing them intensively and extensively belongs not to ethics but to metaphysics. Thus as ethics furnishes morality with its entitlement, and morality supplies entitlement to acts, so metaphysics affords entitlement to ethics, and no system of morality or ethics can be regarded as having disclosed itself fully until disclosure has been made of the metaphysics upon which it rests.

But metaphysics is no more self-justifying than—at the other end—is a single act or a given morality. The justification of metaphysics rests in the ethics, the morality, and the concrete acts it entails. The mistake of looking for the verifiability or falsifiability of metaphysical propositions *in themselves* lies just here, for "in themselves" they are not metaphysical propositions. As metaphysical propositions, what they are consists in the second-order conceptual systems and the concrete actions to which the metaphysical propositions furnish intelligibility and justification. But this furnished intelligibility and justification appear only when the metaphysical propositions are considered in relation to the derivative second-order systems and the endorsed acts, they are not present in the metaphysical propositions "in themselves." Metaphysical principles are not self-evident or self-justifying. They are neither pure intelligibles nor (as Plato and Aristotle supposed they must be) pure active intelligence. The notion that they must be such in order to furnish intelligibility to the world is as mistaken as its current antithesis, that metaphysical propositions are "cognitively meaningless."

A thing is rendered intelligible by disclosure of its antecedents and consequents—causes and effects in the case of physical events, presuppositions and entailments in the case of mental entities, and a combination of these in the case of mixed entities such as historical epochs and personal and collective feelings. Accordingly, metaphysics provides intelligibility to ethics as ethics provides intelligibility to morality, and morality to concrete acts. The function is supportive at each level, which prevents us from supposing that metaphysics extinguishes ethics and morality in its own sovereignty (as was promulgated, for example, by the British Absolute Idealists). The defining characters of morality and ethics are not abolished but rendered intelligible and justified by metaphysics. In the case of morality a defining characteristic is choice, and metaphysics is bound to retain and perfect the nature of choice as well as the meaning of the concept. It does this by rendering choice intelligent, amid intelligible alternatives. This requires the renunciation by metaphysics of its own autocratic proclivities. The projected final outcome of metaphysical endeavor is not a single system of first principles, but a number of alternative and equally viable systems, each of which justifies alternative second-order and first-order systems. Each hierarchy of interdependent first-order (practical), second-order (theoretical), and third-order (metaphysical) systems embraces the totality of experienceable phenomena and is therefore entitled to be termed a world. We have here, then, a number of alternative possible worlds, each of which is complete and incommensurable with the others. By Leibniz's great principle of compossibility (about which more must be said subsequently), the fact of the existence of any thing is proof of the existence of the world in which that thing is implicated. Therefore, at the least, existence comprises one world. And existence also comprises one world at the most, for the obverse of compossibility is incompossibility, according to which alternative worlds are mutually exclusive with respect to existence. In sum, at all times there exists one world, which is surrounded by innumerable possible worlds.*

* For excellent recent work in the logic of possible worlds, with reference to Leibniz, see Benson Mates, "Leibniz on Possible Worlds," in Harry G. Frankfurt, ed., *Leibniz, A Collection of Critical Essays*

Accordingly, the work of metaphysics is twofold. Within a world it functions to afford justification and intelligibility to the aspects of that world, a work we shall call *synchronic* in the broad meaning of "within the system."† Second, metaphysics is responsible for delineating the place of any world amid alternative possible worlds, a work for which we shall use the term *diachronic* in the broad meaning of "between systems." It is important to notice that these two functions of metaphysics implicate one another, for a world can be justified and rendered intelligible only for what it is, namely an alternative amid others of its kind.

The "dangerousness" of metaphysics attends its diachronic function, for it investigates meanings that are inconsistent with "common sense" and established belief. Here metaphysics is the relentless foe of that parochialism that history attests as endemic to human thought and a condition of human life as we know it. By "parochialism" I refer to the supposition that what exists, with its grounds and

---

(Garden City: Doubleday Anchor Books, 1972), pp. 335-364; and Jaakko Hintikka, "Modality and Quantification," *Theoria* 27 (1961), pp. 119-128, and Hintikka, "Studies in the Logic of Existence and Necessity," *The Monist* 50 (1966), pp. 55-76; and Hide Ishiguro, *Leibniz's Philosophy of Logic and Language* (Ithaca: Cornell University Press, 1972).

† I use the terms *synchronic* and *diachronic* somewhat stipulatively, but in accordance with the structuralism of Jean Piaget: see Piaget, *Structuralism*, trans. and ed. by Chaninah Maschler (New York: Harper Torchbooks, 1971). Piaget relies upon the usage of Ferdinand de Saussure's *Course in General Linguistics* (trans. Wade Baskin [New York: Philosophical Library, 1959]), but modifies in the direction of generality to render the terms applicable to systems other than linguistic.

Though it may not be apparent, the two terms retain their temporal reference in our usage. In a Leibnizian "world" of mutual implications, past and future are actual in the present, only implicitly rather than explicitly, and are therefore "synchronous" with it. But in virtue of incompossibility, alternative possible worlds are "diachronous" with respect to actuality (both explicit and implicit) and can exist only at different times.

implications, is exhaustive of possibility, at any rate for "right-minded" persons. Interestingly, it is standard practice by authoritarian governments immediately upon assuming power to take aim at philosophy, rigidly controlling or excising philosophical activity at universities within the nation's boundaries (forceful recent examples are provided by Stalin, Hitler, and Francisco Franco). Think of it!—philosophy, which "bakes no bread" and appears to the casual eye as the most ineffectual of activities. But the eye of authoritarianism is extraordinarily acute, for it is philosophy —and pre-eminently metaphysics—that apprehends alternatives to whatever happens presently to exist. Therefore it is philosophy—and, again, pre-eminently metaphysics—that affords ultimate exemplification of human freedom. The reason for Plato's meticulous control of both poetry and philosophy within the Republic is Plato's recognition, not of the falsehood of these activities, but of their truth. To Plato as poet-philosopher, both poetry and philosophy exhibit "divine madness"—divine because it apprehends highest truths, mad because these highest truths are quite different from what common sense supposes them to be, or the regime legislates them to be.

In the Republic Plato incorporates the psychological principle that men will only work for a truth in the belief that that truth is the exclusive truth. This belief represents parochialism as heretofore defined, and the unbroken reliance upon the principle by history, from Plato's time to our own, is the basis of our suggestion a moment ago that parochialism is "almost a condition of life as we know it." The underlying contention of the present work is that humanity can no longer afford the parochialism of claims to exclusive truth. It has become imperative that each person, each morality, each culture, each state, learn to affirm the equal truth of alternative systems—whether actual or merely possible—and to envisage its own consummation as the consummation of an ultimate individual that is complemented by other and qualitatively different individuals. It may well be that the very meaning of "community," "nation," or "epoch" requires that all activities be ordered by a single set of ultimate presuppositions. But such a commonality requires knowledge of itself for what it is, namely a choice among equally valid alternatives. Provision of this knowledge is the work of diachronic metaphysics.

Synchronic metaphysics furnishes antecedents and consequents to the material (relative presuppositions) of ethics, as ethics furnishes antecedents and consequents to the material (acts and principles) of morality. As morality confers intelligibility on particular acts, so ethics provides intelligibility to morality, and metaphysics to ethics. But metaphysics is destined ever to be without an intelligibility autonomous to itself because its material—ultimate presuppositions—is without logical antecedents. This does not condemn the quest for intelligibility to failure, or propel it into the arms of transcendental providence. It means that metaphysics furnishes intelligibility to a total system of which it is itself a part. And it means that intelligibility works to perfect choice and ultimate diversity, not to abolish these. By metaphysics choice is rendered intelligent through knowledge of its antecedents and consequents together with this same knowledge concerning alternatives. Rather than being transformed into necessity, choice is perfected as choice by knowledge of alternative valid metaphysical systems.

Meanwhile it remains imperative to require justification of acts, principles, and conceptual systems of the second order. Justification presupposes intelligibility as heretofore defined. In the case of an act, it consists in the demonstration that this act fulfills an entailment (a "promise") of a prior act, when both acts are regarded under a given principle. (Moral obligation originates in the promissory character of acts that are acts on principle.) Similarly, principles are justified by their entailments under relative presuppositions. Under this interrogation many acts prove unjustified by their failure to fulfill the promises of prior acts. And many conceptual systems prove unjustified by their inability to stomach their own implications.

From this prologue in behalf of the indispensability of metaphysics we turn now to the metaphysical task at hand. It consists in the explication of two ultimate presuppositions that are distinctive to self-actualization ethics. This ethics presupposes the normative authority of individuated possibilities. Accordingly it presupposes, first, that possibility is an ultimate, underived, and irreducible modality of the real and, second, that possibilities subsist as an incommensurable multiplicity of discrete individuals. We shall also be concerned with a third presupposition, necessary to self-actualization ethics though not unique to it, and left out by some formulations, namely that actuality is the other irreducible modality of the real. From these presuppositions we will derive the following basic principles: (a) freedom as the indeterminate relation between actuality and possibility in the medium of consciousness; (b) possibility as normative authority both within and without the scope of actuality, but necessarily in reference to actuality; (c) the abstract norm of personhood as a perfectible finitude; and (d) the abstract norm of humanity as a perfection of complementary perfected finitudes. We shall begin with the ultimate presupposition that possibility is an irreducible modality of the real.

No person undertakes to do something he knows to be impossible, and no person undertakes to do something he knows to be inevitable. To attempt the impossible is futile, and to attempt the inevitable is gratuitous. All human enterprise, from the least act to the loftiest aspiration, is obliged to presuppose the possibility of its successful outcome and to direct itself by this concretely apprehended possibility. Not successful outcomes but directed activities demonstrate the reality of possibilities. For directed activity we shall hereafter employ the term *development*.

Development is only conceivable if something that is not

yet explicitly actual is affecting change as a goal toward which it is directed. It is certain that actuality includes developments because only in virtue of such inclusions does actuality, regarded as the arena of change, become at all intelligible. For intelligibility consists in the recognizability of antecedents and consequents, but in the absence of development, nothing exists by which to determine which antecedents and which consequents are to be attended to. It is due alone to development that, among all antecedents and consequents to any given thing or event, certain ones can be identified as *its* antecedents and consequents. The degree of intelligibility that change possesses is therefore the demonstration that the arena of change includes developments.

But it must at once be noted that the presence of development is significantly restricted in its demonstrative power. Because the developments are themselves actual, they can demonstrate only the reality of actualized possibilities, and actualized possibilities need not be true possibilities at all, but only necessities in disguise. To see this we must notice that for change to be a development it is sufficient that what it is directed toward does not yet exist. But what does not yet exist may be entirely actual, only implicitly so rather than explicitly. In this case development consists in rendering what is implicit in actuality explicit over the course of time, and if nothing *else* is possible, then this actuality becomes recognizable in both its explicit and its implicit aspects as necessity—a necessity that is simply obliged to spread its self-manifestation over time. We shall term implicit necessity *potentiality* in the Aristotelian sense and distinguish it carefully from possibility, with which it is often confused. "Potentiality" is the character of an actuality that requires time in order to manifest itself. Such potentiality becomes necessity when coupled with the "principle of plenitude,"[1] according to which only those things are possible that do in fact in some measure exist. According to the doctrine produced by this coupling there can be no "free" (unactualized) possibilities. Concomitantly all change is development, for development is actuality, and actuality is all that is (in Aristotle's formulation the formal cause, or end at which becoming aims, is also the efficient cause). Such is the universe of Aristotle,[2] a universe in which nothing new can ever happen, a universe that can be known once and for all by the study of the forms of existing things.

"Dreadful" is the first word from the lips of Etienne Gilson at this "once and for all." Of Aristotle's metaphysics in this respect Gilson concludes, "It is responsible for the immediate death of those positive sciences of observation which Aristotle himself had so happily fostered. For centuries and centuries men will know everything about water, because they will know its essence, that which water is; so also with fire, with air, with earth, with man. Why indeed should we look at things in order to know them? Within each species they are all alike; and if you know one of them, you know them all. What a poverty-stricken world such a world is! And how much deeper the words of the poet sound to our ears: 'There are more things in heaven and earth, Horatio, than are dreamed of in your philosophy.' "[3]

Gilson's response is at once Platonic and characteristically human. For what is most dreadful in the metaphysics of plenitude is its offense against every person's immediate awareness, concerning every course of action he takes and has taken, that "it might have been otherwise." That it ever "might be otherwise" is an intuition of the real alternativity in the universe of being—an alternativity whose foundation rests with the free possibles that surround and suffuse whatever happens at present to be actual. As against Aristotle, the classical spokesman for such alternativity is Plato. But Plato himself did nothing to refute the principle of plenitude, he simply philosophized on his keen intuition to the contrary.

For its refutation, the doctrine of plenitude awaited G. W. Leibniz's principle of incompossibility.[4] With the falcon's eye of philosophical genius, Leibniz recognized that not all possibilities are capable of co-existence. Given the truth of incompossibility, the fact that some things exist demonstrates the subsistence, unactualized, of those possibilities that are incompossible with the things that exist. What prevents that which cannot exist in one place from existing at the same time in another is the singularity of reference implied by the term "the world." All that exists at any given time exists *together* as "the (existing) world." Every existing item finds its intelligibility (in Leibniz's terms, its "sufficient reason") in a set of ultimate presuppositions (metaphysical principles) that afford intelligibility to every other existing item. But by the principle of incompossibility, this existing world is surrounded by non-existing possible worlds that, as fully real, *subsist*.

Recognition of the importance of incompossibility has been hindered by Leibniz's own theology, which rendered it impotent. In the terms of Leibniz's theology, actualization of pure possibles is the work of God exclusively. Because God inevitably acts according to the "principle of the best" it is certain that the existing world is the best of all possible worlds, and it is likewise certain that God shall never find reason to alter his choice.[5] Therefore only those possibles that are actual shall ever be such, and the infinitude of alternative possibles (likewise arranged by compossibility into worlds) that were passed by in God's choice are destined ever to remain unactualized. But in this case why should any human being bother his head with unactualized possibilities? They can neither be actualized nor affect actuality in any way; moreover it is certain on the above account that they are one and all inferior to what is actual. The upshot is that, by his theology, Leibniz manages to nullify the intrinsic interest of his metaphysical principle of compossibility-incompossibility.

The pungency of the principle will be restored if good grounds can be found for disregarding the theology, and such grounds appear in the demonstration—notably by Russell, Couturat, and Parkinson[6]—that Leibniz's metaphysics and his theology are not of a piece but are logically independent. For example the "principle of the best" is not a mere re-wording of the principle of sufficient reason, as Leibniz seems to have supposed.[7] And while the metaphysics demonstrates the necessary existence of something, it does not follow that the something is the Christian God.[8]

By accepting the case for disjunction, we are free to strip away Leibniz's theology, and when this is done the power of incompossibility is restored. Distinct from actuality are infinite possibilities that are possible *actualities*—alternative ultimate principles, alternative second- and first-order systems, alternative ends of every development, alternative life styles and patterns of sociality, perhaps even alternative laws of nature. And under certain conditions these alternatives become available to existing beings. The first condition is that men be able to apprehend free possibles and act upon them. A second important condition is stipulated by compossibility itself, which says that between actuality and free possibility no admixture can occur, but only total exchange. By incompossibility it remains the case that alternative worlds cannot exist simultaneously, but it now obtains that multiple worlds can exist seriatim through the agency of world-exchange.

The reader will be aware that throughout preceding pages the key question, "Are there free possibilities?" has been answered by inference from metaphysical principles. The question of direct evidence of free possibles by immediate apprehension has deliberately been postponed until the tool was in hand to render it answerable. The tool is the concept of world-exchange. Without it the question of immediate apprehension of pure (unactualized) possibles is unanswerable for the following reason. When we apprehend a possible we do so as (ourselves) actual beings, hence the apprehended possible is now an actualized possible, i.e. a potential, and seemingly can offer no evidence that it subsisted prior to the apprehension. To the contrary, does not its actualization by an actual being demonstrate that what is actualized is compossible with the actual world, and therefore that, with the actual world, it has been actual all along, only implicitly so, awaiting explication? Much human discovery is of this sort, representing the explication of implications of antecedent existence. For example the Wright brothers' flight at Kitty Hawk only made explicit certain implications in the mechanics of Isaac Newton, formulated two centuries previously. Such discovery constitutes the extrapolation of the actual. Because the actual world (like every possible world) is a continuum, the change effected by discovery of this type is necessarily continuous, or "evolutionary," change.

What permits identification of apprehensions of free possibles is the recognition, afforded by the principle of incompossibility, that such apprehension constitutes world-exchange. Apprehension of a free possible instantly transforms the entire familiar world into an utterly unfamiliar one in which nothing remains what it was and everything awaits to be discovered afresh. This discontinuous exchange is referred to by the term *revolutionary* change. It occurs because the apprehension of a free possible is at the same time the apprehension of the world of compossibles in which the free possible has its place, an apprehension whose condition is the lapse of the actual world, due to the incommensurability of the two worlds.

Much philosophical interest in and debate about the possibility of revolutionary world-exchange has been engendered by Thomas S. Kuhn's *The Structure of Scientific Revolutions*.[9] I do not wish to enter the current debate further than to remark that the book's most apparent weaknesses, as identified by its critics, are rectified by recourse to the metaphysics of Leibniz. Kuhn's critics[10] rightly charge that he offers no description of world-exchange, and also that he produces nothing in the way of justification or sufficient reason for its occurrence. From Leibniz's metaphysics we have just extracted the description of world-exchange, outlined broadly for our purposes but susceptible of refinement and precision. The justification for world-exchange is a problem because fundamentally every possible world can render intelligible in its own terms everything within it and moreover is, again in its own terms, a plenum, lacking nothing. Thus *why* one world is exchanged for another appears to be an unanswerable question—upon which Kuhn too hastily impales himself by his endorsement of "an apparently arbitrary element, compounded of personal and historical accident."[11]

World-exchange finds its sufficient reason in the metaphysics of Leibniz when Leibniz's theology has been set aside. For of possible worlds, one is *best* only in order that the best can be chosen by God in accordance with his nature. Apart from this consideration there is no reason why all possible worlds may not be equal in quantity of goodness.* The "identity of indiscernibles" precludes only exact replication. It does not speak against a multiplicity of worlds, equal in amount of goodness, but differing in kind. Indeed, Leibniz himself indicates that pure, unactualized possibles are perfections "of a sort,"[12] and perfection logically does not admit of qualification by degree. Consistent with this we can regard each possible world, *qua* pure possibility, as perfect goodness of its unique kind. Sufficient reason for the actualization of alternative possible worlds now appears in the inherent desirability of actualizing all possible kinds of worth. Here, moreover, obtrudes an entirely new question concerning a possible best order for the

---

* Since each, as pure possibility and therefore at the ideal limit of its actual development, is a finite perfection, a "perfection of a kind," and perfection is logically insusceptible of qualification by degree. An infinity of possible worlds is an infinity of kinds of perfection. Nor does this quantitative equivalence in goodness presuppose identical numbers of enworlded persons. As an (ideally) perfect system, a world's perfection is not modified by the numbers of persons who participate in it. It is a boundaried, nondenumerable infinite. Similarly the potential worth of the person is not modified quantitatively by the number of persons with whom he co-exists. Perfection in kind remains perfection whatever may be the number of kinds.

serial actualization of alternative possible worlds. It is the question of the possibility of a diachronic logic—a logic of the relations of incommensurable systems—as against the familiar synchronic logics of development within given systems (as exemplified by all inferential logics). Diachronic logic is a virginal field, but the supposition by critics of world-exchange (and some proponents, notably T. S. Kuhn) that because nothing is known, therefore the process must be arbitrary or fictitious, is clearly non sequitur. More than any other, this question summons fresh logico-metaphysical endeavor. Its only vestige of a precedent lies in Hegel's dialectic, according to which exchange replaces the existing system by its antithesis. But why the antithesis, when alternatives abound? The answer lies in the psychology of rebellion. When one despairs of one's conditions, the first solution that occurs is the inversion of those conditions: if wealth does not bring happiness, poverty will; if learning does not solve everything, then let us sanctify ignorance; if sophistication encumbers, then let us revert to primitive simplicity. But this mere first resort of the cornered animal does not bear hypostatization as the supreme principle of Becoming.

Returning to the matter of the immediate apprehension of free possibilities, we must resist the temptation to work *en gros*, looking to the lives of men of genius and the stories of epoch-making events. For while historical world-exchanges are rare and momentous, the apprehensions that give rise to them are entirely common and unprepossessing. In fact our ordinary mental life teems with such apprehensions, amid which the actual world of established things preserves its stability simply by habit. In everyday life we perceive ordinary things in the ordinary way, but we do so amid a quiet hail of quite extraordinary apperceptions. For example everyone knows the experience of suddenly seeing the commonest word upon the printed page as thoroughly strange and unintelligible. Or again, one knows the experience of suddenly "seeing oneself through the eyes of another." In either case the experience is not that of an atom of unfamiliarity in the familiar world; the strangeness that begins with the word or the self extends everywhere.

Free possibilities swarm in mental life, and what is rare is not our apprehension of them, but our declaration of allegiance to any one of them. For good reason we ordinarily choose to disregard them, and we spare ourselves from perpetual re-choosing by installing the choice as a habit. Unquestionably the actual world imposes severe sanctions against the serious entertainment of alternative possibilities, and exploration will entail considerable cost. Such exploration constitutes world-exchange in the individual. To take its measure we need not set off in pursuit of Einstein or Copernicus, for occasions of world-exchange punctuate the lives of ordinary individuals. I refer to the process of personal growth, within which are to be found the stage-exchanges—of childhood for adolescence, of adolescence for maturation, of maturation for old age. Analysis of the stages of personal development (to be undertaken in the next chapter) discloses that each constitutes a "world" in the deepest meaning of the term, with the transitions between them constituting world-exchanges. Inability or refusal* to undertake these exchanges produces developmental arrest, a common enough condition in the actual world. But assiduous development from stage to stage is manifested by more than a few persons, who thereby afford proximate subjects for the study of world-exchange.

Thus far the argument has sought to establish the subsistence of free (unactualized) possibilities, and it remains now to uncover the inherent characteristics of possibility.

In the first place it is evident that a possible is a possible existent that, without the reference to existence, lapses from possibility to nothingness. For of a thing that is real we must be able to say that it is. But the meaning of "possible"

---

* Whether developmental arrest can be ascribed to refusal, to ignorance, or to some other source or combination of sources, will be treated in the following chapter, p. 169n.

contains on its face a negativity, an "is not." The negation in the possible cannot refer originally to the necessary, to which it is logically prior, nor can it refer either to the impossible or to nothingness, for these are in themselves negations that presuppose something to negate. Again, the possible cannot be conceived as the possibility of itself, for in this case negativity is directed at the only place available to an "is," and the possible destroys itself by self-contradiction. We therefore conclude that for the possible to possess being *qua* possible, it must refer to a being that it is not but can become. This requirement is fulfilled by the modality of the *actual*, by which is meant present matter of fact and its grounds and entailments. In virtue of actuality the pure possible can be said both to be and not to be without contradiction. As possible it is; as actual it is not; yet the actuality it does not possess it can acquire. There is no contradiction here because affirmation and negation have separate referents. At the same time we are forbidden from saying that the possible can not-be as possible. As possible it is eternal.

The demonstrability of the subsistence of free possibles refutes positivism's tenet that actuality is exhaustive of the real.* And the inherent reference of possibility to actuality

* "The characteristic theses of positivism are that science is the only valid knowledge and facts the only possible objects of knowledge; that philosophy does not possess a method different from science; and that the task of philosophy is to find the general principles common to all the sciences and to use these principles as guides to human conduct and as the basis of social organization. Positivism, consequently, denies the existence or intelligibility of forces or substances that go beyond facts and the laws ascertained by science. It opposes any kind of metaphysics, and, in general, any procedure of investigation that is not reducible to scientific method." (From "Positivism," by Nicola Abbagnano, trans. Nino Langiulli, in *The Encyclopaedia of Philosophy*, Paul Edwards, Editor-in-Chief [New York: Macmillan and The Free Press, 1967], vol. 6, 414.)
By employing "existence or intelligibility" with respect to positivism's denial, Abbagnano properly equivocates on the question of whether or not positivism is itself a (covert) metaphysics. Stated

rebukes what Santayana terms the "spiritual pride" of Platonism.[13] For Plato, existence is but an unhappy accident that in itself must ever strive to regain the beatific state of nonexisting, perfect being. But the Forms cannot be conceived except in terms of their possible embodiments, and it is therefore mistaken to envisage them as metaphysically self-sufficient. To stress this, Leibniz speaks metaphorically of possibles as "yearning" or "striving" for an existence that they are incapable of conferring upon themselves.[14]

But Platonism is correct in ascribing to possibilities the status of the eternal: for, in the first place, the actualization of the possible is not its destruction *qua* possible, nor is it the transformation of the possible into something in which possibility no longer remains.* As Leibniz saw, an existent is necessarily "a possible, and something else besides."[15] This means that whatever exists is always susceptible of lapsing once again into the status of unactualized possibility. But by the principle of compossibility, such lapse cannot occur to isolated elements of a world. Within the actual world, items may independently wax or wane in degree of explicitness, but this affects no alteration in their actuality, for when a thing thus "disappears" it remains implicit in what is manifest. Lapse from actuality can only occur to a world as a whole, and by the process of world-exchange. What is meant by "dead history" as distinct from "living history" consists of formerly actual worlds that have lapsed to unactualized possibility through world-exchange. "Living history" is the past of the world that is presently actual; it is continuous with present actuality and recoverable by retrospective inference. But this past is surrounded by

---

minimally, our own position is that whether positivism be epistemology or metaphysics, it has the coercive practical effect of limiting our conception of the real to that which is actual.

* On this point, and for an excellent analysis of possibility in other respects as well, the reader is referred to Nicola Abbagnano, *Critical Existentialism*, trans. and ed. Nino Langiulli (Garden City: Doubleday Anchor Books, 1969), Chs. 6 and 7.

other pasts which, because they are discontinuous with the actual present and its past, are irrecoverable by inference from present principles of actuality. These are "dead pasts," utterly devoid of influence within present actuality because their principles and the principles of present actuality are mutually exclusive. In relation to our own world, examples of dead pasts are to be found in the chivalric code of the Middle Ages or in the ancient Homeric code. Among conceptions implicit in the latter are polytheism, individualism, and moral nobility, each of which is presently precluded by the actuality of incommensurable alternatives. For example, at the center of the concept of nobility is eudaimonia, marking both a special condition of the individual self and the special feeling by which the condition is recognized. The corresponding word for eudaimonia in our language is "happiness," but "happiness" does not denote what eudaimonia denotes. "Happiness" denotes what in our system occupies the place corresponding to the place that eudaimonia occupies in the system of the ancients. In our system eudaimonia has no place, for it derives from first principles that are incommensurable with ours, and it entails an ethics, politics, economics, and finally a common sense that are incompossible with ours.

Nevertheless "dead pasts" are recoverable by a special means. The detailed description of this means remains as yet inadequate, but the foundation for it appears in Wilhelm Dilthey's method of "historical intuition"[16] and R. G. Collingwood's method of "imaginative re-enactment."[17] It consists in exchanging the principles of present actuality for those of the past that is to be recovered.* And successful

* On this conception the historian effects in himself the exchange of his native world for that past world that it is his aim to recover, and his book attempts to effect this same exchange in the reader. By this means (exclusively) a past is recoverable for what it was to itself, rather than for what it appears to have been from the standpoint of the present.

This exchange accounts for the curious psychological effect by exchange demonstrates the eternal subsistence of pure possibles.

Such availability of "dead pasts" also further distinguishes pure possibles from the Forms of Plato. For the Forms are fewer than existing things, and because of the reduction they thereby effect, they function as principles of intelligibility with respect to the actual world. But pure possibles are not fewer in number than actualities but infinitely more numerous, world upon world, hence the intelligibility that actuality manifests cannot be thought to derive from pure possibles of themselves, nor can we suppose that possibles are of themselves intelligence. Intelligibility enters the existing world, not from possibles themselves, but from the ordering effected by the employment of possibles as ends of directed activity by existing things. This requires of a metaphysics that is to account for the intelligibility of the world that actuality be no less real than possibility. Intelligibility arises in the conjunction of actuality and possibility. Because intelligibility is not pure possibility it is not itself an end of activity, but is instead a means for apprehending and attaining ends.

Correspondingly, the worth in the world arises from this same conjunction. It introduces normativity into the world, for it is as elements in patterns of directed activity that acts acquire their inherently promissory character. Rightness originally appears in the fulfillment by a given act of the promise implicit in prior acts, a promise those acts had in virtue of their principle. Goodness originally appears in the

---

which the historian inhabits two different worlds, sometimes preferring the world of the past and experiencing what seems to him its superior reality. In the same way Balzac ended a business conversation by saying: "Well, let us return to reality! Let us talk about Cesar Birotteau."

It must be added that not all historical work requires exchange. Much of it has for its purpose the recovery of the antecedents *of the present* which, as such, are continuous with the present and available to inference, without exchange.

achieved self-identity of the being that, by fulfilling its promises, "becomes what it is." Normativity thus inheres neither alone in possibility nor in bare fact, but in the embodiment by facts of possibilities as the ends of directed development. The metaphysics of self-actualization discloses that every "is" is also an "ought to be" in virtue of its promissory character, its foreshadowing of its own perfection. Affirmation of the actual world by actual beings is at the same time their responsibility to the perfection implicit in that actuality. Moral responsibility is inescapable because affirmation is inescapable. Human consciousness is a plenum, therefore it can contain no negation of the actual world that is not simultaneously the affirmation of an alternative to actuality, and hence a responsibility to the perfection of the alternative. No one can be held responsible to the actual world as against others, nor to possible worlds as against the actual. Even the metaphysician, who is (by nature, according to innatism) responsible for envisaging alternative worlds, can fully satisfy this responsibility by the knowledge he contributes concerning the status of the actual world. But by the medium of world-exchange he, like every other person, is free to exchange his responsibilities to the actual world for another set, qualitatively different but no less exacting. It was Robert Frost's pithy observation that freedom is "running easily in harness," to which we are constrained to add "—having chosen the harness in which one runs."

Within the actual world the primary facts are human acts (all other facts being such as they appear within these), and human acts have their futures within them, active at the present moment. Accordingly an *ought* dwells within every *is*, and the so-called "naturalistic fallacy" (of deriving ought from is, without addition) is a misconception, resting upon an artificially diminished conception of *is*. To constrict *is* to present matter of fact is to treat the world as if it were devoid of patterns of directed activity, in which case it would be entirely unintelligible. That facts are in any degree intelligible is due to their place in patterns of directed activity, and directed activity affirms that the possible *is*. What ought to be *is*, in the mode of potentiality. Ethical intuitionism correctly identifies the referents of ethical terms as real, nonempirical properties, but fatally misconceives them to be, not the inherent potentialities within facts, but existing universals ("good" in the case of G. E. Moore, "right" in the case of A. C. Ewing). Thus conceived they are without intrinsic connection with facts and complete of themselves, asking from us nothing but our admiration.

What remains to be established is that possibilities are ultimate individuals, perfected no less in their differences than in their resemblances. An individual substance is an inclusive and simple finitude, expressing all to which it is related according to its singular principle, while excluding from itself the alternative principles of other individuals. From the individuation of possibilities it follows that the goal of a human individual* is the perfection of his own

* In the course of this study I will not raise the question of the applicability of its concepts and principles to entities other than human beings. My justification for this neglect is that we are studying ethics and not metaphysics, but only so much of metaphysics as the ethics here offered obligates us to set forth. If potentials are distributed throughout existence (as the metaphysics of organicism maintains), it seems clear that in forms other than the human such potentials are properly conceived as Aristotle conceived potentiality or virtuality. But of Aristotelian potentiality Nicola Abbagnano rightly says, it "is a determination of necessity and in fact serves explicitly toward maintaining and guaranteeing the necessity of being in its becoming" (*Critical Existentialism*, p. 119). The freedom that ethics presupposes is introduced by the apprehension of *alternative* potentialities, with the resultant requirement for choice. Such apprehension distinguishes what is apprehended from Aristotelian potentialities, marking them instead as *possibilities*. It is a paramount purpose of the present study to demonstrate that the capacity to apprehend and act upon alternative possibilities is possessed by human beings. But on the basis of the minimal evidence available, it seems to me improper to ascribe this capacity to other entities, for example higher primates. For the best development of

unique finitude, and the goal of humanity is the community of complementary, perfected individuals. But "humanity" is an abstract with respect to individuals, and "its" goal can be the goal of individuals only indirectly, in the respect in which each individual, *qua* individual, is an instance of generic humankind.† The "goal of humanity" is approachable only by means of the self-fulfillment of individuals *qua* individuals, finding its meaning in the objective (social) value of individual excellence.‡ The ethical implications of this structure will be treated in subsequent chapters, but we note here that no room exists for fundamental disparity between social and personal obligations, because social and personal ethics constitute a single system. The intractable conflicts between social and self-interest that cripple both ethical theory and practical life shall be found

the case here suggested, see Max Scheler, *Man's Place in Nature*, trans. Hans Meyerhoff (New York: Noonday Press, 1961), esp. Chs. 1 and 2.

† For the manner in which the individual is "an instance of generic humankind," see Ch. 1, pp. 25-27, and Ch. 8 in its entirety.

‡ The argument may appear to rely here upon what Adam Smith termed "invisible hand" processes—processes that achieve (desirable) ends not intended by those who set the processes in motion. I am not myself in principle disposed against the employment of an "invisible hand" in philosophcal argument, for I believe John Dewey was correct in stressing that outcomes of directed activities necessarily afford occasions of discovery, and that learning from outcomes is an essential aspect of the "method of intelligence." But if "invisible hand" arguments are to be admissible they must of course be used not indiscriminately but criteriologically. A good defense of such use is to be found in Robert Nozick, *Anarchy, State, and Utopia* (New York: Basic Books, 1974), Ch. 1.

I think, however, that the argument here does not imply an "invisible hand," for the self-actualizing individual who knows his destiny knows as well his dependence upon the excellences of others, and the worth of his excellence to them. It is true that neither the good society nor the good of others is his explicit aim, but that the good society is attained by the fulfillment of individuals would occasion in him no surprise, but only the confirmation of what he knew.

to be spawned by conceptual mistakes. And the gymnastics to which ethical theory is put—the elaborate casuistries of sacrifice here for gain there, leading finally to the peremptory banishment of self-interest (as "prudence") from the purview of ethics altogether—are exercises in self-destruction. By its demonstration of the continuity of personal and social ethics, metaphysical individualism offers the primary condition upon which the aim of personal wholeness can be restored as a viable ideal. In modernity, metaphysical individualism finds its surpassing advocate in Leibniz, while among the ancients it achieves expression in the "Pythagoreanism" of Plato.

In Western philosophy Pythagoras and his followers were the first to recognize the ultimate significance of the differences among things. The Ionian philosopher-scientists had searched for the prime matter or the single substance of all things—water according to Thales, indeterminate matter to Anaximander, breath to Anaximenes. Explicitly or implicitly this endeavor pressed toward the reduction of all things to one, and Parmenides "showed once and for all that if you take the One seriously you are bound to deny everything else" (Burnet).[18] But this is a *reductio ad absurdum*, doubtless recognized as such by Pythagoras, who, moreover, found the means to certify the reality of differences in his mathematical studies. The qualitative differences among the fundamental geometrical figures—circle, triangle, rectangle, pentagon, etc.—cannot be attributable to differences in their matter because the ultimate figures themselves are immaterial ideals. Pythagoras was thus led to the concept of numerical form as the complement to matter; and because mathematical form is self-differentiated, differences are hereby shown to be no less real or ultimate than sameness.

But why restrict immaterial forms to the mathematical? For if numbers and geometrical shapes are purely formal determinants, so likewise are the pure concepts signified by words. By thus broadening the conception of forms, Socrates and Plato gave it sufficient scope to comprehend and render intelligible the entire world of experience, and it is in virtue of this extension of the move originally made by Pythagoras that Aristotle can describe Plato as a Pythagorean.[19]

Whereas for Parmenides being is one and undifferentiated, for Plato it is a self-differentiated system of intelligible (and actively intelligent) Forms. In the irreducible differences among the Forms we appear to find ultimate sanction for that definitive moral individualism of Hellas that finds perpetual expression from Pindar ("Various men excel in various ways, but it is meet that a man should walk in straight paths and strive according to his powers of Nature")[20] to Socrates ("Every one chooses his love from the ranks of beauty according to his character").[21] But *are* differences truly ultimate according to the metaphysics of Plato? For as previously noted, the Forms are fewer in number than things in the actual world—there are fewer Forms of trees than actual trees, fewer Forms of virtues than actual virtues; and there are fewer Forms of persons than actual persons. From the latter it follows that not all actual persons are perfectible individuals, whether because some actual persons altogether lack human souls or because some souls replicate others. In either case consequences ensue that are destructive of morality, for justice, under self-actualization ethics, necessarily presupposes the unique and irreplaceable potential worth of every person, and this presupposition is contradicted by the above.

The requirement that the Forms be fewer than actual things is imposed by the supposition that the Forms are themselves principles of intelligibility and goodness. This requirement is set aside by the recognition that intelligibility and goodness subsist, not in the Forms themselves, but in their employment as goals of directed activity by actual beings. Here it makes no difference if the Forms multiply the multiplicity of actuality, for intelligibility is introduced by the choice by an actual being of a single Form as the goal by which to unify its activity.

But the deeper difficulty in Plato is that the method by which the Forms are conceived (the Platonic dialectic) is fundamentally comparative. As such it effects a progressive reduction that can only be halted arbitrarily; and when what can be conceived of the Forms by this method is taken for the exhaustive inventory of the Forms themselves, diversity has been abolished, and the spirit of Parmenides triumphs over that of Pythagoras. As exhibited by the "ladder of love" in the *Symposium*,[22] dialectical method begins by comparing existing things, and ascends to ever greater generality by abandoning differences and retaining common properties. At the level of the Forms, then, multiplicity only once again raises the question of resemblance, and the advisement by Plato that the Forms are alike in their perfection or goodness produces in dialectic the vision of a solitary and consummate Form, the Form of the Good. Plato himself dangles this resolution tantalizingly—notably in his use of the image of the sun in the *Republic*—without overtly endorsing it. On the contrary, in the later dialogues ultimate reality is conceived as a system of interrelated and intercommunicating Forms.[23] By this conception *some* differences are accorded the status of ultimate reality but not all. But the distinction rests upon no apparent principle, leaving it open to Santayana's charge that it is "sentimental." Plato has merely reified those distinctions that Hellenism prized, or that were especially vivid to his own intuition. In Santayana's words,

> Greek minds had rhetorical habits; what told in debate seemed to them final; and Socrates thought it important to define in disputation the common natures designated by various words. Plato, who was initially a poet, had a warmer intuition of his ideas; but it was still grammar and moral prejudice that led him to select

and to deify them. The quality or function that makes all shepherds shepherds or all goods good is an essence; but so are all the remaining qualities which make each shepherd and each good distinguishable from every other. Far from gathering up the fluidity of existence into a few norms for human language and thought to be focussed upon, the realm of essence infinitely multiplies that multiplicity, and adds every undiscriminated shade and mode of being to those which man has discriminated or which nature contains.[24]

In short it is not the vividness of the poetic intuition that is at fault, but the violence done to the discriminations of that intuition by comparative method. Indeed, the initial apprehension of possibilities is not comparative, but immediate and exclusive. In its initial apprehension, each possible floods the world to the exclusion of everything else, thus producing the vividness of the apprehension. Multiplicity is therefore recognizable only seriatim, and the poet "celebrates the world by enumeration."[25] This mutual exclusivity proves to be no eccentricity of apprehension but a profound characteristic of possibilities themselves, namely their incommensurability, together with the implication of each in a dense world of compossibles that is incompossible with other worlds. It is not philosophy's business to betray this initial intuition, but rather to serve it by elaborating discursively, tenaciously, and at leisure what poetic intuition presents instantaneously, "like a flash of lightning in a dark sky."

Plato's unstable compromise on the individuation of Forms is reflected in his equivocality toward the status of the individuation of actual persons. The *Philebus* tells us that souls are alike as subjects of ordinary waking consciousness whose most characteristic function is knowing and whose special excellence is wisdom.[26] But actual persons are incontestably individuated (even by physical characteristics alone, when precisely described—and without resort to fingerprints), and the question is whether such individuation is contingent and remediable or essential and normative. Clearly Plato regards personal differences as highly significant, for he structures the Republic upon differences among *types* of persons, thereby arriving at three classes, and he certainly intends that division of labor according to natural differences obtain within each of the three classes as it does among them. In this way not just class distinctions but personal distinctions disclose themselves to be foundational in the Republic. But from this we can conclude only that Plato regards individuation as natural (innate and irremediable) throughout the span of one lifetime. It must be remembered that by Plato's doctrine of reincarnation every soul has many embodiments or "lifetimes." So far as we are told, what distinguishes one incarnate soul from another derives from the distinguishing features of only its most recent visit with the Forms—the one preceding its present incarnation—together with those impediments to its memory of the Forms imposed by its present incarnation. Describing these differences, Plato becomes fragmentary and allusive, but the general tenor of his words bespeaks contingency and inessentiality. In the *Phaedrus*, for example, we are told that incarnated souls "do not easily recall the things of the other world" because "they may have seen them for a short time only, or they may have been unfortunate in their earthly lot, and having had their hearts turned to unrighteousness through some corrupting influence, they may have lost the memory of the holy things which they once saw."[27] And from the *Republic* we learn that the debilities of the soul are only apparent, and that they are owing to the fact that the soul is "marred by communion with the body."[28]

From such clouded sayings it is impossible to grasp firmly Plato's meaning, but it would seem that we are being invited to infer that the soul's perfectibility leaves individuation behind. Individuation is the product of accidents of one kind and another; indeed, existence itself is but an unhappy accident that befalls otherwise perfect essences. The purified soul perfectly sees all Forms in a perpetual present, or rather—if intellectual intuition is an identity of knower and known—becomes one with eternal reality. Since replication of perfection is gratuitous if not contradictory, the number of such souls reduces to one, and likewise the Forms. On this reading Plato's "Pythagoreanism" amounts to nothing more than a debt in Plato's beginning, of which no trace is to be found in Plato's final formulations.

But this outline is the extrapolation of Plato's thought by what may arguably be said to be its internal momentum. Plato himself resisted this momentum, and we may conjecture that his scruples for so doing were two, the first logical, and the second moral. The logical defect in the above "Parmenideanism" is its inability to account for even the appearance of diversity. An undifferentiated One simply is what it is, without distinction between seeming and being. The incapacity of the One in this respect renders it a mystery or an absurdity. But if Plato was first a poet, he was soon after a moralist, and just as essentially. The conjunction of the two produces a poet-moralist who is "rapt in amazement" at his visions of the Good, and enlisted permanently in the service of those visions. If an account originally aimed at understanding those visions should somewhere along the way begin to threaten them, so much the worse for the account—it is the original loyalty that endures.

Such scruples are expressed in Plato's retention of the principle of the self-differentiation of the Forms and in his conception of ultimate reality as a system of interrelated and intercommunicating individual Forms. In the *Lysis* we can glimpse the attendant conception of humanity, for there, as the condition of friendship, persons are shown to be alike in aspiring to goodness, but individuated by the differences in the kinds of goodness to which they aspire. Here is the prototype of metaphysical individualism, for it means that, while some differences among actual persons are contingent and remediable, others are ultimate and normative. To cite Plato's failure to provide an adequate principle for discriminating between contingent and normative differences is merely to confirm that here, as elsewhere, the inauguration of an idea will not be its consummate statement. Much of the work at the elaboration of implications must fall to successors, hence the necessity of *tradition*, by which successors are bound to the improvement of what they inherit. By tradition, self-actualization ethics of today is responsible for improvement upon its foundations as laid down in classical antiquity, and notably in the metaphysics of Plato. Just now we are striving to refine and fortify those respects in which Plato's metaphysics justified Greek moral individualism.

Unfortunately it is these very respects that are immediately undermined by the metaphysics of Aristotle. To "bring the Forms down to earth," Aristotle transformed them into entailments of present matter of fact, and thereby into implicit actualities. By this transformation all that is possible is said to be already actual, the possible in the strict sense is abolished, and potentials reveal themselves to be necessities under the disguise of time. And while Aristotle professes to be interested in individuals exclusively, his metaphysics affords them no place. He says that what is real is not man, but only this man and that,[29] but what is real in this man and that is only what every man is, namely the species-form.[30] Individuals are such, he says, in virtue of their matter. But thus conceived, individuating differences are no more than insufficiencies resulting from failures of the various matters to fill their forms adequately. Since the goal of individuals of the same species is the species-form, the true goal of every human being is identical to that of every other. Inasmuch as the distinguishing characteristic of man is intellect, the proper goal of all individuals is the contemplative life, a single *nous* or intellect,*

* Concerning Aristotle's identification of human beings exclusively with that which distinguishes them from other things—their reason —see Thomas Nagel, "Aristotle on Eudaimonia," *Phronesis* 17

which moreover exists. It is God who, as contemplation of contemplation, is wholly indifferent to existence beneath him with its diversification and its conflicts.

Somewhere Ortega y Gasset remarks that Aristotle thus represents God not, to be sure, as a first-rate philosopher, but as a tenured professor of philosophy, long since neglectful of everything but the phantoms of his own mind.

How quickly did Plato's original mistake come home to roost! I refer to the mistake of identifying man with his reason, thereby setting in motion a reductive mechanism that ends by identifying reason with being and positing it as the singular end of all existence. Reason is not being but the relation between being and being—being in the modality of actuality and being in the modality of possibility. In this status it cannot constitute the end of existence but instead offers itself as the means for apprehension and attainment

---

(1972), 252-259. Nagel says of it, "This lands us in immediate difficulty, for the inference seems unsound. If the feature of life unique to humans could exist in the absence of those features which humans share with the beasts, the result would not be a human but something else. And why should we take the highest good of a rarefied individual like that as the ultimate end for complicated and messy individuals like ourselves? One would expect at the very least that the *interaction* between the function that differentiates us from animals, and the functions that we share with them, would play a role in the definition of *eudaimonia*" (p. 253). The "rarefied individual" with whom man is identified is of course Aristotle's God, and Nagel summarizes the result by saying, "Aristotle believes, in short, that human life is not important enough for humans to spend their lives on" (p. 257). But the thrust of Nagel's analysis demonstrates Aristotle's *indecision* between this "intellectualist" account of man's nature and end and a "comprehensive" account by which those functions man shares with other forms of life are retained. It is the comprehensive account, the present book argues, that eudaimonism today must advocate. Not life in the service of reason, but reason in the service of life. Reason does indeed "transcend" the lower functions of human life, as Aristotle recognized. It does so in the sense of escaping their dictations. But it does so, not for the purpose of abandoning the other functions of life, but for the purpose of organizing them into the best possible life.

of ends. Far from asking persons to transform themselves into disembodied ideas, the ends of human activity are living embodiments of perfected personhood. As ends they are individuated by the requirement for their determinacy as goals of directed activity, and the directed activity itself is individuated by its end. In short, persons are individual not in the beginning and contingently, but in the end and normatively. The ultimate end of the individual life confers simplicity upon that life by integrating everything that appears within that life as means to or expressions of itself. But of itself it does so only ideally and potentially. The integration becomes actual only if the actual person recognizes the unique end within himself and learns to conceive the world in its terms. He thus actualizes himself as what Leibniz termed a monad—a self-identical point of view upon all things.

By his conception of persons as monads, Leibniz drives wedges of incommensurability between possibilities and thereby preserves their individuation against the reductive tendencies evident in Plato. In the metaphysics of Leibniz, the actual world is made up of compossible possibilities, i.e. possibilities that are capable of co-existence. It is in virtue of their nature as monads that these actualized possibilities cannot be commensurated, for as a monad each is the distinctive principle of a perspective upon the entire world. Between principles there can be no intermediate positions because each principle implies nothing less than the entire world in its own aspect. Therefore any intermediate position, say, between Monad A and Monad B is apprehended by A in its A-aspect and by B in its B-aspect. Because no medium exists in which the conjunction of A and B can occur, no mediation is possible between A and B, and likewise no synthesis. Put figuratively, the separate principles of human individuals cannot be thought to converge at some point on a distant horizon because each principle is infinitely extensible. Within every person at a given time the future and the past of his principle are contained, but implicitly.

(This is Leibniz's "predicate-in-notion principle," according to which the complete concept of an individual substance "embraces all the changes it has undergone and will one day undergo."[31]) This future becomes explicit by the activities of the individual, which consist in progressively clarifying, refining, and extending his principle, toward the goal of a perfect but finite world-perspective. His principle is changeless because it derives from an eternal possibility. And eternal possibilities are individuated because they are possible actualities, capable as such of serving as goals of directed activity. By employment of an eternal possibility the acts of the actual person are conjoined by mutual entailment, and every individual act becomes "promissory." *Sensu stricto* the life of the individual thus becomes a single act, manifesting itself over a span of time.

In this conception of the person there are three sources of differentiation (three "imperfections" in Leibniz's language), two of which are remediable by his own efforts while one is not. The two remediable sources are vagueness and incompleteness in the world-perspective that he is, while the irremediable source is the finitude—the qualitative uniqueness—of that possibility of which he is the partial actualization, and which constitutes his essence. Here it will be well to note the propensity by certain of Leibniz's critics—in recent times, Bertrand Russell and Montgomery Furth[32]—mistakenly to identify vagueness (of perception and expression) with essential finitude. It is unquestionably mistaken, for degrees of vagueness are entirely commensurable and therefore tractable to human initiative. Certainly if what individuates possibilities is only their differences in degrees of vagueness or clarity (and we may well ask, "Of what?"; for possibilities as such do not act, and therefore can neither perceive nor express), then such differences are resolved by God, in whose being no vagueness exists. Noticing this, those critics who identify vagueness with essential difference accuse Leibniz of being a covert Spinozan, believing at bottom in a being that is one and unindividuated.

But this Spinozising of Leibniz is the critic's work. For Leibniz himself stresses that God himself is powerless to remove the "essential and original limitation" of each possible by which it is distinguished from every other.[33] It is in virtue of this ultimate individuation that God himself can bring the world into existence only as a system of finite compossibles.

Here then, Leibniz offers a principle by which to distinguish contingent and remediable differences from essential and normative ones. Commensurable differences are resolvable, incommensurable ones are not. Commensurable differences are confined to the differences among states and conditions of the individual within a given stage of his life; incommensurable differences distinguish the stages of the individual life, and likewise distinguish each individual from every other.* The moral task of the individual is set by the identity that is achievable in the stages of his life. Conversely he is obliged by incommensurability *not* to seek to actualize an identity other than that which is his in virtue of his innate potential and his stage of life.

The explication of this principle is one fundamental advance by Leibniz upon the metaphysical individualism of Plato. The second is that, by the metaphysics of Leibniz, every person, and not select persons only, is affirmed as an essential and perfectible individuality.

In Leibniz's wake, what remains to be cleared up is his equivocality over the relative worth of perfected individuals. Is it the case that the inherent worth of some persons is inferior to others? To the popular belief that some persons are inherently more "gifted" than others, Leibniz offers both support and opposition. Opposition appears in his conception of possibles as finite perfections. As such they must possess equivalent worth, for perfection cannot be qualified by degree.

---

* This reference to the incommensurability of the stages of the individual life will be refined following our detailed consideration of the stages in Chapter 6. See esp. pp. 210-215.

On the other hand he supports the thesis of innate disadvantage by his contention that the actual world is necessarily the best of all possible worlds since it has been chosen for actualization by God. This introduces gradations of inherent worth among pure possibles, for it asserts that, among the systems of pure possibles, one is better than others, and the others are left, presumably, to vary among themselves in degrees of worth. This line of thought arms Leibniz with a means to account for the evil in the actual world in accordance with Christian teaching. To adhere to Christian teaching, evil in the world cannot be remediable by human efforts alone and must therefore be essential rather than contingent, while at the same time it must be conceived in such a way that it cannot be attributable to God. By resort to the notion of deficient possibles (above), Leibniz's theodicy fulfills the Christian conditions, not perfectly, but perhaps as well as the conditions themselves permit. For accordingly, the "best of all possible worlds" need not be perfect, and may contain essential deficiencies for which God cannot be held responsible, provided only that among possible worlds nothing better is to be found. God is thus absolved of responsibility for the essential deficiencies of the world at only that small cost to his omnipotence that a scrupulous logic will demand—namely that his choice be limited to what is possible. And Leibniz is consistently scrupulous in this respect, for he insists (against Cartesians) that God chooses the good, rather than creating the good by his choice. Likewise God's omniscience has a logical limitation—he knows, not everything, but everything that is knowable. And Russell to the contrary notwithstanding,[34] according to Leibniz God does not create possibility by his choice, but chooses the best among antecedent possibles (though whether this limitation upon his omnipotence is by metaphysical or moral necessity is not clear).

In the existing world, deficient possibles appear as persons who, as perfected, obstruct the perfection of the world.

To illustrate this, Leibniz employs his famous Judas-example. In the best of all possible worlds Judas betrays Christ, and the betrayal is unavoidable, for it is the essence of Judas. If some one asks "whence comes it that this man will assuredly commit this sin," the reply "is easy, it is that otherwise it would not be this man."[35] Betrayal is the essence of Judas, and the perfection of Judas is the perfection of betrayal. God is not ultimately responsible, for the world is a set of compossibles that by logical necessity must co-exist, and therefore to actualize the world is necessarily to actualize Judas. Would Christ be Christ had he not been betrayed?

But we are left with a fundamental contradiction in Leibniz's thought, for possibilities are finite perfections, and perfections cannot be qualified by degree, nor (by the impossibility of self-contradictory reals) can there be "perfect imperfections." It follows that the implicit end of every actual life is equivalent in worth to every other; specifically it is the perfection of worth of its unique kind. But what also follows is that every possible *world* is equivalent in worth to every other. This conception is implicit in Leibniz's metaphysics, but is never explicitly endorsed by him. It does not fall victim to the identity of indiscernibles, for such worlds are inherently self-discerned as perfections of worth of unique kinds. What it decidedly interferes with is the necessity (moral, but strict nonetheless) by which God chooses the best. For among possible worlds as just conceived, none is better or worse. In this situation Leibniz's conclusion will be that God's choice can have no sufficient reason, lacking which it can only be arbitrary. But a God who chooses arbitrarily is self-contradictory and hence impossible.

It is true that if alternative possible worlds are equivalent in amount of potential worth, the actualization of just one of them, forevermore, will be without sufficient reason. But sufficient reason will obtain in the actualization of all possible worlds, for it represents the actualization of all varieties of worth. Moreover, while such multiple actualization can only be seriatim (by the principle of incompossibility), it remains to be determined whether there may not be a best order for the series. In either case the metaphysical principle of sufficient reason is vindicated, and we are free to endorse these implications in Leibniz's metaphysics. We are hereby obliged to regard every actual person as *in potentia* a qualitatively unique excellence, equivalent in amount of worth to every other person. The present chapter has provided metaphysical justification for this presupposition. It is this presupposition that generates self-actualization ethics in both its personal and its social aspects, and the scrupulous examination of this ethics and its derivative moral principles shall be our task in the chapters to follow.

Many of the abstract considerations of this chapter find proximate and concrete exemplification in the succession of stages—childhood, adolescence, maturation, old age—that constitutes the life of the human individual. The doctrine of the stages, previewed in Chapter 3 as formulated by Kierkegaard, will now be developed and refined in light of the metaphysical considerations in hand. That the metaphysics possesses explanatory power will be apparent when we conceive each stage in the development of the individual as a "little world" that is related to the stage preceding and the stage to follow by world-exchange.

6

The Stages of Life:
Childhood, Adolescence, Maturation,
Old Age

It is no mere coincidence that the world's two great self-actualization doctrines, the Greek and the Hindu, share the thesis that personal growth proceeds by incommensurable stages—youth, maturity, old age; "student," "householder," "retirement," "sage."* Self-actualization entails a doctrine of stages of life because, by its cardinal terms, childhood and old age are exempted. Aristotle prefaces his *Nichomachean Ethics* by observing that its content does not apply to children, who are "not yet capable of such acts."[1] The imperative, "Know Thyself," presupposes the autonomy of the

* While not strictly of the same logical order, the terms "student," "householder," "retirement," and "sage" are established English names of the Hindu stages thanks to Heinrich Zimmer's authoritative *Philosophies of India*. In Zimmer's words: "According to the Hindu dharma, a man's lifetime is to be divided into four strictly differentiated stages (*āśrama*). The first is that of the student, 'he who is to be taught' (*śiṣya*), 'he who attends, waits upon, and serves his guru' (*antevāsin*). The second is that of the householder (*gṛhastha*), which is the great period of a man's maturity and enactment of his due role in the world. The third is that of retirement to the forest for meditation (*vanaprastha*). And the fourth is that of the mendicant wandering sage (*bhikṣu*)." Heinrich Zimmer, *Philosophies of India*, ed. Joseph Campbell (Princeton: Bollingen Series XXVI, Princeton Univeristy Press, 1969), p. 44.
Hinduism does not figure further in our study because in its dominant formulations it denies the ultimate reality of individuation, calling for the dissolution of all differences in the undifferentiated unity of Atman-Brahman. Hinduism is therefore not a normative individualism.

158

subject both as knower and as object of knowledge. As such it cannot be addressed to a child, for childhood lacks such autonomy. Because the child depends for his identity upon external sources, the imperative passes through his being to lodge instead in these sources. And old age, if judged by the actualization-criteria of maturity, appears as pure deterioration, thereby contradicting the basic self-actualization thesis.

Accordingly self-actualization theory has two options, each of which is a stage-doctrine. It can regard normativity as restricted to the period of life we term *maturity*; or it can conceive of personal development as a succession of stages each of which is (normatively) a law unto itself, exacting its distinctive kind of actualization. Historically, the first option has predominated in the literature of self-actualization, but we intend to demonstrate the truth of the second. The body of this chapter will be devoted to disclosure of the exclusive values, virtues, and obligations of the distinctive stages of personal development. But beforehand some clarification of the general doctrine of the stages is in order.

By a "stage of life" we mean a span of time in the life of the individual that is autonomous in the sense that its regulatory principles are intrinsic and unchanging in their application throughout. A given stage is preceded and followed by other stages, governed by sets of principles that are incommensurable with the principles of the given stage.* Development within a stage consists in continuous explication of implications of the stage's principles by means of progressive clarification, extrapolation, and refinement. It constitutes the type of change we term "evolutionary." On the other hand development between stages consists in the exchange of incommensurable sets of principles. The incommensurability of the sets precludes intermediate positions, therefore such exchange can have no temporal

---

* The incommensurability of the stages, referred to previously on p. 154, will be considered in detail in our summary on the concept of the stages, pp. 210-215.

spread; it is necessarily instantaneous, a change of the "revolutionary" type.* Stage-exchange in the life of the individual is analagous in historical process to what are called
"epoch-making" events, by which one epoch, as a unified
historical sensibility, is succeeded by another. We shall
want to be on the lookout for the "epoch-making" events of
personal life.

"But we cannot live the afternoon of life according to the
programme of life's morning; for what was great in the
morning will be little at evening, and what in the morning

* Between incommensurate terms there can be no intermediate
or transitional positions, for intermediacy requires combination (as
orange is intermediate between red and yellow, for example), which
presupposes commensurability. For this reason the instantaneousness
of stage-exchange is to be understood *sensu stricto*. A thesis ex-
pounded in the following pages is that stage-exchanges are marked by
illuminations that instantly transform the perspectival world of the
individual; thus the inner illumination "Someday I must die" instantly exchanges the world of adolescence for the world of maturation without remainder (see pp. 188ff.).

The notion of instantaneous exchange may seem contrary to the
personal experience of many persons, but this can be accounted for
by several factors. In the first place, while the initial illumination
of the new stage is instantaneous, the process of explicating the
implications of the illumination is slow and continuous, proceeding
by degrees, and that all that is hereby explicated was antecedently
revealed "in a flash" is likely to remain—with the exception of an
occasional *déjà vu* experience—unrecognized. Second, the illumination of the new stage may not be acted upon by a given individual,
but followed instead by a resumption of the old terms of life, with
the new stage being tentatively re-opened from time to time until
it finally is adopted. Thus vacillation may give to exchange the
appearance of gradual transition. Third, stage-exchange by an individual usually goes unrecognized by his acquaintances, companions,
and relatives, who behave toward him as before; and since one's
self-image is partly the product of the attitudes of others, we find
here a strong conditioning in favor of continuity. Finally, by its
nature, retrospection perceives only continuity, for it perceives prior
stages according to its own principle, thereby commensurating them.
Prior discontinuities are therefore invisible to retrospection. They
are available only to the exceptional procedure of participatory re-
enactment.

was true will at evening have become a lie."[2] C. G. Jung voices the insight that founds history's repeated attempts to formulate a workable doctrine of stages. Unfortunately the conception of the stages has been largely ignored ("snubbed" might be the better term) by ethical philosophy. Resolutely, ethical theory has sought to subsume the whole of life under a single set of normative principles. The result has been a wholesale perpetration of what I shall name the "fallacy of anachronism." Grasping the genuine moral terms of one stage of life, philosophy imposes them unrestrictedly, thereby imposing them upon stages of life where they do not belong. Most often it is maturity that is hypostatized, but alternatively the whole of life is represented as moral childhood by those doctrines that assert man's perpetual dependence—upon God, for example, or upon metaphysical necessity of one kind or another. The theoretical consequence is blindness to the intrinsic truths of the misused stages. The practical consequence is that, by such rude imposition, individuals living within the imposed-upon stages are asked to falsify themselves, and frequently enough comply. Youths are expected to exhibit the temperance of maturity, while hoary age is sent over the hurdles once more.

"The curve of life is like the parabola of a projectile which, disturbed from its initial state of rest, rises and then returns to a state of repose."[3] Jung captures in an image the first and tersest empirical truth pertaining to the stages of life. The powers of the individual wax in the first half of life, wane in the second. This evident fact, accessible no less to earliest men than to ourselves, is responsible for the two-stage or *akme* model of life that first finds formulation in the "heroic code" of Homeric Greece. It is a code of relentless moral vitalism, tying virtue to physical powers as tested in battle and games, and celebrating life's noon. Ascendent life is value, descendent life disvalue. Best is the life that achieves its *akme* and its end simultaneously; its archetype is the hero slain in battle. Hence the archaic practice of killing kings and great men at their noontime, thereby sparing them the moral anguish of their own debilitation.* A life denied its *arete* (excellence) from the first by deformity of body or spirit had been better not begun, thus the archaic practice of setting afflicted infants out to die of exposure.

But the problem of locating life's *akme* soon proved more difficult than first supposed. As civilization advanced, the bellicose virtues had to be supplemented by civil ones, and the *akmes* of these two classes of virtues do not chronologically coincide.

Attendant revision of the simple *akme* model is evident in Aristotle, who notes that normally a man's body reaches its prime between the ages of thirty and thirty-five, while his mental powers culminate at "about forty-nine."[4] Confronted with this double *akme*, Aristotle takes the simplest resort. In effect he merely connects the physical *akme* to the intellectual *akme*, forming, so to speak, a plateau at the mountain top. But by so doing he transforms the *akme* of the individual's life from a moment into a stage of some fif-

---

* We speak here not of the classical period but of archaic Greece, culminating in Homer. For the practice of killing kings and semi-divine heroes at the height of their powers, see Sir James G. Frazer, *The Golden Bough* (*The New Golden Bough*, ed. Theodor H. Gaster [New York: New Amercian Library Mentor Books, 1964], Nos. 189-191, "Putting the King to Death"). On the heroic code, see Lewis Richard Farnell, *Greek Hero Cults and Ideas of Immortality* (Oxford at the Clarendon Press, 1921).

The conception of old age as pure degeneration is unquestionably softened in the classical period, as attested most notably by the place of the Council of Elders in the public life of city-states (see Bessie Ellen Richardson, *Old Age Among the Ancient Greeks* [Baltimore: Johns Hopkins Press, 1933], esp. Ch. 3). But by no means is the archaic view erased, for as Ms. Richardson observes, concerning old age "Greek literature almost uniformly paints a gruesome picture" (*op. cit.*, p. 2). If the Cult of Geras be cited, it must be borne in mind that Geras was often depicted as a grotesque (Richardson, *op. cit.*, Ch. 6). On the whole it seems safe to regard Aristotle as faithful to the classical view in this matter, and in his characterization of old age (*Rhetoric* 2.13) this stage of life appears exclusively as degeneration, without redeeming virtue.

teen to twenty years' duration. And this is a contradiction in terms. For right living, according to Aristotle, is progressive actualization of one's innate potentiality, and such actualization constitutes "ascent." Therefore the plateau-image is a serious misrepresentation. The man who has ceased to ascend is not living well, he is spiritually dead.

Worse still, the analytic method that produces two *akmes* thereby only warms to its work, and will proceed to proliferate *akmes* to absurdity. Besides an intellectual and a physical nature, man may be said to possess a religious nature, an aesthetic nature, a sensual nature, a passional nature, etc., etc.—each with its distinct *akme*. And is not "physical nature" a rude lump, refinable into such aspects as rate of cell replacement, sexual potency, beauty of appearance, strength, grace, athletic prowess—all with corresponding *akmes*? Likewise for "intellectual nature," within which can be distinguished receptivity, comprehension, retention, wisdom. Similarly knowledge possesses properties of precision, scope, and depth, analytic power, synthetic power—again, with divergent *akmes*.

The akme model will be resurrected from this melancholy plight only by a strategy that restores his unity to the individual and centers developmental interest here. The standpoint that treats persons as integrated structures of faculties, acts, and aspects is the moral standpoint. It is therefore moral development that must henceforth be the profound theme of stages of life.*

---

* It may avoid a possible confusion if we distinguish the meaning of "moral stages" as herein employed from these same terms as they are employed in the current developmental researches of Lawrence Kohlberg. Kohlberg is more narrowly concerned with the types of moral judgments made by individuals in different stages of their lives. Our concern is for life as a whole within each of the stages, and by identifying the stages as moral we refer to implicit normative principles regulating life as a whole within each stage. Thus the terms of the well-lived adolescence are implicit within adolescence itself, as so for other stages. For a good summary of Kohlberg's work see Lawrence Kohlberg, "From Is to Ought: How

Rescued by this recognition, the doctrine endures in Western thought. For our purposes, a most instructive modern proponent is Friedrich Nietzsche. Nietzsche advocates the ancient two-stage *akme* model without alteration. The sole intrinsic value is waxing life understood as growing power of personhood ("will to power"), while the sole intrinsic disvalue is waning life, diminishing power of personhood. Ideally all consummations will be endings and all endings consummations, but nature is decidedly clumsy in this respect, either hesitating or intervening prematurely. Over her premature intervention we have no final control, but such is not the case with the tardy death that leaves on the tree "overripe apples, yellow and shriveled."[5] At the attainment of one's *akme* the part of honor is to stand thereafter aside, leaving the management of affairs to persons in their ascendency.

But something is amiss here, and we put our finger upon it if we sense that vital virtues are virtues only when complemented by virtues of repose. If old age were to make itself invisible, as Nietzsche proposes, the remaining enactment would not be nearly so uplifting as Nietzsche envisages. We would instead be treated to an unrelieved spectacle of striving, agitation, competition, resentment, and insecurity. For there is an incipient harshness in maturation, stemming from its obligation to make of itself *causa sui*. Where old age is oblivion, self-actualization confronts the abyss, and the self-caused person becomes nothing but his own arbitrary construct—a groundless invention. In this condition he will pillage the world for purposes of self-support.

In the words, again, of C. G. Jung, "A human being would certainly not grow to be seventy or eighty years old if this

---

to Commit the Naturalistic Fallacy and Get Away with It in the Study of Moral Development," in Theodore Mischel, ed., *Cognitive Development and Epistemology* (New York and London: Academic Press, 1971), 151-235.

longevity had no meaning for the species. The afternoon of life must also have a significance of its own and cannot be merely a pitiful appendage to life's morning."[6] Here, Jung's supposition that nothing exists without good reason need not ruffle us. For if "sufficient reason" is today regarded as dubious metaphysics, it remains invaluable methodologically. By supposing that there must be an intrinsic meaning of old age, Jung remains undaunted by contentions to the contrary and must look for himself. Our approach shall be the same. Where old age is judged by the critera of maturation, it exhibits itself to be mere deterioration. But to him who will dispense with such criteria and look upon old age with fresh eyes, it displays evidence of a rebirth under novel criteria.

Thus far our assessment has not mentioned childhood, and we must now determine whether this omission is to be defended or rectified. Neglect of childhood characterizes Western ethical philosophy, and the reason is not far to seek. As ordinarily conceived, ethics presupposes both a freedom and a self-responsibility that are incommensurate with the fundamental dependence of childhood. It would therefore seem necessary to defer ethics until, as the Greeks liked to say, "a young man's beard begins to grow." Thus Aristotle, for example, ignores childhood in the three-stage scheme of the *Rhetoric*, and he addresses the whole of the *Nichomachean Ethics* to life's middle stage, with the remark that none of it is applicable to mere boys, for they are "not yet capable of such acts," and deserve approval and disapproval only "by reason of the hopes we have for them."[7]

We do not question the essential dependency by which Aristotle characterizes childhood. Childhood is directed toward ends of which it can have no comprehension. But the fact of such dependence does not mean that childhood can have no autonomus virtues, values, and responsibilities, it only means that such autonomous moral qualities as it may have are insufficient to define it. Aristotle himself acknowledges that one may properly predicate goodness or badness of "natural slaves."[8] The natural slave is one who intrinsically lacks *autarkia* (autonomy—the subsistence of one's end within oneself) and is therefore fundamentally dependent. Within this meaning, good dependence consists in fulfillment of the definition of dependence, and can be judged without reference to the external end. Very well: children are natural slaves who are destined to outgrow their servitude. Correspondingly their dependence possesses an intrinsic normativity, and this establishes childhood as a moral stage of life. Nor is childhood's normativity the mere diminutive of adulthood's, for by the incommensurability of the stages, the only future childhood can see is the future of itself, the only past the past of itself. Therefore its intrinsic morality will be exclusive to itself, and not derived from what childhood will one day become.

If we summarize our results thus far, we find that the original *akme* model of personal development has been substantially altered. It ascribed positive value to a single stage of life—maturation—while we are compelled to seek intrinsic positive values also in the stages of old age and childhood. Moreover these additions conduce to a conception of the equivalence of the stages, each with its distinctive normativity. Accordingly we shall be prepared to seek, not a single moral *akme* of the individual life, but an *akme* or consummation within each stage.

But our conception of the stages remains demonstrably incomplete, for if we juxtapose childhood and moral maturity we see immediately that the exchange of the former for the latter is impossible. Moral maturity presupposes self-responsibility, which in turn presupposes self-determination by means of free choice. The choice in question is that of the self one strives to become. But a necessary condition of free choice is knowledge of alternatives, which, in this case, mean alternative ultimate possibilities for living, alternative life-styles, alternative "destinies" (in the classical Greek sense). And where will knowledge of such alternatives have been acquired? In maturation? But maturation *begins* with the choice that presupposes such knowledge. Then in childhood? But the dependence of childhood precludes this very kind of knowledge. For we speak here of knowledge of the alternative persons that one may (by the inherent possibilities within the self) choose to become. The child can have no knowledge of its own alternative identities, for its dependence is an identity-dependence: it receives its identity from sources external to it and responsible for it. It cannot choose what to become, but can only become what has been chosen for it. Correspondingly it cannot perceive those alternatives from which that choice has been made. Where a precocious child is exposed (by residence abroad, perhaps, or movies, or early acquaintance with literature of cultural anthropology) to alternative ultimate life-styles, he does not perceive them *as* ultimate alternatives, but necessarily perceives them through his own received perspective.

We thus arrive at the need in the well-lived life for a period for exploration between childhood and maturation. It is the stage we term *adolescence*. That the individual is an adolescent after childhood and prior to his adulthood will come to no one as fresh news. What should be news, however, is the incontrovertible evidence that adolescence is not a temporary aberration in an otherwise sensible life, but a profound moral stage with its autonomous values, virtues, and obligations—a stage that, like other stages, must be true to *itself* if it is to manifest worth in the world.

Our preliminary inquiry into the stages of life herewith delivers into our hands a conception of four successive autonomous stages, to be designated "childhood," "adolescence," "maturation," and "old age." It remains to render these abstractions concrete by uncovering the moral logic of each stage. But, first, it will be well to summarize some of the more telling implications of the doctrine of the stages as thus far developed.

According to the thesis of the stages, the well-lived life

is neither a pure continuum, perpetuating the same, nor discontinuous, a speckle of unrelated or contingently related acts. It consists instead of periods of continuous development (the stages) broken by discontinuities of stage-exchange. This means that change, in personal life, is of two fundamentally different sorts. Within stages we can expect to find continuous change, represented by the clarification, extension, and refinement of unchanging principles. But between stages change constitutes the exchange of one set of principles for an incommensurably different set, and incommensurability dictates that such exchange be instantaneous. By such exchange the entire world of the individual is transformed, and he must learn to make his way anew.

Discontinuities between stages render logics of inference inoperative. Specifically, from the character of moral life in one stage, no inferences can be made concerning the character of moral life in other stages. To thus infer is to impose a given set of moral conditions where they do not belong, to the detriment of the true conditions of the imposed-upon stage. We have named this process the fallacy of anachronism, and hold it accountable for the most serious errors of morality and ethics.

Our investigation will disclose that what represents a virtue in one stage of life can be a crippling defect at another stage. It will likewise divulge a hidden and impeccable logic to certain characteristic stage-behaviors that appear to common sense as bizarre and unintelligible. The doctrine of the stages places inquiry under the fundamental obligation to study each stage in its own terms, and by so doing, to contribute to the basic work of life—that of living each stage in its own terms. Such inquiry will reveal that the singular word *love*, for example, has essentially different meanings in each of the four stages, each meaning being normative for its stage and no other. In the life of the individual, then, subsist not one but four meanings of *love* to be lived and fulfilled. No less is this the case for each of life's

168

profound meanings—notably justice, freedom, and death. In each case the fullest meaning to the child or adolescent is not merely a lesser degree of the meaning of the concept to the adult or old person, it is a qualitatively different meaning, perfectible within its stage just as are the adult and aged meanings.

The intrinsic requirements of each stage relinquish their hold only when they are fulfilled, hence neglect or the attempt to bypass a stage produces developmental arrest.* The forty-year-old adolescent is a familiar figure because in our culture adolescence is systematically thwarted by the imposition upon it of anachronistic demands, both from childhood and adulthood. The individual who remains developmentally adolescent only pretends to maturity; his

---

* To determine the precise dynamics of developmental arrest is the business of psychology, but we may comment upon an obtrusive question, namely: To what extent is responsibility for an individual's developmental arrest to be ascribed to the individual himself? Unquestionably a culture or family that fosters perpetual dependence either positively—by idealizing and rewarding it—or negatively—by withholding the necessary conditions of autonomy—must bear a large measure of responsibility for fostering perpetual dependents. But I doubt that the intuitions of new conditions that mark the stage-exchanges can ever be wholly precluded to any individual in this way. In the preponderance of instances of developmental arrest, I believe that the individual experiences the illumination that the terms of his life are changed, but chooses—with the complicity, perhaps, of culture and family—to perpetuate his life in the old and familiar terms. Such a perpetuation is inevitably made hollow by the brief glimpse of new requirements, but for supporting hollow enterprises our capacity at self-deception is limitless. If it be noted that stage-exchange marks the requirement to begin *de novo*, learning the requirements of living anew, it will be small wonder that it causes hesitation in the strongest of individuals.

The illumination marking stage-exchange is the recognition that new requirements apply, but between this introductory recognition and the fulfillment of the new requirements lie the long years that constitute the living of the stage. By no means is the stage lived in the illumination, but rather may the living be avoided by reversion to the terms of the prior stage.

adolescent behavior is ever likely to outcrop disastrously. Likewise old age is undermined, directly by our refusal to affirm its exclusive virtues and responsibilities, and indirectly by unfulfilled remnants of prior stages. In Jung's words, "So for many people all too much unlived life remains over —sometimes potentialities which they could never have lived with the best of wills, so that they approach the threshold of old age with unsatisfied demands which inevitably turn their glances backward."[9]

CHILDHOOD

Common sense and folk-wisdom together identify childhood as the condition of dependency, and in this instance they are not contradicted by refined scientific study, but corroborated and deepened. The observation that infants and young children are dependent upon others for the satisfaction of their basic needs is available to all. Developmental psychology deepens the conception of childhood's dependence by demonstrating that the child's very identity necessarily comes to him from without and that one major class of the child's needs is necessarily determined socioculturally. Philosophy completes the picture by disclosing that the concept of "need" implies a judgment of which childhood itself is incapable.

Those needs that are evident at birth for the survival of the infant we shall term "first-order" needs. They include needs for nourishment, warmth, cleanliness, rest, light, comfort, and the recent tendency has been to extend first-order needs to include, for example, a need for love and a need for visual and aural stimulation. But consider such "needs" as are represented by bowel and bladder control, or the "need" to adjust hunger to mealtimes, or to begin to learn arithmetic. These needs are not of the first-order, for they are not present at birth, and moreover they do not originate in the child but are ascribed to him by parents and community. At the same time, to regard them as purely conventional would be unwarranted, for at least some of them are likely to manifest themselves autonomously in later development. In this sense parents act in behalf of the persons their children shall one day become, but it is they, and not their children, who are responsible for the conception of this personhood, and it is therefore they who are responsible for those needs ascribed to childhood by this conception. Needs that have this origin shall be termed "second-order."

But our argument is for childhood as radical (unqualified) dependence, and we are thereby recalled to the category of first-order needs. And we discover that first-order needs are no more child-determined than are second-order needs. For the term *need* bears within itself a judgment, one which the child himself is incapable of making. That a child needs love, for example, is the judgment that he should be aided to grow to be the sort of person for which the receiving of love in childhood is a necessary condition. Judgments of this form are implicit in every first-order need of childhood, including even the need for physical nourishment. For while it is a fact that without nourishment the child will die, to call nourishment a need is to judge that the child ought to live—and this *is* a judgment. Moreover it is a judgment that contains implicit reference to the person the child will become—necessarily so, for such reference is implicit in the meaning of *child* itself. In sum, childhood's first-order needs are such only by a reference that lies beyond the reach of childhood, and for which the child is strictly dependent upon others. Indeed, *need* represents nothing in the datum of human life, nothing immediately "given." Rather it constitutes a discrimination among givens that, as such, expresses a principle of discrimination. Among the multifarious and disorderly impulses within a child, the child himself can initiate no arbitration, for the principle of such arbitration can only be derived ex post facto, while the child's situation is not *post* but *ante*. If needs were given, my son's need to ingest cigarette stubs would triumph handily over the claims of his oatmeal, and arithmetic would constitute a need of almost no children.

Having defined childhood as essential dependence, we must carefully avoid the suppositions commonly associated with dependence, namely that the nature of childhood is inherently passive, or that childhood is a tabula rasa, devoid of an intrinsic nature.

Dependence does not connote passivity, and observation indicates that much child-behavior (feeling, thinking, wishing, willing, anticipating, remembering, acting) is not responsive but spontaneous. The dependence-autonomy issue concerns regulated behavior, and childhood's dependence is confirmed in the recognition that child-behavior does not embody its own regulatory standard.

Nor does dependence connote that childhood is a tabula rasa upon which "environment" can write with impunity. A viable alternative is the innatist hypothesis that childhood is a nature subsisting for the most part in the mode of a potentiality whose time for actualization is not yet. This means that the dependence of childhood is a provisional dependence, and it is this provisionality that lends normative qualification to the authority that is exercised over children. Because that authority is trusted, it must make itself trustworthy. Because it is required to function unquestioned, it must be (for the child) unquestionable. And because childhood's dependence is provisional, the authority over it must be provisional authority, containing from the first the anticipation of its own demise. In due course we will show that these requisite characteristics of authority are not mutually contradictory.

Authority forecasts its own demise by directing children to the cultivation within themselves of the materials of eventual self-regulation. In brief, this means that the child must learn about the world and about himself, and the primacy of this task determines the essential virtue of childhood to be that of receptivity. Receptivity constitutes the

positive contribution of what genetic psychologist Jean
Piaget calls the "unilateral respect" of early childhood.[10] In
early childhood respect flows exclusively from the child to
its mentors, rendering the child susceptible to their influence. Piaget identifies a subsequent stage of childhood that
is characterized by "reciprocal respect,"[11] but we must not
be misled by mere terminology. Unlike love, which affirms
potential worth, respect is the affirmation in feeling of actual worth, and actual worth always carries its degree of
authority. But the reciprocal respect of which Piaget speaks
mitigates neither the exclusive authority of adulthood with
respect to children nor the strict dependence of childhood,
for it appears only in the relations of children with one another. Under reciprocal respect, the child experiences himself as entitled to the respect of his peers in his interpretation of principles received from the unquestioned authority
of adulthood. In short he experiences himself as entitled to
respect for what he is, namely a dependent creature, hence
for those virtues *of dependence* that he manifests. Thus by
the essential meaning of childhood as dependence Piaget's
two "stages" are commensurated, disclosing themselves to
be, not true stages of life, but distinctions within a stage.

It is a cardinal principle of the pedagogy of later life that
every student's own principle of interpretation is to be re-
spected (this is by no means to say that it is uncritically
accepted), for the work of later life begins in the acquisition and nurture of these very principles. But when it is directed to childhood this same respect commits the fallacy
of anachronism by according to the child capacities that he
cannot possess. The respect that can responsibly be accorded to childhood is confined to the virtues of dependence, foremost of which is receptivity. Childhood is not
receptive "by nature." Rather, it is spontaneously expressive
of pandaimonic impulses, each of which obstructs receptivity, while together they create an impenetrable din. Receptivity must be acquired, which is to say it is not a fact but

a virtue. It does not in the least connote passivity—for the simplest act of learning *is* an act—but instead implies directed activity according to received principle.

Anachronistic respect of a child's own authority, while it sometimes masquerades as enlightened generosity, in fact disenfranchises childhood of the condition of its own worth. Nor is this deep injustice unrecognized by children themselves. I think of the recent period when contemporary painting was influenced by primitive African art, and countless children were told that their random color-splotchings were "as good as Picasso." If encouragement was the intent of this fatuity, its effect is profoundly the contrary, for it puts the child himself in charge of his own future development at painting and, by analogy, at life itself, and for this the child knows himself to be profoundly unready.

Its essential dependence precludes to childhood the determination of standards of excellence and all deliberation upon the ultimate regulatory principles of life. This means that by its nature childhood is entitled to be furnished with such principles, and injustice obtains wherever they are not forthcoming, and also wherever such principles as are forthcoming are such as to call themselves into question by mutual inconsistency. When the ultimate principles given to childhood are themselves inconsistent, the inevitable result is an inconsistent childhood, impossible to fulfill.

Childhood is entitled to unquestionable authority because by its very nature questionable authority appeals to higher authority, and this, if nowhere to be found, devolves upon the child himself, asking of him what he cannot find within himself to give. This does not mean that the child's parents must represent unquestionable authority to him, and the attempt by parents to set themselves up as such only perpetrates the injustice just identified, for parents are inevitably perceived as fallible by their children, and much earlier than is commonly supposed. This is because children at an early age are entirely capable of formulating profound questions to which no parent can have a satisfactory answer. Indeed, I am myself persuaded that the most intractable metaphysical paradoxes present themselves to every child by the age of six or seven.[12] Appearance–reality lurks in the child's puzzlement over his own dreams, and in the experience of himself lying; the contingency of existence is harbored in his recognition that any situation might be other than it is; and the paradox of the conception of nonbeing appears in the question put by the child to its parent, "Where was I before I was born?" Indeed, what has often been regarded as the ultimate metaphysical question —Why is there something rather than nothing?—was not first formulated by Leibniz, but was long asked of parents by children.

That an authoritative answer to such questions exists is the child's assurance that these are not his problems in the sense that they appeal to him for solution. He knows full well that he cannot solve them; that his parents cannot solve them he perhaps knows (or will shortly discover). But the absolution that his childhood requires is the reassurance that someone, somewhere, *can* solve them, and moreover already has done so. This being the case, the inherent obligation the problem imposes is antecedently met, and does not fall upon the child.

Precisely the knowledge of something that "I, alone, must do" is the ground of each individual's conviction of his own noncomparative intrinsic potential self-worth in adulthood. But the child must be preserved from the conditions that give rise to it, for as a child there is nothing he alone can do. The apprehension of an unsolved problem imposes an individual responsibility that is incommensurable with childhood. Therefore no unsolved problems can in justice be allowed to appear, and every problem the child and his parents cannot solve must be regarded as solved by higher authority for which parents act as imperfect spokesmen.

It is sometimes supposed that the first doubt of the finality of parental authority casts the young person upon his own resources, but early development is not nearly so ruthless. A young child learns that at work his father has a "boss," that his mother reads and consults authorities by other means. Gradually he thereby gains a sense of what Henri Bergson terms the "shadowy presence" of an authority beyond parenthood.[13] It is the vested authority of the community at large, of which every child has a vague but forceful awareness. As adults we know that this authority is imperfect. But if we bear in mind that we seek only the authority that, without deceit, will provide the condition for childhood to be childhood, Bergson's "shadowy presence" is perhaps sufficient and well-suited. It is sufficient because its fallibility does not disclose itself to childhood. It involves no fundamental deceit, because the disclosure of its fallibility is at the same time the child's discovery of himself as no longer a child, but a constitutive part of the "shadowy presence"—its problems are henceforth authentically his problems. At this stage the concept of absolute and independent authority is revealed for what it is, a concept of childhood. Not only is it no longer needed, but it is actively dysfunctional, interfering with the new enterprise of attaining to self-responsibility, excellence, and self-authority. Its retention in succeeding stages commits the fallacy of anachronism.

Conversely, a concept that is functionally essential to later stages but dysfunctional in childhood is that of personal mortality, as embodied in the recognition of one's own eventual death. Recognition of life's finitude founds the practical imperative, "What is to be done must be begun at once." But the imperative has force only on the supposition that something is to be done by the individual that none other can do. For childhood, nothing of this sort is to be done.

Indeed, investigations of childhood disclose that it is intrinsically protected against anachronistic recognition of "the death that is one's own." Death is the termination of life, but the life the child lives is (in virtue of childhood's essential dependence) not his own, hence the death the child recognizes likewise will not be his own. If he were to die, the death would not be his own but another's—the death of the person he is yet to be, and, in virtue of parenthood's intrinsic responsibility, and the death of that responsibility, a "little death" within his parents. Confirmation of this "otherness" of death in the psychology of childhood is forthcoming from clinical studies that attest that, for children, death appears as entirely alien and outside life, often personified as a strange and hostile figure, wholly unlike persons of the child's circle.[14] This natural immunity calls for cultural support, not for cultural rectification in the misguided interest of realism.

But childhood possesses no comparable immunity concerning the deaths of others. Indeed, normal childhood is permeated by nonempirical apprehensions of separation that are its indirect witness to its own dependence. Moreover the loss through death of someone the child loves is a genuine possibility for which every child must be prepared. At the same time such loss cannot be allowed to appear to the child as absolute, for two reasons. The first is the fact that the child's dependence is absolute, and he must know that responsibility for him will continue. The second is that love—even children's love—is profound willing of the immortality of what is loved, and the extinction of the love-object inevitably implies the failure of one's love. Such an implication is commensurate with adulthood and promotes appropriate actions, for example one's reaffirmation of responsibility to the dead person by one's efforts to keep his ideals alive. But childhood is incapable of manifesting responsibility to its beloved dead, and must, therefore, be safeguarded from that feeling whose only resolution consists in such manifestation. Every child needs to know that the death of persons he loves does not mark their extinction. Childhood requires a belief in immortality.

If supernatural religion, alone, could justify belief in immortality, then the most crippling anachronism that could be imposed upon childhood would be pinpointed in Erik

Erikson's citation of the "many [who] are proud to be without religion whose children cannot afford their being without it."[15] Likewise the question of religion will have suggested itself earlier when we relied upon what Bergson termed the "shadowy presence" of community authority, for behind this authority might be introduced the unquestionable authority of God. The difficulty is that the traditional omni-omni-omni deity of supernaturalism vitiates an ethics of self-actualization and self-responsibility. The absolute authority of such a God subsumes adults no less than children, rendering them moral children, responsible only for obedience (however much the circumlocutions of doctrine may obscure the fact). But the parenthood to which we refer throughout is the parenthood constituted by principles of self-actualization, and if it is inconsistent with supernaturalism, then it cannot offer supernaturalism to its children without inconsistency and deceit. In the matter of authority we have supported the judgment that the community is in this respect sufficient to the requirements of childhood, and involves no deceit. Likewise it is our belief that so-called natural or social immortality is sufficient to the requirement of childhood for belief in immortality of loved persons. Again, no deceit is involved, but only the subsequent discovery by the (former) child that for such immortality he himself must bear a portion of responsibility.

ADOLESCENCE

"They are changeable and fickle in their desires, which are violent while they last, but quickly over."[16] So thoroughly truistic seems Aristotle's description of adolescents that our minds yawn and look about for better company. But surely this bespeaks the somnolence of our minds rather than the transparency of Aristotle's statement. It is scarcely trivial that a synopsis of the adolescence of 2,500 years ago remains apt today. And if we look carefully into the simple characteristics set forth by Aristotle we shall discern there the hidden logic of a fundamental stage of life.

Fervent commitments abruptly abandoned. Adult judgment upon adolescence characteristically divides according to whether the fervence or the haste should be condemned. But both qualities are entirely efficacious and necessary to the intrinsic demands of adolescence itself.

Adolescence begins in the discovery of autonomy—"I am alive; I am an authentic living being, not a derivation. From this moment forward it is I myself who must do my living; no longer is there any other who can do my living for me." The implications of this recognition are revolutionary, transforming not merely the individual but the entire world. By this single recognition the world of childhood is exchanged for the world of adolescence.

The texture of this discovery has been set forth previously[17] and will here be only summarized. Characteristically the original awareness is that of being misrepresented by those authorities—typically parents and teachers—who had heretofore spoken for us infallibly. Implicit in this misrepresentation is the novel presence of one's own internal authority. In these terms, misrepresentation cannot occur in childhood, for childhood possesses no internal authority. Where misrepresentation is felt by a child, it consists in conflict between two or more external authorities and is resolved by the child by reference to the highest of the conflicting authorities—normally parental authority. But the misrepresentation felt by adolescence refers in its obverse not externally, but to something within the adolescent for which he alone can speak, hence the typical adolescent feeling of being misunderstood by *everyone*. Here is the discontinuity that demonstrates that adolescence is not a sum or synthesis of child identities, nor any sort of dividend from them, but a novel presence that supplants in its entirety the dependence of childhood. Childhood is the mode of life for which others must speak. Adolescence (uniquely among the stages) is the mode of life for which no one else can possibly speak.

While in truth it constitutes internal authority, at the outset the "inner voice" of adolescence does not speak authoritatively, but timorously and tentatively. At first it is scarcely audible, and this is why the dominant feeling of adolescence is the seemingly negative feeling of being misunderstood, from which the presence of internal authority must be inferred. But this dominant feeling must not mislead us into supposing that the fundamental problem of adolescence consists in its relations with others. C. G. Jung has defined childhood as the period in the life of the individual when he is a problem strictly for others. Very well: adolescence begins with the moment at which the individual, having been exclusively a problem for others, becomes a problem to himself.

The terms of the problem that adolescence is appear in the timorousness of its "inner voice." At the outset, internal authority is largely potential and only minutely actual. The essential task of adolescence consists in that nuture of its internal authority aimed at making it authoritative and trustworthy. This authority will ultimately be exercised over the self—its functions are self-knowledge, self-responsibility, and self-fulfillment. But none of these can be attained introspectively—for introspection is inherently retrospection, capable of apprehending only what has antecedently been actualized, while adolescence is everything in possibility, nothing in actuality. By an inherently internal purpose adolescence is therefore directed outward, into the world. But the world it sets about so voraciously to discover is in no sense the in-itself world of objective knowledge. By enactment of the actual alternatives the world offers, adolescence actualizes possibilities within itself one by one, rendering them available to introspection and susceptible of reflective judgment.

From the perspective of adulthood, the work of adolescence can be recognized as acquiring knowledge of the alternative ultimate principles of living, as the condition of genuine choice. Shall one choose a profession with internal knowledge of but one or two? Shall one choose marriage or bachelorhood with living knowledge of neither? Shall one have children without knowing all that having children means? Shall one choose a wife or husband without experience of the diversity of temperaments, proclivities, capacities, and tastes among individuals of the other sex? Shall one choose a friend without this same knowledge? Shall one pursue pleasure without knowledge of the qualitative diversity of its sources?—or worth, without this same sort of knowledge? From the perspective of adulthood, the work of adolescence is to acquire living knowledge of the alternatives available to choice, but to do this work adolescence must be carefully preserved from every least intimation of the eventual requirement of choice. (And the impatient demand upon the adolescent that he "choose something and stick to it" is a suffocating anachronism.) He is preserved from knowledge of the requirement for choice by his inherent non-recognition of the eventuality of his own death. The requirement for choice is dictated by the finitude of the individual as imposed by death, therefore ignorance of "the death which is one's own," as ignorance of personal finitude, is immunity from the requirement for choice. By hearsay the adolescent of course "knows" that one day he will die, but notoriously he behaves as if he were immortal—he dallies, he dawdles, he takes incredible risks, he is careless of others, he cannot conceive of irreversible consequences of his actions. Above all he is a universal dilettante, behaving as if exploration might go on forever. Precisely so, for exploration is adolescence itself. Where exploration knows itself to be instrumental, mistakes count, prudence intervenes —and contradiction is introduced into exploration itself. For in this case the end of exploration is already within it, the decision already (implicitly) made. Such exploration, itself a means, can be exploration only of alternative means for the given end. But to adolescence the end of exploration

—the person it shall in maturation become—is not given, and only because this is so can it *be* its explorations. In short, only thus can adolescence be adolescence.

To be its explorations is the intrinsic requirement of adolescence, for the options it successively enacts in the world are at bottom the objectifications of its own possibles. Its work consists in enacting these options and thereby actualizing the corresponding possibilities in itself. This work is effectively served by the three qualities of adolescence that adulthood insistently decries—its extremism, its inconstancy, and its insolence.

Extremism here refers to the intensity of adolescent commitments together with their distance from the familiar. Intensity, when coupled with another adolescent characteristic—its clannishness—has led some commentators[18] to identify the mind of adolescence as inherently "ideological," but the appearance is misleading. We shall see that adolescent clannishness is not the adoption of a group identity but a cloak drawn over a profound and fully self-aware solitude. And the identification of intense commitment with an "ideological mind" is canceled by adolescence's notorious inconstancy. Ideology demands unconditional commitment. The adolescent's commitment to each new fancy *appears* frighteningly total, but the ease and rapidity of their succession is the clue to the defining characteristic of adolescence—its total absence of commitment other than to the process of exploration itself.

Consider the distancing of adolescent interests from the familiar. Impetuously the adolescent plunges into activities that are at the furthest remove—geographically, psychologically, philosophically—from home ground. If he has been reared in the city he announces that he has found a summer job in the wilderness of northern Idaho. If he has been reared under the tenets of strictest rationalism he becomes a devotee of witchcraft. If he has been reared indulgently he adopts the asceticism of a medieval monk. It is the same logic that sent the Portuguese navigators to the opposite side of the globe—the logic of inversion, which is the logic of exploration itself. To find virgin ground requires that one shun not merely the paths upon which one has been set, but surrounding lawns and fields as well. To discover one's authentic responses, stripped of all conditioning, it is necessary to overleap not only familiar concepts and attitudes but all that these entail. Of course, the opposite of the familiar is also entailed by the familiar (but psychologically, not logically—for we shall not repeat the mistake of Hegel). But it is the effective starting-point of exploration, and exploration will be such where this starting-point is not fixedly clung-to (as by the psychology of rebellion) but only serves as introduction to the full array of possibilities.

And extremism in respect of distantiation is canny in a second respect, for home ground is invariably a middling position. By its extremism adolescence seeks the poles of possibilities, thereby establishing at the outset the scope of its exploratory task.

Meanwhile the intensity of adolescence's investment in each new possibility is likewise functional, for what it must explore is lifetimes, yet it does not have a bundle of lifetimes at its disposal—therefore it requires successive "cram-courses" in which intensity substitutes for duration.[19] By participatory enactment adolescence in a week traverses the course of a lifetime. Certainly from an independent standpoint there is no equivalence here but only symbolic representation; but adolescence itself cannot recognize the disparity. Here appears the flagrant *insolence* by which the adolescent quickly "sees through" your arduous lifetime endeavor and mine. Indeed, the complete measure of this insolence is not taken until we notice that it is not ordinary lifetimes but the lifetimes of the world's greatest men and women that are thus outworn in a rush and cast aside—Socrates's, Shakespeare's, Newton's, Gandhi's, Picasso's. Once again, however, the tactic has an inexorable logic. Every course in life is determined by aspiration to an end; every ultimate end is a perfection; and the lives of the world's greatest men and women more nearly approach the perfection that inspired them than do ordinary lives. Therefore the lives of the greatest have more to teach about ends.

Of course such high-handedness inspires our wrath and we severely remind the youth that as yet he amounts to nothing, that he has not made his way in the world, and therefore that the judgments he so cavalierly and volubly expresses are worthless. But we forget that his judgments are not of actualities in the world but of possibilities within himself. They are of the form, "If I were to choose to pursue such-and-so, then I would be likely to experience such-and-so, and be in a position to contribute such-and-so." True, the adolescent behaves as if he supposes himself to be judging actualities. Fantasizing himself amid the great personages of history leads him in this stage to judge his father poor company and to rate himself worthy of honor in virtue of his fantasies. We intend to show that in truth he deserves honor for his "fantasies" for what they are, namely participatory explorations of life's possibilities. When we recognize them for what they are, we will not be threatened by them, and our righteous wrath will subside—though there is no antidote for unrighteous wrath. Insolence is necessary as the backside of two necessary virtues of adolescence, hopefulness and daring.

As distinguished from actuality, possibility bears none of the scars and decrepitude of existence, and this gives youth that "hopeful disposition" of which Aristotle speaks, which "makes them think themselves equal to great things—and this means having exalted notions."[20] A "hopeful disposition" is necessary because what must be explored consists in ultimate ends, perfections, which a resigned disposition discards as "unrealistic." A resigned or "realistic" adolescence is properly intuited as unnatural, for it is a contradiction in terms.

Here is the ground and vindication of the further insolence by which adolescence disavows solidarity with the rest of humanity. It is disgusted by the infirmities of old age, announcing its intention to "die by the age of fifty." It disavows its own childhood as the history of an utter stranger (which by incommensurability is morally the truth). It splashes brimming contempt upon adulthood's inevitable compromises. It wants it known that the lessons of history do not apply to its own case. In short it behaves as if it were an immaculate conception without precedent upon the earth—and necessarily so. When Erik Erikson says that "the danger of this stage is isolation,"[21] we are provoked to the counter-assertion that isolation is adolescence's definitive condition and its salvation. The assessment of pure possibilities is possible only to a being that is itself uncontaminated by the inherent infirmity of existence. Such exemption belongs to adolescence in virtue of its status as everything *in potentia*, nothing in actuality. To preserve this innocence adolescence must deny its solidarity with actual humanity.

But what of adolescence's manifest clannishness—does it not preclude real solitude by substituting a group-identity? Let us scrutinize this characteristic with care.

The prevailing form of adolescent sociation is the homogeneous small group—the unisexual clan, club, team, or fraternity; so much so that there is good reason to identify this form of sociation as an adolescent invention.[22] The name we give to the relationships subsisting within such groups is comradeship, and the defining characteristic of comradeship is its principle of exclusion. Comradeship is a "we" against "them."

In his seminal studies, Georg Simmel locates the paradigmatic setting of comradeship in the secret society. Of the Gallic Druids, for example, he says that their long training in absolute secrecy "tied every single member with incomparable closeness to the group, and made him feel that, were he severed from this substance, he would lose his own and could never find it again anywhere."[23] The secrets can be of several sorts. Sometimes the very existence of the society itself is the primary secret. Sometimes the existence of the society is public knowledge, but its membership is secret. In other cases both the existence of the society and the names of its members are publicly available, but secrecy surrounds the society's creed and ritual practices. Concerning substantive secrets, no one who has by hook or crook gained access to them—those of the Sufis, for example, or the Carboneri, or the Freemasons (or the Kiwanis, or Lions, or a college fraternity)—will have failed to have been struck by their paltriness and triviality. Yet here is the clue to the deep truth about secrecy—the secret is everything before it is revealed, nothing after. The power of the secret lies not in what it is but in what it does; it divides the human community into two groups, the knowing and the unknowing, the *cognoscenti* and the *ignoranti*. Simmel's analysis thus confirms that in the essence of comradeship is a principle of exclusion that works inter-individually to distinguish some persons from the rest. By this feature comradeship isolates adolescence from the rest of the human race according to the necessity heretofore described.

Moreover comradeship's principle of exclusion works intra-individually, restricting what each individual presents of himself to that which obtains in common among members of the group. The effective device here is ritual, including creedal recitation. To the extent to which behavior and belief are ritualized, nothing of individual differentiation appears. This exclusion has led some commentators to define adolescence as a stage devoid of individuation. Thus Ortega y Gasset says of adolescence "The isolation of infancy breaks down, and the boy's personality flows out into the coeval group. He no longer lives by himself and for himself; he no longer feels and wishes as an individual; he is absorbed by the anonymous personality of the group which wishes and feels for him."[24] Similarly Erikson points to adolescence's "apparent complete loss of identity . . . [in] cliques and crowds."[25] But Ortega and Erikson here foist upon adolescence the meaning of comradeship in adulthood. The comradeship of adulthood can achieve loss of identity of the unique individual, thereby providing escape from self-responsibility. But when we look carefully into adolescent comradeship we discover it to be a cloak, well-contrived to nurture within its folds an individuation that cannot yet bear exposure to direct sunlight. Beneath the bravado and gregariousness of adolescence is a hidden but fully self-aware solitude. In the group the adolescent knows himself to be not *of* the group. Behind his resolute conformity he is absolutely alone, and he fears the discovery of himself in this condition, for he knows himself to be—in the profoundest sense of the term—*unprepared*. In the strictest sense, here is the origin of shame in human beings. It is the feeling that attends the anticipation of being discovered naked, not in body but in spirit. Shame originates in adolescence, where it serves to signify that the unique self is in this stage of life nascent and unclothed. Borrowing a biological image, Abraham Maslow likened this nascent self to the "growth-tip" of the plant, its tenderest part.[26] Comradeship affords to the "growth-tip" of personhood the shelter within which to gain strength toward its entrance into the world. In any case, the world tramps heavily upon the delicacies of individuation, but without the hidden horticulture of adolescence nothing but thorn and bracken could survive.

Nurture of the "growth-tip" of unique personhood is the work of adolescence, and the means is the exercise of preference among options in the world as the expression of an innate inclination within the individual (termed by the Greeks one's "destiny"). In his landmark study, *Formalism in Ethics and Non-Formal Ethics of Values*, Max Scheler calls attention to the fact that preferring, in this sense, occurs independently of "all conation, choosing, and willing."[27] Preferring (including "placing after" and rejecting) is the appearance in the world of the innate inclination that is the inborn essence or given nature of the individual. The materials of preferring are possibilities, not actualities, and preferring expresses one's own possibility, having the status of one's innate potentiality. Preferring is not willing or choosing, for it can be discerned in the absence of willing and choosing, as when we say (in Scheler's example) "I prefer roses to carnations," without thinking of a choice; and preferring does not contain the reflexivity of willing and choosing, but is "lost in its object." Right willing and choosing are founded in preferring and are right by accordance with the individual's innate potentiality as expressed in preferring. By its exemption from all willing and choosing, adolescence is the training-ground of preferring. Within its span, preferring requires transformation from its initial timorousness and tentativeness to the hardiness and unequivocality that ground choice in the world.

Adolescence is the stage of life when the individual, having heretofore been spoken for by others, must learn to speak for himself and, by speaking for himself, discover himself. By this internal requirement adolescence may be judged without anachronism.

MATURATION

"Choose yourself"—Seneca's *"Praebere se fato"*—is the imperative announcing life's third stage, whose definitive moral quality derives from its intrinsic obligation upon each individual to "Become what you are."

As adolescence opens with the revelation "I am alive—I am an original living human being," so the onset of adulthood is correspondingly announced in the revelation, "Someday I must die." Again the implications are revolutionary, transforming both the individual and his entire familiar world into utter novelties. Maturation consists in learning to make one's way in this new world by progressively enacting the implications of the instigatory revelation. The most urgent and immediate of these implications is that because life is not endless, what is to be done must be begun at once.

The inner demand to begin at once what must be done is the requirement upon the individual to choose what is to be done by himself. The choice cannot be made for him by the world because from the standpoint of the world what needs to be done is everything, and the answer to the question by whom it is to be done is "everyone." But the impetus to the doing of the third stage of life is an individuating factor. His recognition of his own eventual death renders a person acutely aware of his own finitude: he is not "everyone," but rather a finite one among others; what must be done by "everyone" affords nothing to him in the way of a necessity in which to ground the "must" of "what must be done." Nor is such ground provided by that which can just as well be done by another, for in such cases it can just as well be left to the other to do.

The moral necessity in "what must be done" rests in the conviction of a "something which I, alone, can do," a conviction that is the product of adolescent exploration and that has been furnished by exploration with concrete knowledge of the distinctive quality of the particular "something." The individual's choice of what is to be done by himself is the choice of his ultimate possibility, a possibility that *is himself* as a fulfilled person. This choice can be made either explicitly or implicitly. To choose explicitly is to identify, amid alternatives, that end or final consummation (in form, a perfected person) that will henceforth be served by all of one's acts, and that will in turn serve them by giving them their meaning. To choose implicitly is to resolve to fulfill the implications of a given concrete activity, thereby adhering to the implicit principle of the given activity ("keeping one's promises") and advancing toward the ultimate possibility from which the principle derives.

In either case the choice is in no sense arbitrary, but acknowledges an absolute criterion in innate inclination. It is the choice of that end that from the birth of the individual is implicit in his actuality. Right choice is choice that accords with innate inclination, wrong choice is choice at variance with innate inclination. Between the ultimate pos-

189

sibility that is innately the individual's own and the actual individual whose ultimate possibility it is lies the relationship of potentiality. Between this individual and all other human possibilities—though they likewise subsist within him—no such relationship exists. The relationship of potentiality manifests itself in concrete experience as love, in the classical meaning of *eros*. In this meaning love is aspiration to the good—not, however, to the universal and indeterminate Good, nor to one good or another indiscriminately, but to the determinate good that will fulfill and complete the given individual *qua* individual, and that is accordingly to be conceived as the good that is his own. In Plato's words *eros* is "*tiktein en tô kalô*," desire for generation and birth in beauty, where generation is growth and beauty is the good life. The individual who strives in accordance with his innate inclination does all that he does out of love. The individual whose striving is at variance with his innate inclination lacks the moving power of love, and acts upon such surrogate motivations as need, desire (including the desire for "pleasure" or "happiness" for himself or others), vanity, guilt, shame, or extrinsically imposed "duty."

Is success in life possible to an individual who lives contrary to his innate inclination? This question must be met with the counter-question, What is meant by success? This is not an intellectual dodge, but a recognition that conceptions of success are many and various. In particular a distinction must be identified between what the world may judge to be a successful life and the judgment of the individual whose life is in question. Eudaimonism contends that, where disparity exists, it is the individual's judgment that must sustain him in the end. The internal reward that consummates the life lived in accordance with innate inclination is the concluding recognition, "I lived the life which was my own." Such a life has found its necessity, and by this means has overcome guilt, regret, and fear of death. It would exchange places with no other. In particular it would not exchange places with any of the countless lives that are judged successful by others, but that lack this internal conviction.

Worldly success is entirely possible, and perhaps even likelier, to the individual in whom duplicity operates, but his own harvest is this very duplicity—he cannot know whether it would have been better had he done otherwise; he is unremittingly bedeviled by his "otherwise," fearing the judgment upon his life in virtue of it, and fearing death as an ultimate "otherwise." And well he may, for his "success" is not founded in the objective worth of his life but in public misconceptions that, while ubiquitous indeed, are highly unstable. Manifestation of worth in the world— even of what the world mistakes for worth—requires cohesion, discipline, tenacity, for which a powerful motivation is required. In the case of the individual who is living in truth to himself, this motivation is love in the eros-meaning, which, as the aspiration to higher value, is the intrinsic, profound, and original movement of life. Where the motivation of love is lacking, its place must be taken—if "success" is to be achieved—by an equally powerful motivator of a different kind. The existence of such substitutes for love is indisputable, but when we set out to catalogue them—ambition, avarice, guilt, competitiveness, hatred—we see immediately that they are distinguished from love by the fact that their true aim is not the maximization of value, but something quite different from this and in certain cases the very opposite, namely value-degradation. But value-maximization cannot be achieved by indirection, much less by the opposite intent (however well it may be disguised), and by contrast to love, these substitute motivators are guaranteed by their very nature in greater or lesser degree to impoverish the world. And this is what the relentless "otherwise" of dysdaimonia signifies.

Returning to the choice with which the stage of maturation begins, we have seen that it is the adoption of the ultimate end of the individual life either explicitly, by selection among alternative ultimate ends as experienced imaginatively by participatory enactment, or implicitly, by a decision to be faithful to the implications of a preferred activity in the present.

It should next be noted that this choice is both "hard" and corrigible. There can be no a priori certitude concerning it because its entailments are never to be fully known except by enactment. As was said earlier, the best judgments of the rectitude of choice are made a posteriori, for possibilities within the self become discernible only when they are in some degree actualized. The experiments of adolescence are conducted largely by an imaginative participation, the very capacity for which adolescence serves to cultivate, and which is by no means infallible but only better or worse. It follows that mistakes will sometimes be made in the choice with which maturation begins. And no one is condemned to the perpetuation of a choice he subsequently recognizes to have been mistaken. At all times it remains possible to revoke one's choice in the interest of choosing anew. But here appears the sharpest difference between adolescence and maturation. Adolescence is the stage of life in which the individual is not to be held to his promises. He is not to be held to his promises because he does not choose—he experiments and explores—and therefore, *sensu stricto*, he does not promise. If from the manner in which an adolescent presents himself this week we infer what to expect of him next week, the mistake is ours. The adult's original choice, however, renders his every action genuinely promissory by the principle with which his choice invests his actions. The man or woman of principle is the person of whom certain things are rightfully to be expected, namely those future acts entailed by past and present acts according to the principle that he or she is. Therefore to revoke one's choice of one's ultimate possibility is to default on promises, the anticipated fulfillment of which is in some part the basis of the actions of others. In this situation some extreme rigorisms[28] admit no moral exception to the keeping of one's promises, but they unpardonably overlook the crucial distinction between right and wrong promises. The worth the individual manifests in the world is the expression of right living and right promising and not otherwise. In this light it will be apparent that every promisee has a fundamental interest in the intrinsic rightness in reference to the promiser of what is promised to him. (For an exaggerated example: if I, who am ignorant of auto mechanics, promise to help you repair the engine of your car, you will be ill-served by the fulfillment of my promise.) The datum of the morality of promising, in short, is right promising, and toward the goal of right promising morality and ethics cannot in self-consistency pose immovable barriers.

At the same time no one who has truly promised can with impunity default on his promises. The very act of promising is itself the promise to promise well, therefore wrong promises can morally be revoked in favor of right ones, worse in favor of better. Persons whose legitimate expectations are thwarted by the re-choosing of a given individual are to be compensated by new promises (the entailments of the new choice) whose fulfillments are worthier than the old in virtue of their superior truth to the promiser. There can (morally) be no revocation of an original promising that is not at the same time a re-promising.

In addition the very act of re-choosing contains its own deterrent to promiscuity. The actualization of personhood is progressive, requiring, in Nietzsche's words, "long obedience in the same direction."[29] To re-choose is to annihilate all accomplished actualization stemming from the original choice; it is a re-beginning out of a lapse into indeterminacy. As such it poses to the life in question the spectre of final indeterminacy as a life without identity or necessity—a life that in the true meaning of the term has failed to exist.

In sum, the corrigibility of ultimate choice is restrictively conditioned from within. In accordance with this the choice itself is "hard" in two distinct but interrelated respects: it is of necessity "wholehearted," and it forecloses all possibilities but the possibility that is chosen.

Where the choice is one's life, logically one cannot choose with reservations for there can be nothing in reserve. By the law of the excluded middle what can be reserved can only be another and incommensurably different life (for what can be commensurated with a given life is entailed by it, and included within it as an implication). And it is reserved by choice, which means that by the choice "with reservations" two lives have been chosen, in which condition no choice has been made. Kierkegaard identified the condition as "double-mindedness" (or triple- or quadruple-mindedness), and it precludes attainment to the self-identical life for the same reason that it precludes the enactment of a self-identical act. The reason is the finitude of both acts and lives. One cannot act in two different ways at once; and because a lifetime is the expression throughout a span of time of a single act (by progressive explication of implications), one cannot live two lives. To attempt to live two lives or to act in two different ways at once is necessarily to fail at the actualization of either option by contradiction. And to choose "with reservations" is precisely this attempt, whether what is reserved is in any degree overtly acted upon or not.* With respect to the ultimate possibility of the individual, only the wholehearted choice *is* a choice.

Doctrines of "commitment" are regularly met by the sardonic and "worldly" remark that nothing in the world warrants wholehearted endorsement, but the remark altogether misconceives the terms of the structure of ultimate choice. What is chosen does indeed appear in the world—first because, as we have shown, possibilities in the self are initially apprehended by participatory enactment of actualities in the world and, second, because the self necessarily acts into the world. But what is to be chosen "wholeheartedly" is nothing actual, being instead a pure possible that certain actualities in the world deficiently express. Hence the recognition that everything actual is deficient is no deterrent

* An epitome of the choice "with reservations" is Pascal's famous "wager."

to wholehearted commitment to those finite perfections that are pure possibles.

Moreover it must be stressed that the object of wholehearted commitment is not the world but oneself, as the moral task of self-actualization. This must be stressed because of the frequency with which persons in the situation of choice objectify the determinants of choice and neglect themselves. In effect such persons look to the world to make the choice for them by exhibiting a course of action that is objectively best. They forget that what is to be decided is not what is, but what is to be done, and not what is to be done by the world but what is to be done by themselves. That a given course of endeavor in the world is up to now less estimable than others says nothing against an increase in its estimability by the contribution of the person who is just now in the situation of choice. The possibilities of choice are not first in the world but initially in persons, appearing in the world as actualizations of choices. What one chooses wholeheartedly is the self one shall strive to become, a becoming that contributes actual worth to the world.

The choice of one's ultimate possibility is also "hard" in that it necessarily forecloses all other possibilities. In ordinary language the person who is "becoming what he is" is "no longer available" to the options. Perpetual availability, the native condition of adolescence, constitutes essential distraction in adulthood: it is to belong to the world rather than to oneself, to contingency rather than necessity. On the contrary: as the wedding-band on one's finger forestalls unwanted solicitations, so the purposeful man wears his purpose upon his face, to the same effect. He will keep his promises by living in fidelity to his choice. All good things that can be expected from adherence to other choices belong to others to give.

Choice forecloses other possibilities because by the condition of finitude one cannot do two different things at once, and the attempt results in failure to do either successfully.

But surely one can do two different things seriatim? Not so, when the lifetime of the individual is recognized to be the progressive explication of implications of a single act. To do two truly (incommensurably) different things is to act seriatim on two different principles. But as Leibniz was the first to see, each principle is a perspective upon everything that is—each substance "expresses the universe conformably with [its] view."[30] Therefore what is implicit in an act on principle in given circumstances is nothing less than the expression of this same principle with respect to all other circumstances the world affords. It follows that to act on different principles seriatim is to default in one's responsibility to the implications of the first principle. Because the implications of any act-on-principle extend to the limit of the lifetime, to act on two different principles seriatim is to attempt to act in two different ways at one time, the *one* time that is the lifetime.

Concretely exemplified: if I, by choice a philosopher, at the conclusion of the writing of this book were to choose to enter, say, political life by winning elective office and fulfilling its requirements, I should henceforth be in default with respect to a number of distinct promises this book implicitly makes (and which were antecedently implied in my original choice of philosophy). One of these is the promise of a thorough metaphysics in accordance with the principles sketched in Chapter 5. Another is the promise of an epistemology of "participatory enactment," a concept used here only allusively (but which will be developed sufficiently for present purposes in Chapter 8). Another is the promise of an explicit aesthetics in accordance with scattered implications in the present work. Still another is the promise, under the unwritten rules of philosophical professionalism, to utilize the ethical principles of the present work in present debate concerning more narrowly circumscribed ethical dilemmas, to "show how they work." In these and other respects the present book is promissory, and my responsibility for the book is my responsibility for the fulfillment of its promises. But I have chosen only the illustration that in my case lies nearest to hand. Analogous entailments obtain for every act that, as the act of a person in the stage of maturation, is an act on principle.

Adolescence marks the appearance of the self as a problem to itself, and maturation constitutes the solution of the problem of the self by choice of the ultimate principle that affords identity and necessity to the life of the individual. The fundamental virtue of maturation is self-truth—truth to one's choice and one's promises, predicated upon the prior truth of one's choice to one's innate potentiality. Generically this virtue is named loyalty or fidelity, and the word for the species of fidelity that is reflexive, as fidelity to self, is integrity. It is the thesis of ethical eudaimonism that this "duty to oneself" is the ground of every interpersonal, social, and objective duty.

It should be emphasized that "choice" and "integrity" as they apply to maturation by no means necessarily imply a narrow life. The most heterogeneous-appearing activities and interests can be integrated by a life that is sufficiently strong in its principle, for we must bear in mind that what is thus integrated is not the activity objectively considered, but its meaning to the individual in question. To exemplify this I cannot resist an anecdote. The little tale stems from my personal acquaintance with R. M. Hare, distinguished Professor of Moral Philosophy at Oxford. In due course I learned, first (from him) that he spent part of his time clambering over the roofs of his college, plugging leaks; and, second (from his wife, Catherine) that for many years he has made leather sandals. Now, we would be hard-put to name activities as disparate as moral philosophy, roof repair, and sandals-making. But my response to Catherine was, "And I'll bet he shows the same scrupulous concern for the quality of the sandals he makes as he does for the quality of his writing." She replied, "Oh, yes indeed, and do you know, the sandals he made for me eleven years ago are still in fine condition?"

The correlation, of course, is not between sandals and philosophy, but between Hare-made sandals and Hare-made essays and books. In general it centers in scrupulous craftsmanship with economy of means and a lasting result, but these qualities are further refined to distinctively Hare-craftsmanship, such that I believe, out of my familiarity with his writing, I could identify the Hare-made sandals among a dozen pairs by different makers.

Likewise the roof-clambering is integrated by the meaning of stewardship with respect to our cultural heritage, in which, for Professor Hare, both Oxford and philosophy have a large place.

By the virtue of integrity, every act by the individual, no matter how seemingly insignificant, expresses personal principle, and thereby expresses the whole person. In Sartre's words, a person "is a totality and not a collection."[31] Nor can we afford to overlook (as does Sartre, for example), the profound generosity integrity implies. By expressing himself in each of his acts the integral individual appears in the world, giving of himself for what uses others can make of him. Nor does he penuriously retain control over his expressions by legislating their meaning, but rather his expressions invite the best meanings they shall have for others. Thus the music of Haydn, for example, is a gift that, while conditioned by its specific qualities, is nonetheless amenable to an infinitude of meanings by which to be integrated into countless lives.

The generic quality of life within the stage of maturation is perhaps best characterized by the term "eudaimonic aspiration." Eudaimonia as a subjective quality is the specific theme of the chapter to follow, and shall be deferred here with but a brief word. It is the feeling of inner necessity, of "being where one must be, doing what one must do." Aspiration, deeply considered, is the meaning of eros according to Plato, *tiktein en tô kalô*, a desire for generation and birth in beauty. Specifically it is the desire to become the worthy individual one can become, experienced in the becoming.

Because all virtues have defects for their obverse side, maturation can also be understood by the harsh, compulsive, and compassionless striving to which it has a native vulnerability—in the manner of Santayana's fanatic, who "redoubles his effort when he has forgotten his aim."[32]

A revealing leitmotif of the third stage of life is its perpetual torment by time. Time appears here in the image of the hourglass whose sand is irreversibly running out. Time does not "drift," or "pass," but presses, thanks to the recognition that the time allotted to the individual is measured, and the goal is distant, the way arduous. In the work of self-actualization there can be no precocious successes, for actualization includes a strengthening of vision and judgment that all the more clearly perceive the distance between what has been achieved and what remains to be done. Uniquely, for this stage death acquires a "right time." The right time for death is after the consummation of the great work, the work that "I, alone, can do." Correspondingly fear of death is qualified as apprehension of the death that comes too soon, the death that pens the period to life "before the sentence is finished."

A concomitant to this leitmotif is the *economy* cited by Schopenhauer as the most readily discernible difference between the adult and the youth. In Schopenhauer's words, "A grave seriousness now takes the place of that early extravagance of spirit; and the change is noticeable even in the expression of a man's face. As long as we are young, people may tell us what they please! we look upon life as endless and use our time recklessly; but the older we become, the more we practice economy."[33] In the interest of his singular objective, the individual shuns everything that he cannot utilize. He sheds acquaintances, does not offer himself to friendship, and must be besieged if friendship is to occur. He deems his own illnesses as annoying distractions, and will disregard them as far as he can. He measures his sleep and his recreation. He wastes no words, and is filled with chagrin by the recollection of his garrulous youth. In speech he is scrupulously truthful, not from conventional moral considerations, but because lying wastes time and ingenuity, it is the vice of aimlessness. To return to Schopenhauer's description:

> In my young days I was always pleased to hear a ring at my door: ah! thought I, now for something pleasant. But in my later life my feelings on such occasions were rather akin to dismay than to pleasure: heaven help me! thought I, what am I to do? A similar revulsion of feeling in regard to the world of men takes place in all persons of any talent or distinction. For that very reason they cannot be said properly to belong to the world; in a greater or less degree, according to the extent of their superiority, they stand alone. In their youth they have a sense of being abandoned by the world; but later on, they feel as though they had escaped it.[34]

We shall reserve our consideration of the specific form of sociality that maturation manifests to Chapters 9 and 10, except to note that the quality of life herewith described is rendered congenial by certain factors. Its congeniality appears, in the first place, in the profound generosity expressed by integrity in the form of culture. A second congenial factor is the exemplification integrity affords of the meaningfulness and worth of life. A third factor is the ascription of worth (potential and actual) to others by the integral individual, on the analogue of his own self-worth. These factors are not additions to the generic sensibility of maturation, they are maturation itself in a native dimension.

Nevertheless the congenial factors are sometimes lacking in given individuals, as aspiration to the good is not infrequently displaced by harsh and compulsive striving. This is the phenomenon termed by F. H. Bradley the "peevish enemy,"[35] propelling individuals by dissatisfaction from behind, and issuing in blind competitiveness and resentment. It is clearly not maturation but a pseudomorph, yet it is a pseudomorph that claims a proximate relation to maturation by the intrinsic precariousness of maturation itself. For maturation cannot erase, in the being which is *causa sui*, the anxiety over its own groundlessness. It is precisely here that old age is efficacious. But this efficacy of old age is thwarted by our resolute propensity to mistake the third stage for the whole of life, dismissing old age as pure deterioration.

The inherent anxiety of maturation is gratuitously aggravated by our disrespect for other stages. Thus the child is conceived as a miniature adult, adolescence is a temporary aberration, and old age is asked to make itself invisible. By this conception adulthood is suspended between two oblivions—the one of an adolescence that has been suppressed, and the other of an old age that is the awaiting of death. So conceived, the enterprise of adulthood is doomed, for its burden is too heavy for it alone to bear. Here the pseudomorph finds its foothold, and the self-caused individual, fearing that he is nothing but his own arbitrary invention, turns to pillage for support.

OLD AGE

"Age takes hold of us by surprise"—thus Goethe expressed the manner of arrival of the final stage of life. "Why, what has happened?" wrote Aragon; "It is life that has happened, and I am old."[36]

The surprise by which old age arrives is taken by Simone de Beauvoir to be a striking feature, calling for explanation. To account for it she contends that age is akin to a costume in which we appear to the public, but which we ourselves cannot directly see. In her words, "Our private, inward experience does not tell us the number of our years; no fresh perception comes into being to show us the decline of age." Hence the revelation that we are now old will first be given in the behavior of others toward us, for which we can have no inner preparation. In virtue of this, old age is fated to remain "an insoluble contradiction between the obvious clarity of the inward feeling that guarantees our unchanging quality and the objective certainty of our transformation. All we can ever do is waver from the one to the other, never managing to hold them both firmly together."[37]

Mlle de Beauvoir's account is admirable for its fidelity to the manifest empirical paradoxes of old age everywhere in the Western world, but to explain empirical paradoxes as the manifestation of inherent contradiction smacks of the essentialist fallacy ("explaining" appearances by positing corresponding essences). It in no way increases the intelligibility of the phenomenon in question, which means that no philosophy has been done. And in the present case it underrates that moral necessity by which persons can give coherence and meaning to their lives. In obedience to the philosopher's principle of sufficient reason[38] we must look beneath appearances for an implicit logic of old age, whose disclosure will likewise call to prominence a number of empirical features of the stage that are overlooked by de Beauvoir.

Thanks to human freedom, chronological age is only contingently correlated with developmental age. Hence, while it is correct that inner experience "does not tell us the number of our years," nothing follows from this concerning the stage of our lives. On the contrary, inner experience infallibly identifies the present stage of our life. And de Beauvoir to the contrary notwithstanding, a "fresh perception" most certainly announces to us our commencement upon the final stage of life. It is the sudden perception that we, the aged person, no longer have a future. Implicit in this perception is the logic of old age together with its exclusive values, virtues, and obligations. Our present task is to render this logic explicit.

This inner perception prompts the surprise with which old age takes us, hence the surprise has nothing to do with other persons but is intrinsic to the stage. Moreover, with respect to surprise, old age is structurally identical to every other stage. As late maturation is "surprised" by old age, so adolescence is "surprised" by adulthood and childhood is "surprised" by adolescence (and pre-natal life, if you will, is "surprised" by birth, as antecedent being is "surprised" by conception). Surprise arises from the discontinuities subsisting between stages, precluding anticipation of the stage to come. Each stage is a vital principle by which to experience the entire world, and an exchange of stages is an exchange of principles of enworldment. To exchange stages is to be reborn to a novel world—no less when the stage entered upon is old age than in previous stage-exchanges.*

De Beauvoir valorizes the old age that remains "still full of projects."[39] She regrets the lapse of enterprise that commonly attends old age, and commends the perpetuation of aspiration, striving, planning. At bottom the old age that wins her approval is the reiteration of the stage of maturation. By this anachronistic norm, old age is condemned to a pathos of pure debilitation, for the very capacities whose

* In this sense there is a childhood with respect to each stage of life, and likewise each stage has its old age, when the terms of the stage are worn out and the individual longs for fresh challenges. Concerning the "childhood" of old age, Ms. Maggie Kuhn (70-year-old National Convener of the Gray Panthers, and leading advocate of the virtues of old age) says that old age produces an abundant renewal of energy as a result of the transformation of the world of the individual. A new world waits to be explored, and poses the requirement for new terms of living, and the newly old person—if he is not locked away in a nursing home—will experience a renewal of energy proportional to the work. Ms. Kuhn also says that old age is the time for "dangerous, risky living," and the correlation of this with my proposition that old age is without a future seems to me clear. Without a future, one has nothing to lose, and in this condition he experiences, as Ms. Kuhn says, a new kind of freedom. It is what Abraham Maslow has termed "post-mortem life." As Robert Frost somewhere says, "I leave it to anyone to condemn me to death, so long as he allows nature to carry out the sentence." When we have reached old age, then it is clear that nature carries out our sentence, and our vulnerability at the hands of our enemies vanishes. (I report here on conversation with Ms. Kuhn, related to her address at the University of Delaware, November 11, 1975, entitled "Death and Old Age.")

strength and resilience are depended upon by maturation—analytic and synthetic intelligence, single-mindedness, integration, physical endurance—are eroded by old age. The virtues of the third stage of life are born of that freedom that conceives the future independently of the historical past. But old age is the stage by which life is shorn of its future. In the words of the French writer Michel Leiris, "When one no longer looks upon being wiped out by death or senility as a fate but expects it as an evil that is about to strike, then—and this was the case with me—one loses even the smallest wish to undertake any new thing: one reckons the very small amount of time that lies ahead—a throttled time that has no relation with the days when it was unthinkable that any undertaking should not have space enough to develop freely; and this puts out one's fire entirely."[40]

Here is the internal recognition that distinguishes old age as a unique and comprehensive perspective. Here, too, is the key to the manifest empirical paradoxes of old age as it is presently lived—in our very ambivalence to the principle of old age as just enunciated. We doubt whether such a life is acceptable or bearable, yet it shall be ours. The empirical paradoxes of old age result from the disparity between old age that is lived as chosen and old age that is unwillingly undergone. The old age extolled by de Beauvoir for being "still full of projects" is in truth engaged at self-denial.

Let us take care to avoid the common error. Old age is not distinguished by ending in death, for every stage of life dies in its own surpassing. The difference appears when we notice that prior stages of life are present to themselves as infinitely extended but old age does not so present itself. *Qua* stage, old age is that stage that has no future, and this self-contained horizon migrates forward to bar the advance of the present by death. In the words of C. G. Jung, "Dying, therefore, has its onset long before actual death."[41] On this point the empirical testimony of old age agrees—it cannot "look forward to life," it cannot "live by hope."

The conclusion to be drawn is that the fourth stage of life

begins in death, and reveals to us death that is not the mere negation of life but is instead death that is to be lived.

As thus defined can the fourth stage of life be chosen? For answer we return to the ambivalence cited a moment ago. By scores our aged seek every means to deny their agedness. But these same persons in alternate breaths announce to the world their rebirth as new persons—persons now released from former requirements, with whom relations must be renegotiated. Typically they do this by loudly or softly flaunting those conventions that bound their prior lives. Having previously hoarded time, the newly old person extravangantly wastes it. Having heretofore lived energetically, he now claims his right to idleness. Having unfailingly recognized (in both the literal and the diplomatic senses) other persons, he now indulges his right to withhold recognition (again, in the two senses), perhaps invoking his deafness or failing vision in support. By such signs as these he expresses his inner conviction that "the rules no longer apply." Frequently he experiences the heady feeling that "all is permitted," signaling an interim between the lapse of the old order and the acceptance of the new. But intrinsic to the stage of life that has no future are special values, virtues, and obligations that shortly begin to assert themselves.

The work reserved exclusively to old age consists in the recovery of the past as the foundation of present and future living. The past old age recovers is not the past of the given present but the eternal past. It is not the past of the individual but the past of humankind, the past of the world, the past of historical being.

Wherever we meet the old we find them wrapped in recollections of times past. In Aristotle's words, the old "live by memory rather than by hope: for what is left to them of life is but little as compared with the long past; and hope is of the future, memory of the past."[42] Above all it is this characteristic which is thought to render the old tiresomely self-indulgent. It is supposed that by substituting the past for the present old people stand in life's way, obsolete and obstructive. But this belief is superficial and opportunistic. In the first place it is not the present for which old age requires substitution but the future. But the aim of substitution is itself impossible and misguided, appearing as such no less to old age than to its critics. It is a resentment motif, resulting when the true objectives of old age are thwarted by external factors. Chief among these factors is the robbery from old age occuring in the assertion of dominance by the succeeding generation. The newly dominant generation commandeers the present for the sake of the future and so leaves old age homeless, for old age has no future. If the old retreat to their memories, then, it is not because they have abandoned the present but because they have been driven out: It is a self-destructive choice, for the past that stands against the present is the dead past, and irrecoverable. The resort to the dead past is described by François Mauriac when he says, "A very old man's memories are like ants whose anthill has been destroyed. One's eyes cannot follow any single one of them for long."[43]

Notice, however, that the present from which old age is driven out is narrowly constituted; it is the present that maturation owns, and like maturation itself it is constituted by maturation's chosen future. As present it requires foundation in a past, but the past on which it draws is *its* past, which likewise is constituted by maturation's chosen future. Thus this entire structure of past, present, and future is founded in choice, and is therefore unstable, for the burden is too much for choice to bear. For choice is a vital activity that, as such, must lapse. Yet *as* choice it demands assurance that what is chosen does not lapse with the lapse of choice, but continues to be. It is for this reason that choice contains within itself the requirement of rectitude—it is inherently criteriological. Right choice contains the assurance that what is chosen does not die with the chooser.

We are now prepared to recognize the profound service old age can uniquely provide to the prior stages of life through recollection. It can substantialize the world of the chosen present by supplying it with a past that is independent of choice, thereby affording it foundation.

The past that the old person is set by old age itself to recover is not his individual past, for individuation lapses with the lapse of the choice of one's future. Likewise it is not a former present disguised as past, nor a past as past, nor even an aboriginal past from which the world might be conceived to have begun. Rather it is the universal and eternal past that, as the past of every present (including every past that once was present), is the ground of the present as such. It is this past that is invoked in Santayana's definition of piety as "man's reverent attachment to the sources of his being and the steadying of his life by that attachment."[44]

The sacredness that many primitive cultures believed to invest old age has two sources. In the first place it attends the elders' knowledge of tribal traditions, songs, myths, customs and ceremonies; second it marks the proximity of elders to the spirits of the dead whose numbers they will soon join. Concerning the first of these sources, investigators commonly conclude that the replacement of the oral tradition by written records depletes such sacredness by usurping the function of the memories of aged persons. But this is a misconception, for it was never mere knowledge of past facts that conferred sacredness (a young man who is an adept student can make himself expert regarding ceremonial life), but rather a special perspective upon those facts that is available only to old age, namely reverence for those facts as sacred facts.

By ritual the present is impacted with the meaning of the past, and if we regard old age as the creature of habit we but dimly reflect the truth that old age is responsible for ritual. For what is meant by "habit"? In the common meaning, habit is the unthinking perpetuation of established patterns of activity. But thus understood, habit characterizes the seniority of every stage of life, and the inauguration of old age, far from instituting the sovereignty of habit, overturns the habits of the previous stage. Further, by the common meaning habit obviates choice, yet the old clearly indicate that their repetitious behavior is their choice, obstinately "clinging to their habits." Indeed, ordinary habits as unthinking perpetuations of patterned behaviors are no match for any explicit self-interest with which they conflict, whereas the exasperating feature of the habits of the aged is that they clearly obstruct the best interests of the aged themselves. In the middle years habit is a principal device of vital economics, conserving energy and time. How utterly different are the "habits" of the old, which do not conserve time but expend it liberally as if the supply were inexhaustible. No one has failed to notice how the old person extends his trivial little tasks by routines that serve no useful purpose. We mutter to ourselves that he wastes time when—good Lord!—so little of it remains to him. Is this not conclusive evidence of his senility?

It is nothing of the sort, but only evidence of the disparity between the true perspectives of maturation and old age. To life's third stage, time-wasting is indeed irresponsible. But in the absence of a future, the economics of the third stage does not apply, and time in old age becomes the "moving image of eternity."[45] In this aspect time is expressed by repetition, cyclical movement, the drawn circle, ritual. Ritual sanctifies life by expressing the eternal within it, and this sanctification is the responsibility of old age. My grandfather's fond daily attentions to three possessions—his pipe, his pen, and his pocketknife—invested hastening time with the touch of the eternal, as did his meticulous daily gardening and his inviolate Tuesday trolley excursions "downtown"—ostensible shopping trips on which he purchased only trifles. Amidst changes in the family pattern these things endured, conferring substance and weight.

The habits of the middle years are aimed aloft, representing the discipline of ascent. The ritual of old age is the recovery of the ground beneath our feet. Accordingly inertia is not the plight of old age but its virtue and its aim. In the words of the aged Victor Hugo, "I have the massive, haughty immobility of the rock."[46]

As the gift of old age to life itself, the substantialization of the human world expresses the definitive virtue of life's fourth stage, namely the profound generosity that is the expression of its mode of being. As inertia is generosity with respect to action, and silence is generosity with respect to speech, so death is generosity with respect to existence. Old age is the stage of *Gelassenheit*, or universal "letting be." Its loss of a future is loss of the principle of self-actualized individuation, and this loss is the occasion for the re-discovery within the individual of his common humanity. Loss of the principle of individuation means lapse of the instrumental meanings that were assigned[47] to all things in the world by the principle. This loss is therefore the occasion for all things to appear, not for what they are with respect to the principle, but for what they are otherwise. But with respect to other persons, it is more than the mere occasion for such appearance, for the re-discovery within the old person of his common humanity is the foundation of that mode of love, termed "sympathy" or "fellow-feeling," which affirms all humankind, hence the good old age does not merely occasion the appearance of others for what they are but is the active encouragement to such appearance.

What empirically we know only too well as the vices of old age—its indifference and its petty self-indulgence, its obdurateness and its bigotry, its niggardliness and its obstructivism, are not qualities inherent in the stage but inversions of inherent qualities produced by blockages to the expression of the originals. Doubtless the systematic robbery of old age, as practiced in our society, contributes to such inversion. But the central question remains, shall our old age be wrung from us or lived by our choice, and the individual himself is finally responsible for his answer. To give while being methodically stripped, bound, and gagged may be difficult, but it is not impossible. For reflect: the resolve to live with integrity (truth to the requirements of the stage of one's life) meets vigorous opposition in each stage of life, and the old person who has lived with integrity in prior stages is sinewy and resourceful. Against him thievery will prove helpless—for how does one steal what has in advance been given to him and every other?

As always, the issue finally rests with the inner adversary. The good old age cannot be stolen, but only mislaid or forfeited. It is forfeited by complicity with the thieves, by the erection of impregnable defenses, and by unfulfilled conditions of prior stages of life. Of such cases, the third is the foundational one. In the words of Max Scheler, "The process of ageing can be fruitful and satisfactory if the important transitions are accompanied by free resignation, by the renunciation of the values proper to the preceding stage of life."[48] This free resignation of prior moral conditions is found in their fulfillment, and is not to be gained otherwise.

The inquiry into the stages of life is a fundamental and neglected province of philosophical anthropology.* In this large sense the foregoing sketch can hope at most to be indicative of it *as* a philosophical field, in need of attention as such.

Our primary and restricted aim has been to delineate the stages as they derive from the basic principles and presuppositions of the ethics of self-actualization, in order to learn what further principles and what refinements of established principles may be uncovered by such explication. The following summarizes our findings.

The moral life of the individual is not unitary but fourfold, consisting in the separate sets of normative determinants (values, virtues, and obligations) of the four stages. Within each of the stages life has a different meaning and the

---

* I do not mean to ignore the evidence of a small stirring of philosophical interest found in Theodore Mischel's edited collection, *Cognitive Development and Epistemology* (New York and London: Academic Press, 1971).

world a different appearance. The meanings of such fundamental normative terms as love, freedom, justice, truth, and
death are incommensurably different within the different
stages of life, and we must learn to distinguish scrupulously,
for example, the love and justice of childhood from the love
and justice of adolescence, adulthood, and old age.

A difference between two terms is commensurable when
the terms are capable of being expressed essentially as
members of a single series or variants of a common measure
such that between them lies an uninterrupted series of intermediate positions. By this definition it is obvious that between commensurables continuity obtains and inference
operates, such that to be in possession of one of the terms
together with the principle of the series or the common
measure is to be able to infer the other term. But an incommensurable difference is a difference between terms that
are not members of one series and between which no common measure exists. Hence between incommensurables
discontinuity obtains and inference is inoperative. The
stages of life are incommensurable because each is the principle of a separate series, and events in different stages are
incommensurable because for their intelligibility they must
be referred to separate principles. But by precluding commensuration and a "linear" logic of inference, incommensurability need not be supposed to preclude all relationship,
for commensurability—and its underlying goal of identity
—is not exhaustive of possible relationships. In particular,
in the previous chapter we introduced the idea of a "diachronic" logic, a logic of succession. In this unexplored
field,* it seems just possible that the order of the stages of
life may provide us with a key to the understanding of suc-
cessions of other sorts, i.e. that within it may lie a metaphysical truth.

It deserves re-emphasis that the meanings and normative
requirements of each stage of life are intrinsic to the stage

---

* We may term it this, I think, with all due respect to the dialectics,
respectively, of Plato and of Hegel.

itself, and not imposed from without. The inception of each stage is announced by the individual's inner perception of an utter novelty—the perception of being fated to be misunderstood that opens adolescence, the perception of the death that is one's own that opens maturation, and the perception of the foreclosure of one's future that opens old age. Implicit in each of these perceptions are the normative terms of the given stage, and in each stage the well-lived life consists in actualizing the implications of the original inner perception. Because the stages are determined from within, and because fulfillment of the requirements of each stage is problematic but nonetheless the condition of entrance upon the subsequent stage, chronological age has no necessary correlation to developmental age.

With the exception of eudaimonism, all objective moral systems and ethical theories in Western life have been unitary, representing the life of the individual as subject to a single set of commensurate normative principles.[49] Insofar as such systems contain a partial truth, they achieve their unity by hypostatizing the principles inherent in one or another of the four stages of life, imposing them upon the life of the individual in its entirety. By so doing they institutionalize the fallacy of anachronism, demanding of life in incommensurate stages what it cannot possibly give, and what it can attempt to give only by self-falsification. Indeed, self-actualization ethics especially emphasizes the normative terms of life's third stage, but it is uniquely able to do this without overriding the moral autonomy of the other stages, for its principal imperatives, "Know thyself" and "Become what you are," emphasize the autonomy of other stages by their restricted applicability.

The question remains, where lies that internal continuity that common sense supposes the individual's life to possess? If it is to be sought in the terms of Mlle de Beauvoir as "the inward feeling that guarantees our unchanging quality," the response must be that it cannot be found, for no inward feelings can provide such a guarantee. The reason is that feelings are interpretations that, as such, are constituted by the separate principles of the distinct stages. Our impression of the unchanging quality of a lifetime derives from the unlimited extension of the perspective of each stage. Accordingly the continuity that appears in each stage is a product of a retrospective inference that *transforms* the previous stage in accordance with present principle, together with the prospective creation of a consonant future. Whether in feeling or idea, memory or will, the continuity that appears to each stage is only apparent, to be replaced by a different appearance in other stages.

Eudaimonism's answer to the question of continuity throughout the lifetime of the person is that continuity obtains twofold. In the first place each person possesses continuity as a generic human being rather than a unique individual in virtue of the unchanging subsistence within him of "common humanity" (whose form shall be investigated in Chapter 8). Second, he possesses continuity as a unique person, in virtue of the continuity of his inborn potentiality. But this potentiality contains both prerequisites and consequents to its actualization that, for their actualization, preclude co-temporaneous actualization of the innate potentiality itself, thereby introducing the requirement for prior and succeeding stages. The fact that unique potentiality is destined to subsist merely implicitly in stages other than the third attests that the aforementioned continuity produced by actual feelings, memories, etc., of a given stage is illusory.

Stage-exchange by no means implies the sudden abandonment of all interests, talents, and endeavors that obtained before. Such an objective asseveration would be bizarre indeed, and is by no means implied by the incommensurability of the stages. What is implied by incommensurability is that interests and activities that persist through stage-exchange undergo a radical transformation of meaning. Thus a given individual may well participate in athletics—say, at tennis, or swimming—lifelong, but for quite different reasons: to display prowess in youth, as an exercise in self-discipline in maturity, and for reasons of health thereafter.

This is ancient Hindu teaching, and neglect of it is responsible for the grossest misconception by Westerners of the Hindu stages. When Hinduism teaches that the youthful desire for sexual enjoyment is replaced by the desire for worldly success it must not be thought that sexual enjoyment ends (at the age of twenty-five years, or thereabout!). On the contrary, sexual activity and sexual enjoyment continue and may very well increase, but stage-exchange transforms their meaning. From having been the dominant end and organizing principle of personality, they take the place and the meaning assigned to them by a new organizing principle.

We have, then, an objective continuity, across stage-exchange, of "strands" of interest and activity. But it would be naïve to suppose that somewhere in the life of the individual is to be found such a strand running from beginning to end, by which to reduce his life to identity. To the individual, such strands are his with respect to their *meanings*, and it is precisely in their meanings that stage-exchange produces transformations. What middle-age tennis playing is to be correlated to is not adolescent tennis playing, but other activities and interests of the given individual's middle-age.

The light of eudaimonism discloses the four stages of life for the moral stages that they are, therefore an exhaustive treatise in eudaimonism is required to offer equivalent studies of each of the stages. Such an enterprise exceeds the limitations of a single book, and shall not be undertaken here. Concerning childhood, adolescence, and old age, the brief sketches offered by the present chapter must suffice. What follows will concentrate on maturation, as the stage of life that claims theoretical priority for its explicit and normative rendering of the unique individuality of the person. In the next chapter we will endeavor to depict the quality and texture of moral life in the stage of maturation, amplifying the sketch of this stage in the present chapter, and refining features described in a preliminary way in Chapter 1. Chapters thereafter shall be devoted to the explication of the pattern of sociality entailed by self-actualization in maturation.

7

Eudaimonia: The Quality of Moral Life in the Stage of Maturation

"No one chooses to possess the whole world if he has first to become someone else."[1]

Aristotle's words epitomize a radical disparity between the moral sensibilities of his time and our own. For surely the motto of our time runs, "Show me how to possess the whole world and I will become whomever you please."

The disparity is accounted for by the modern loss of a condition of personal life, and a feeling attendant upon the condition, with which the Hellenes were intimately familiar. Their name for both the condition and the attendant feeling was *eudaimonia*. Literally, eudaimonia is the condition of living in harmony with one's daimon or innate potentiality, "living in truth to oneself." It is marked by a distinctive feeling that constitutes its intrinsic reward and therefore bears the same name as the condition itself. Provisionally we will describe the feeling of eudaimonia as "being where one wants to be, doing what one wants to do."

As disclosed in previous chapters, the precondition of eudaimonia is the unique, irreplaceable, potential worth of the person. It is his readers' sense of this personal worth on which Aristotle relies in his confident assertion that no one would wish to exchange himself, even "to possess the whole world." Today we are without this sense, and rush to exchange ourselves at the prospect of the most trivial rewards. To persons who have no knowledge of who they are, much less of anything in the way of irreplaceable personal worth, nothing is to be lost by such exchange.

Portions of each of the preceding chapters have described the condition of eudaimonia, and that description will be supplemented here only in certain details. Our present task is to concentrate upon the feeling of eudaimonia and thereby to reveal the generic quality of moral life in the stage of maturation.[2]

But how can a feeling be meaningfully described when it has not been felt by persons to whom the description is offered? The quixotic appearance of the present task will be diminished by sharpening the *en passant* observation of a moment ago that eudaimonia is lost to modernity. It is indeed lost to modernity as a cultural possession and therefore it goes uncultivated, undiscussed, and largely unrecognized. Nonetheless it is fully recognized and cultivated by a handful of individuals who live within the interstices of the cultural fabric—among them those persons termed "self-actualizers" in studies by Abraham H. Maslow[3]—and who would not exchange place with any other, even "to possess the whole world." But apart from these few, and despite eudaimonia's lack of cultural sanction, our exposition shall presuppose that every person has experienced eudaimonia, at least momentarily, at a specific juncture in his life. The juncture to which I refer is the death of childhood and the birth of adolescence. It appears as the first free act by which the adolescent oversteps the boundaries of dependent childhood. As set forth in Chapter 6, it is the act of self-discovery *in* self-actualization, and as such it is inevitably attended by the feeling of eudaimonia. Frequently the first autonomous act is followed by reversion, brief or lengthy, to the mode of childhood dependence, and in this case the initial experience of eudaimonia will be momentary. Furthermore the feeling experienced will be that of generic eudaimonia, not the qualitatively individuated eudaimonia of maturation, for as a stage of life adolescence precedes the choice by which individuated personhood becomes manifest. But this feeling of generic eudaimonia is experienced in perfect purity, for (as subsequent analysis will disclose) it is eudaimonia's nature to be fully present in every occasion of it.

Accordingly the following description of eudaimonia presupposes that every person knows the feeling being described, though a given individual may not know that he knows. And these are the conditions of Platonic "recollection."

At the outset, eudaimonia must be strictly distinguished from "pleasure" and "happiness"—more especially because of our relentless practice of translating it as such. By our legacy from the associational psychology of the Enlightenment,[4] "happiness" means a "sum" or "balance" of pleasures or "pleasure in the long run," while "pleasure" is the feeling that attends the gratification of desire. Here the orthodox inquiry ends, and it is astonishing that the enormous Anglo-American preoccupation with pleasure fails to recognize that, while some pleasures are consonant with the natures of the persons whose pleasures they are, others are dissonant. The resulting mischief, today pervasive, is epitomized in Jeremy Bentham's famous conclusion that, "quantity of pleasure being equal, pushpin is as good as poetry."[5] The decisive question—undreamed of by Bentham—is, "For whom?" For the poet? I do not know whether any poets have been ruined by pushpin, but it is certain that poets have been ruined by pursuit of pleasures equally diversionary. Indeed, any poet who gives equal weight to pleasures resulting from the gratification of desires of every kind, and therefore no precedence to the desire to make a poem, is no poet whatever.

The mischief is only compounded by John Stuart Mill's introduction of qualitative distinctions among pleasures, for Mill's distinctions concern pleasures conceived abstractly, in disregard of persons whose pleasures they may be. Because (according to Mill) intellectual pleasures are inherently higher than sensual pleasures, they ought to be and *will* be chosen in preference to the latter by everyone who "knows both sides."[6] That the descriptive part of Mill's contention is plainly mistaken he might have informed himself by reading, for example, Erasmus's *In Praise of Folly*, or Giordano Bruno's *In Praise of the Ass*. More, history discloses whole epochs that mistrust rationality, seeking salvation elsewhere—our own time for one, and post-Hellenic Greece for another—and no genetic quirk can be supposed to have deprived the leaders of such epochs of the capacity for intellectual pleasures. When Mill says "No intelligent human being would consent to be a fool,"[7] he forgets the notable example of Diogenes, who chose to emulate the life of the dog—one step beneath the fool in Mill's hierarchy. Nor is the normative part of Mill's contention in a better way than the descriptive (wholly apart from the illogicality by which Mill rests the former on the latter, arguing that the fact that persons who "know both sides" do choose the higher pleasures demonstrates that they ought to so choose). When Mill says "It is better to be Socrates dissatisfied than a fool satisfied,"[8] we must once again ask, "For whom?" And we reject the answer implied by Mill, "For everyone" (Mill would restrict this to everyone who has the intellectual capacity; but in Mill's terms it would clearly be better if everyone had the intellectual capacity). Certainly it is better for Socrates to be Socrates. But for Mill to be Socrates (or try to be, since the proposal constitutes an impossibility) is distinctly worse than for Mill to be Mill, and correspondingly for you and for me.

Pleasures are not objective, intrinsic goods, distributable like horses to which we shall hitch our wagons. As conceived abstractly they are valueless, acquiring value or disvalue accordingly as the desires they reflect are commensurate or incommensurate with the persons whose desires they are. Because pleasure attends the gratification of commensurate and incommensurate desires alike, pleasure is not a value-indicator. That office belongs to eudaimonia.

Concerning those goods "with which prosperity and adversity have to do," Aristotle reminds his readers that "taken absolutely [they] are always good, but for a particular person are not always good."[9] For example, the desires for material wealth or political power, entirely commensurate with certain natures, are incommensurate with the nature of the philosopher. For him they constitute what Nietzsche termed "glittering and loud things," distractions from his true course. This does not mean that they cannot be gratified. It means that their gratification by the man who is essentially a philosopher will be at the expense of what he is. The affective result is nonetheless pleasure (understood as the feeling of gratified desire), but the pleasure, like the desire, is at odds with the individual's nature. Disparity here appears between what this individual is and what he ought to be. The disparity constitutes an actual contradiction because that which he ought to be he also is, *in potentia*. It registers subjectively as a tension that underlies pleasure and displeasure, qualifying them both, a qualitatively specific tension for which the Greek term is *dysdaimonia*.[10] The *locus classicus* of the description of the feeling of dysdaimonia is the *Nichomachean Ethics* (9.4). According to Aristotle dysdaimonic individuals feel (and are) "at variance with themselves, and have appetites for some things and rational desires for others." In this condition the "soul is rent by faction, and one element in it . . . grieves when it abstains from certain acts, while the other is pleased, and one draws them this way and the other that, as if they were pulling them in pieces." The possibility of the *condition* of dysdaimonia finds its ground in the self's dual nature as actuality and possibility. Dysdaimonia (as condition) is the actual contradiction resulting from incommensurable disparity between desires and innate inclination. In the eudaimonic individual subsists the disparity between actuality and possibility, but it is a commensurable disparity* in virtue of the fact that possibility affords aim

* In the meaning here employed, a difference is commensurable when its terms are capable of being expressed essentially as members

and measure to actuality. As an aim, an ultimate possibility is capable of commensurating everything in the world (rendering each person, as Leibniz says, a "little world"[11]) except an alternative ultimate possibility and its derivative secondary and tertiary aims. Desires are incommensurate when they constitute the expressions of divergent ultimate aims. The dysdaimonic individual is at every moment impelled to two different acts at once, and in this condition he cannot move, or else (where the impulsions are of different strengths) can move only lamely.

Dysdaimonia is self-contradiction. If this condition is not thoroughly familiar to us today, it is because dysdaimonia is but the first step in the path leading to that self-alienation with which we are entirely familiar.

To the trained eye the outward signs of dysdaimonia are unmistakable. The dysdaimonic individual is perpetually distracted, being only in a part of himself where you find him while part of himself is somewhere else, his "here" and "there" being not continuous but contradictory. Lucretius refers to this characteristic when he speaks of "you [who] always desire what is absent and despise what is at hand."[12] The same feature is marked by Montaigne's words, "We seek for other conditions because we understand not the use of ours, and go out of ourselves forasmuch as we know not what abiding there is."[13] The man who is apologetic about his work or his station in life, hastening to inform us that he is on the brink of something better; the person who characteristically overspeaks himself; the individual who dissociates himself from his habitat, insinuating that its paucity of culture (say) does not reflect upon him in virtue of his spiritual home elsewhere—New York City, perhaps, or London, or Vienna; the woman who at cocktail parties disavows her husband by saying to us, "I met George on the rebound," or "I was so young and inexperienced when Ray-

---

of a single series or variants of a common measure such that between them lies an uninterrupted series of intermediate positions.

mond proposed to me"—such individuals are signboards of dysdaimonia. Or again the dilettante, who by his rapid moves prevents our grasping him in any of his acts. A diaphanous Don Juan is he, putting us on notice that the whole of him is nowhere to be found in any of the parts—as indeed it is not, for in him wholeness is absent, the parts being but fugitive and disparate moments.

Dysdaimonia's contradiction is protean, appearing now in the disparity of parts, again in the discrepancy between end and means, or yet again in the misrepresentation of subjective contents by explicit behavior. But in these and its numerous other case-types the fundamental structure of dysdaimonia obtains as heretofore described.

As the contrary of dysdaimonia, eudaimonia is best expressed as that "wholeheartedness" by which it was identified earlier in our account,[14] and which shall here be carefully scrutinized. The eudaimonic individual experiences the whole of his life in every act, and he experiences parts and whole together as necessary, such that he can will that nothing be changed. But the necessity here introduced is moral necessity, deriving from his choice. Hence we may say of him interchangeably, "He is where he wants to be, doing what he wants to do," or "He is where he must be, doing what he must do." In either case the characteristic is outwardly unmistakable to the trained eye. On the other hand what the untrained eye must be on constant guard against is the habit of analogical inference, i.e. of inferring the subjective contents of other persons from one's own case by correlation of behavioral signs. Specifically, if we are to recognize eudaimonia in others, we must avoid substituting our own feelings with respect to where they are and what they are doing. In the forefront of eudaimonic individuals of my acquaintance I think of Wally, a painter, who lived in a loft in New York's East Village. The loft was vast, dusty, and barren, punctuated only by an exposed toilet in the exact center and a battered stove and refrigerator in one corner, while the perimeter was lined with paintings stacked face-to-the-wall. On the day in question one of Wally's wealthy patrons paid a surprise visit to the loft, and was instantly and thoroughly appalled. With urgent generosity he sought to bestow upon the artist a carte blanche two weeks in the Bahamas, and could not comprehend why the would-be beneficiary refused. The patron could not comprehend because he was unable to recognize that Wally was where he wanted to be, doing what he wanted to do. Anything different held for Wally no attraction.

Eudaimonia's "wholeheartedness" means that the whole person is present in each of his acts. This is so because the individual's choice of his ultimate possibility establishes a principle of entailment whereby his future and his past are implicit in his present, and thereby are within his present act. Because his "there" is within his "here," he is devoid of that condition of semi-distraction that is the common attendant of personal life. Structurally, such distraction resolves into two sorts for which I shall informally use the terms "spatial" and "temporal." By "spatial" distractions I refer to distractions that are co-temporaneous with the individual. These consist, first, in objects, privileges, and rewards that are incommensurate with his ultimate choice and hence with the person he by choice is. By his lingering susceptibility to them he demonstrates that his choice was not truly such, and he subsists in the condition of indetermination. In his actuality he is "no one in particular." The second sort of "spatial" distraction consists in the lives of persons around him. Insofar as an individual lives by received belief, substituting the judgments, goals, and feelings of others for his own, he lives a surrogate existence by choice of others.

By "temporal" distractions I mean those grappling hooks thrown into the personal present by the personal past and the personal future, dragging it away. The severest temporal distraction afforded by the past appears in that "determination by the primordium" by which the present merely repeats the past endlessly. The eudaimonic individual manifests freedom from determination by the past through the inclusion within his present of a chosen future that decides the meaning of his past.

Concerning the theft of the present by the future, we know it well in the restless dissatisfaction that characterizes a certain sort of striving, termed by F. H. Bradley "the peevish enemy."[15] Here the envisagement of the perfection that lies at the end of striving reduces all relative attainments to ashes. Gradually the incentive in such striving shifts from love of the good to be attained to hatred of the imperfections of what has been achieved—love of the ideal generates hatred of actuality as its correlate. Nothing done is enough; nothing that ever can be done shall be enough. This condition incites the previously cited words by Lucretius—"You [who] always desire what is absent and despise what is at hand." To this we must add, "And when what was absent is brought to hand, despise it."

Eudaimonia is distinguished from "peevish" striving by the presence of its end within it and the presence within it likewise of the gratification of good endings. In familiar terms the end is within the means, and likewise the means within the end. For as we have previously seen the life of the integral individual to constitute but a single act spread over time,[16] so end and means are logically one and the same thing in different expressions. The difference between end and means is a temporal one, stemming from restrictions imposed by temporality itself, namely that a thing cannot present itself all at once. Accordingly eudaimonia does not tolerate the distinction between intrinsic and merely instrumental goods. An "instrumental" good is only good if it contains its end within itself, in which case it is an intrinsic good. "Peevish striving" is the clear indication that the end within the striving is not a true good for the individual whose striving it is. It is, so to speak, advance notice that this end will prove to be ashes upon attainment. "Peevish striving" points to a fundamental mistake in the individual's choice of ends, and constitutes the call for re-choice.

Implicit in what has just been said are two basic characteristics of eudaimonia as a feeling. The first is that eudaimonia is a feeling of the whole person, and the second is that eudaimonia presents itself always as a total feeling.

The two paramount characteristics of personal wholeness are, first, that the past and the future of the individual are contained within his present, and second that, without exception, his analytically separable acts are related by mutual implication. A moment ago we saw that, by the chosen principle of his personhood, the past and future of the eudaimonic individual are contained implicitly in his present. Concerning the second characteristic, every act by the eudaimonic individual derives its meaning from his ultimate possibility. (For example, his diversions and recreations are chosen for their complementary or compensatory relationship to his ultimate possibility and the actual enterprises that presently express it.) Accordingly these separate (strictly, "analytically separable") meanings are expressions of his ultimate possibility under differing situations and differing degrees of personal development. Wholeness is therefore part of the meaning of eudaimonia as a condition, and the feeling of eudaimonia is necessarily a feeling that qualifies the whole. With this in mind we shall term the feeling of eudaimonia a personal feeling. It differs from sensory feeling (itch, tickle, sensory pain) inasmuch as the latter is externally conditioned and spatially localized (it is our thumb that hurts, and from the hot iron). It differs from vital feeling, e.g. pleasure, anguish, happiness, sadness, in that these qualify but a part of the person. It is evident, for example, that disappointment cannot be complete, not only because it cannot qualify the future, but because it requires hope—if only remembered hope—to be what it is, and finally because it cannot qualify and transform the sensory feelings, such as sensory pain. On the other hand pleasure might be thought to be complete and therefore a personal feeling—until it is recognized that as the feeling of gratified desire, pleasure marks a terminus of activity and cannot qualify that perpetual activity that living as a whole is. By contrast, eudaimonia qualifies not the end of activity, but activity itself. Finally, as a personal feeling eudaimonia differs from an emotion, of which love and hate are the paramount examples. For as the term implies, emotions are essentially vectorial, they are themselves movements. Love is the movement to higher value, hatred the movement to lower value: in the words of St. Augustine, "My love is my weight; where it goes, I go."[17] But eudaimonia, while it is the feeling-concomitant of a movement, is not itself a movement. Thus while love includes within itself the lack of that which will fulfill it (Plato, *Symposium*),[18] eudaimonia contains no lack but is pure sufficiency. Indeed, as we shall see, eudaimonia is a superabundance by which personality overflows its native confines to become that environment we shall call personal culture.

As pure sufficiency eudaimonia cannot be qualified by degree, being fully present in its every occasion. In complete purity it attends the activity of living in truth to oneself, no less for the individual who has just set foot upon his path than for the accomplished genius of self-actualization. It can be conceptually analyzed but it is phenomenally simple, appearing completely or not at all. By this characteristic eudaimonia is categorially divorced from sensory feelings and vital feelings. This categorial distinction renders eudaimonism insusceptible to the charge that the life it advocates is one of perpetually dissatisfied striving. Because this charge has often been laid at eudaimonism's door it will be well to put it to rest by pinpointing the misconception in its root.

Consider T. H. Green, a friend of eudaimonism who plays into the hands of its adversaries by perpetrating the misconception in question. For Green, satisfaction attends a person's "consciousness of having accomplished his work."[19] But a person's true work is nothing less than the "complete fulfillment of [his] capabilities,"[20] and this result cannot be attained in a lifetime. In view of this, Green believes that all satisfaction is precluded to living persons. He acknowledges that the aim of fulfillment is approachable, and that resolute individuals can and do move a good way toward it. But he observes that degree of satisfaction does not parallel degree of fulfillment, and he thinks that very likely it is inversely proportional. The basis for this belief is his observation that "probably just in proportion to his elevation of character"[21] an individual is *denied* satisfaction, and he concludes by saying that "We cannot indeed describe any state in which a man . . . would find rest for his soul."[22] On the basis of this line of thought Green deems eudaimonism incomplete without a doctrine of personal immortality, said doctrine functioning to promise the satisfaction that life withholds.

Green thus plays into the hands of eudaimonism's adversaries, notably Henry Sidgwick. Concerning satisfaction, Sidgwick commends to us the proverb, "A miss is as good as a mile."[23] By so saying, Sidgwick perpetuates the mistake fostered by Green. It is the mistake of conceiving all feelings on the model of sensory ones. The Greeks were familiar with this mistake and had a name for those who perpetrated it. They called them worshippers of "belly gods."[24] Supposing that I am just now very hungry and am making my way across town to a favorite restaurant, my hunger does not diminish with the diminution of the distance between me and my meal, and to push open the door of the restaurant, or even to take my seat at a table, affords no least satisfaction of my hunger. For both sensory and vital feelings, the example is a paradigm, because satisfactions of both these kinds are confined to the end of the activities that lead to them. But by our previous argument, personal feelings are not so confined, and as the satisfaction that is a personal feeling, eudaimonia qualifies not the end of activity, but the activity itself. As the feeling of living in truth to oneself, eudaimonia qualifies not the terminus of perfect self-fulfillment, but the relationship of congruence between one's possibility and his actuality—a relationship that must be ceaselessly active. In the last of the above citations from Green, "satisfaction" is equated with "rest for [one's] soul." But the satisfaction termed *eudaimonia* is not found in rest, but in right activity.

Stripped of the misconception just noted, Green's observation about "elevation of character" contains some truth. The individual who progresses at self-actualization does not experience increase of eudaimonic feeling. Necessarily, "elevation of character," in this meaning, includes heightened perspicacity that sees ever better how much remains yet to be done. In this sense the (perceived) horizon recedes as one moves, and the smugness of the novice becomes the humility of the man of accomplishment. This feature is captured in the well-known words by Isaac Newton shortly before his death: "I do not know what I may appear to the world, but to myself I seem to have been only like a boy playing on the sea shore, and diverting myself in now and then finding a smoother pebble or a prettier shell than ordinary, while the great ocean of truth lay all undiscovered before me."[25]

Newton's words are poignant and deeply revelatory, but to suppose that they affirm Green's conclusion that all satisfaction is precluded to mortal men and women is to betray utter ignorance of eudaimonia. Eudaimonia does not increase with degree of achievement, nor does it diminish, for as a personal feeling eudaimonia is fully present in its every occasion.

Earlier we noted in passing that as a personal feeling eudaimonia is distinguished from vital feelings by its capacity to qualify and transform sensory feelings. (That eudaimonia qualifies and transforms vital feelings has previously been exhibited in instances of dysdaimonic and eudaimonic pleasures.) To explicate this capacity we shall choose the sensory feeling of pain, and for a situation we shall revert to the occasion in which every person experiences eudaimonia—the onset of adolescence. This juncture appears in the first free act by which the individual oversteps the boundaries of dependent childhood. His motive in this act is the self-expression that furnishes material for self-discovery (for self-discovery is necessarily a posteriori[26]). In this interest, sensory pain appears as a privileged sort of evidence, for it was first of all as a protection from pain that the individual's childhood was controlled by others. The high school cross-country runner relishes the pains in his legs and chest as evidence that his activity is self-determined. And if his parents condemn the enterprise, his pain (vital feeling) at this he likewise relishes for the same reason. Some of the exhilaration of fighting, war, and physical risk is always, I suspect, attributable to this source. Such experience disallows Kurt Baier's contention that "if there are sensations which we ordinarily dislike but on some occasions like having, then we do not call them pains on those occasions on which we like having them."[27] At this juncture, pain is enjoyed as pain.

If we broaden our scope we find that the above provides an intelligible account of the phenomenon sometimes referred to as "noble suffering." In the words of Moritz Schlick, noble suffering appears "in those cases where a 'higher' but sorrowful life is contrasted with a 'lower' but happy one, and praised as the more valuable."[28] Schlick accepts the evidence that "the great man himself . . . can feel the value of an heroic existence so strongly that despite his 'unhappiness' he would change with no one to whom life's joys came in less adulterated form."[29]

Thus understood, "noble suffering" is a perennial bane to psychological hedonism,[30] but it is entirely consonant with eudaimonism's principles of the psychology of feeling. As herein set forth, the personal feelings of eudaimonia and dysdaimonia underlie and qualify all sensory and vital feelings, including the vital feelings of pleasure and pain. Because it is personal feelings and not vital feelings or sensory feelings that constitute normative indicators, dysdaimonic pleasures are avoided by the person who knows himself and lives in truth to himself, and eudaimonic pains are either welcomed (as in the example from adolescence) or at least accepted within the eudaimonic recognition that these particular pains are rightfully one's own, to be avoided only at the cost of acting in untruth to oneself. Where pleasure and pain are employed as normative indicators, acquaintance with eudaimonia and knowledge of self are lacking. Suppose a man to be walking along a path that contains a pitfall just ahead. A fall into it will likely break his leg, and he skirts it carefully. Now we ask him why he did so. If he is a man with no special place to go, he will tell us that he avoided the pitfall because a broken leg is painful. But if he is bent on getting somewhere, he will tell us that he avoided the pitfall because a broken leg would hinder his getting where he wants to go.

To this parable must only be added that on every path certain pitfalls are unavoidable. They introduce the requirement for the resilience and resourcefulness to clamber out, mend one's leg, and hobble onward—eudaimonically.

At this point in our explication it will be well to distinguish the eudaimonia of adulthood from that of adolescence. In both contexts the term refers to the feeling-concomitant of the condition of integral living. But adolescence precedes the choice by which the individuated self is actualized, hence the self to which the adolescent is to be true is an unindividuated self of generic adolescence, and the attendant feeling is that of generic eudaimonia, undifferentiated among persons. On the other hand by his choice and adherence to the principle of his personhood each adult is profoundly a unique individual, and the eudaimonia he feels is uniquely qualified. This qualitative uniqueness reflects no admixture of non-eudaimonic feelings. Rather, eudaimonia, like subjectivity, is originally a genus that is susceptible of individuation. In a like sense every human activity is susceptible of either generic or individuated performance. The religion a person espouses, the philosophy he enunciates, are often no more than the common belief; his dancing and courtship may be simply à la mode. But in the case of the person who is a unique individual, the philosophy he enunciates will be both generic philosophy and uniquely his, and likewise his dancing and courtship. That the eudaimonia of adulthood is both generic and individuated is but the reflection of the general truth (to be analyzed in Chapter 8) that every person is both generic humankind and the unique individual he is.

Concerning the integration achieved by eudaimonia, Abraham Maslow offers from his clinical studies of self-actualizing persons that, for them, the conventional dichotomy of work and play is "transcended totally. . . . If a person loves his work and enjoys it more than any other activity in the whole world and is eager to get to it, to get back to it after any interruption, then how can we speak about 'labor' in the sense of something one is forced to do against one's wishes?"[31] We can readily distinguish the eudaimonic individual from his caricature, the compulsive careerist, when we remember that the basic "work" of the former is nothing less than his life, while the compulsive person invests himself in what is demonstrably only a part of his life, to the neglect of other aspects. Nor can we allow ourselves to suppose from the Maslow citation that play is renounced by eudaimonia. Instead it is de-compartmentalized and infused throughout productive life as that ludic spirit Plato called the "best part" of man.[32] It is the sublime laughter and delight of all originality. As such it banishes the *gravitas* that envelops "labor," weighing down the spirit so as to preclude its dance.

Nor does integrity preclude play more narrowly conceived but instead includes it by conferring upon it its meaning. Suppose just now we come across dignified Professor Z, and what is he doing but bicycling frenetically, hair flying and elbows and knees thrashing. Or suppose there he is, gleefully playing softball and hollering in very unprofessorial fashion. Incongruity, yes, but only to our eye. For Professor Z has chosen the "unprofessorial" activity to complement the sedentariness and judicious restraint of his vocation, and for him (we shall say) it nicely serves. In the same fashion other apparently disparate activities can be commensurated with an individual's ultimate possibility by deriving their meaning for the individual from that source.

What Kierkegaard called the "will to one thing" is no crabbed asceticism. It is a principle of unrestricted scope, capable of assimilating and rendering congruous everything that the world presents and experience affords—except an alternative principle. Why then does Nietzsche warn of "glittering and loud things"? Because, regarded practically, no person is so strong in his integrity as to be wholly proof against certain distractions that, by his choice of his personal principle, are particularly compelling distractions for him. With this in mind Nietzsche issues his specific warning to philosophers to beware of "fame, princes, and women"[33] —popularity, patronage, and passion. These three things he rightly perceives to be both particularly destructive to the doing of philosophy, and particularly compelling to the philosopher. At the same time each of them *can* be commensurated with a philosophical destiny, but to achieve this will require an exceptional integrity.

But philosophy is Nietzsche's example simply because it is to him home ground. Every other principle of personhood has its peculiar seductions. By seduction is meant an inducement to an alternative principle of personhood. A thing in the world is a seduction, not (*per impossible*) when it exhibits an alternative principle of personhood, but when it exhibits a facet of meaning that is revealed by an alternative principle of personhood. This diversionary capability presupposes the presence within every person of ultimate possibilities and principles of personhood alternative to his chosen ultimate possibility and principle. It is in this sense (to be set forth in Chapter 8) that each person is within himself generic humanity, as well as a distinctive individual. By his choice of his ultimate possibility and principle, each person establishes what for him will constitute his "glittering and loud things." These special seductions are overmatched against the tenacity of a person who is well-advanced at self-actualization, but the beginner is highly vulnerable to them and must be ever watchful.

Extension of the above answers the practical question of eudaimonia's situation. The question concerns the extent to which eudaimonia is situation-dependent. Is it attainable under adverse conditions—in a slum or a prison, for example—or only under conditions so delicate in their prescription as to render eudaimonism impractical? At first glance two contradictory answers appear. On one side it is clear that the eudaimonic individual is exceptionally sensitive to the elements in his situation. This characteristic expresses the necessity for his situation to be *his*, the necessity for the accouterments of his situation to constitute personal culture. By this internal requirement he is, in Robert Frost's words, "instinctively thorough / About [his] crevice and burrow."* This sensitivity is panoramic, extending for example to topography and climate, as in Nietzsche's advice that "Nobody is free to live everywhere; and whoever has to solve great problems that challenge all his strength actually has a very restricted choice in this matter. The influence of climate on our *metabolism*, its retardation, its acceleration, goes so far that a mistaken choice of place and climate can not only estrange a man from his task but can actually keep it from him: he never gets to see it. His animal *vigor* has never become great enough for him to attain that freedom which overflows into the most spiritual regions and allows one to recognize: *this* only I can do."[34]

Nietzsche also stresses the cumulative debilitation produced by minor disparities. Integrity "commands us not only to say No when Yes would be 'selfless' but also to say *No as rarely as possible*. To detach oneself, to separate oneself from anything that would make it necessary to keep saying No. The reason is that whenever defensive expenditures, be they ever so small, become the rule and a habit,

* "A Drumlin Woodchuck"

they entail an extraordinary and entirely superfluous impoverishment."[35]

On this authority it is clear that eudaimonia's situational sensitivity is the very opposite of that for which it is sometimes mistaken—the blindness to situation of the compulsive neurotic. By the overflow of personhood that it is, eudaimonia constitutes the affirmation of each of the constituents of situation in that aspect that corresponds to personal principle. And on the advice of Nietzsche, situations and aspects of situation that do not admit of this affirmation (because the aspects which correspond to personal principle constitute disvalue) must be changed or abolished.

But against all this, have we not seen that the eudaimonic individual is uniquely free of circumstances? Have not circumstances been forced to relinquish their hold by his self-determination? Is this not corroborated by our insistent intuition concerning such an individual that in whatever conditions we may next find him—in prison, say, or selling watermelons from the back of a truck in Boston's Haymarket Square—his distinctive élan will be visible, he will be "where he wants to be, doing what he wants to do"?

Imagine the frustration of Gandhi's adversaries at their discovery that he enjoyed imprisonment and made keenly satisfying use of his time there; he read and wrote. When books and paper were taken away from him, he conversed productively with fellow prisoners and thanked his captors for the opportunity. When social contact was precluded, he meditated—again thanking his captors for the opportunity. Notice how the strategy here employs situation. Gandhi's captors sought to have their way by progressively impoverishing his situation, and Gandhi turned each new restriction into an advantage by choosing an activity that the situation fostered, thereby choosing the situation.

In extremis, again, eudaimonia appeared in the Nazi concentration camps in the persons of Bruno Bettelheim and Viktor Frankl, who made special use of the experience afforded by their imprisonment toward the construction of their respective psychologies of man.[36]

Where does this leave the situational fastidiousness that Nietzsche ascribes to him "who has great tasks to perform"? To neurasthenia? Indeed, the prima facie contradiction lodges in Nietzsche himself, for within the space of just a few pages of *Ecce Homo* he first says, regarding his conduct of certain early years, "I shall never forgive myself," and thereafter we read: "I do not want in the least that anything should become different than it is; I myself do not want to become different. But that is how I have always lived."[37]

But the contradiction is merely appearance. At depth we find the mutual entailment of poles of a continuum. The polar terms are these: the paragon of self-actualization possesses such power of personhood as to be invulnerable to the most antithetic of situations. Conversely some situations are so imposing as to guarantee their triumph over all but the paragon just identified. But by far the preponderance of living lies on the continuum between these extremes, and what is critical here is the ratio between the challenge of the environment and the personal power of the individual. It is this ratio that fully warrants the fastidiousness of the Nietzschean treatment.

An example or two may make this concrete. The rigid "muffin-tin" pattern of departments within the American college or university unquestionably daunts those students whose grasp of themselves is nil or tentative. The rare self-directed student, however, by no means succumbs to it, but like a buccaneer raids the compartments successively, carrying his booty to his private hideaway for sorting and weighing.

Or again, no institution is more coercive upon individuals than that of ordinary language usage. To the student it is completely authoritative, and by far the majority of adults remain subservient to its dictates throughout their lives. What can be expressed in accordance with ordinary language usage, however, is limited to ordinary thoughts and feelings. Only he who surpasses this ordinariness by making language a means for the expression of the extraordinary is a writer in the profound (eudaimonistic) meaning of the term. And thanks to the formidability of the institution of ordinary language usage, he must be possessed of an extraordinary inner conviction.

We shall conclude our consideration of eudaimonia as the quality of integral living by directing some remarks to what is sometimes supposed to be its bête noire, "the death that comes too soon." In Chapter 6 we sought to demonstrate that the well-lived life effects a reconciliation with the death that is one's own, but this reconciliation constitutes old age. In the terms set forth, a good old age presupposes a good maturation, and, to be good, maturation must achieve the consummation of its aim, the aim of self-actualization. But what of the death that does not wait patiently for old age but runs forward to seize the individual before the work of maturation is finished, before that voluntary relinquishment of striving that marks the exchange of maturation for old age?

Opponents of eudaimonism have sometimes argued that its perfectionism insures death's victory over life. For according to eudaimonism the aim of the individual life, as well as the source of its meaning and worth, is a qualitatively unique perfection (termed by us "ultimate possibility"). But perfection is precluded to actuality; therefore by eudaimonism death is conceived as the stroke fated to terminate life short of its goal. And (it is argued) this conception renders eudaimonism self-defeating.

Against this charge, we earlier saw that satisfaction is not precluded by the "death that comes too soon." For as the intrinsic reward of integral living, eudaimonia is not reserved to the conclusion of the process of self-actualization, but in full measure attends every step of the process. Similarly meaning and objective worth are not confined to the terminus but are manifested within the process of self-actualization and—unlike eudaimonia—increase as self-actualization increases. In the words of Bernard Bosanquet, "The great enemy of all sane idealism is the notion that the ideal belongs to the future."[38] Eudaimonism consists not in living for the future, but in subsuming one's future within one's present. One's ultimate possibility is the source of one's worth, meaning, and intrinsic reward, but each of these is actualized by the process of self-actualization, not reserved to perfection.

To the restless striving promoted by the "peevish enemy," death always comes too soon, for all worth has been reserved to the end by the divorce of means from ends. Such persons bargain nervously for time. "I do not admit death" was a regulatory principle in the life of the elder Goethe, who turned his back on death's every reminder, avoided the subject in conversation, and shunned the funerals of his dearest friends. When death came to him at the age of eighty-three, evidence suggests that he was still unready for it. His physician, Dr. Vogel, reported that "His glance expressed the most horrible fear of death."[39] Yet his endemic procrastination likewise endured to the end, serving paradoxically as the invitation to death to interrupt the work short of completion. And if to Goethe's incessant demand for more time the question be put, "For what purpose?," the answer must be: "To do that for which more time will always be required!"

Goethe said to Eckermann that he would not know what to do with an afterlife if it did not provide new tasks and new opportunities. This extrapolative propensity is supported by certain distinctive theories of immortality as exemplified in the thought of Immanuel Kant and Josiah Royce. According to Kant's "moral" argument, immortality is a necessary postulate of the practical reason because the true good consists in the union of virtue and happiness; and although happiness is attainable in this world, virtue consists in an infinite progress of the will toward identity with the moral law—in short it is perpetual progress toward an unattainable perfection. For virtue to be possible it is necessary to postulate the prolongation of life to infinity, affording an infinitude of striving toward perfection.[40] Similarly for Royce, immortality is demanded by the ever-aspiring, never contented moral nature of man. Death cannot be conceived to end this perpetual striving for perfection, for death itself must be purposeful in a purposeful universe. It follows, according to Royce, that the death that terminates a lifetime of striving must give birth to another lifetime of striving, to be followed by another, and another—the apparently separate lifetimes in truth constituting stages in the development of the true individual.[41]

Where lies the consolation in an immortality of striving? It holds none for the youth, for he as yet knows nothing of the "that which I, alone, can do," and in the mode of the adventurer he disdains whatever does not afford quick rewards. An infinitude of striving cannot charm him whose patience is exhausted in a week. Nor is it attractive to old age, which has bid wry goodby to arduousness itself, and will not be lured back to it. To judicious old age such an immortality represents regression.

An immortality of striving is a compensatory expression of a torment by the brevity of time that arises from the adult recognition that worthy achievement necessitates "*obedience* over a long period of time and in a *single* direction."[42] But this torment by the brevity of time is no sensory or vital feeling that can be subsumed and transformed by eudaimonia—it is the personal feeling of dysdaimonia, marking the divorce of striving from its proper goal. In the words of Kierkegaard, "For that which absorbs men's time when they complain about the lack of time is irresoluteness, distraction, half thoughts, half resolutions, indecisiveness, great moments—great moments. It was because of this that we said: to be and to remain loyal to, so that the commitment should not be confused with the extravagance of an expansive moment. The person, who in decisiveness wills to be and to remain loyal to the Good, can find time for all possible things. No, he cannot do that. But neither does he need to do that, for he wills only one thing, and just on that account he will not have to do all possible things, and so he finds ample time for the Good."[43]

As we have noted previously,[44] the mature lifetime of the integral individual is a single act, spread over time by the condition of existence that a thing cannot present itself all at once. But in a profound sense, integrity hereby abolishes time by containing its past and its future in its present. It would make good sense to say that to set foot upon one's path is as good as arriving at the end, provided we recognize that a condition of being upon one's path is to be engaged at walking.

The past and future of the eudaimonic individual are contained in his present in the mode of that moral necessity conferred upon his life by his chosen principle of personhood. Accordingly he would change nothing that he has done, and he has left undone nothing that he ought to have done. At the same time the inclusion of the future in his present means that each act is right for its occasion, and as such it is a mini-consummation, a "little completion." It follows that the individual who is living in truth to himself is ready to die at any time. The sense of this is conveyed in a report by Abraham Maslow of his feelings upon completion of what he identifies only as an "important" piece of work. "I had really spent myself. This was the best I could do, and here was not only a good time to die but I was even willing to die . . . It was what David M. Levy called the 'completion of the act.' It was like a good ending, a good close." What follows the good close is termed by Maslow "post-mortem life." He says, "I could just as easily have died so that my living constitutes a kind of extra, a bonus. It's all gravy. Therefore I might just as well live as if I had already died." What comes next in Maslow's account sounds a new note. "One very important aspect of the post-mortem life," he says, "is that everything gets doubly precious, gets piercingly important. You get stabbed by things, by flowers and by babies and by beautiful things—just the very act of living, of walking and breathing and eating and having friends and chatting. Everything seems to look more beautiful rather than less, and one gets the much-intensified sense of miracles."[45]

For myself, I cannot imagine a better evocation of the wonder that must have filled Adam in the moment when he first opened his eyes upon the world.

But it must be stressed that in the integral life the aspect of a "little completion" attends every act, no matter how minute and insignificant. It is by no means restricted to major works such as Maslow describes.

By the eudaimonic individual death is not feared as the "period" by which a tragic fate cuts short the unfinished sentence. In the biography of the good life every sentence is a fitting epitaph and *is the epitaph* until it is succeeded by the next sentence. "Little completions" are in some parts of the world called "little deaths," and this should be understood in more than a figurative sense. To account for this manifestation of death within life, Freud has suggested that after Eros has been diminished by a satisfaction, Thanatos has a free hand.[46] In every case but one, this "little completion" is followed by new requirements for rightness in new occasions, constituting a "little rebirth." In light of this we must broaden Socrates's observation that all philosophy is a preparation for death. Every mature act, when well done, is an appearance of death in life.

Therefore to the good life death is no stranger, no alien event opposed to life, and death does not "take us by surprise," as Sartre says, nor "alienate us wholly in our own life."[47] Death is life in its consummation, and because consummation is perpetually within the well-lived life, so likewise is death within that life. The conception of death as alien to life is the product of a death-aversion which, by attempting to banish death from the sphere of life, precludes to life its consummation and its worth.

8

Our Knowledge of Other Persons

The purpose of this chapter and the two that follow is to make explicit those normative principles of sociality that subsist implicitly in the ethics of self-actualization. Our general thesis asserts the strict continuity of personal and social ethics. Conceived ethically, the personal, the interpersonal, and the social stand not as separate spheres, independently regulated, but as concentric circles of a single figure. In virtue of continuity no conflict of principle is possible between true personal interest and true social interest, and social- and self-responsibility are distinguishable aspects of an identical set of requirements. In particular the amputation of personal interest from the domain of the ethical, as is intended by some uses of the term "prudence," cannot be tolerated.

How glibly men discourse about "humanity," "society," "the Germans," "the French," "politicians," "scientists," "the rich," "the poor"—and how haltingly each man truly speaks of himself! But surely to speak meaningfully of many persons is to compound the difficulties of speaking meaningfully about a solitary individual.

The key to the disparity lies in this, that in our discussions of collectivities no persons appear but only integers, which as such present few problems to the mind and offer no resistance to collectivization. On the other hand, to himself each person is a locus of the most exasperating problems. With what relief, then, are persons dispensed with in favor of unproblematic masses. But what entitles the manipulators to reduce persons to integers, and whence comes the inducement to the integers to accept such representation?

Depersonalization is sanctioned by the well-entrenched supposition of common sense that "personality" is a strictly private affair, unavailable socially. No one can feel another person's toothache, and likewise for his joy, his sorrow, his desire, even his ideas. Perhaps there are "sympathetic feelings" such that the joy of another produces joy in us who witness it, but what we feel is our joy, not his. Certainly there are ideas that persons can hold alike, but such ideas are social, not personal; they are "everyone's." The conclusion drawn by common sense is that one can have no immediate knowledge of the private side of another person. The most one can do is to infer what others may think or feel from their visible and audible behavior. But in this case one can know nothing of the other apart from what one already knows from his own case. By this means of "analogical inference" the only person to appear is oneself, and what one terms "others" are merely replications of oneself in other bodies and locations.

As Santayana observes, there are cases "in which the pathetic fallacy is not fallacious."[1] Analogical inference affords genuine knowledge in certain gross cases of public response, for example crowd fear. Additionally it affords knowledge where individuals act out of the residuum of the shared subjective content within every person. And doubtless analogical inference must ever be utilized where nothing else is available. But to rest sociality upon it is to preclude unique personhood, thereby precluding to sociality the irreplaceable worth of true individuals, and insuring that, with respect to social regulations, each individual privately makes an exception of himself. Such sociality is that of interchangeable integers, and it most certainly exists. But by the precepts of self-actualization ethics it is to be superseded by an interpersonal sociality built upon the complementarity of unique persons. This interpersonal sociality presupposes the communicability of unique personhood, and we must here demonstrate the possibility of immediate, internal knowledge of other persons where "other" means not merely numerical but qualitative difference.

Consider the everyday occurrence of misunderstanding between two persons. In its root instance, person A witnesses an act by person B ("act" is here used broadly to include any perceptible behavior, thus spoken words are verbal acts, witnessed aurally) and ascribes to it a meaning that is not B's but (in the common case) would be A's if the act were A's own. Here is ordinary misunderstanding, and we shall suppose that it becomes apparent to B, i.e. that A acts on the meaning that he mistakenly ascribes to B's act, and that the inappropriateness of A's response is recognized by B. Perhaps A responds belligerently, where no offense was meant by B.

Insofar as B's act was a personal expression and not a mere usage (which, as what "everyone" does, is strictly anonymous), B's recognition of misunderstanding occurs as a perceptible shock, the shock of the experience we refer to as "seeing oneself through the eyes of another"—a phrase we shall find to be no idle figure of speech. The shock attests to the juxtaposition of two incommensurable meanings. Under B's meaning B's act coheres with antecedent and subsequent acts by B; under A's meaning it is incongruous in this context. B's meaning derives from the locus of meaning that is B's person, while every alternative meaning of the given act adheres to a different locus of meaning that is a different person. The meaning A ascribes to B's act commensurates the act with A's person and at the same time renders the act incommensurate with B.

The shock of incommensurability contains nothing hidden but instead registers a two-fold awareness. B wanted to be seen in a certain way but in fact is seen differently. The two-fold recognition by B is possible because *independently of A's empirical presence*, A's meaning for B's act is known to B as a possible meaning of the act. Thus it is that when A presents his meaning for B's act it is possible for B to recognize it, saying, "Yes, I might have meant that by my act, but in fact I did not." It is only in virtue of such recognition that misunderstanding can appear *qua* misunderstanding, i.e. in both its terms.

What this discloses is the presence within every person of meanings alternative to his own. Indeed, for "his own" to be applicable in the full (self-responsible) sense, the meaning that is his must constitute a selection from a spectrum of possibilities. Normally such selection is intuitive or habitual, and scarcely evident to introspection or reflexive awareness. But it becomes fully evident—sometimes painfully so—in novel situations wherein one must, as we say, "sort out" his feelings. In such situations we try out one feeling after another in search of the feeling that is ours. Often in confusion we withdraw from the situation for a time, returning later for a fresh start. Throughout such experimentation we are aware that the feelings (attitudes, ideas, aims) we try out are possible feelings for the situation. We discard them because we are not comfortable with them. Our discomfort signals that the feeling in question is incommensurate with our other feelings (etc.) and will, if adopted, require significant revision throughout the rest. Such thoroughgoing revision is by no means impossible. Where it is undertaken, we speak of a "conversion" and of the initiating feeling as an "illumination" or "revelation." But conversions are extraordinary happenings. Normally in the novel situation we hunt down the feeling that at least roughly commensurates with our other feelings and thoughts, identifying it as our own. Meanwhile the feelings that have been felt but rejected are such as to commensurate with persons not ourselves, they are feelings belonging to other persons.

For future reference we may note here that the absence of "our" feeling with respect to a given situation is not in the nature of a true lack but is, on the contrary, a superabundance. This finding can be generalized as the principle of subjective plenitude: in consciousness no voids exist, every absence connoting the presence of content other than that which was sought.

As a subjective event a feeling is a meaning, and the presence within the person of alternative possible feelings is the presence of alternative possible meanings. This attests to the presence within him of alternative ultimate possibilities and principles of personhood. With respect to this presence the words of Terence are a profound truth: "*Nihil humani a me alienum puto*"—for nothing human is alien to any person. Within every person are all human possibilities; here is each individual's generic humanity. It subsists, not as an amorphous universal, but as the constellation of discrete human possibilities.

In standard form, the problem of knowledge of other minds has two parts: how can a person know that minds other than his own exist? And how can he know the present concrete content of another's mind? We are now prepared to outline the answers to both questions. To begin with the first: a given individual knows of the subsistence of minds other than his own immediately and autonomously, for they subsist within himself as principles of personhood alternative to his own and are available to him as such. In virtue of this, a hypothetical Robinson Crusoe, having lived entirely without human contact, would yet know himself to be inherently a social being. But what thus subsists within constitutes only possible others. Others' existence is demonstrated only by their actual presence as the actualizations of their respective possibilities.

Here it will be well to allay the superstition that what appears to us in lieu of other persons is their bodies. Against it, P. F. Strawson correctly insists upon the "primitiveness of the concept of the person,"[2] as Max Scheler rightly insists upon the "altogether primary givenness"[3] of the whole person, of which the body is expressive. At first encounter with another, such personal phenomena as friendliness or unfriendliness, "withness" or "againstness," are perceptually prior to physical traits or movements. This priority of expressive phenomena is demonstrated by the ubiquitous animism of primitive peoples and of our own children. Sophistication delimits the field of the expressive phenomena of personhood, but by no means eliminates it. Blond or black hair, blue, green, or brown eyes, pug or aquiline noses would not warrant a tenth of the interest they hold for us but for their expressive function, and so a forteriori for gesture and movement.

The priority in perception of persons is further attested by the strenuous effort required in those exceptional circumstances where the presentations of the other must be restricted to body alone—e.g. in medical practice and in the sustaining of sexual lust. To restrict his patients' presentations to pure body (or due to specialization, to pure spleen, heart, lungs, etc.) the physician must actively police their demeanor in the examination and consulting rooms until they learn to police themselves. Meanwhile the physician's own powers of abstractive attention will be exercised to the full. In the matter of sexual lust (defined as the desire for pure flesh), it is a rare and precarious phenomenon in human beings, requiring guileful gymnastics to sustain. The reversion from concrete human relations to pornography and sadism; the tactic expressed in Don Juan's perpetual cry, "To horse and to spur!"—these and the other devices employed by lust are eloquent testimony to the intrusiveness of personality. It was Freud's considered judgment that lust requires the active degradation of its object.[4] That the other must be reduced to pure flesh is conclusive evidence that he or she does not originally appear as such.

But our account of the primary givenness of personhood differs from Strawson's in one important respect. For Strawson, while the concept of the person cannot be reduced to mere body, neither can it be reduced to a disembodied consciousness, or "Cartesian ego." But for us the concept of the person is originally that of a purely conscious entity, for in its primitive form it is the concept, not of an actual, but of a possible person.

What Strawson means by the concept of a person "is the concept of a type of entity such that *both* predicates ascribing states of consciousness *and* predicates ascribing corporeal characteristics, a physical situation &c. are equally applicable to a single individual of that single type."[5] The reason for the necessity of the corporeal character is that, for Strawson, it is the only available determinant of the "otherness" that is, he thinks, requisite to the ascription of states of consciousness. His "central thought" is that "it is a necessary condition of one's ascribing states of consciousness, experiences, to oneself, in the way one does, that one should also ascribe them, or be prepared to ascribe them, to others who are not oneself."[6] But the states of consciousness one is to ascribe to oneself and to others are identical (in Strawson's terms, the ascribing phrases are identical, and they are used "in just the same sense when the subject is another as when the subject is oneself"[7]). This means that the only differentiation is the material differentiation of separate bodies. In Strawson's words,

> If, in identifying the things to which states of consciousness are to be ascribed, private experiences are to be all one has to go on, then, just for the very same reason as that for which there is, from one's own point of view, no question of telling that a private experience is one's own, there is also no question of telling that a private experience is another's. All private experiences, all states of consciousness, will be mine, i.e. no one's. To put it briefly. One can ascribe states of consciousness to oneself only if one can ascribe them to others. One can ascribe them to others only if one can identify other subjects of experience. And one cannot identify others if one can identify them *only* as subjects of experience, possessors of states of consciousness.[8]

Against this, however, we have shown that one *can* distinguish *in himself* between states of consciousness that are his own and states of consciousness that are others. The basis of this distinction is qualitative difference in the states of consciousness. When one hunts for and finds the feeling that is his own, he distinguishes it from other feelings by its specific quality, by which it commensurates with the person he is. And he discards alternative possible feelings by recognizing their alternative qualities to be incommensurable with the person he is. Thus person X recognizes that he might experience pleasure at the misfortune of an acquaintance but in fact he does not; person B might experience discouragement at the failure of a piece of work, but in fact does not. In such cases the rejected qualities of feeling stand as "other" to the person in question, representing the self-differentiation of subjective contents, a differentiation wholly independent of the spatial distribution of bodies. To repeat what has been said earlier, such differentiation constitutes the recognition of other persons only as possibilities, not as actualities. Recognition of their actuality requires their actual presence, and experience teaches that embodiment is a condition of such actual presence. I have no intention of pursuing the remaining logical possibility of the actualization of disembodied minds. Crucial to our position as against Strawson's is that by the differentiation just noted, other persons are shown to differ from ourselves not merely numerically but also qualitatively.

The person of the other appears to us as an "altogether primary givenness," and we recognize him both as qualitatively different from ourselves and as the unique person he is on the ground of the alternative possible persons within ourselves. For on the conception herein developed every person is a universal–particular; he is both a unique destiny and "humanity" in the form of the total constellation of human possibilities. The resulting structure of interpersonal relations can be clarified with the aid of a diagram.

Within each person all human possibilities subsist, one alone of which has been actualized as a potentiality (represented by the capital letter at the center), constituting the locus of meaning that this individual is, while the others

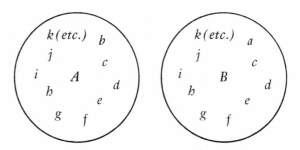

The figures represent two persons, A and B.

(represented by lower case letters) remain unactualized. In the confrontation symbolized above, B can be known immediately by A by the actualization within A of possibility b. The process of such knowledge is termed "participatory enactment" by Max Scheler, *Verstehen* by Wilhelm Dilthey, and "imaginative re-enactment" by R. G. Collingwood.*

---

* "Participatory enactment" appears tantalizingly in Thomas Nagel's recent inquiry, "What Is It Like to Be a Bat?" *Philosophical Review*, 82, No. 4 (Oct. 1974), 435-450. As the definitive characteristic of consciousness, Nagel offers the following: "But fundamentally an organism has conscious mental states if and only if there is something it is like to *be* that organism—something it is like *for* the organism." All experiential facts of an organism embody the point of view of the organism. To know the experience of another organism (a bat, in Nagel's example; but equally another person) or even to form a conception of it, one must be able to adopt its point of view. On this ground Nagel argues that objective knowledge of the experience of other organisms cannot be had by any procedure that disregards the point of view from which the experience is had. "It is difficult to understand what could be meant by the *objective* character of an experience, apart from the particular point of view from which its subject apprehends it. After all, what would be left of what it was like to be a bat if one removed the viewpoint of the bat." Nagel concludes this line of thought with a "speculative proposal" for a "new method" by which to obtain objective knowledge of consciousness, an "objective phenomenology not dependent on empathy or the imagination." Its goal would be "to describe, at least in part, the

The major limitation upon it is imposed by the incommensurability of *a* and *b* as organizing principles of alternative total perspectives or "points of view." It means that the actualization of possibility *b* within *A* requires the temporary lapse of *A*'s actuality. (Without this lapse, *B* can only appear to *A* as the meaning he has for *A*.) By his actualization of *b*, *A* is introduced to an alternative world of meanings. No jeopardy to *A*'s identity results, for *A*'s innate potentiality remains what it was, ready to be reassumed.

What requires the *empirical* presence of one person to another is not internal knowledge of others per se, but only the coincidence of our knowledge of another with the actual

---

subjective character of experiences in a form comprehensible to beings incapable of having those experiences."

But this is an impossible goal: for Nagel acknowledges that "At present we are completely unequipped to think about the subjective character of experience without relying upon imagination." This means that we are equally incapable of thinking about a new science for this purpose that does not rely upon imagination. What Nagel says of physicalism—that it "is a position we cannot understand because we do not at present have any conception of how it might be true"—rebounds upon his "new method" in a *tu quoque*.

But if, as Nagel (correctly) suggests, it is by imagination that we take up other viewpoints, why indeed must we cast about for a "new method" that is "not dependent" upon imagination? Agreed, the method of imagination is, as we know it, loose and undisciplined: but the logical recourse would seem to be to give our careful attention to the cultivation and discipline of imagination as the method of "participatory enactment." Such is the proposal offered at the end of this chapter. The criterion of objectivity with respect to conscious experience will then be found in the ability of all persons to take the point of view of the given subject with respect to the subject's experience.

Concerning knowledge of other persons (I have nothing to say about bats), Nagel gratuitously aggravates the problem by describing it as knowledge of experiences that is to be had by "beings incapable of having those experiences." But there is no such incapacity. For it is the profound truth of the maxim of Terence—*Nihil humani a me alienum puto*—that any experience by any person is available to every other person (by "participatory enactment").

person whom on a given occasion we wish to know. Suppose that just now person Z is viewing a sunset from the high windows of his New York City apartment at the conclusion of a strenuous day. The subjective contents that constitute "his" response to the sunset will be consistent with the person he is. But at the same time he is pelted by a quiet hail of foreign essences, each implicated in an alternative response. His response to the sunset will be consistent with the person he is because such consistency is a necessary part of the meaning of personhood. In virtue of it, each present moment invokes a consistent past and a consistent future, transcending that "solipsism of the present moment" that would otherwise obtain, and that is inconsistent with personhood. But the meaning of each present moment represents a selection amid alternative possible meanings.

Ordinarily the quiet hail of foreign meanings goes unrecognized precisely because in relation to the person in question—in our example person Z—the meanings are foreign. To acknowledge one of them would be to experience a moment shorn of past and future, a "moment out of time." When such recognition occurs it constitutes the experience we term a "revelation" or "illumination." Such an experience seems to afford a glimpse, usually brief and fugitive, into an alternative world. As discontinuous with the familiar world it lacks apparent utility with respect to that world.* Yet for the individual who is prepared to relinquish his familiar world for a time, it affords access to another world, the world constituted by a different mind according to an alternative principle of meaning. In this case the "il-

* Its underlying utility with respect to the familiar world is certified, however, by for example the actress, who for purposes of self-criticism learns to view her performance from the standpoints of different types of persons constituting her audience; or the writer, who learns to read his work from the standpoints of representative critics. Such activities as these involve the exchange of incommensurable perspectives, and are straightforward instances of "seeing oneself through the eyes of another." Concerning the use here of *types* of persons, more shall be said subsequently.

lumination" is seized upon as the starting point for memory, anticipation, and inferential reason, thereby divulging a qualitatively novel continuum.*

The important points here are that such novel continua constitute the topographies of other minds, and that the foreign essences that afford access to them are continuously available to every person. Every person therefore has continuous access to minds qualitatively different from his own. Here is the foundation for the immediate, non-inferential knowledge of the actual other persons who appear before us. Lately we have seen that others appear to us not as bodies to which personhood must be attached by inference, but immediately and fully as persons. However this is not to say that the actual other is known to us immediately and at the outset as the other person he is (for if such were the case sociality would be inherently destructive of the integrity of individuals), but only that from the outset he appears to us immediately as the distinctive interpersonal problem. For such is the profound tenor of the interpersonal—it is the region of the fundamentally problematic. By contradistinction from nonpersonal things and events, the presence before us of another person is an invitation to enter a perspectival world alternative to our own.† To accept the invitation is to undertake to correlate an unactualized possibility within us with the actual person who presents himself to us. The process of such correlation is falli-

* But not a metaphysically superior region. It is the mistake of intuitionists such as Plato and H. Bergson to have restricted intuitive apprehension to but one alternative to the actual world, and to have regarded that alternative as metaphysically superior to actuality. The alternatives available through intuition are not metaphysically superior to actuality but strictly alternative.

† By no means is it the violent expropriation of our world by "the look" of the other, as Sartre maintains in *Being and Nothingness*, Part III. Sartre overlooks counterindications, notably the pure generosity that inheres in selfhood and is expressed as personal culture. "The look" cannot steal what the individual perpetually gives. The adoption of the viewpoint of another is the paradigm of the purely voluntary.

ble and groping, consisting in the imaginative enactment of one possibility after another, but it lends itself to the acquisition of efficiency and skill. And the mark of success is patent, consisting in discovery of the other's internal necessity such that his actual past and future are contained in our present recognition of him. From our initial illumination a continuum unfolds that is confirmed by the other's existence as the continuum constituted by his personal principle. Herewith we possess what Leibniz called the "complete concept" of the other person.[10]

It will be apparent that knowledge of other persons on the model here described presupposes the individuation and integrity of the persons concerned, and therefore that the sociality for which this knowledge is a condition likewise presupposes individuation. But we have seen in Chapter 6 that individuation derives from the choice with which maturation begins, and is not actual theretofore. Does this commit us to the view that sociality itself is a late emergent in human development? But demonstrably every person is social before he is individual, and there are forms of sociality that presuppose nothing in the way of individuation. In recognition of this we must now attend to a categorial distinction between two broad kinds of sociality, to be termed antecedent sociality and consequent sociality. Every human being is social in the beginning and social in the end, but the two socialities are radically different in kind in virtue of the intervening attainment to individuality. The first is a received sociality to which the person (as child and adolescent) is responsible; the second is a constituted sociality for which he shares responsibility. The sociality that follows from the choice of oneself in no way compromises this choice but extends and fulfills it. It asks for no sacrifice of individuality to the collective interest but exemplifies the principle of the complementarity of true individuals.

The normative principles of sociality implicit in principles of self-actualization pertain exclusively to consequent sociality. But consequent sociality should be viewed in developmental context, hence we must sketch the antecedent sociality from which it is emergent.

We have spoken of the subsistence within every person of differentiated possibilities constituting the personal principles of other individuals, actual and possible. But also contained within every person, even the most highly individuated, is a residuum of undifferentiated common content that is *sensu stricto* not his own but "everyone's," belonging to no person more than another.

To uncover this content, we may consider, for example, the writer, who must scrupulously distinguish in his manuscript between his own ideas and borrowed ideas that he must credit to others. This can be confidently done only in rare instances, e.g. direct citations. Most often the responsibility is mixed. Another's loose suggestion has congealed a set of thoughts on which our man has been knitting for some time. Or the idea in question is clearly borrowed, but not from an individual so much as from a "school" of thought, spread over time and geography, but nonetheless in this respect "of like mind." The insolubility of the problem is acknowledged informally by our agreement to regard the preponderance of ideas as "in the public domain," and formally by the stricture of copyright law that ownership can be predicated, not of ideas themselves, but only of particular formulations.* In general, most ideas are considered to belong no more to one person than to another. Now notice that the arena in which such difficulties are encountered is the head of the writer of whom we speak. Here is a second refutation of common sense's supposition that "a man can think only his own thoughts" (". . . and feel only his own feelings"—but feelings remain to be considered). In the subjective life of every individual is much that is in

---

* "The copyright protects the language used and the development, treatment, arrangement and sequence of the ideas and facts contained in the copyrighted work. Ideas and facts as such are not subject to copyright." Harriet F. Pilpel and Morton David Goldberg, *A Copyright Guide* (New York: R. R. Bowker Co., 1969), p. 5.

no distinctive sense his own. When Kierkegaard issues the judgment "the crowd is untruth,"[11] he directs it to the crowd that is within every person. The judgment of its untruth derives from normative individualism.

The source of the residuum of common content is not obscure, for it is childhood itself. Childhood is dependence and receptivity, lacking autonomy and origination. This does not connote passivity, but it means that the expression of childhood must be furnished with forms and content—words, concepts, judgments, feelings. The materials supplied to childhood are the common property of the community, and they are supplied to every child alike. Necessarily every child learns to use language as "everyone" uses it, and likewise he learns to judge as "everyone" judges, and to feel as "everyone" feels. The judgments that he learns to offer constitute the "common sense" of the community. From the outset such judgments are adopted by the child in the mode of received beliefs. And if the pronouncements of common sense often go unquestioned throughout later life, by no means does this demonstrate their indubitability (as for example G. E. Moore has claimed).[12] They go unquestioned because they have become entrenched as habits of belief before such questioning is possible.

Likewise for feelings—but the prevalence of the superstition that feelings are somehow personal and self-originated from the outset necessitates a demonstration of their derivation. Against this superstition the evidence that "the feelings" are the product of the learning that characterizes antecedent sociality is twofold. In the first place we have direct evidence that small children "do not know their own feelings" and must be taught to identify them. Second, evidence from cross-cultural studies strongly suggests that such identification-training constitutes actualization of a limited repertoire of feelings from a much wider spectrum of possibilities of feeling.

Even such (to us) fundamental feelings as pleasure and happiness require identification-training. A young child cannot identify in himself the feeling of happiness, and will often ask its parents what happiness is, sometimes inquiring plaintively, "Is what I am feeling now 'happiness'?" The parent teaches the quality of feeling the word denotes by arranging the conditions under which the feeling is likely to appear. Perhaps mother takes the opportunity of the child's approaching birthday and arranges a party for him, telling him that what he will feel on that occasion is happiness. But in the midst of the party the child's feelings are likely to be in fact kaleidoscopic. At the moment he asks mother, "Am I happy now?" he may well be anxious and in tears. Reading the signs, mother will make adjustments in the situation. Perhaps after considerable manipulation she perceives the signs that enable her to say, "What you feel now is happiness." The method of definition here is operational, consisting in guiding the child to the conditions under which the feeling appears.

Historical and cross-cultural studies furnish abundant evidence that the repertoire of common feelings varies remarkably from age to age and from culture to culture.[13] Such formerly foundational feelings as were marked by the Greek eros and eudaimonia, or the Latin *amor fati*, are now unrecognized and unactualized, while the feeling we Americans associate with romantic love—and take great pains to cultivate—is not widespread, and *anomie*, "alienation," and "estrangement" are localized twentieth-century phenomena. The inescapable conclusion is that what a given culture regards as "the feelings" is but a narrow band of subjective qualities, elicited by the culture in question from a much more extensive potentiality for feeling in human beings.

Conversely, every culture precludes unwanted feelings by forbidding the situations in which the unwanted feelings are prone to arise. Thus our own culture works to curtail erotic feelings between parent and child of opposite sex by prescribing separate bedrooms in the home, avoidance of unnecessary genital contact, and a "closed door" bathroom policy. By situational regulation it also constricts feelings of tenderness between men, aggressive feelings in women, nonretrospective feelings of self-worth in the aged, and the asexual feelings of comradeship between men and women. To deliberately preclude certain feelings, of course, requires prior recognition of those feelings, but only initially. Customary practice over the years loses all trace of its origins, and the feelings in question disappear.

Moreover, by its common sense categories, a given culture insures that of the feelings had, only selected ones are retained while the rest are eliminated by inattention. Feelings that "fall between the cracks," so to speak, of common sense categories go uncultivated, undiscussed, and unreflected-upon, and in this condition they prove highly fugitive. The case is analogous to that of dreams, which are highly fugitive under the working supposition of common sense that dream-life is insignificant compared to waking life. If these priorities become altered—perhaps by undergoing psychoanalysis, or simply by reading Freud, Adler, or Jung—an immense amount of dream-content is recovered that had theretofore been unavailable. That the same result obtains for "day dreaming," or reverie, is demonstrated in studies of the subject by such investigators as William James, Henri Bergson, Marcel Proust, James Joyce, and Gaston Bachelard. And so it is for directed consciousness. In particular, feelings retained in self-awareness are but a small proportion of the feelings had, because the common sense of a given culture cannot, if it is to perform its simplifying and ordering function, retain and interrelate all feelings that are had. According to the independent studies of Mircea Eliade and Abraham Maslow,[14] Western life today is hereby shorn of an entire class of feelings that it can ill afford to do without—the "religious" feelings such as joy, ecstasy, awe, reverence, the sense of the sacred, of the sublime, of the daemonic. By what Eliade calls the "desacralization" of modern life, common sense has progressively pushed out the feelings of the sacred. Maslow's specific contention is that such feelings are necessary to meaningful living, and are not inherently connected to doctrinal super-naturalism. He urges that a viable naturalistic humanism must undertake to recover them on natural ground.

Given the constriction that characterizes the received common subjectivity with which the encultured lives of persons begins, one source of the materials of subsequent individuation is immediately apparent. It is the reservoir of possible feelings, sensations, desires, intentions, and concepts, unactualized by childhood training, that may later be actualized by novel situations and cultivated under altered priorities. But of equal importance for individuation is that modulation of aspects of the common subjective content, provision for which is contained in the very notion of a common content.

The foregoing bears directly on the "private language question" and arguments deriving from it. As childhood receives a common subjective content, so it receives the common language. But a condition of a common language is the relative indeterminacy of its terms. The term "pain," for example, is a genus-word for a generic feeling. To be sure, Strawson is correct when he points out that the dictionaries give but a single set of meanings that is to apply without discrimination to everyone's pain. But the scope of the feeling denoted by the term is susceptible of an infinite variation of instances. In childhood the generic term is legislative, and variation can be ignored, for childhood is in essence unindividuated, being individuated only contingently. But the quality of pain of the true individual is unique to himself, while yet remaining within the scope denoted by the generic term "pain." So, too, for all other substantive terms of the common language, whether their referents be objective or subjective. The modulated meanings of "table," "typewriter," "automobile," "love," "hate," "justice"—alike derive their modulation from the ultimate possibility of the individual, and will be qualitatively unique in cases of true individuals. Accordingly private languages are not only possible but invariably actual in true (unique) individuals. And they are recognized as such by their users, notably by the effort to which such an individual will sometimes be put to use ordinary terms in the ordinary way. Nor is private language by any means lacking in practical utility. It has paramount utility for personal growth as the language of the inner dialectic, the language in which one speaks to oneself, the language of self-criticism and self-advancement. But no less importantly, private language constitutes the *limit* of the modulation that is expressed, in lesser degree, in the specialized meanings for ordinary terms that characterize our distinctive disciplines and schools of thought.* The susceptibility to modulation of ordinary language is the invitation to disciplinary specialization and perspectivism, and a prime condition of the advancement of knowledge. And finally, private language is communicable by the means to knowledge of the individuated other herein described. To know another is to know the modulations which make up his private language by actualizing their principle.

Dictionary meanings catalogue the content of antecedent sociality as individuated meanings constitute the content of

---

* I intentionally represent common language, disciplinary language, and private language, as stations on a continuum of refinement. Disciplinary language, like common language, but unlike private language, expresses a shared point of view. Unlike common language, but like private language, it does not in principle embody a relative indeterminacy of terms, but aims at precision. Both disciplinary language and private language are arrived at, not by a radical infusion of the subjectivity of individuals, but by controlled modulations of ordinary meanings according to special interest and perspective. They begin by refining the meanings of common terms, and thereafter may coin new terms where the disparity of meanings is great.

I do not wish to misrepresent disciplinary language by overplaying its resemblances to private language, but to overlook these resemblances is to misrepresent it no less. In particular, disciplinary language expresses a point of view to which alternatives exist. The notion that it, uniquely, is viewpointless, and thus the language of independent "reality," is but a chauvinism associated with pretensions to "presuppositionless science."

consequent sociality. Concerning the question whether one can "start from one's own case" for knowledge of other persons, the distinction between antecedent and consequent sociality must be invoked. An example of the misconceptions that result from failure to take account of this distinction is provided by Strawson's argument against the possibility of starting from oneself. "There is no sense," Strawson says, "in the idea of ascribing states of consciousness to oneself, or at all, unless the ascriber already knows how to ascribe at least some states of consciousness to others. So he cannot argue in general 'from his own case' to conclusions about how to do this; for unless he already knows how to do this, he has no conception of *his own case*, or any *case*, i.e. any subject of experiences."[15] This contention is entirely correct with respect to the terms of antecedent sociality—in short it is true for children. For the self of the child *is* a "one among others like itself" and therefore cannot be known apart from the "others like itself." In the case of the child there can be no otherness within the subjective content of the individual, for childhood antedates the process of individuation that produces such subjective differentiation. Therefore *in this situation* (the situation of antecedent sociality) corporeality, as Strawson says, must be part of what is meant by "person," for it is exclusively by corporeal characteristics that otherness arises. The states of consciousness that are ascribed to others are the identical states of consciousness that one ascribes to oneself, and they are ascribed to others and to oneself "in just the same sense."[16]

But none of this holds for individuated adults for whom, as we have seen, the process of individuation introduces the distinction within the subjective contents of the individual between those that are his own and those that belong to others. Because the individual has immediate access to the whole of this differentiated subjective content, it constitutes what is meant by the individual's "own case" in the ordinary sense. And under this meaning the individual's knowledge of others is indeed achieved by starting with his own case.

He discovers others within himself in the form of subjective content that resists self-ascription because it is incommensurable with the unique person he is. But the content he thus ascribes to others is therefore *not* the same content he ascribes to himself, but qualitatively different content. It is in this fundamental respect that the "others" of consequent sociality are different from the "others" of antecedent sociality. Hence if Strawson were to be re-affirmed on the ground that, because childhood precedes maturation, the "start" to which we have just referred is not strictly such, we would respond that within antecedent sociality the term "others" can have but the attenuated meaning of numerical difference, and the start to which we refer is strictly such with respect to "others" in the full meaning of persons qualitatively different from oneself in terms of subjective content and its organizing principle.

Wittgenstein's denial of the possibility of starting from one's own case is closely tied to what he takes to be the impossibility of private language.[17] By private language he means a language grounded in first-person psychological statements applicable exclusively to the given person himself. But such a language rests upon the ability of the solitary individual to identify in himself determinate subjective qualities—for example a pain, an annoyance, an anger—and this identification requires a means for distinguishing between correct and incorrect instances. But for the solitary individual no such means exists. He cannot look to his own behavior, for his behavior follows from (or *is*) this identification. Nor can he look to memory for such a criterion, for what check has he on his own memory? If he has consistently misidentified his own subjective qualities his memory will only perpetuate the error. In sum, the solitary individual has no way to distinguish between correct and incorrect identifications, and in the absence of such a criterion the notion of identification is empty.

To avoid the appalling implication that the plethora of first-person psychological statements in daily discourse is a monumental mistake, Wittgenstein offers a covering suggestion: "Here is one possibility: words are connected with the primitive, the natural, expressions of sensation and used in their place."[18] According to Norman Malcolm the meaning of this is that first-person psychological statements have "nothing to do with recognizing or identifying or observing a state of oneself."[19] Moreover on Malcolm's reading of Wittgenstein, self-reference is not the intention of ordinary persons when they make such statements. But surely, by those who strain at the gnat we are here being asked to swallow a camel. I submit that in Wittgenstein here and throughout, we have an example of highly individuated language use, to which full entitlement has been affirmed by our argument of preceding pages. But the claim that such use is the common usage, or ought to be, has no entitlement whatever.

In this connection a basic question arises concerning the program of linguistic analysis as philosophy. The program seeks by analysis to establish precise meanings of significant words, together (sometimes) with the ascertainment of the natures and logical properties of concepts. Insofar as it limits its scope to the establishment of meanings (etc.) for a specific employment—in a given book, for example, or within a determinate school of thought—it is faultless and merely reiterates a responsibility of philosophy that has been explicitly acknowledged since the time of Socrates. But as the Wittgenstein–Malcolm example illustrates, the intent of programatic linguistic analysis is more ambitious. It undertakes to establish linguistic specifications for all philosophy. But where programatic linguistic analysis equates itself with philosophy without remainder, it follows—whatever analysts themselves may say about the matter—that its intended governance extends more widely still,* namely to

* This follows from the recognized distinction between use and analysis. If philosophy itself is analysis exclusively then it is not use, and must rely for use upon nonphilosophical sources. What it says about use must thus be construed as directed to these sources.

ordinary usage as a corrective to its notorious vagueness and ambiguity. This ambition contradicts the necessary condition of common language identified heretofore, namely the relative indeterminateness of its terms, which leaves them open to modulations by schools of thought and individuals, with resulting interactions among alternative refined meanings.

This "relative indeterminateness" condition, touched upon earlier, can be further elucidated by comparison to the "open texture" and "systematic ambiguity" that Friedrich Waismann uses to distinguish natural languages from formalized languages. Waismann contends that an experiential statement is not conclusively verifiable, in part because of the "open texture" that is a distinguishing feature of empirical terms. "If, in geometry, I describe a triangle, e.g. by giving its three sides, the description is *complete*: nothing can be added to it that is not included in, or at variance with, the data." But empirical terms and concepts cannot be correspondingly closed because experience itself is open to a future in which "something quite new and unforeseen may occur."[20] According to Waismann this necessary deference to the future is responsible for the open texture of terms "which is so characteristic of all factual knowledge."[21]

In accordance with Waismann's thesis we may say that, thanks to "open texture," when we use an empirical term we cannot know exactly what we mean. But such is not the case with the trait of ordinary language that I have named "relative indeterminateness." Relative indeterminateness affords, within the generic meaning of a given term, a multiplicity of alternative closed meanings. Meanings are "closed" because we are speaking of moral meanings that derive from choice and adherence to choice. The relative indeterminateness of such a term as "freedom" or "law" in its common usage affords latitude for each integral individual to work out his own precise meaning. But he must not claim that his refined meaning is the only true meaning, for to do so is to deny the identical rights of other individuals. Rather, he is obliged expressly to condone alternative refined meanings as they are employed by other integral individuals and alternative schools of thought.

What organizes alternative refined meanings within the generic meaning of the same common word Waismann calls "family likeness"[22] (we shall not pause to compare this with Wittgenstein's cotemporaneous "family resemblance"). Waismann perceptively adduces some of the many established senses in which we use words such as "reality," "existence," "knowledge," and "fact" as support for his contention that the words are "systematically ambiguous," and he uses "family likeness" to describe the relations of alternative meanings of the same word. As described by Waismann, "family likeness" is what relates the alternative meanings of any word as given by dictionaries; it is objective in the sense that it is independent of the word users. But attention should also be given to the "family likeness" that will obtain among the meanings of all the different words that are used by a given person (where the person is an integral individual) in virtue of the unity of the person and the singularity of his personal principle. Not only will the integral individual possess distinctive meanings for basic terms, but in virtue of his personal unity his meanings for the terms will cohere. Their coherence will not exhibit a strict mutual entailment because they are meanings whose content is experiential and therefore "open" to what the future may bring. They cohere by the reflection in each of this individual's singular principle of personhood.* And this level of "family likeness" underlies Waismann's because the differentiation of objective contexts, used by him to authenticate differentiated meanings of a given word, itself derives from the differentiation of persons. Of itself the world offers no contexts, and to persons who were identical there could

---

* This is the sense in which meanings are closed. They express a chosen attitude to whatever the future may bring. Thus the honesty of the honest man is not conditional upon future experience.

be but a single context (and the term "context" could have no meaning).

To disambiguate the meanings of common terms for one's own use is part of the process of becoming an individual, and entirely legitimate provided one recognizes the right of other individuals to alternative refined meanings. In addition one can offer his refined meanings as instances of a distinctive species of meaning, for use by others who wish to see the world similarly (for example it is to this end that the distinctive meanings embodied in this book are offered). But such others must be affirmed in their freedom to work out their own modulations within this species-meaning. Meanwhile the partisans of alternative perspectives must be affirmed in their entitlement to their alternative species-meanings, with the proviso that these alternative meanings be well wrought.

Where linguistic analysis aims at the reform of ordinary usage by the disambiguation of its terms, it foolishly works to eradicate a necessary condition of common language. Where it more narrowly seeks to disambiguate the terms of discourse of philosophy, it aims to extinguish all other styles of philosophical thinking. By so doing it attacks the condition of its own existence.

Returning to first-person psychological statements, not only do we ordinarily intend them to be self-referential, but we are justified in so doing, for by our choice of our ultimate possibility and principle of personhood we choose the distinctive qualities of our subjective contents. We are able to identify our unique feelings (for example) as modulations of the genera corresponding to the generic feeling-words of the common language. In the problem of acquiring knowledge of other minds, one starts with one's own case, and one can do so because one's own case is a determination within the general case. It retains within it the general case as a residuum; and by the process of individuation it also contains the finite principles of all other persons, actual and possible, in the mode of unactualized possibilities. In the problem of acquiring knowledge of other persons one begins with one's own case as the immediately actual case, and proceeds by exchanging it for alternatives. As the product of choice, one's own case is self-evidently an alternative among alternatives, hence it is true, as Scheler says, that "one's own self can only appear by contrast with some other or alien self."[23] But this is very different from Strawson's contention that one learns to attribute states of consciousness to oneself and to others simultaneously. For what is thus attributed, according to Strawson, are identical states of consciousness, and they are attributed to all parties in "just the same sense." Accordingly for Strawson there can be no differentiation of the consciousness of different persons *qua* consciousness, all differentiation between persons being instead attributable entirely to their different bodies. But the contrast of which Scheler speaks is the qualitative difference of contents of consciousness owing to difference of organizing principle, and such contrasts subsist within the field of consciousness of every true individual as well as between individuals.

The "quiet hail" of foreign essences that perpetually besieges the individual is a condition of individuated life and constitutes the continuous availability to the individual of qualities of feeling, sensation, volition, and cognition alternative to his own. In addition individuals are involuntarily subject in greater and lesser degree to those momentary actualizations of alternatives we term "illuminations" or "revelations" or "insights." But internal knowledge of another person is the sustained participatory enactment of his possibility, and as such it is a strictly voluntary matter. No one can be compelled to such an exchange. To produce knowledge such exchanges must make use of skills that require careful nurture. What Ortega y Gasset aptly terms the migratory soul[24] is no miraculous gift of nature to a handful of the elect; and I find it ceaselessly astonishing that persons who readily acknowledge the requirement for intensest training in the pursuit of knowledge of atoms, stars, or chromosomes, should look upon knowledge of other persons as calling for no special effort.

A fulfilled adolescence serves as the foundation of the "migratory soul" of adulthood, for the imaginative enactments by which the adolescent explores the spectrum of available life-styles are the prototype of the exchanges that in later life are requisite to knowledge of other persons. In adulthood the required skill is cultivated by performing such exchanges experimentally and learning to systematize by classifying possible persons according to types. Notice that such typology is consistent with an intermediate stage of personal development, for from his beginning as a numerical instance of common humanity (before his unique potential is actualized), each person must become a distinguishable type of person before he achieves unique individuality. In the intermediate stage his own ultimate possibility and principle of personhood is available to him only as a type, and he is knowable to others according to type. As his individuation progresses, he is knowable according to discriminations within the type that are of the same kind as was the prior type-discrimination. Thus, for example, within the type "voluntarist" are numerous species, with individuation appearing by refinement upon speciation.

Experimental exchange does not require the actual presence of another person. It can conveniently begin by isolating a judgment of one's own, inverting it, and then seeking the principle of the inverted judgment. For example, consider the conventional judgment that to be reared in an urban ghetto is to be personally disadvantaged. Earlier, in considering Sartre's thesis that man is free to choose the meaning of his situation (p. 100), I spoke of a young, black politician who argued for the advantage of such a rearing, as against the insularity of the typical suburban childhood. Here is the inversion of the conventional judgment. The mere enunciation of it does not produce perspectival exchange. But if we uncover the principle of which this view is an expression, then we will be able to explicate for ourselves its implications for other situations and conditions of life, and this explication by us constitutes participatory enactment at the conceptual level that becomes participatory enactment at the practical level by living out these same implications. In this case the principle is the moral autonomy and self-responsibility of the person. A corollary is that training for autonomy should begin earlier than it does for "advantaged" youth in our culture. A further corollary is that excessive protection constitutes disadvantage.

Inversion is merely a convenient introduction to perspectival exchange, for possibilities are not limited to antithetical pairs, but swarm the intervening region. A book, for example, that consistently expresses a perspective alternative to one's own may be dredged for its interpretive principle, the principle being thereafter extended by participatory enactment. And great help in the cultivation of a "migratory soul" may be obtained from the creative arts, especially the theater and the novel. Both theater and the novel invite an exchange of perspectival worlds—ours for that of the protagonist. By means of such exchange we perceive familiar things—love, work, play, death—through different eyes. We thus discover in them a novel aspect, and by the coherence of aspects are led to the principle that is its source. It is barely an overstatement to say that some of our greatest novels are complete training-courses in personal exchange.* I think for example of *The Brothers Karamazov*, and of *The Magic Mountain*. By the latter the reader is immersed successively in the incommensurable worlds of the bourgeois Hans Castorp, the humanist Settembrini, the ascetic Naphta, the daemonic Madam Chauchat, the life-worshipping Herr Pieperkorn.

Additionally, self-training in personal exchange is available by means of the sudden and discordant "illuminations"

---

* I know of two novels that have been deliberately designed to this purpose—André Gide's *The Counterfeiters* and Aldous Huxley's *Point Counterpoint*. I find them less successful, but why this would be so is a question for better critics of the novel than I.

that intrude occasionally upon the daily lives of most persons. The categories of common sense sentence such intrusions to disregard. But they are well worth conserving as an introduction to alternative interpretive principles. For example, a common sort of illumination is the "familiarity experience." One enters a city, a building, or a room for the first time and is overcome by the feeling that he has been there before; or he meets a person for the first time and is troubled by the feeling that he knew the person in a remote past. Such experience is concrete ground of the Eastern doctrine of reincarnation, and likewise of Plato's related doctrine that all true knowledge is "recollection" (*anamnesis*). These doctrines are remote from our common sense and seemingly inaccessible to us. But by invitation of the "familiarity experience" they become available to us for participatory enactment. The same holds true for every doctrine of every possible world-perspective, no matter how exotic it may appear from the standpoint of current common sense.[25]

Should we have acquired some degree of skill by means such as the above, the terms by which to apply personal exchange to the problem of knowledge of a given actual other person are broadly the following. Each isolated expressive act by the other is inherently ambiguous, affording in itself no clue to distinguish its actual meaning—its meaning for the actual other—from the infinitude of its possible meanings. But its actual meaning is the aspect that expresses the principle of the other's personhood, and by this meaning the act coheres with the person's other expressive acts. What we seek, therefore, is the meaning of each act that produces coherence with other acts, and the principle of this meaning. Enactment of this principle is participatory enactment of the other person, affording immediate, internal knowledge of him. The other's principle can be abstractly stated and externally known, as it is by scientific classification of personality types and refinements within the type, or as one may "know Shakespeare" by analysis of his plays and sonnets, but such knowledge is necessarily an interpretation based upon a principle of its own, and because this principle is not the personal principle of the other, it does not enable the expressive acts of the other to cohere; thus, they remain a mere collection. Coherence of the other's expressive acts can be achieved by one means, by participatory enactment of the other's personal principle. It is achieved in two steps: first, the scrupulous observation of the objective characters of the other's expressive acts; and, second, by successive enactment of alternative principles of personhood within the most promising type, in search of that principle that affords coherence of meanings.* By this means immediate internal knowledge of the unique other is attained, including knowledge of him for what he is to himself, and knowledge of the world for what it is to him.

What attests to the availability of the other not merely in his type but in his uniqueness is the fundamental nature of human being as *ekstasis*. In the Greek sense *ekstasis* means "standing out from . . . and into. . . ." The meaning here is that man lives from himself into the world; the world is the medium into which man must live; it is, in Dilthey's sense, "objectified *Geist*." To live is to live in the world, and living in the world is expressive of the nature of him whose living it is, not merely generically—as human being—but as individuated human being. Even an individual's concealments are expressive acts (which is by no means to say that deception is impossible, but only that it cannot in the end withstand a refined hermeneutics).

Indeed, it is the true individual who among human beings is most expressive and thereby most available, for he is "wholly present in each expression" (Kierkegaard, *Purity of Heart Is To Will One Thing*, p. 60). The acts of the frag-

* Discovery of the right principle has the character of what gestalt psychology has termed the "ah ha!" experience, because the new-found meaningfulness floods all of the assembled phenomena (objective characters of the other's expressive acts) at once.

mented or "double minded" individual do not integrate on a single principle. Yet the fragmented individual *can be known in his singularity* by the person who loves him, for such is the ultimate service of interpersonal love. Therewith, however, love is no all-accepting embrace, but the resolute corrective to disintegrity, awakening the beloved to what in his own best interest he *ought* to have done in the disjunctive instances.

By our knowledge of the personal principle of another we cannot predict what he will do in given conditions, but only what he ought to do if he acts in truth to himself. On the other hand, concerning the rare individual of keen integrity, one can—if one possesses the appropriate principle—predict what he will do under given conditions, for in such an individual what is done and what ought to be done are made one and the same by moral necessity.

To conclude, it will be well to summarize the conditions of immediate, internal knowledge of other persons. In the first place this knowledge is in general possible only if both persons are true individuals. Concerning the individual to be known, we have just seen that this condition can be obviated by love, but in the absence of love the fragmented individual is incomprehensible by the means we have set forth, as indeed he is to himself. If the knower is not a true individual, alternative possible principles of personhood will be unavailable to him, for it is by his own individuation that differentiation of his subjective content is achieved.

Second, it is in general a practical condition that, to be known, the other must make himself available by expressive behavior, he must develop and utilize the capacity for what Martin Buber calls "personal making-present."[26] This availability can be withheld by a pattern of actions that are calculatedly nonrevelatory, or by lack of expressive ability—for personal expression is an art. This condition holds practically and in general despite what has been noted about the expressiveness of the modes of concealment chosen by the individual. Strictly speaking concealment is impossible, for not only are its chosen means revelatory but it is the inadvertent behaviors—exhibited by even the most controlled persons—that are the most revelatory. (Clearly an issue arises here in the ethics of discretion, but we shall only refer the reader to telling passages on the subject by Georg Simmel.[27]) But such considerations could be held to overcome the condition of "personal making-present" only by presupposing a widespread expertise at refined hermeneutics that does not presently exist.

Again, immediate internal knowledge of others will be a practical impossibility for individuals who are insecure in their own identities, for in this circumstance identity-exchange involves high risks. One does not adventure upon foreign soil without confidence that home ground remains where it was, to be regained at will (adolescence is a categorial exception, for in this respect it has as yet nothing to lose). It follows that if our time is correctly characterized as a widespread crisis of identity—as by Erik Erikson and others—then the "migratory soul" will be a rarity among us.

But the weight of these conditions does not constitute an argument for the practical unworkability of immediate internal knowledge of others in sociality, nor can unworkability be inferred from the *analytical* complexity of the process of such knowledge. For the conditions are fulfilled in the course of the personal growth whose stages have been described in Chapter 6. If their fulfillment is uncommon, correctives are available through systematic attention to the problems of growth on the basis of presently available knowledge.

And the analytical complexities of the method must not be allowed to obscure the method's experiential simplicity. To "see oneself through the eyes of another" and to "see the world through another's eyes" are phenomenally simple events. The correlation of such perspectival exchange with given actual persons who are to be known calls for skill. But the acquisition of this skill is greatly facilitated by simple typologies of personality—Plato's tripartite distinctions

among intellectualist, voluntarist, and sensualist temperaments; Galen's fourfold classification of sanguine, phlegmatic, choleric, and melancholic dispositions; medieval
classifications according to dominant "humours"; the
recent endomorph-ectomorph-mesomorph categories of
W. H. Sheldon; the introvert-extrovert and archetypal categories of Carl Jung. On the strength of prior efforts of this
kind, J. S. Mill proposed the full-scale development of
"ethology" as the science of human character,[28] and today
this effort proceeds under the name "characterology." As
we have indicated, such objective endeavors cannot themselves afford internal knowledge of others, but they serve
the purpose of such knowledge by supplying categories that
narrow the field of possibilities to be experimentally actualized in particular cases.

We have also seen that persons reared in the same culture share a residuum of common subjective content and
achieve individuation (with rare exceptions) through modulation and refinement of this common content. In such
cases the residuum of common content, patterned by objective categories of the culture, affords individuals ready access to one another.

It remains the case that by comparison with, for example, the analogical inference we have described, the number
of persons an individual can know immediately is restricted, for knowledge of the latter kind requires a special
endeavor in each case, while knowledge of the former sort
is but the generalization of one's own case. But a few instances of immediate internal knowledge are sufficient to
establish what we term *consequent sociality*. To generalize
from these instances is to regard every person as both like
all persons (as an instance of common humanity) and as
qualitatively unique, the bearer of an irreplaceable value
that he alone can manifest. It is by the inclusion of a place
for the unique contribution of every person that consequent
sociality is categorially distinguished from antecedent sociality and the latter's merely numerical individuation.

The opportunity of knowledge of other persons as unique individuals is the possibility of the participation of qualitatively unique personhood in sociality. It is this form of sociality that is normative for self-actualization ethics, and not a numerical sociality from which true personhood has been evacuated. The justice within consequent sociality is of just persons, not of just non-persons; the love within consequent sociality is not impersonal love but the love by persons as persons, of persons as persons; and the division of labor within consequent sociality derives not from abstract assignment of integers by an impersonal agency, but from choices by persons according to the unique persons they are. The remaining chapters of our book shall explicate these terms of consequent sociality.

9

Social Entailments of Self-Actualization: Love and "Congeniality of Excellences"

In this chapter and the next we shall delineate significant features of the distinctive social ethics that follows from the principles of self-actualization. The distinctiveness of the social ethics of self-actualization lies in its double-aspect criterion of moral acts: that they be acts in accordance with principles that are both universalizable and also expressive of unique, individuated personhood. To exhibit the praxis of this criterion we shall investigate its workings with respect to three foundational manifestations of personal interdependence—love, division of labor, and justice. At the same time our delineation is intended to lay to rest the careless supposition by numerous critics of self-actualization—based, it would seem, on nothing more telling than nomenclature—that it is devoid of social ethics.

This hasty supposition lurks in Pitirim Sorokin's softly put suggestion that "Eros always has difficulty in finding room for love to man."[1] It appears sharply in the observation by Irving Singer, summarizing his study of eros in Plato and Aristotle, that "it could not account for the love of persons."[2] Still more explicitly, Morris Ginsberg states that "the formula of self-realization leaves out of consideration the central problem of ethics—that of the relation between self and others."[3] In similar vein Gordon Allport says of the priority ascribed by eros to self-love, "If this assumption is sound, the outlook for improving human relations is of course dim. Rationalize our self-love as we will, we remain frauds. Human relations cannot be improved; they can only be prettified."[4]

If the social entailments of the principles of self-actualization have not always been made explicit by proponents of the doctrine, critics are not relieved of their responsibility both to read and to think about that which they propose to criticize. Of itself, and without the addition of other motivational factors or conditions, self-actualization constitutes social contribution in four distinct respects. First, the integral person of the self-actualizing individual appears in the world as an objective value, where by "objective" is meant, in principle, valuable to all persons. This contribution receives unequivocal affirmation in the words of J. S. Mill: "And if it may possibly be doubted whether a noble character is always the happier for its nobleness, there can be no doubt that it makes other people happier, and that the world in general is immensely the gainer by it."[5] Indeed, Mill is altogether too plain-spoken; for the objectivity of personal value certifies only that other persons *can* gain by the manifest worth of the noble character, not that they inevitably *do* so gain, or are made happier thereby. It must not be overlooked that the presence of integrity strips opportunism and deceit of their favorite self-justification, namely that everyone else does likewise, or would if they could. For this reason the existence of nobility of character is not universally received as welcome news. But if nobility of character is the standing exposure of opportunism and deceit, this is itself a significant social service, the contrary opinion of the unregenerate deceiver notwithstanding.

Second, the actualization of personal worth by any individual exemplifies the potential personal worth of all persons in virtue of the isomorphism of personhood. Recognition of isomorphism forbids the practice of conceptually segregating "geniuses" as a class distinguished from the ordinary run of human beings by birth. It calls for the replacement of worship (and resentment) by *emulation*.

Third, the integral individual affords to other persons the occasion of a participatory enactment by which to fulfill vicariously a possibility whose direct fulfillment in themselves is precluded by their obligation to their own potentiality. In this way reading a good novel, listening to a good piece of music, or witnessing a good athletic performance can be personally enriching as well as (under the first contribution) the apprehension of an objective value, to be appreciated or utilized. Such vicarious enrichment is parasitic only for individuals who are not themselves engaged at self-actualization. Among integral individuals, it constitutes that division of labor that expresses their profound interdependence, the interdependence of autonomous, self-responsible persons.

Fourth, the integral individual is in his person the cardinal principle of social justice, for he lays claim only to those distributable goods to which his distinctive destiny entitles him. In Nietzsche's terms, he "pleases our senses, . . . he is carved from wood that is hard, delicate, and at the same time smells good. He has a taste only for what is good for him; his pleasure, his delight cease where the measure of what is good for him is transgressed."[6] Beyond this restricted entitlement he not only disavows his claim to distributable goods but he actively wills such goods to the persons who possess natural entitlement to them, thereby expressing social justice in his person. This derivation of social justice from self-actualization will be the theme of Chapter 10.

While these four social contributions are distinguishable analytically, they coalesce phenomenally as the sociality of personal acts. To avoid abstractionism we shall not further develop the four aspects separately; instead, we shall employ the concrete themes of love, justice, and division of labor to explicate these aspects conjointly. But before embarking on this adventure it will be useful to lay bare the criteriology of normative individualism by which moral acts are required to be both universalizable and personal.

In the first place, to term this a "double-aspect criterion" is to stress the inseparability of universalizability and individuation as aspects of a single criterion that in no circumstances can be regarded as separable criteria. Misconception of the aspects as separate criteria has produced, first, the motivational separation between egoism and altruism that thereafter becomes an antagonism and, second, a bifurcation of the realm of morality into social morality and "prudence." When "prudence" is subsequently excised from the domain of morality altogether, the motivation of self-interest is either explicitly precluded to morality—thereby rendering the question "Why be moral?" unanswerable—or else it must first be laundered by such gymnastic contrivances as "veils of ignorance," "impersonal standpoints," or the magical transformation of persons into ideal observers from whom every interest but that of impartial benevolence has been removed. About these exercises in self-renunciation something more will be said in due course. Meanwhile we must note that, by its opposition to bifurcation of the moral realm with subsequent excision of the motive of self-interest, normative individualism does not propose to derive morality from self-interest. Such an undertaking is an attempt to squeeze blood from a bloodless abstraction. For "egoism" and "altruism," "prudence" and "morality" (as the term is used in contradistinction to "prudence") are not concrete phenomena originally, but analytical distinctions reflecting the mind's ability to conceive an aspect of a phenomenon in isolation from other aspects. I say they are not concrete phenomena *originally*, but once the conceptual distinctions have been made it becomes entirely possible for persons to live them, thereby transforming themselves into abstractions. Yet this does nothing to dispel the original simplicity of concrete moral motivation, which consists in the aim to do the right and manifest the good, wholly without distinction between the good for others and the good for oneself. To the person who is engaged at doing what he truly thinks best, the question, "But what do you hope to gain from it?" is incongruous.

Given the reassertion of undissected, concrete moral

motivation, the question "Why be moral?" is answered "Because I am a person." But in this answer lies the conjunction expressed by the double-aspect criterion, for, as heretofore considered,* to be a person is to be irreducibly a "universal–particular." Accordingly a morality is a morality of persons only when both aspects are affirmed to function normatively. It is morally significant that the individual is in certain respects like others, and it is no less morally significant that he is in certain other respects unique.

In the interest of universalizability a substantial amount of ethical theorizing declares all individuating features of personhood morally irrelevant. This is sometimes done simply by employing trivial differences as paradigms, e.g. "Can I say that the fact that I have a mole in a particular place on my chin entitles me to further my own interests at others' expense . . . ?"[7] Alternatively it is proposed that all differences between persons consist in, or are reducible to, their numerically different physical bodies. This is the effect of P. F. Strawson's contention that material particulars are "the basic particulars," for while Strawson argues that persons are also "primary particulars," the ground of the particularity of persons is their possession of material bodies.[8] A similar contention appears in Thomas Nagel's requirement for an "objective standpoint"—an impersonal standpoint from which moral situations are to be described by participants. For while such description must, according to Nagel, be supplemented by "the personal premise," he stresses that the latter adds nothing but the opportunity to use token-reflexives and thereby locate individuals spatio-temporally, i.e. as numerical individuals.[9] Likewise the reduction to numerical individuality occurs in the imposition by John Rawls of a "veil of ignorance" upon the persons of his "original position" who are to choose the principles of justice of their subsequent association. The purpose of the veil is to banish from them all knowledge of "particulars"

---

* E.g. Chapter 8, pp. 248-250 and *passim*.

(individuating features). According to Rawls such ignorance is the condition of right choice because "If a knowledge of particulars is allowed, then the outcome is biased by arbitrary contingencies."[10] Finally, proponents of the ideal observer theory of moral determination, from David Hume and Adam Smith to such recent formulators as C. I. Lewis, Roderick Firth, and David Haslett,[11] conceive that all persons, when sufficiently "idealized," will have been rendered qualitatively identical by being emptied of all subjective content except for an even-handed benevolence. Speaking of choice by individuals of the life they wish to lead, Haslett says "It must be emphasized that if the choice is to be one from such an ideal standpoint, absolutely *nothing* else such as tastes, prejudices, superstitions, idiosyncrasies, philosophic theories, etc., must have any effect upon the choice whatsoever. Consequently we may say that two different individuals who each make a choice on the same lives from this ideal standpoint would have to make the *same* choice, for by definition their choice would be based upon or caused by identically the same factors. We would simply have a case of same cause, same effect."[12]

The propensity shared by the above formulations is for a depersonalized morality, a morality not of persons but of non-persons. It achieves the universalizability of moral judgments and principles by presupposing that all individuating features of personhood are morally irrelevant. Against it, normative individualism demands recognition of the moral significance of the fundamental individuating feature of personhood, namely the innate, qualitatively unique potential worth of every person. As developed in previous chapters the argument for this tenet consists, first, in the demonstrable objective worth of some persons, coupled with the evidence for the basic isomorphism of persons *qua* persons. Additionally we are in this chapter and the next engaged at ex post facto "vindication"* of this tenet by

* "Vindication" will be recognized as Herbert Feigl's term for the justification of which ultimate epistemological and ethical

examination of the social ethics it founds. Specifically our claim is that the justice, love, and division of labor that this tenet fosters are morally superior to the justice, love, and division of labor that are furnished by alternative ethical principles. Moral individuality is moral irreplaceability; it means that each person is in himself an irreplaceable end in a system of ends. Ideal sociality is the system of complementary, perfected individuals; and the denial of the normativity of individuality—as by the above types of ethical theory—at bottom precludes true sociality by offering replication in place of complementarity.

---

principles are susceptible. These ultimate principles are necessarily presupposed in the "validation," respectively, of particular knowledge claims and particular acts, but are not themselves susceptible of validation. They are susceptible of "vindication" (or "pragmatic justification") by the consequences which derive from their adoption. (Herbert Feigl, "Validation and Vindication, An Analysis of the Nature and Limits of Ethical Arguments," in Wilfrid Sellars and John Hospers, *Readings in Ethical Theory* [New York: Appleton-Century-Crofts, Inc., 1952], pp. 667-680.

Feigl's "vindication" bears striking resemblance to the "logical efficacy" that justifies the "absolute presuppositions" of metaphysics according to R. G. Collingwood, and also to the "decidability" that applies to ontologies and *Weltanschauungen* according to J. O. Wisdom. See R. G. Collingwood, *An Essay On Metaphysics* (Oxford at the Clarendon Press, 1940), especially Ch. IV; and J. O. Wisdom, "Scientific Theory: Empirical Content, Embedded Ontology, and Weltanschauung," in *Philosophy and Phenomenological Research*, 83, no. 1 (Sept. 1972). Wisdom's article contains a useful summary of recent thinking on these lines by Joseph Agassi, Mario Bunge, T. S. Kuhn, Imre Lakatos, J.W.N. Watkins, and others.

As ultimate normative ethical principles, principles of normative individualism are implicit courses of action that, to be explicated, must be acted upon. The justfication to which they are susceptible is therefore necessarily ex post facto and "pragmatic." But it is not essentially comparative, for comparison requires an independent standard, and the term *ultimate* as applied to underived ethical principles attests to the absence of such standards. Accordingly the ex post facto "vindication" of ethical principles takes the form of an answer to the question: Does acting upon them fulfill what they promised?

As against the manufactured, depersonalized unanimity produced by "veils of ignorance," "objective standpoints," and the like, we affirm "diversity in the pursuit of ends" to be not only a moral possibility but a moral necessity in virtue of the innate, morally relevant diversity of persons.

The possibility of moral individuation is logically demonstrated by R. M. Hare's recent work, the effect of which is to show that moral judgments predicated upon an irreducible diversity of ultimate goods are nonetheless universalizable. According to Hare a judgment is universal when it "logically commits the speaker to making a similar judgment about anything which is either exactly like the subject of the original judgment or like it in the relevant respects. The relevant respects are those which formed the grounds of the original judgment."[13] To judge that one's responsibility under a moral rule is unique is to make a universalizable judgment if one acknowledges that all persons have unique responsibilities under moral rules. The reason is that uniqueness is a universalizable predicate, while the quality of each individual's uniqueness is singular. Therefore, to universalize our behavior under given circumstances is *not* to hold that under these circumstances all persons ought to behave in identical fashion to ourselves, but rather to hold that every other person ought to act so as to express his unique personhood with respect to these circumstances, as we ourselves do.

Unique obligation under a moral rule attests that the rule does not determine behavior unilaterally, but only in conjunction with persons. There can be no moral acts without rules and principles, but likewise there can be no moral acts without agents, and agents of the sort we call persons. As Hare says, a person who accepts a principle "has not thereby had all his moral problems solved for him; he has to do something further in order to obtain his . . . maxims, namely, exercise his autonomous, rational will by 'making laws for himself' which are of the form prescribed by the . . . principle, but are not of themselves formal." In other words,

Hare says, maxims are not deduced from a principle, they are "framed in accordance with it." And he proceeds to show that the maxims that may be framed in accordance with a given principle are not limited to one (as Kant may have thought), but are infinite.[14] In the terms of normative individualism, the principle "Actualize your innate potential excellence" will be adhered to in an infinite qualitative diversity of lives.

Most moral systems are made up of principles and rules to which everyone privately regards himself as the exception, and it is of special interest that in normative individualism the exceptionality of individuals is affirmed and contained as exceptionality *under* the principles and rules of morality. That an individual is unique does not exempt him from the principles and rules of normative individualism, but renders him responsible for what he alone can do. Exceptionality *under* a rule is universalizable in virtue of the universalizability of uniqueness, while the claim to exemption from the rule is not universalizable, for its universalization destroys the rule. To make a universalizable claim to one's exemption from a rule is to challenge the rule as a rule (and it is by their tacit recognition of this that persons for the most part keep silent about their feelings of exceptionality with respect to conventional rules). Logically, the claim of exemption from a valid rule can only rest upon singular properties, and it therefore fails of universalizability. If I were to claim exemption from a moral rule "because I live at 6 Windflower Drive, Newark, Delaware," I cannot make the claim universalizable by the words, "and I acknowledge the exemption of anyone living at that address," for the predicate in question has singular applicability. But singular acts and judgments are universalizable *under* a principle or rule in virtue of the uniqueness of every moral agent.

With the possibility of moral individuation established, we shall next argue for its necessity, using for our benchmark P. F. Strawson's paper, "Social Morality and Individual Ideal." Strawson identifies himself as an advocate of a "diversity in the pursuit of ends" such that "the steadiest adherence to one image [end] may co-exist with the strongest desire that other and incompatible images should have their steady adherents too." He adds, "To one who has such a desire, any doctrine that the pattern of the ideal life should be the same for all is intolerable; as it is for me."[15] We note that in this depiction the very diversity of ideals appears as a meta-ideal, and one that Strawson at least *feels* should be the same for all.

In Strawson's meta-ideal we grasp the very kind of ultimate formal moral principle required by normative individualism, a principle that incorporates both the universality and the individuation of moral agents. Of all persons alike it requires steady adherence to an ideal, but each person can qualify as an exception *under* the principle in virtue of the ideal that is distinctively his.

Strawson himself does not construe his "diversity in the pursuit of ends" in this way, however, and it will repay us to discern the ground of his reluctance. For Strawson, "diversity in the pursuit of ends" does not govern ideals as what we have termed a "meta-ideal." Rather it is offered as merely one ideal that, as such, is in free competition with those ideals for which exclusivity is claimed.

Strawson confines himself to this reduced claim because he treats ideals as extra-moral supplements to moral life rather than as integral to it. In this light he cannot require others to acknowledge diversity in the pursuit of ends, for such acknowledgment is not a moral requirement, it is a matter of taste. Here is the harvest of Strawson's metaphysics according to which personal individuation is ascribable to bodily individuation. This leaves individuation devoid of morally relevant ground, and the individuation reflected in (I should say, founded in) adherence by persons to diverse ideals is without moral foundation—it expresses mere taste.

Indeed, Strawson's handling of ideals suggests that their use by persons is largely accidental and confined, moreover, to persons who are "imaginatively restless and materially cosy."[16] This excision of ideals from the domain of morality draws Hare's passing objection, "I think it inadvisable to confine the word 'moral' so narrowly."[17] That it is not merely inadvisable but disastrous will be apparent if we look to Strawson's meaning of morality.

Strawson's announced intention is to provide a "minimal interpretation" of morality as a "useful analytical idea." To this end he proposes that morality be conceived as "the sphere of the observance of rules, such that the existence of some such set of rules is a condition of the existence of a society."[18] Now this is a conception of morality—minimal or otherwise—only on the presupposition that the rules in question are moral rules. But Strawson's job is not to presuppose morality but to offer a conception of it, and this he has not done. He subsequently acknowledges this in his consideration of the sanctions of social rules: "if no interest of mine is safeguarded by the system of demands to which I am subject, then, in fulfilling a demand made upon me, I may indeed, in one sense, be doing what I am obliged to do; but scarcely what I am *morally* obliged to do."[19] This recognition moves him to offer an "enriched" minimal conception of morality in which the "demands" of a "socially sanctioned" system are "not merely enforced as demands, but [are] also at least in some degree generally acknowledged as claims by those subject to them."[20] Such acknowledgment presupposes, according to Strawson, that "members have *some* interest, not merely in there being a system of socially sanctioned demands, but in the actual system of demands which obtains in that society."[21]

In the first place, however, by Strawson's admission, he is no longer entitled to regard his "minimal interpretation" as an interpretation or conception of morality, for no hint of morality can be found in it. Exactly the same holds true for his "enriched" minimal interpretation. To term a system of rules "moral" because the rules express interests and acknowledged claims is once again to presuppose morality, not to define or describe it. The decisive question is still whether the claims are morally rightful claims and the interests morally rightful interests.

Meanwhile as we saw, Hare objects to Strawson's excision of ideals from the realm of morality. But while Hare himself includes both ideals and interests in the moral domain he insists that they be kept distinct, being understood as two different grounds on which we can commend or condemn actions.[22] The consequence of maintaining this distinction is that while Hare acknowledges that the individual must add "something further" to the universalizability criterion in order to obtain moral rules,[23] the possible sources of this personal addition—interests, wants, desires, and inclinations—are without moral character. This is because, on Hare's own authority, interests, wants, and desires are non-universalizable.

> In this respect wanting [desiring, needing, having an interest in] is like assenting to a singular imperative, not to a moral or other value-judgment. If I am trying to make up my mind what to do, I may simply ask myself what I most want to do; or I may ask myself what I ought to do. If I want to do A in these circumstances, I am not committed to wanting anyone else placed in exactly or relevantly similar circumstances to do likewise. But if I think that I ought to do A in these circumstances, I am committed to thinking that anyone else similarly placed ought to do the same.[24]

("Inclinations," as the term is ordinarily used, represent established patterns of interests, wants, and desires.[25])

The way to render interests, desires, wants, and inclinations as moral factors is by recognition of their universality —not, however, by the mistaken claim that at bottom all persons are alike with respect to them, but by connecting them to ideals. The means by which to acknowledge the normativity of individuation is the recognition that ideals

286

in their essential nature are individuated, and social ideals are systems of individuated, personal ideals.

Interests, desires, and wants are *moral* when they are constituted by ideals, and they are *right* in the moral sense when the ideal by which they are constituted is the innate ideal of the person whose interests, wants, and desires they are—the ideal that marks the limit, in a finite perfection, of his innate potentiality.

Moral motivation, then, is founded in the desire to become the good person that in potentiality one uniquely is. The crux here is each person's desire to manifest in the world the worth that is both his, and *real*, and which as such is susceptible of recognition and affirmation by others. No one desires to manifest a worth for himself alone, for such a worth would be a merely apparent worth, rendering the life in question a thoroughgoing self-deception. And no one desires to manifest a worth exclusively for others, for relative worth is genuine worth only where it is intrinsic worth, i.e. worth to itself. But the desire that the worth one manifests be real worth contains the self-imposed requirement that one's desires, interests, and wants be right desires, interests, and wants; and to be such they must be constituted by ideals. Ideals are apprehensions of real worth, and by no means is such apprehension confined to the "imaginatively restless and materially cosy." A normal adolescence is an imaginative exploration of ideals as alternative ends of life; and every desire to do what one ought, and do it well, is necessarily informed by an ideal. Indeed, the educability of children is an expression of this very motivation, but in this case the ideals that serve as standards to judge the work must be supplied by external agencies, and "heteronomy" obtains. By its exploration of ideals as alternative ends of life, adolescence avails itself of the condition of moral autonomy, and self-responsible moral life commences to be lived with the choice of the ideal by which future needs, desires, and interests shall be constituted.

287

Not only must ideals be accorded an essential place within the domain of morality, but within this domain they are inseparably connected with interests. The fundamental reason for the denial by Hare and Strawson of this essential connection is their apprehensions of fanaticism. By an appalling irony, however, the respective stance adopted by each man out of this apprehension is such as to court fanaticism, while what follows from normative individualism with respect to fanaticism is ready identification and unequivocal moral condemnation.

Strawson's excision of ideals from the domain of morality renders his own ideal—"diversity in the pursuit of ends"—a mere taste, and it accords this same status to the most bigoted, cruel, and totalitarian ambition that can be imposed upon a people. The extent of Strawson's self-debilitation as moral critic is apparent in his wan remark concerning such a society that it will "evidently be subject to at least some stresses from which a liberal society is free."[26]*

Nor is Hare in a better way. For he confirms that on his conception of moral arguments a true fanaticism cannot be touched. Next he strives to assure his readers of the "fortunate contingent fact that [fanatics] . . . are extremely rare."[28] He concludes with the advice that "In his war with the fanatic, the best strategy for the liberal to adopt is one of persistent attrition," adding that "if he keeps fighting and does not lose heart, [he] will cause all but a small number of hard core fanatics to relent."[29]

But such reassurance fades in the face of Hare's definition

* The reader will recall that by Strawson's "enriched minimal conception" of morality, social rules are required to be in the interests of individuals. But nothing here avails against totalitarianism, under which it is most emphatically in persons' interests to conform. Nor can we afford to forget that totalitarianism serves some significant antecedent interests. As Santayana says, "The constant compensation tyranny brings, which keeps it from at once exhausting its victims, is the silence it imposes on their private squabbles."[27] To be told what to do and what to think is welcomed by all persons sometimes, and by some persons at all times.

of fanaticism, for to Hare the fanatic is an idealist for whom "the ideal in question is made to override all considerations of people's interests, even the holder's own in actual or hypothetical cases."[30] The acid test employed by Hare is that the fanatic wills the fulfillment of his ideal even when his own interests must be sacrificed to it. Thus, to distinguish the merely opportunistic Nazi from the fanatical Nazi, Hare asks that a given Nazi be made to suppose that genealogical research discloses him to be in fact a Jew. He is a fanatic if under these circumstances he would will that he be sent to Buchenwald. Hare is persuaded that, by this test, genuine fanatics will prove to be very few.

But, setting aside for the moment the example of Nazism, we may hope that persons who can pass Hare's test are not so few as he supposes, for what the test identifies is not fanaticism but moral idealism. As a straightforward case, consider the ideal of sobriety to a reformed alcoholic; it is evident that if he is to *be* a reformed alcoholic this ideal must assert itself perpetually over his immediate desire to have a drink. Bearing in mind that interests are not of themselves moral (by Hare's demonstration that they are not universalizable), we will realize that a requirement of moral ideals is that they *must* "override all considerations of people's interests, even the holder's own." For as we have previously seen, it is the function of ideals to establish *moral* interests and maintain their priority over nonmoral ones. To will the fulfillment of one's ideal where it contravenes one's interests is therefore to will the fulfillment of one's moral interests against one's nonmoral interests—the characteristic, not of fanaticism, but of moral integrity. Concerning the nonmoral interests of others, moral integrity likewise consists in adherence to one's moral interests against these. But by the nature of ideals, to will the fulfillment of one's moral interests is at the same time to will fulfillment of the *moral* interests of all other persons, and it is to affirm the alternative ideals from which the moral interests of others derive. Such is necessarily the case because one's own ideal is a finite perfection that subsists in the relationship of complementarity with other finite perfections. Because the realm of the ideal is a democracy of finite, complementary perfections, to live by an ideal is necessarily to affirm "diversity in the pursuit of ends." Accordingly the "liberalism" espoused personally by Strawson and Hare is very far from the expression of mere taste that they take it to be; it is the metaprinciple of moral life.

In these terms Nazism is condemned as immoral because of its program of suppression or extermination of persons who decline allegiance to it. Its self-aggrandizing ambition is not an ideal, standing instead as dire warning against inflated interests that remain uninstructed by ideals. Such usurpation is no morally optional idealism but flagrant immorality, identified as such by the constraints of idealism. These constraints require affirmation of equal validity of alternative ideals, and acknowledgment of the intrinsic potential worth of every person *qua* person. Under these constraints the absolute suppression of any person—much less of an entire race—is morally condemned. Any infringement of the basic rights* of another, as for example by his imprisonment for a crime, requires justification in the form of concrete aids toward that person's discovery and manifestation of his unique potential worth.

We have spoken, first, of recognition of the unique worth of individual others; second, of affirmation of their worth as worth; and third, of willing their fulfillment of the unique worth that is theirs. Psychologically these factors are distinguishable as knowledge, respect, and love of others. Logically these three factors subsist in relations of mutual entailment, and in a perfect person they resolve to identity, but in the development of personhood of which perfection is the limiting ideal they appear in the genetic order here indicated, the capacity for love presupposing capacities for both knowledge and respect. In Max Scheler's words love

* Rights obtaining from birth in virtue of potential worth, to be considered in Ch. 10.

is "a movement tending to the enhancement of value."[31] The thrust of our present argument is that in consequent sociality the true interests of others are to be secured with each individual, not by depersonalization by means of "veils of ignorance," "impersonal standpoints," and the like, but rather by the love that is the expression of developing personhood.

As described in Chapter 8, individuation of subjective contents through personal choice is the essential condition of recognition and knowledge of other individuals *qua* individuals. In his exploration of alternative possible ends of life, what identifies the ideal that is innately the person's own is the upsurge of love as aspiration to enhanced value. This love identifies that which the individual fundamentally lacks and which constitutes his fulfillment, thereby connecting actuality with possibility in a movement, an e-motion. This love is eros—Plato's *tiktein en tô kalô*—in its genetically original manifestation as self-love. To suppose that self-love precludes love of others, as Gordon Allport does, is unpardonably to confuse eros with egoism. By asserting the primacy of the actual self, egoism overrides both the interests of others and the self's moral interests. On the contrary, the self-love of eros, by embracing the finite personal ideal, transforms the actual interests of the individual into moral interests. By recognition of the personal ideal as a member of a family of complementary perfections, the self-love of eros generates knowledge, respect, and love of other persons.

As the will to the maximization of value, love is in principle universalizable, affirming the potential worth of every person, and willing the actualization by each person of his own worth. In actuality the scope of an individual's love of others will correspond to his degree of self-knowledge and self-actualization. But if we are to avoid an empty abstractionism we must bear in mind that this knowledge and love of others is an emergent that, as such, is subject to the dictates of genetic order. The love of which we speak is a love neither of abstractions nor of collectivities but of unique individuals who can be known only one by one. It follows that self-love cannot leap to a "love of humanity" by means of facile generalization, but must make its way concretely and step by step. What follows self-love in the genetic order is love of the singular other individual. This love need not be reciprocated, but the unilateral instance is an incomplete form. We shall therefore give our attention to reciprocal love between two persons as the expression of the principle that consequent sociality must begin à deux.

Reciprocal love between two persons consists not in unification, nor in imposition, nor in essential sacrifice, but in the conjoint willing of fulfillment of two distinct and complementary individuals. On the precondition of self-knowledge and self-love, each knows the other for what he or she essentially is, a unique potential perfection, and each by his love wills the fulfillment of that perfection by the other. The nature of this love will be brought to sharpened focus by contradistinction to three common pseudomorphs, namely "imposition," "appropriation," and "unconditional love."

By "imposition" we mean the lover's substitution for the beloved of an ideal of his own devising. Stendhal bestowed literary immortality on this pseudomorph by his famous theory of "crystalization."[32] The theory derives its name from a phenomenon associated with the salt mines of Salzburg. When a bare branch is thrown into the unused workings and allowed to remain there for a time, it is transformed into a thing of exquisite beauty by a coat of shimmering crystals. In like manner, says Stendhal, the mind of the lover adorns with perfections the object of his love. The perfections are entirely the invention of the lover, and beneath them the true nature of the beloved remains entirely hidden from him. The imposition Stendhal describes undoubtedly occurs frequently in human affairs—for example it typifies adolescent "loves"—but it has nothing to do with love, being merely a disguised egoism.[33] By its renown,

Stendhal's theory has had the pernicious effect of abetting the popular fallacy that love is blind.

By "appropriation" we mean the enterprise on the part of the lover who truly knows his beloved to actualize her potential worth by his own efforts. Like imposition, this pseudomorph unquestionably exhibits a prevalence in human affairs, most notably in the relations of caring adults with their children. Often, indeed, the aims of child rearing are bluntly imposed by adults in the manner of crystalization. But just as often these aims are scrupulously inferred from the nature of childhood itself, and perhaps even with consideration for the distinctive inclinations of the individual child. Here knowledge of the child's own good replaces blind imposition. But if it is attended by the resolve of managerial adults to achieve, themselves, the ends for their children—"sparing them the mistakes we ourselves made"— then the gain is erased, for it is a condition of a personal goal that it must be achieved, it cannot be received. The reciprocal love that just now concerns us is no affair of childhood, nor yet of adolescence, for it presupposes individuation by choice and therefore awaits the stage of maturation. The virtue of the stage of maturation is integrity, consisting in fidelity to one's choice by faithful enactment of the implications of that choice. Integrity is the enactment by which potential worth becomes actual worth, and an individual can possess actual worth in no other way. This means that the lover's effort to actualize the worth of his beloved in her stead is at bottom calculated (intentionally or not) to preclude to her all actual worth, confining her to a perennial condition of a merely potential worth. This is the condition of childhood, but a monstrous childhood from which the prospect of growth has been stripped away. By a final irony such a "lover" denies love to himself, for from the recognition that the other is an incommensurably different person from himself—the recognition that distinguishes appropriation from imposition—he knows that his

enterprise in her behalf is at the expense of his own fundamental self-responsibility. The cost to him is both his self-
love and his worthiness of the love of others. Thus do the
pseudomorphs of love prove breeding-grounds of resentment and hatred.

As a "movement tending to the enhancement of value" the
love of which we speak cannot be "unconditional" with
respect to actual persons, for every actual person is an amalgam of virtues and defects. In this amalgam normative individualism identifies the object of love as the ideal of perfection, implicit within the individual, which his actual
virtues reflect. This love, then, includes the other's actuality
to the degree to which and in the respects by which his
actuality expresses his innate perfection. By no means does
this love embrace the other's lapses, defects, and infirmities,
but rather it works with respect to these as perpetual critic,
calling for their rectification. This "conditionality" has
called down upon eros (to give our love its name) the
charge that it lacks charity and compassion. But in truth
a love that loves defects is not charity but complicity, rivet-
ing the other to his defects by identification. Let us notice
first that a person who loves us "unconditionally" thereby
sets himself at cross-purposes with our own self-love, for by
the latter we are in no least measure rendered either blind
to our deficiencies or enamored of them, but rather are we
alerted to them and bent upon transcending them. In this
light I submit that an unconditional love of which we ourselves are the object will strike us as at best ignorant, and
at worst morally mischievous. And we must notice that,
while eros shuns pity and self-righteous forgiveness, it is
rich with the profoundest consolation possible—the consolation of its unwavering apprehension of the other's consummate potential personal worth. It re-teaches him of this
worth when in dark moments his own conviction is lost to
despair, and it recalls him from the unconditional self-
affirmation of egoism.

Eros's exclusive affirmation of the good produces Irving

Singer's contention that it cannot include love of persons. "We do not love someone *as* a person," he says, "if we are merely in love with her perfections."[34] Singer's view is that actual persons are integrated, indivisible wholes, containing both perfections and imperfections, and a love confined to perfections is a love of abstractions from this whole. But the whole person of whom Singer wishes to be solicitious is not actual but ideal. In actuality each of us is but a loose and ill-coordinated assemblage of parts—roles, faculties, needs, hopes, attitudes, principles—fraught with dissonances and contradictions. Integration and wholeness are not natural facts of personhood but moral ends, and our degree of actual wholeness derives from adherence to these ends. In short, love of persons as integrated wholes is precluded, not by eros, but by Singer's blindness to the necessary place of ideals in true personhood. Confusion is compounded by Singer's references to "perfections" in the actual beloved, for perfections—and we must speak strictly—are not found in actuality. My beloved's eyes, or voice, or bearing may be exemplary indeed, but they are not perfect. Had Singer been inclined to place quotation marks around the word *perfections* he might have recognized that ideality has already appeared in his description of what he insists is pure actuality. Foremost among such ideal perfections is personal wholeness, whose reflection by actuality constitutes the virtue of integrity.

In the genetic order, self-love gives rise to reciprocal love between two persons, and here the paradigmatic forms are friendship and romantic love. Concerning the relative value of these two forms, Montaigne surely expresses the judgment of humanity when he admonishes romantic love as "more precipitant, fickle, moving and inconstant; a fever subject to intermissions and paroxysms, that has seized upon but one part of us," whereas friendship is "a general and universal fire, but temperate and equal, a constant established heat, all gentle and smooth, without poignancy or roughness."[35] More especially has philosophy given preference to friendship, while condemning romantic love as the subverter of reason and judgment. Nevertheless from the genetic point of view romantic love takes precedence, as signaled by its notorious exclusivism as a relation between two persons and no more. This genetic priority is confirmed by the recognition that, while romantic love requires more of the individual in the way of developed capacities than comradeship, it requires less of him than does friendship.* Moreover by a powerful mechanism romantic love uniquely renders the individual precocious with respect to a requisite capacity that otherwise must await substantial maturity and self-discipline. It is the capacity for intense and sustained attention to a single object, and the mechanism for its precocious attainment is passion.

This mechanism and this capacity confer upon romantic love the appearance of an irrational obsession and earn the list of epithets addressed to it by the ages—"a madness," "a fit," "a rage," "a delusion." This uproar is directly provoked by romantic love's blatant perceptual and judgmental distortions. The lover sees perfections in his beloved that the rest of the world does not see, and through passion he chooses her in preference to and against the world. Here we discern the cardinal feature by which so much concerning romantic love becomes explicable—its intemperance. Romantic love is the implacable foe of the commonplace. As Socrates says, the lover is "like a bird fluttering and looking aloft and careless of the world below."[36] In Emerson's words, romantic love "extrudes all other persons from [the lover's] attention as cheap and unworthy."[37] It is an extraordinary condition that befalls an ordinary man or woman, and within it both beloved and lover become extraordinary persons, while the daily world suffers active devaluation—

* Therefore it is unsurprising that some of the world's renowned romantic lovers have been incapable of friendship, whereas the capacity for friendship inevitably includes the capacity for romantic love—though it may indeed choose to shun the occasions of it, and not without reason.

the best of it together with the worst. To Schopenhauer's keen displeasure, love "sometimes embarrasses for awhile even the greatest minds, does not hesitate to intrude with its trash interfering with the negotiations of statesmen and the investigations of men of learning, knows how to slip its love letters and locks of hair even into ministerial portfolios and philosophical manuscripts. . . ."[38]

Think of it! Even the exalted stations of philosophy and ministry of state are trampled upon. Indeed, love has been known to seize a philosopher by the heels and shake him until his categories rattle and his postulates spill out upon the floor.

Intemperate love makes sport of the entire temperate world—career, family, friends, obligations, duties, honors, alliances, all are trampled upon. And the ordinary world responds in kind. It first seeks to tame and domesticate passion by throwing the weight of the world upon it, the institution of marriage serving the purpose. Failing this, untamed loves are excised, as the Greek philosopher Democritus is said to have plucked out his eye when it had fastened upon a passing woman. The world brands love mad.

For our part, shall we side with passion or with the world and "common sense"? But is common sense anything more than shared prejudice? Is ordinary living ever more than half awake? Ordinary perception is, after all, unremittingly self-interested, and disgracefully careless even in this. It has no idea what the true self is, nor what may be its genuine interest. Such is its perpetual restlessness and distractability that it can fix upon nothing in the world long enough to penetrate the refractions of its surface and discover its underlying essence. Against this desultoriness, prodigious feats are achieved by the extraordinary power of attention of artists, scientists, artisans, and athletes—indeed by any individual who truly loves his work; for in truth love is the secret of that self-discipline whose core is a power of sustained attention. But we speak here of a self-discipline that is long in the making and attained by only a minority of persons. If consequent sociality—the sociality of individuals as individuals —were to rest upon this attainment, then the practical man would be obliged to judge consequent sociality far-fetched, a refined art cultivated from so tentative a natural base as to hold promise only for the salons. But as if it were made for the purpose of disarming this judgment, romantic love appears at the outset of life's third stage to confirm that consequent sociality possesses a profound and universal natural base. By the passion of its first phase, the rudest neophyte at individuation is thrust to the outermost limit of self-discipline, exhibiting a power of concentration that would do credit to a master of Raja Yoga.

As Ortega y Gasset says well, passion is "an abnormal state of attention which occurs in a normal man."[39] Ordinary attention roams restlessly, focusing briefly and incompletely upon one object after another against a background of indistinct presences. But into this undisciplined diffusion comes a paroxysm, a seizure that rivets attention upon a single object, intensifying it and sustaining it for an abnormal period of time. Passion thus bestows upon youth an instrument that must otherwise await a cultivation of years. By means of it he is able to penetrate the refractory surfaces, perceiving what is forever concealed from the world and common sense—the precious essence of his beloved. A profound truth bequeathed by Plato to the ages is that love's "madness" is divine, affording apprehension of the perfections in things that subsist in the mode of innate possibilities and that are hidden from the eyes of the nonlover by the refractory surfaces of the actual.

Moreover passion produces a re-centering by which the background is oriented with respect to the beloved rather than the lover, and so too for the lover himself. Suppose that just now my beloved is absent from my side and I find myself touring an art gallery and examining its paintings— what I demand to know is not my responses to the works but hers. Likewise in the countryside, the green or gold of the field, the sun's warmth, the sweet smell of honeysuckle

—these things must tell me of her if they wish to receive my gratitude. Under her spell I discover my own feelings and responses to be an intolerable annoyance, interfering as they do with the disclosure of her. This unique impetus to the suspension of our own responses identifies an irreconcilable disparity between love and ordinary perception. Under the latter our own interests are relentless and we perceive exclusively in accordance with them; all things are pragmata deriving their meaning from us. But under the impetus of passion the interests of the beloved supplant our own, and the world finds its meaning in her.

Yet this precocious ripening pays a penalty whose cost is measured—though never by the lover—in passion's exclusivism. To achieve its penetrating intensity, attention has had to sacrifice its scope. No less than the beloved, all persons possess implicit perfections, but passion has eyes for one alone. Therefore it chooses its beloved not in the world but against the world, and herein lies its deadliness, for by excising both beloved and lover from the world, passion deprives them of the medium necessary to their existence. Though the fire of passion will appear to them a higher sustenance, it is of a kind with the flush upon the cheek of the victim of advanced consumption, foreshadowing death. The proximity of passion and death is timelessly told in the legend of Tristan and Isolde. In Simone de Beauvoir's words, the meaning of the legend is that "Two lovers destined solely for each other are already dead: they die of ennui, of the slow agony of a love that feeds on itself."[40]

But the legend reveals that Tristanism is not love, for love is life itself in its ascendancy. Is passion therefore antithetical to true love, as such philosophers as Epicurus, Montaigne, and Denis de Rougemont have alleged? No, for passion performs the inestimable service we have just described, a service both to love and to life. What we are led to recognize is that passion, while not identical to love, is the necessary first stage of that form of love that follows upon self-love in the genetic order. By its penetration and re-centering, passion precociously effects that exchange of incommensurable personal principles that constitutes internal knowledge of the other by participatory enactment, and that maturity can achieve without passion's aid. It remains the destiny of romantic love to move through passion to a restoration of the world, but a restoration by which the world is transformed through the personalization of its individual human beings. We may therefore proceed with our description, but carefully and step by step to avoid abstractionism.

A person in the throes of passion looks eagerly to his beloved for indications that his condition is replicated in her. This is not because passion per se is beautifying or ennobling. Love is indeed beautifying and ennobling; it also enriches, vitalizes, and enlarges. But passion is none of these things, but the very opposite—it is constriction, stupefaction, paralysis. Nothing is more tiresome to observe than two individuals convulsed by a mutual passion. They endlessly repeat to each other a handful of tedious phrases; they sit motionless together for hours; they move as if their bodies were filled with sand; they rapturously twirp and tweet over trifles. Yet an individual who is thus stricken will wish his unbeautiful condition on his beloved, and why? Because passion has a reflexive side that renders the individual totally vulnerable. Together with internal perception of the other, it affords total disclosure of the individual to the other. This reflexive dimension produces in him a brief but inevitable hesitation. For remember, we are speaking here first of youth and by passion youth is required to unveil that which the whole of adolescence has sheltered and nurtured in darkness—the tender growth tip of individuation, of unique personhood. This hesitation manifests itself as the search for signs of reciprocity in the other. It is his reassurance that he can relinquish himself without risk of being summarily swallowed. In this condition he will be rightly distressed by her attentions to others, her pursuit of standing interests in friends, career, bridge, or items in the daily news. For these are signs that her original world remains coolly intact, containing a place for him that he is being trimmed to fit. These terms will not appear either too canny or too prudential for youthful passion if we bear in mind the extreme shyness and vulnerability of youth in respect to the very thing summoned forth by passion.

But that passion is only the preliminary and first stage will now be put beyond doubt if we address to it the following question. Supposing that reciprocity exhibits itself to passion's complete satisfaction, does passion continue indefinitely to demand of the beloved the constricted and paralytic condition that is passion itself? The answer veritably shouts itself. It does not want this but something very different, namely the prosperity and fulfillment of the beloved as the unique and precious enterprise that passion reveals her to be.

In this light Tristanism is recognizable as the developmental arrest of romantic love in its first stage—it is forcibly truncated love. To illustrate this, the model of a cone will serve. The world, full and brimming at the top, is attenuated by passion to a single object. Passion knots a cord around the throat of the world, constricting it to the point that is the beloved. Yet this point, if penetrated by the intensest concentration, reopens into a brimming world very different from the original world for, as against the commonplace world, this new world is the personal world of the beloved. Such is the transformation effected by the passion that becomes love. But Tristanism vows to preclude the appearance of the world ever after, thereby arresting this process at the stage of passion. By so doing it constitutes a sentence of death and reveals itself to be, not love, but a life- and world-renunciation that uses passion to this end.

A person is not a pinpoint in a void but an organizing center of a singular world of meanings, and because this is so, romantic love must be understood to intend the re-admission of the world. To love a person is to love an environment, an environment that is the world for her and by her, the world as it appears in her meaning and under her principle. Its richest elements are those things that are closest to her, in which she has invested herself and which in turn permeate her. Can we love a painter without loving inclusively her paintings and the sources in her experience from which they are made? But this is impossible, for they are inseparable from her being. We shall long to know her house and the things within it which are her treasures; her books, and the passages in them from which she draws sustenance and delight; the music she loves and lives with and by; the friends whose lives are mixed with hers. By feeling, thought, perception, intention, and imagination she lives both from and into things, persons, and events, and she can only be embraced inclusively, by embracing them.

Likewise the environment that she is includes her past. One day it strikes us with the force of a blow that her childhood escapes us, and immediately we begin to reclaim it by asking her to relive it with us. More especially does this environment include her future, for its present meanings are constituted by her destiny, and by her destiny we are introduced to its implicit perfections. We love her distinctive possibility* *as her possibility*, and by our love we will the fulfillment of that possibility by her.

Thus arises the intemperance responsible for hostilities between romantic love and the world. By no means does romantic love scorn enworldment per se, nor can we afford to suppose, as have countless critics, that it abolishes the "real" world in favor of a chimera. It abolishes the anonymous and impersonal common world in order that the world of another person may unfold. The "chimera" the ordinary world ascribes to romantic love is the latter's apprehension of the immeasurable preciousness of the person. By introducing us to the preciousness of another person, romantic love bridges antecedent sociality and consequent sociality—the sociality of sameness and the sociality of com-

---

* As opposed to Sartre, for whom love is enslavement precisely because it amputates the other's possibilities.[41]

plementary differences. If romantic love is notably ungentle in its onset, and in significant respects mechanical, by these traits is it outfitted to break the iron bonds of egoism. But by the very characteristic that achieves its purpose—its exclusivism—romantic love is itself rendered unfit for the recognition upon which the further development of consequent sociality depends, namely the universality of preciousness in persons as unique individuals.

Where the meaning of love is eros, universal love must have its foundation in universal value, and this love—to be termed, perhaps, "fellow feeling" or "caring"—will inevitably be largely abstract. For as love of persons as persons, its concrete instances are restricted to persons of whom one has actual internal knowledge, and these will be relatively few. One's love of persons other than these will be abstract because it is empty of knowledge of their potential excellences, but this recognition does not diminish the significance of universal love. In the absence of knowledge this love is expressed as the presupposition of the intrinsic, implicit preciousness of all persons, a preciousness that demands respect no less in the absence of concrete knowledge. It is an epitomizing case of the wisdom of St. Augustine's *"credo quia intelligam"*—believe, in order to know. However abstractly held, the conviction of persons' irreplaceable potential worth is an inducement to the manifestation of that worth. The employment of this presupposition as the wellspring of policy in education, government, and community life can be expected to produce transformations as profound and far-reaching as they are moral.

Intermediate between romantic love and universal love is friendship. The structure and aim of friendship are identical to the structure and aim we have discerned in romantic love, consisting in reciprocal willing of fulfillment of the individuals as individuals. But friendship lacks romantic love's passion and therefore its exclusivism. While romantic love in its essence affirms one other to the exclusion of the rest, friendship exhibits no corresponding restriction, though the number of the persons with whom an individual can simultaneously be friends is directly proportional to the strength and coherence of his personhood. Friendship is thus relieved of a trait in romantic love that constitutes the latter's limitation from the standpoint of sociality. But the cost to friendship of its victory over exclusivism is the loss of passion's special services. What passion furnishes automatically—rupture of egoism, encounter with the innermost being of the other, disclosure of one's own innermost being—in the case of friendship must be achieved by cultivated skills of personal character. To be a friend one must know how to suspend voluntarily his own perspective with its attendant needs and interests; he must know how to discover the principle that is the innermost being of the other; he must know how to use this principle to explore the personal world of the other; he must possess the discretion to will his friend's fulfillment without abrogating his friend's self-responsibility; and he must himself be capable of profound self-disclosure. He must manifest the will to do these things. The will to friendship expresses the recognition that one is in oneself not the totality of goodness but rather an aspect—an aspect that in its actualization summons complementary aspects, willing their actualization together with its own. The abilities requisite to friendship are encapsulated in romantic love, awaiting disclosure by reflective analysis. But in the case of friendship they are manifested by the initiative and ingenuity of the individual or not at all. Referring to the conditions of friendship, Martin Buber says,

> If we want to do today's work and prepare tomorrow's with clear sight, then we must develop in ourselves and in the next generation a gift which lives in man's inwardness as a Cinderella, one day to be a princess. Some call it intuition, but that is not a wholly unambiguous concept. I prefer the name "imagining the real," for in its essential being this gift is not a looking at the other, but a bold swinging—demanding the

most intensive stirring of one's being—into the life of the other. This is the nature of all genuine imagining, only that here the realm of my action is not the all-possible, but the particular real person who confronts me, whom I can attempt to make present to myself just in this way, and not otherwise, in his wholeness, unity, and uniqueness, and with his dynamic centre which realizes all these things ever anew.[42]

The work of which Buber speaks is, in our terms, the cultivation of consequent sociality, the sociality that presupposes the unique potential excellence of every individual and is predicated upon the rational principle of the complementarity of excellences. By generalizing each individual's knowledge of his own worth, friendship provides the concrete foundation for consequent sociality's ascription of worth to all persons. It overturns the contrary supposition, founded in acquaintance, that worthy persons are few while the unworthy are legion. Such, indeed, is the unequivocal testimony of actuality. Its refutation consists in friendship's demonstration that actuality does not contain persons until it is transformed into potentiality by the inclusion of possibilities.

Antecedent sociality achieves the harmony that sociality requires by emphasizing the resemblance of persons at the expense of differences. It teaches individuals to regard themselves as fundamentally alike, and only epiphenomenally diverse. In support of this teaching and the presupposition on which it rests (that likeness is the condition of harmony), antecedent sociality rebukes a resolute individuation and invokes moral sanctions against it, branding it "selfish" and "anti-social." This is why, in Buber's words, "The perception of one's fellow man as a whole, as a unity, and as unique—even if his wholeness, unity, and uniqueness are only partly developed, as is usually the case—is opposed in our time by almost everything that is commonly understood as specifically modern." It is why "In our time there predominates an analytical, reductive, and deriving look between man and man. This look is analytical, or rather pseudo analytical, since it treats the whole being as put together and therefore able to be taken apart—not only the so-called unconscious which is accessible to relative objectification, but also the psychic stream itself, which can never, in fact, be grasped as an object. This look is a reductive one because it tries to contract the manifold person, who is nourished by the cosmic richness of the possible, to some schematically surveyable and recurrent structures."[43]

From the genetic standpoint, antecedent sociality is entirely legitimate for what it is, namely a necessary stage in the development of sociality. But its opposition to meaningful individuation evinces an unpardonable self-reification. By mistaking itself for the final truth of sociality, it poses an obstacle to further development and thereby to life itself. The ground of its antagonism to individuation is its conviction that, for sociality to obtain, resemblance among individuals must prevail over differences. In this interest it conspires resolutely to diminish individuation to its minimal meaning as the merely numerical.

But even the Hellenes recognized that a higher ground of social harmony obtained in the complementarity of qualitatively distinct excellences. The principle of this higher, individuated sociality finds first formal expression in Plato's "congeniality of excellences." Concerning friendship, Plato demonstrates that its condition cannot be the bare likeness of the individuals, for in this case neither person can do for the other anything that the other cannot do as well for himself. "And if neither can be of any use to the other, how can they be loved by one another?"[44] Nor can the condition of friendship be pure difference between individuals, for in such a case no relationship can possibly obtain. The conclusion drawn is that the condition of friendship is neither pure resemblance nor pure difference, but is instead the "congeniality" that obtains between persons who are alike in loving the good, but different in respect to the particular

good each loves. It is this principle of the congeniality of
finite goods, personal excellences, that fulfills the condition
of a sociality of persons. In terms set forth at the beginning
of this chapter, to be a morality of persons a social morality
must accord equal significance to likeness and to differences
among persons. A society manifests goodness in the degree
to which it is founded in a morality of persons.

In modern times the principle of the congeniality of excellences finds consummate theoretical formulation in Leibniz's Principle of Compossibility. Precisely stated, "compossibility" is the principle of possible co-existence. For a thing
to exist, it must first be possible, i.e. its concept can not be
self-contradictory; but it is also necessary that it be capable
of co-existing with all other existing things. Compossibility
is a logico-metaphysical condition, which is to say a matter
of essences. As for Plato, so for Leibniz essences are ends
of activity. They are perfections embodied in and aspired
to by active substances. As active substances persons are
aspirants to perfections—in Plato's terms they are "lovers
of the good." But Leibniz stresses that the perfections that
persons embody are qualified in two fundamental respects.
By the Principle of the Identity of Indiscernibles they cannot replicate one another but are of necessity qualitatively
diverse. Each is bound by "the essential and original limitation of the created thing,"[45] a limitation that is limitation itself, or finitude. To be what it is, each pays the price of not
being everything else—it is an essential individual. In these
terms the perfection of the world consists in the perfect harmony of qualitatively diverse, finite perfections. This ideal
is implicit in the actual world as the end to which actuality
is destined by moral necessity, an end it imperfectly expresses. Conflict in the actual world reflects, not conflict in
moral ends, but the imperfect expression by actuality of its
ends.

Against the social principle of the congeniality of excellences, it is commonplace to construe conflict in the world
as essentially the product of mutually antagonistic ends.

The proposition the congeniality principle endorses is that conflict is not of essences but of appearances, the result of our imperfect apprehension of ends. Phenomenological evidence of this appears in the worthy man's typical respect for his worthy opponents. From this standpoint the will to suppress one's opponents is identifiable as a mistake of immaturity that inevitably fails in its purpose because failure is what it is in and of itself. *Per contra* the worthy man wills not the suppression of his opponents but their fulfillment together with his own, by which opposition is extinguished in the complementarity of perfections.

The will to suppress one's opponents has been sufficiently demonstrated by Nietzsche and Scheler to be typically a *ressentiment* phenomenon, the resort of persons lacking a conviction of self-worth, devoid of self-love.[46] With (as they believe) nothing in themselves to be gained, they conceive their gain to be the degradation of others, and they set themselves to this purpose. But a second source of the will to the suppression of others arises with a self-love that, while accurate in what it knows, as yet perceives none of the implications of its knowledge. I refer to egoism's supposition that its own truth is the truth exclusively, its own worth the exclusive good. In this condition it demands of others a discipleship that the worthy man hastens to forbid.* Together, *ressentiment* and egoism find their only true correctives in moral education—education in self-worth in the case of *ressentiment*, and education in the universal implications of self-worth in the case of egoism. The course of learning is laid down by the natural development of love, from self-love to exclusivistic romantic love to friendship and universal love of persons. It is love of persons that is expressed in the worthy man's pleasure in worthy opponents. Such is his strength that he wills not his

---

* E.g. the Buddha to his followers: "Be ye lamps unto yourselves . . . . Those who, either now or after I am dead, shall rely upon themselves only and not look for assistance to anyone beside themselves, it is they who shall reach the very topmost height."[47]

adversaries' demise but their perfection, thereby to out-grow adversity in the congeniality of excellences.

Implicit in the smallest impulse to self-actualization is the will to the actualization of unique worth by every person, and in itself this will is its own measure of responsibility for securing the conditions of such actualization. Here is the foundation of social justice. The worthy person fulfills his social responsibility initially and foremost by living his own life justly. But he is in himself the expression of truths that, by an epistemic "lag," are elsewhere only implicit, and as such he bears his measure of responsibility for achieving and maintaining the conditions that promote their emergence. In his measure he is responsible for the installation of these truths in the institutions of society, foremost among them the institutions of education, division of labor, the law, and the penal system. His responsibility must be exercised with patience, for to expect a precipitous transformation of antecedent, impersonal sociality into the consequent sociality of true persons is to commit the fallacy of anachronism. What maturity owes to prior stages of development is not a suddenly bestowed maturation, but rather the conditions by which self-maturation can be achieved, together with the example of mature, worthy living.

10

Intrinsic Justice and Division of Labor
in Consequent Sociality

Justice is the paramount virtue of society, as integrity is the cardinal virtue of personal life. Justice, in the first instance, subsists in principles for the allocation of goods and responsibilities within a social grouping. Concerning the source of these principles, normative individualism contends that they subsist implicitly within every person, rising to explicitness as the person attains integral individuation.

In this conception, the foundation of justice is the presupposition of the unique, irreplaceable, potential worth of every person, and forms of sociality that neglect or contradict this presupposition (we will shortly take notice of several) deal justice a mortal wound at the outset. This presupposition disallows the conventional belief that so-called "natural talents" are haphazardly distributed. In their root meaning as potential personal excellences, "natural talents" are universally distributed* but haphazardly recognized and, in consequence, haphazardly cultivated. It likewise disallows the supposition that "natural talents" are blessings, gifts, or gratuities, to be idly enjoyed. Fundamentally they are taskmasters, thematic responsibilities that for each individual constitute his meaningful work. Here we arrive at the centrality of "work" to the true concept of the person. Within this concept, "work" is no mere appendage, contingency, or burden. In its profound meaning "work" is not man's punishment for the sin committed by Adam and Eve in a workless paradise, nor is it the provisional imposition of a natural evolutionary process moving toward a

* We shall subsequently say something about "birth defects."

workless paradise. The concept "person" is incompatible with a workless paradise for the reason that a person can never be a fait accompli. Rather, a person is irredeemably and essentially a future to be made present, a potentiality to be progressively actualized, and it is this task of actualization that furnishes the term "work" with its profound meaning. Insofar as "work" historically has a poor press among humankind this is because so little of the work to be done has been done by the individuals whose true work it is. And this historical fact bespeaks deep-rooted injustice, for the subsistence within every person of a discrete potential excellence is his natural entitlement to meaningful work —the work that, were he entirely free, each person would do in preference to every other kind of work, and in preference to doing nothing of value, or nothing at all.[1]

The source of the justice here invoked is not God, or the state, or a contract that individuals may enter into—it is the essential nature of the person as an individual. Each person *qua* person possesses natural entitlements in virtue of his worth, a worth that is (for actual persons) both potential and actual. As a perfection of a kind, each person's potential worth is absolute, while his actual worth is qualified by degree. Because it is qualified by degree, actual worth furnishes differential entitlement, while worth as pure potential establishes a lower limit of entitlement that is alike for all. At the lower limit (minimum actual worth) each person is entitled to the necessities for actualization—to food, shelter, decent treatment by other persons in acknowledgment of his potential worth, to the materials of self-knowledge and of factual knowledge of the world. At the upper limit he is entitled to those *commensurate* goods whose potential worth he can maximally actualize in accordance with his destiny, his "meaningful work."

Justice here originates noncomparatively, in an intra-individual dimension. This is necessarily the case. For consider an essentially comparative conception of justice, e.g. the egalitarian, requiring "equal treatment for equal cases."

The principle will be adhered to by treating equal cases equally badly, and "badly" can logically have the meaning of "unjustly" in the sense that the particular treatment is undeserved by any of the individuals so treated. That bad treatment is undeserved *equally* does not render it just, despite the honorific halo of the word "equal." In short, comparative justice is justice only when justice obtains in the individual case.

The derivation of justice from integral personhood renders it uniquely self-sustaining, for individuation itself implies voluntary disavowal of claim to certain distributable goods. We will develop this point with a concrete example.

As a philosopher I have just claim to certain distributable goods, and I am without just claim to others. For example I have no just claim to a Ferrari sports car. Moreover, for reasons much sterner than its $30,000 price tag I cannot "afford" to own the car and should not consent to receive it as a gift. The piece of machinery will go 160 miles an hour, corner like a leopard, and hold direction in a four-wheel drift. These capabilities will not be utilized in my daily commutes to my office. In addition, to utilize them requires a discipline no less arduous than that of philosophy, and for me to undertake it will necessarily be at philosophy's expense. As a philosopher I ought not undertake it, and we revert to the equally unjustified situation in which the Ferrari's capabilities go unactualized because of my ownership. This is a waste of potential value, and a wise person knows there can be no pleasure in it. But we must speak strictly. The wise person knows that the intrinsic reward of *doing* is confined to the doing that one does well, while the doing that one does badly is intrinsically costly. But "well" and "badly" as applied to doing are not measures of mere efficiency; they likewise gauge the relation of what is done to the individual who is doing it. For this reason the wise person disregards pleasure and pain as signals, turning instead to the feelings of eudaimonia and dysdaimonia. Pleasure is the feeling of gratified desire and is indiscriminate with respect to the desires that are gratified. Eudaimonia is the feeling attending *right* desire, not only in its gratification but equally in its inception as desire and in every step leading to its gratification. Accordingly there are eudaimonic pains as well as dysdaimonic pleasures, and the wise person (the integral individual) accepts the former while shunning the latter. To the true individual the feeling of eudaimonia constitutes the intrinsic reward of doing what is his to do, and doing it well. Conversely to do what is not one's own is intrinsically costly, being at the expense of oneself, and to desire what is not one's own is to wish to be someone other than one is. This is the condition of dysdaimonia—a condition that does not preclude pleasures (it may give me pleasure that, crouched at my curb, the Ferrari causes passersby to misidentify me as a race driver or a millionaire), but it prevents these pleasures from constituting intrinsic rewards.

Returning for a moment to the conception of waste of potential value, we have implied that it constitutes injustice, and it is important to see specifically how this is so. The injustice of waste is clear where the waste of a resource by one individual deprives another of a resource to which he is entitled. For example, to waste food when the world contains starving people is unjust. But to tie the injustice of waste to the consequent deprivation of others is to predicate justice upon an economics of scarcity. While this predication has often enough been made,[2] it remains fundamentally mistaken. Not only does it commit the previously noted fallacy of rendering justice essentially comparative, but it perpetrates a fallacy of "misplaced concreteness" by grounding justice in distributable goods rather than in persons. The question of justice appears in the world with persons, and remains so long as there are persons in the world. Neither the superabundance nor the utter lack of distributable goods can eliminate the problem of justice. Indeed, to treat distributable goods as if they were independent variables in this context is rightly ridiculed by Robert Nozick as a "manna-from-heaven"[3] conception of distributable goods that ignores the investments of persons in the production of such goods. Nozick's concern is to demonstrate an antecedent entitlement that must weigh in any distribution or redistribution, and in due course we must attend to his "entitlement conception of justice." Just now we want to insist on a point more basic still, namely that distributable goods are not independent variables in the matrix of justice, but instead are the products of life and work, and it is therefore in terms of the productive life that the problem of justice originates. An inquiry into the meaning of justice touches bottom, not in the "recipient justice" of "who gets what," but in the productive justice of who shall do what and contribute what, in regard to which recipient justice exhibits strictly instrumental status.

By the theory we espouse, injustice consists in deprivation of what is claimed with entitlement, and in advancement of unentitled claims. It rests in personal worth, and the productive work that personal worth, as potentiality, requires for actualization. Our hypothetical Robinson Crusoe, alone on his island and entirely without experience of other persons, nevertheless inhabits a setting where the conditions of justice are present and the question of justice arises. The potential excellence that Robinson Crusoe possesses as a person constitutes his natural entitlement to the material and circumstantial requisites for the manifestation of this excellence.* Where the lack of such requisites precludes the actualization of Robinson Crusoe's personal excellence—e.g. where no food is to be found and he starves to death—injustice obtains. But, alternatively, Robinson

---

* This exhibits a certain kinship to William James's proposition that "without a claim actually being made by some concrete person there can be no obligation, but that there is some obligation wherever there is a claim." But we differ from James by our insistence that only *rightful* claims create obligation. (See James's "The Moral Philosopher and the Moral Life," in *The Will to Believe, and Other Essays in Popular Philosophy* [New York: Longmans, Green & Co., 1897], pp. 184-215).

Crusoe possesses no entitlement to goods that he cannot utilize toward the actualization of his personal excellence. His use of such goods will be misuse, wasting their potential value. This waste is injustice—the injustice of acting upon unentitled claims. At work here at the deepest level is the principle that goodness has a right to exist. Because waste destroys the potential worth of distributable goods it commits injustice by violating this right.

An important implication of the correlation of waste and injustice concerns what can be called the "maximizing principle of material benefits," a principle offered as a principle of justice by a certain type of theories of justice. The principle calls for the proliferation without limit of the material holdings of persons on the grounds that of such goods "each [person] prefer(s) a larger to a lesser share."[4] But the indeterminacy of both the principle and this alleged preference render them disproportionate to the nature of the individual. Individuation is determination according to the Spinozan principle, *omnis determinatio est negatio*. As a finite creature a person's entitlements are strictly finite both quantitatively and qualitatively. In order to manifest his determinate worth in the world, an individual needs not all kinds of distributable goods, but only goods of certain kinds; and the amount of these goods he can utilize to his qualitatively determinate purpose is limited. The maximizing principle bespeaks injustice by sponsoring indeterminacy against the determinate nature of personhood. The desires it expresses are those of the non-individual—the ignorant, undisciplined, and uncommitted man, who wants everything, believes himself entitled to everything, and begrudges others their smallest gain. It should now be clear of what type those theories are that espouse the maximizing principle as a principle of justice. They are theories that attempt to squeeze justice out of ignorance, as exemplified most recently by the "veil of ignorance" that John Rawls uses to preclude all knowledge to the persons who, on his contractarian theory, are to choose the principles of justice of their subsequent association. It is indeed to be expected that persons who are utterly without knowledge of their own identities will endorse the maximization of benefits without limit. Since to their knowledge they are no one in particular, each must regard himself as potentially anyone, with a potential need for anything, and with as much of a claim to anything as anyone else. This ignorant omnivorousness is inscribed everlastingly within the conception of justice of Rawls's contractarianism by his stipulation that the principles of justice be chosen under the veil of ingorance.*

Such is not the condition of the self-aware individual. As a finite, determinate potentiality he knows his entitlements to be correspondingly determinate. By no means does he claim all goods, in unlimited amounts. He claims only those goods whose potential worth he can maximally manifest in the course of manifesting his own determinate worth, and he claims them only in utilizable amounts. He shuns "maximization" out of his moral abhorrence of waste. And he shuns goods that are incommensurate with his determinate destiny in the knowledge that for him, such goods represent distractions, impediments to self-actualization, in short: waste of himself.

In my life-style as a philosopher, the effect of the Ferrari

---

* In an argument related to mine, Andreas Esheté identifies the latent contradiction between "maximization" and meaningful work, contending against Rawls that at relative abundance the former must be abandoned for the latter (and therefore that Rawls's conception of justice fails of universality). See Andreas Esheté, "Contractarianism and the Scope of Justice," Ethics, 85, no. 1 (Oct. 1974), 38-49. Our (stronger) contention is that "maximization" is a false principle per se, fostering injustice under any economic conditions by fostering ignorant omnivorousness against due proportion. Conversely, meaningful work is a universal principle of justice, irrespective of economic conditions: indeed, it is the best possible guarantor of productivity, for to live meaningfully is to live productively. Meaningful work presupposes individuation and self-knowledge, and is therefore de facto confined to consequent sociality. But consequent sociality universalizes itself by supplying to all the conditions of individuation and self-knowledge.

would be that of a large lump that unbalanced the whole, like the eccentrically placed lump of lead in trick golf balls that causes them to describe weird arcs in the air and land anywhere but the point of aim. The highly refined piece of machinery would force me to keep a mechanic on retainer, or become one myself. Meanwhile my subconscious will have become a simmering cauldron of premonitions—of bruising one of my $80 Pirelli tires against a curb, for example. In my bed at night, asleep, my ears will be sleeplessly attuned to sounds of the Ferrari's stealthy rusting, rusting.

Pursuing individuality's implications for justice further, let us suppose that I shun the Ferrari: does it follow that I begrudge the machine to another? Not if the other is Mario Andretti or Emerson Fittipaldi, for either man can maximize the capabilities of the car to the benefit of every fan of racing, myself included. Likewise I do not begrudge the engineer his slide rule, the biologist his electron microscope, the diplomat his entertainment budget, or the movie star his splendid clothing. I disavow these distributable "goods" because I recognize them to be incommensurate with the person I am, and because I know that possession of such incommensurate goods will distract me from my course, set me at odds with myself, and impede the manifestation of my own worth. At the same time I recognize that goods that are incommensurate with my particular destiny are commensurate with the destinies of certain others, and in the interest of the maximization of value I actively will such goods to those persons to whom by natural entitlement they belong. By no means is justice here in any respect grudging, but rather is this active willing what is meant by the love of justice, and the justice of love.

But I do these things upon condition of the recognition of my own entitlements, which is to say, upon condition of confidence in my own potential worth. Here is why we insisted at the outset that the presupposition of the intrinsic, irreplaceable potential worth of every person is the indispensable condition of social justice. Without this presupposition, voluntary relinquishment of incommensurable goods will not occur, and justice loses its natural foundation and its self-subsistence. Here arises that make-believe justice that is "no respecter of persons," and that, in the absence of persons, must found itself in some such merely numerical formula as "each to count for one and only one."

Concerning the crucial condition of scarcity, it appears to disclose a distinct advantage in conceptions of justice that accord differential entitlement, as opposed to egalitarian and numerical conceptions. This appearance is deceptive, but it will be worthwhile to expose it as such.

Scarcity here means the condition that obtains with respect to a distributable good when the supply of the good is insufficient to satisfy all entitled claims to it. With respect to a scarce good, the advantage of conceptions of justice that affirm differential entitlement is that they appear to be able to select which, among competing claims, possesses greatest entitlement. If this is so, then distribution of scarce goods can be determined *within* the meaning of justice. But for egalitarian and numerical conceptions of justice, no distribution of a scarce good can be more just than another, and this means that such distribution must be made by means which are alien to justice as thus conceived. An abused in extremis example* is the "lifeboat" situation—three persons adrift in a lifeboat with food enough to sustain only one of them for the interval likely for discovery and rescue. Which of the three shall be given the chance for life? By the equality of the merely numerical, the question cannot be decided, and resort must be made to some such

---

* In extremis examples are regularly abused in philosophical debate. The proponent of a theory is asked to show how his theory would handle a certain extreme situation. His answer is patently weak, and his theory suffers the indicated judgment. What remains unsaid and usually unrecognized is that the in extremis situation is handled weakly, and perhaps more weakly still, by all rival theories. The proper conclusion to be drawn is, I think, that in extremis situations are an in extremis critical resort. Of immensely more interest is how a given theory handles common situations.

means as a drawing of lots. Despite the contentions of egalitarians and numerologists, however, the drawing of lots is not rendered just by the equal chance of all participants. Our clear recognition of the disparity is indicated by the fact that we would not tolerate the judgment by lot of those accused of crimes, or the awarding of honors by lot, or the apportionment of responsibility by lot. The resort to lots is the resort to chance, not justice, and we confuse the two at our peril. When a theory of justice resorts to the determinations of chance, it identifies its own limitations.

The question, then, is whether a conception of justice that affirms differential entitlement is in a better way. Suppose the lifeboat contains two unexceptional persons and Albert Einstein. Does not Einstein possess a greater entitlement to life than his two companions? And suppose that all three are by conviction normative individualists who, moreover, will not abandon their principles in extremis. May we not expect them to agree to award the chance of life to Einstein, as the individual whose continued life is likeliest to actualize a large measure of value, to the benefit of mankind?*

---

* *Noblesse oblige* calls for consideration here, both as a feeling and as a moral concept. As a feeling it is frequently very powerful, such that it is not unlikely that under its sway Einstein, in our example, would be the first to volunteer to sacrifice himself. But just here, I think, the feeling betrays its untrustworthiness, for to ask self-extinction of nobility is to conspire to the sovereignty of mediocrity. It is the validity of the *concept* of *noblesse oblige* that normative individualism asserts, and the concept disconfirms the feeling when the feeling works to diminish nobility in the world. The heavy obligation that nobility (in the moral sense) bears is that of perfecting itself while extending its own conditions to ever greater numbers of humankind.

In support (as he believes) of Albert Schweitzer and John Rawls, Herbert Spiegelberg argues that nobility owes compensatory benefits to ordinary persons and that ordinary persons have a moral right to expect compensatory benefits from nobility. But this contention is calculated to extinguish moral nobility unless the proviso be added that the benefits to be expected from nobility are strictly those which nobility of itself confers, in truth to itself. For if the ordinary per-

Correspondingly, in less spectacular distribution of scarce goods, differential entitlement means that, in principle, claims can be arranged hierarchically and thereby adjudicated within the scope of justice, obviating a resort to extraneous means.

On closer inspection, however, differential entitlement cannot claim this superiority. For it must be borne in mind that goods are scarce, not by reference to all claims upon them, but rather by reference only to true claims upon them (and thus we are able to distinguish between genuine and false scarcity). But all true claims are absolute, and therefore a conception of justice that affirms differential entitlement holds, at our present level of analysis, no advantage over egalitarian and numerical conceptions. By the tenets of normative individualism, entitlements are differentiated both qualitatively and quantitatively. By qualitative differentiation, one person may be entitled alone to a good to which several persons lay claim. By quantitative differentiation, one person may be entitled to more of a certain good than others. But the quality and amount of goods to which any person is entitled he is entitled to absolutely, not more or less. Thus while Picasso is entitled to linen canvas in

---

son is endorsed in whatever he himself may demand of nobility, it will be found that those who are themselves most devoid of nobility require above all the extinction of nobility, thereby to erase the standing evidence of their own moral inferiority. In Chapter 9 we saw what nobility confers upon others in truth to itself, and therefore without self-debilitation.

"Compensation" is called for by Spiegelberg's supposition that nobility is either an "accident" of birth or an instance of cosmically bestowed "good fortune." But either supposition is pernicious, for it divides the sheep from the goats inalterably. The truth of the matter is that moral nobility is earned by the effort of the individual, coming about in no other way; it is available to all persons. For it consists not in the characteristics that are the individual's from birth, but in what is wrought from these characteristics by the individual himself. (See Herbert Spiegelberg, "Good Fortune Obligates: Albert Schweitzer's Second Ethical Principle," *Ethics*, 85, no. 3 [April 1975], 227-234.)

large amounts, and the beginning student of painting is entitled only to cotton canvas in lesser amounts, that canvas to which the student is entitled he is entitled to absolutely, and any shortage constitutes injustice. In the lifeboat example, each of the three persons is entitled to life in virtue of his innate potentiality, and because the entitlement is in each case absolute, the conception of justice offered by normative individualism cannot decide to whom the opportunity of life shall be given, and extraneous means must be employed. Likewise with less spectacular distributions of scarce goods, where the claims are genuine (backed by entitlement), normative individualism's conception of justice is rendered impotent by the absolutism of all genuine claims.

But normative individualism is in this respect at no disadvantage by comparison to alternative conceptions of justice, for no conception of justice can subsume distributions under conditions of genuine scarcity. Where a good is scarce with respect to genuine claims, injustice is inevitable; and this suggests that conceptions of justice must be held responsible, not for achieving justice where it is not to be had, but for the more far-reaching effect of meliorating the conditions inimical to justice. Here, the differential entitlement conception of normative individualism holds surpassing promise. It works to alleviate scarcity, in the first place, by the distinction it introduces between true and false claims to distributable goods. By honoring all claims as equal, egalitarianism fails to distinguish between true and false claims, thereby institutionalizing injustice; for where self-knowledge is lacking, the individual himself cannot distinguish between desires that are in his true interest and those that are not. Under normative individualism the final ground of the distinction between true and false desires is the nature of the individual himself, and he himself is the final authority. But by the emergent nature of individualism the exercise of this final authority by the individual is deferred until true individuation is attained, and meanwhile others must share with him the responsibility for the determination of his true interests. The test of judgments of others with respect to the true interests of an emerging individual is whether their judgment supports or retards his emerging individuation.* The number of claims upon scarce distributable goods is diminished, in the first place, by the voluntary forebearance of integral individuals who recognize that they themselves are in the given instance without entitlement. It is likewise diminished by the identification by authority of unentitled claims among claims made, said authority being bound by the principle that it must further the self-responsibility of the persons over whom it is exercised. To revert to a previous example, I do not lay claim to a Ferrari because I recognize that I possess no entitlement (I cannot actualize the potential worth of this distributable good in consonance with my own destiny). If my sixteen-year-old son were to advance his claim to a Ferrari I should deny it, on the same ground and the same logic. But were he to show a glimmer of promise as a race driver, justice would dictate that he be allowed to see what he could do with a used Triumph Spitfire (say) and some instruction in race-driving and mechanics.

The justice of normative individualism works to alleviate scarcity, second, by setting upper limits to the entitlements of individuals, as against such limitless conceptions as the

---

* By the tenets of normative individualism, the authority of one individual over another is restricted to that amount and kind of authority that enhances the individual in his exercise of self-authority. Because normative individualism affirms the essential dependence of children, and because it also affirms that at any developmental level the true interests of an individual may be known better by another person than by himself (hence the supreme moral service that love can render), it might be suspected that normative individualism wittingly or unwittingly succors paternalism. But the opprobrious meaning of paternalism is an exercise of authority intended to preserve dependents in their dependence, and such exercise is identified and condemned by the principle of normative individualism enunciated above.

previously mentioned "maximizing principle of material benefits." By sanctifying the ideal of superabundance for all, a maximizing principle effectively endorses the superabundance of those individuals who possess it, while encouraging all persons to aspire to this condition. But the condition is nonuniversalizable in virtue of the finite supply at least of material (and, I would argue, of nonmaterial) goods. The practical result is the moral self-satisfaction of the enormously wealthy, together with a moral onus upon others to do as well for themselves. An unlimited acquisitiveness is here institutionalized which, given the finite supply of distributable goods, amounts to the institutionalization of aggravated and ubiquitous scarcity. *Per contra*, the justice of normative individualism condemns superabundance *in itself* as unjust, on the ground of the individual's finitude and the waste of potential value that superabundance therefore represents. Superabundance is renounced in favor of proportionality, and entitlement acquires an upper limit in the quantity and quality of goods whose potential value the individual can maximally actualize in accordance with his finite destiny as the individual he is. Under this conception scarcity will be alleviated both by the limitation of claims, and by the redistribution of superabundant holdings.*

The third feature serving toward the alleviation of scarcity in the justice of normative individualism is subtler than the two just mentioned, but at the same time more pervasive. It lies in the exchange of a consumption-oriented economy for a production-orientation. For normative individualism, entitlement is not logically ultimate, but derives from the potentiality of every individual for value-actual-

* The redistribution I have in mind would be gradual and largely voluntary, extending over perhaps three or four generations, as the result of changes in education in the meaning of justice. I myself distrust revolutionary expropriation and redistribution. But I grant that the issue remains arguable. I simply have not found revolutionaries who care to offer cogent arguments.

ization. Essentially every person is just such a potential, and the fundamental meaning of living is the production of value in the world by self-actualization. If we suppose that this conception of the person is teachable—and normative individualism argues that it is the most teachable, because the truest, being received characteristically as "what we knew all along, but didn't know that we knew"—we may be sure that the effect of such re-education will be to diminish both real and artificial scarcity in the world.

The justice of normative individualism alleviates scarcity; the "justice" of egalitarianism and the merely numerical artificially exacerbates scarcity, thereby spreading injustice. But the injustice to persons that is inflicted by their interchangeability as merely numerical individuals has as yet barely appeared. To take its measure we examine in some detail the conception of justice currently espoused by John Rawls.

According to Rawls's contractarian theory, justice subsists in the appropriate principles that would be chosen by individuals who expect thereafter to engage in ongoing social cooperation. The appropriate principles assign basic rights and duties and determine the division of social benefits. The choice is to be made from an "original position" by individuals who are "free and rational persons" and "moral equals."[5] It is Rawls's conception of the requisite equality that holds special interest, and we shall begin with a description of it.

Rawls starts from the incontestable fact that any existing social system abounds in inequities among included individuals. Those relevant to the determinations of justice and "especially deep," according to Rawls, are the differences fostered by "economic and social circumstances," by the "political system," and by the "natural lottery"[6] (the distribution of natural talents at birth). Such differences, he says, "cannot possibly be justified by an appeal to the notions of merit or desert,"[7] yet they will influence the choices made by the differentiated individuals themselves, biasing these choices by "arbitrary contingencies."[8] This means that if justice is to reside in principles initially chosen by individuals, the situation of the choice cannot be any actual situation but must instead be a rectification of actuality. What Rawls terms the "original position" is a result of such rectification. The tool by which rectification is achieved is a "veil of ignorance" that requires persons who are about to choose the principles of their subsequent association to conform to the following self-description. "First of all, no one knows his place in society, his class position or social status; nor does he know his fortune in the distribution of natural assets and abilities, his intelligence and strength, and the like. Nor, again, does anyone know his conception of the good, the particulars of his rational plan of life, or even the special features of his psychology such as his aversion to risk or liability to optimism or pessimism. More than this, I assume . . ."[9] (but the citation is now sufficient for our purposes).

The veil of ignorance is expressly intended to nullify "bias by particulars" as heretofore described. Of course the ignorance is functional merely, to be obtained not by vacuum-cleaning the minds in question but only by employing the appropriate constraints on arguments. But in whatever terms, the supposition that *all* particulars are biases requiring elimination reduces the "individuals" of the original position to merely numerical instances of the generic "man." As Rawls painstakingly delineates, these "individuals" will think alike, act alike, need alike, aspire alike, and —to be sure—choose alike. (What they choose "with a single voice" as we may well say, are the two principles of justice and the two priority rules espoused by Rawls, but the substance of these is not our present concern.) They are each replaceable without loss; and while Rawls concedes that all talk of justice would be gratuitous without the existence of conflicts of interest, the only source of conflict that passes the tight mesh of the foregoing stipulations is quantitative. Of the "primary goods" with which justice is concerned, and which all persons (Rawls says) desire alike, "each [individual] prefer(s) a larger to a lesser share."[10]

To grant what Rawls has said thus far would be to agree with him that "the first principle of justice" is "one requiring an equal distribution."[11] For by reducing the persons of his original position to a merely numerical individuality, Rawls has eliminated every possible ground of differential entitlement. But if we bear in mind that this reduction has occurred *prior* to the appearance of justice, it will be apparent that means by which to defend the reduction itself are scarce.* In these straits Rawls calls upon everyone's "intuitive" support. That justice requires equal distribution is, he says, "so obvious that we would expect it to occur to anyone immediately."[12]

The circularity in the argument is only one of the troubles here. Another concerns the need for the rectification of "bias by arbitrary contingencies," if everyone "intuitively" agrees in advance to what it is intended to achieve. Yet another is just what this intuition—yours, mine, everyone's —may be, which somehow remains proof against bias in order that Rawls may rely upon it. But I mention these only in passing. I will myself consult our "intuitive" sense of justice in order to show that basic features of Rawls's conception offend it. But by "intuition" I shall mean nothing in the way of occult authority, but only the abrupt anticipation of the outcome of discursive thought. I shall submit that the "intuitions" upon which Rawls relies are put to rout by discursive thought.

The locus of that sense of the just and the unjust that (as Aristotle says) is the distinction of men lies not in a comparison ("equality," "inequality") but rather in each individual's conviction of his own intrinsic, irreplaceable, potential worth—a conviction that obliges him to resist to the death his reduction to mere numericality under Rawls's veil

---

* Indeed, Rawls himself acknowledges that the design of the Original Position cannot be ethically neutral (pp. 584-585). Bluntly put, Rawls commits the fallacy of presupposing the consequent.

of ignorance. Included in this intuitive conviction is his right to decent treatment by others *in virtue of* his potential worth, and his right to those distributable goods that constitute necessary conditions for his actualization of his potential worth. The most powerful forces of injustice in society—envy and resentment—originate in the denial by others of the inalienable worth of the individual. What must be discerned in resentment is its seething sense of injustice. The "little man" (in Nietzsche's phrase), whose replication into the majority comprises every historical population, feels cheated of something. He therefore begrudges others their every gain, and will revenge himself wherever he can. The assassins of the Kennedys and Martin Luther King were clearly imbued with a feeling of the *righteousness* of their acts. The "little man" feels himself *entitled* to his resentment of distinction or advantage in virtue of the egalitarian supposition that at bottom all men are alike.

To control expressions of resentment we call upon "retributive justice," meting out punishments for social offenses. But retribution only breeds the very resentment it is intended to correct. Publicly we wonder at and deplore the astounding "recidivism" rate among former convicts, but no one wonders at this who has gained the confidence of prisoners themselves, for each of them is an Ancient Mariner with a tale to tell of the injustices that put him where he is—a treacherous girl friend, a sadistic sheriff, a faithless friend, a set of circumstances for which he is in no way responsible, yet they blamed him. On the strength of these real or imagined injustices, these individuals are awaiting their release in order to revenge themselves upon the society that has wronged them, and their vengeance will be aimed no more accurately than their sense of injustice.

What the "little men" have in truth been cheated of is recognition of their own individual, irreplaceable potential worth as persons. It is this deprivation that produces resentment of every advantage of others together with omnivorous acquisitiveness. By contrast, the individual whose unique worth is recognized does not intuitively believe himself entitled to everything, but only to what he needs and can maximally utilize. And the determinacy of this entitlement implies the determinate entitlements of others.

Classically termed "proportion," this commensuration of goods and persons that characterizes our original, intra-individual, "intuitive sense of justice" is likewise constitutive of justice comparatively. Suppose that just now I am contemplating the situation of a person who is more "advantaged" than me with respect to the distributable goods he possesses. Unless prior circumstances of the sort just described have made me a reservoir of resentment, I do not immediately begrudge him his advantages. Nor do I start (as Rawls says I am to do) by searching for benefits to me of his advantages. What I immediately want to know is whether he deserves his advantages, in the sense that, as the person he is, he maximally manifests their potential worth. I ask, is he worthy of them; and my comparative sense of justice is satisfied if available evidence suggests that he is as worthy of the goods he possesses as I am worthy of mine. In short the equality of comparative justice no more lies in replicability of distributable goods than the equality of persons lies in their replication of one another. Rather it consists in equality of the proportion between goods and actual personal worth. Differential entitlement is hereby seen to obtain in virtue of differences of persons with respect to actual worth. These differences are both qualitative and quantitative. Qualitatively, differential entitlement of actual persons derives from qualitative distinctions among their potential excellences. Quantitatively, differential entitlement obtains in virtue of differences among persons with respect to their degree of self-actualization.

To my knowledge, nowhere has attention been called to the fact that egalitarianism's ubiquitous suspicion of advantage precludes to its adherents our natural delight in the presence of persons of surpassing moral excellence. I say "natural delight" in full awareness that the response in question is at present quite rare, for I take this rarity to reflect both the rarity among us of persons of high integrity and the prevalence of a "morality of the commonplace" that instinctively mistrusts exceptionality of any sort. But these countervening factors do nothing to diminish the profound Platonic truth that the natural response to excellence is love. Such love expresses the deep human interdependence formulated by Plato as the "congeniality of excellences," which resentment cannot acknowledge. The integral person requires the company of others of surpassing excellence whom he respects and loves (but neither worships nor imitates), and where they are unavailable to him in actuality he invents them—thus the tragic hero upon the Greek stage, the archetypes of literature (of all genres except, perhaps, the "naturalistic"), and thus that imaginary company that integral individuals often privately keep. By "rendering mediocrity the ascendant power among mankind," as John Stuart Mill said,[13] the egalitarian presupposition serves both to diminish instances of integral individuality and to shift our natural response to such persons from love and gratitude to suspicion and resentment. The foreclosure to us of such occasions of affirmative valuational feeling is not the least of the injustices perpetrated by egalitarianism.

Our natural response of joy in the surpassing excellence of another reveals the essential poverty of conceptions of justice based on "reciprocity" as "returning in kind" (e.g. Rawls, pp. 464, 494, and *passim*), for it affirms benefits that are measureless and ask for no return. The contrast appears effectively in the imagery of José Ortega y Gasset: "A billiard ball colliding with another imparts to it an impulse in principle equal to its own; cause and effect are equal. But when the spur's point ever so lightly touches its flank, the thoroughbred breaks into a gallop, generously out of proportion to the impulse of the spur."[14] Surpassing excellence confers a measureless benefit upon those capable of recognizing it, not by doing measurable practical services for which it asks equal in return, but simply by being. Disproportionate benefits conferred by one person upon another are properly regarded as gifts and expressions of generosity, but as such they are not exempt from the determinations of justice. The prevalence of theories that affirm such exemption attests to a quantification of the concept of justice, beginning with the reduction of persons to merely numerical individuals, which finds itself unable to handle what cannot be measured, weighed, counted, divided, etc. In his recent book, *Anarchy, State, and Utopia*, Robert Nozick exempts gift-giving from the determinations of justice on the ground that entitlement includes the right to dispose of one's entitled resources as one chooses.[15] But surely this right is not unqualified, for if entitlement includes the conception of "being worthy of what one possesses," then a part of being worthy consists in being able to distinguish between better and worse uses of one's possessions, and gift-giving is clearly susceptible of such distinction.* Moreover to exchange the "recipient" model of justice for the "productive" model is to recognize integral living as the archetypal gift-giving, productive of surplus value. To suppose that this surplus value can with impunity be wasted or bestowed capriciously is to undermine justice at its foundations.

By Rawls's "strongly egalitarian" conception of justice, "an equal distribution is to be preferred"[17] such that the distributable goods in the possession of any individual might be exchanged for those of any other individual without loss to either person. (By this conception, if Rawls's typewriter and Phil Esposito's hockey skates are of equal value, then no injustice is committed if a redistributing

---

* Nozick's contention that gift-giving must be left unconstrained (and justice therefore "unpatterned"[16]) finds prima facie support in the conventional conception of justice as external regulation, on the model of positive law. It is true that important aspects of living —gift-giving among them—must be exempted from external regulation. But the reason for this is not that they go unregulated, but in order that they can be regulated by the normative principles of individuals themselves.

agency assigns the typewriter to Esposito and the skates to Rawls, and no reason will exist for Esposito and Rawls to work out an exchange.) Exceptions to equal distribution are allowed, however, by a "difference principle" according to which unequal distribution is just if and only if it is "to the greatest benefit of the least advantaged."[18] But surely here is a riddle: for since in matters of justice we are asked by Rawls to speak only of "primary goods," which in his meaning are desired by all men alike, then "least advantaged" (if relevant to justice) can only mean possessed of fewer primary goods, i.e. "least benefited," and the unequal distribution is required by the difference principle to be "to the benefit of the least benefited." This is self-contradictory.

But doesn't Rawls intend to distinguish between present and future advantage? Thus, present disadvantage to the least advantaged group can be justified by showing that it promotes their future advantage. This seems to be Rawls's intention, for at times he refers to "the expectations of the least advantaged,"[19] and his sole illustration stresses incentive. He says that inequalities can be justified by showing that they "set up various incentives which succeed in eliciting more productive efforts."[20] But in Rawls's ("recipient") conception of justice, advantage is not in "productive efforts" as such, but only in "primary goods." In these terms the expectations of the disadvantaged are logically exhausted by three possibilities, namely expectation of future advantage, of future disadvantage, and of future equality. To aspire to future disadvantage is irrational. To aspire to future advantage is an unjust aspiration, not to be justified by the "benefit" to the remaining disadvantaged that by this example they too shall be encouraged to aspire unjustly; and a system that fosters unjust aspirations is an unjust system. The only rational and just aspiration, then, is the aspiration to equality. But supposing equality to be one day achieved, the disparity that has existed meanwhile has diminished the justice of the system relative to one in which equality is instituted from the outset.

331

Perhaps it will be supposed that the incentive introduced by inequality will elevate total productivity, increasing the distributable goods of the system? But by Rawls's fundamentally comparative standard, gains that are everyone's go unperceived, like the universe in which everything doubles in size overnight. Such a consideration is expressly precluded from determinations of justice, both by Rawls's principle of "mutual disinterest" ("the parties take no interest in one another's interests"[21]) and by the stipulation of the difference principle that the justice of the system is decided, not by the standing of the whole, but strictly by the standing of the least advantaged group.[22]

The impotence of the difference principle is attributable to the qualitative identity and numerical equality Rawls inscribes upon justice at the outset by his stipulative design of the "original position." The same justice to which other than numerical differences are offensive in the beginning cannot be made to smile upon such differences in the end.

I submit that Rawls resorts to the difference principle because he is displeased by the unfolding implications of his original reduction of persons to mere numerical integers. So am I. But this means that the purported "intuition" on which Rawls rests the original equalization is no intuition at all. For either an intuition is (as previously defined) an abrupt anticipation of the outcome of discursive thought, to be tested by discursive thought (and the experience that furnishes content to discursive thought), or else it is an occultism that, as such, is forbidden to philosophy.* The "intuition" relied upon by Rawls cannot stomach its own implications, ergo it is not a valid intuition. Moreover it is not to

* Rawls's uncritical reliance on "intuitions" is documented and criticized in R. M. Hare, "Rawls' Theory of Justice—1," *Philosophical Quarterly* 23, no. 91 (1973), 144-155. But as an offense to reason it is rivaled or surpassed by Rawls's conception of the choice of the principles of justice from the Original Position. For not only are these principles to be chosen in ignorance (under the "veil"), but they are to be adhered to in complete disregard of what the experience of living in accordance with them may teach.

be found in very many minds posing as an intuition. Our "intuitive sense of justice" does not tell us that differences are per se unjust. It tells us that, of differences among individuals, some are unjust, some are just, and some are irrelevant to considerations of justice. This intuition is supported by discursive thought. According to normative individualism, all persons possess an equal but limited* entitlement in virtue of equivalence of potential worth, while differential entitlements accrue among individuals according to differences in degree of self-actualization. Here justice presupposes, not ignorance and the eradication of qualitative individuation, but knowledge and the progressive development of individuation.

Strictly speaking Rawls is correct when he insists that persons cannot be said to deserve their natural endowments, but the reason for this is that persons cannot be conceived independently of natural endowments, hence the question of desert cannot arise logically, and Rawls's re-

---

* Entitlement conferred by merely potential worth is limited because potential worth confers upon the individual a responsibility for its actualization. The natural foundation for potentiality as a distinct entitlement is childhood, which must be provided for, and of which self-knowledge and self-actualization are not to be expected. The level of this entitlement can be termed "subsistence," provided the term is used to include the necessary conditions for growth, and not for mere stasis. In virtue of the inalienability of potential worth, persons are entitled to the requisites of subsistence lifelong. No human being can be without such entitlement, for to possess potential worth is the minimum definition of "person," and all human beings are in this sense persons. Concerning human beings who are marked by what we term "birth defects," most are entirely capable of setting goals and achieving them, and are thereby from the moral viewpoint to be regarded fully as persons. I stress fully, because the presupposition that what such persons are capable of is morally inferior is appropriate only to omniscience. Regarding the lesser numbers who appear to be incapable of any degree of actualization, we have a choice. Either we deem them nonpersons, e.g. "vegetables," or the like, and treat them accordingly, or else we regard them as children who in all likelihood will remain such. I think the latter course is dictated not by charity alone, but likewise by prudence and reason.

liance on such a conception convicts him of abstractionism. One might as well ask if persons deserve to be born. For persons are in part potential, "possessing their futures within them, active at the present moment."[23] This "presenting future" is the root meaning of "natural endowment," hence what can be conceived in independence of natural endowment is not a person. While it may be amusing to propound a theory of justice for nonpersons, such an endeavor is culpable to the degree that it persuades persons to relinquish their personhood. What leads Rawls to suppose that the question of desert arises with respect to natural endowments is the belief that natural endowments are differentially distributed, some persons being richly endowed at birth while others are endowed poorly or not at all. This belief is endorsed by common sense, which rests it upon the evidence that persons of actual excellence are uncommon in the world. But, in the first place, the said evidence by no means demonstrates that endowments are sparsely distributed, being equally compatible with the supposition that endowments are universally distributed but often go unactualized. Second, it seems not unlikely that we have here further confirmation of the notorious somnambulance of common sense, which has won for it the disesteem of such philosophers as Plato, Schopenhauer, Nietzsche, and Kierkegaard. As a ritualized obeisance, to ascribe excellence to such of our historical monuments as a Socrates, a Ptolemy, a Leonardo, a Michelangelo, or a Newton requires no discernment. But to recognize personal excellence in one's daily associates requires much in the way both of discernment and of generosity. Whether the qualitative improvement of human life—the aim of moral endeavor—is advanced or retarded by monument-worship is an open question. But it is incontrovertible that a *program* of such qualitative improvement is strictly dependent upon a progressively more widespread cultivation of the capacities to discern and appreciate proximal excellences.

The cultivation of capacities of discernment and appreciation of diverse excellences claims top priority in a sound moral program, but it encounters the prima facie obstacle of the finitude of both individuals and cultures. The meaning of the finitude of the individual in this regard is that no person, *qua* individual, can be capable of recognizing and appreciating all possible determinate human excellences or —to speak practically—even a preponderance of those excellences that may be manifested by persons who are proximate to him. But here we must bear in mind that, if justice is to be workable and not an untouchable ideal, then it, too, must be tractable practically to the extent of being attainable by degrees. As the cornerstone of justice, the presupposition of the unique, irreplaceable, potential worth of every individual requires concrete affirmation in the recognition of an individual's worth by others. In principle it is true that an individual's unique worth is susceptible of recognition by every other individual.* But to contend that each actual individual is entitled to concrete recognition of his own unique worth by every other actual individual would be to commit the perfectionist fallacy. Under the condition of practicability, what each individual who manifests an excellence is entitled to is recognition of that excellence, not by all others, but by *some* others. This entitlement invokes, as the context for its fulfillment, the community. The community is the indispensable instrument of justice so long as the individual cannot be sure of concrete recognition of his unique worth by every other individual (which in practical terms is to say, forever).

What of the finitude of the community, which in analogous fashion constricts the range of the diverse excellences that can conceivably be recognized within it? What of the analogous finitude of nations and cultures? As before, resolution lies in the recognition that what one cannot do, others shall. An indispensable instrument of justice is the patterning of nations, cultures, and communities, such that all indi-

---

* The demonstration of this is implicit in the structure of personhood as set forth in Ch. 8, see esp. pp. 248 and 249.

vidual excellences shall have their place. Clearly it is only with the advent of worldwide communications and travel that such patterning on a global scale becomes significant. Formerly the options available to any individual were largely confined to alternative communities included within a given nation, and the workability of this restricted patterning depended on the reflexive conditioning of individuals by the prevalent options—in Pericles's words, "What is honored in a country will be cultivated there." But under today's changed conditions it becomes imperative to extend our conception of the requisite patterning worldwide. To some extent, by "invisible hand" processes, such patterning already exists in those compossible diversities we term "the English way of life," "the Scottish way of life," "the Danish way of life," "the capitalistic system," "the communistic system," "the agrarian life style," "the industrial life style," and so on. It remains to conceive of this diversity, not as the countless ways of going wrong, but as a precious commodity to be emphasized, rendered more cogent, and made openly available to choice.*

* The reader who wishes to pursue the conception of comprehensive patterning can be directed to the "Utopia" section of Nozick's book. Starting from individualism's tenet that differences among persons are inalienable and normative, Nozick contends that the only viable conception of Utopia consists in a framework of alternative utopian communities, affording "a wide and diverse range of communities which people can enter if they are admitted, leave if they wish to, shape according to their wishes; a society in which utopian experimentation can be tried, different styles of life can be lived, and alternative visions of the good can be individually or jointly pursued" (*Anarchy, State, and Utopia*, p. 307).

Because Nozick is close to the present study, both on the nature and meaning of individuation, and on the social principle we have identified as Plato's "congeniality of excellences," it is worthwhile to mark key distinctions between his "framework" and our "patterning." His conception is clearly utopian in a sense that ours just as clearly is not, namely that "the framework" is to be a *de novo* construction, whereas "patterning" already exists, very imperfectly, in the nations and cultures of the world, and the distinguishable

This conception of patterning relies upon the truth of Plato's principle of the "congeniality of excellences," and something must be said about a formidable obstacle to our recognition of the principle. It lies in humankind's resolute parochialism, by which any germ of truth is mistaken for the truth exclusively, and used to disparage alternative glimpses of truth. Here an investigation of motives would be illuminating, but such an investigation is psychological and we must eschew it for lack of competence. We must notice, however, an objective factor that goes far to account for the historical effectiveness of disparagement. Finitude itself provides disparagement its foothold, for finitude contains an essential vulnerability, and it is such that it does not diminish but is instead magnified by an individual's attainment of worth. As Santayana says, "In the end our distinc-

---

communities within these nations and cultures. I stress that patterning, and the consequent sociality of which it is a part, is nonrevolutionary, involving neither radical transformation nor *de novo* beginning. It is to be actualized by degrees on the foundation of existing patterning. Nor does such actualization presuppose a making of "converts to the cause," for, as evolutionary, it can be significantly advanced by those individuals who presently are living by the principles of normative individualism, through the example of their lives, the rearing of their children, and the influence they can have upon educational and governmental affairs in their communities.

Second, Nozick wants it understood that by the framework, no common goals are implied or instituted among the included alternative utopian communities, whereas our patterning presupposes the tenets of normative individualism, and arises to organize the diversity these tenets cultivate. With all due respect to Nozick's "see what will happen" approach, we *are not* starting *de novo*, and stand to lose more than we gain by pretending otherwise. We are too old by centuries for trying out anything that anyone may wish. We are called by the moral requirement to maximize the quality of human life by endeavoring to actualize the potential worth of every human being, and harmonizing the result. This book has sought to show that to this end we possess much of the requisite knowledge, due in good part to the host of our worthy predecessors. To pretend to be starting *de novo* does insolent and profound injustice to this host.

tion and our glory, as well as our sorrow, will have lain in being something in particular, and in knowing what it is."[24] The achievement of a given identity is necessarily at the cost of all else that one might have been, but cannot be, in consequence of being what one is. It makes no difference how freely one wills this "all else" to others if they do not avail themselves of it, for in this condition they will long to dispossess the worthy individual of his profoundest possession. He is vulnerable to their intent through the negations that are the obverse of his identity.

Ready illustration exists among philosophers previously cited in these pages—Scheler, Simmel, and Santayana. Each of them did philosophy in a distinctive manner, and each was subjected to lifelong criticism by his colleagues for not doing "real philosophy" (meaning, of course, philosophy in the manner approved by the critics). Scheler and Simmel were on crucial occasions denied academic appointment or advancement for being "unsystematic," while Santayana was hastened into self-exile by carpings that he was too "literary." Now each of these men manifested in his work unique virtues for which we must be everlastingly grateful. By his love of ideals and his refusal to petrify them by an effort of precise description, Santayana awakens in us the recognition that life is immensely richer with meanings than any of us take it to be. Scheler and Simmel, *because* they are "unsystematic," serve as provocateurs to any reader who possesses the least mental initiative. In a book by either man insights wink on and off like fireflies. The greater number go undeveloped, and none is developed exhaustively (John Dewey, for example, might have written a library out of one of their chapters, for Dewey's virtue is not insight but tenacity). This does the reader the immense honor of supposing that he can do some of this work for himself.

In each of these cases—Santayana, Scheler, Simmel—the specific virtue is manifested only at the cost of alternative virtues. Thus disparagement's strategy is clear. It devalues the man by ignoring the determinate virtue he manifests, measuring him instead by virtues he lacks. Disparagement succeeds because "the public," having no conception of qualitative individuality, can see no reason why anything is not to be expected of anyone. Scheler lacked tenacity? Santayana lacked precision? Well, then. . . .

By the dictates of finitude, everything is not to be asked of anyone, but only that which is his own to give. If the propensity to disparagement of alternatives is to be overcome, it shall be achieved not by eliminating or correcting the condition upon which disparagement relies, nor by denying that condition. In the end it can be overcome only by the establishment of justice such as to awaken the disparagers to the supreme importance of the work that is their own to do.

Robert Nozick points to an ambiguity in Rawls's contention that natural endowments are "arbitrary from a moral point of view." Nozick says "It might mean that there is no moral reason why the fact ought to be that way, or it might mean that the fact's being that way is of no moral significance and has no moral consequences." He then observes that in respect to such natural endowments as rationality, the ability to make choices, etc., absence of moral reasons in the first sense does not imply absence of moral significance in the second sense. Then why should such implication be thought to obtain in respect to other types of natural endowment?[25]

Of an individual's natural endowments it is permissible to say that they were conferred *libero arbitrio* in the sense that he himself had nothing to do with the fact that they are his. But from this we cannot infer that it is a matter of moral indifference what he does with his endowments. By his obligation to the better person he can become, he is morally obliged to actualize his endowments and not waste them. In any confusion of the two senses of "morally arbitrary" Nozick discerns dire jeopardy to morality itself.

If nothing of moral significance could flow from what was arbitrary [first sense, above], then no particular person's existence could be of moral significance; since of the many sperm cells, which one succeeds in fertilizing the egg cell is (so far as we know) arbitrary from a moral point of view [first sense]. This suggests another, vaguer remark directed to the spirit of Rawls' position rather than its letter. Each existing person is the product of a process wherein the one sperm cell which succeeds is no more deserving that the millions that fail. Should we wish that process had been "fairer" as judged by Rawls' standards, that all "inequities" in it had been nullified? We should be apprehensive about any principle that would condemn morally the very sort of process that brought us to be, and that therefore would undercut the legitimacy of our very existing.[26]

As previously cited, the stance of normative individualism toward the question of whether or not natural endowments at birth are deserved is that the question cannot logically arise. This is so because the question of justice presupposes the existence of persons as persons, and potentiality, as the root meaning of "natural endowment" is an inseparable part of personhood. Instead, justice arises on the foundation of natural endowments as the entitlement of natural endowments to the necessary conditions of their fulfillment.

It is in virtue of finite individuation—the determinateness and qualitative differentiation of natural endowments—that distributions under our control become susceptible of the predications "just" and "unjust," and justice itself becomes self-supporting. No one is entitled to goods qualitatively incommensurate with the person he as an individual is, and no one is entitled to disproportionate amounts of any distributable good, his proportion being determined as that of which he can maximally actualize the potential value, in consonance with the person he is. The finitude of persons disallows claim to an unlimited "more," authorizing only the claim to "enough." "Enough" is the amount that can maximally be utilized, an amount that varies according to the degree of actualization of the individual but is objectively determinable. No one, for example, is entitled to waste food, whether through spoilage or overeating. No one is entitled to waste land, as measured by non-use or deterioration of the land itself where land is abundant and no competing claims exist and, where competing claims exist, as determined by comparative degrees of actualization of the potential value of the land. By the actualization-of-potential-value criterion it is objectively determinable, for example, that I possess entitlement to one typewriter but no more than one, and to a rather larger number of books than ordinary, including some that I do not presently own, but excluding a few that I own but am unlikely to put to good use. My minimal needs as a person are extended and qualitatively refined, first by the type of person I am, and next by the individual I am within the type. As a philosopher my shelter entitlements will include an insular area for my study, and if walks in the countryside are beneficial to my work, then I possess entitlement to the use, whether by ownership or by a formal or informal rights-of-way arrangement, of suitable land in the useful amount. If clothing is of little importance to me then my just claim here is minimal, but if I derive stimulation from, and can give stimulation by expressive and changeable dress, then I have entitlement to more. I have just claim to the tools I need—the aforementioned books and typewriter, together with paper, pens, and the rest. And if I can write material that is worth reading I am also entitled to the best use I can make of the complex machinery of printing and publication. Likewise with respect to social goods—friendship, love, companionship, sexuality—I have just claim to the kinds and amounts that I can assimilate and valuationally maximize without unbalancing myself or being diverted from myself thereby.

How much food is too much? How much sex is too much?

341

How much conviviality, or fame, or influence? The true authority resides within the individual himself, and were self-knowledge perfect no other authority would be necessary or desirable. Because self-knowledge is imperfect and in many cases non-existent, however, claims must be susceptible of objective validation. The maximization-of-potential-value criterion is objective for it is a performance criterion. A claim by me to the Ferrari is disallowed by my handling of the car. A claim by me to my typewriter is validated (I hope the reader will agree) by the contents of this book. On the other hand I know a writer who simultaneously works on as many as three books, fully utilizing the capabilities of three typewriters and two secretaries. His performance validates his claim to them, while a similar claim by me would be invalidated by the observable fact that I write slowly, one book at a time.

We may object to a performance criterion because of its necessarily a posteriori character. To test my claim to the Ferrari, the car must be put in my hands. But this feature does no damage if we bear in mind that the performance criterion pertains to entitlements according to actual worth, which supervene upon nonperformance entitlements according to potential worth. Between nonperformance entitlements and performance entitlements there is an overlap owing to the fact that what is to be sustained by the former is the growth of the persons so sustained, and not their stasis. In virtue of the inclusion of potentiality within the meaning of personhood, the conditions of subsistence by definition extend beyond the actual needs of persons at any given time, and this overlap is available for the experimental determination of performance entitlements.

To the objection that a performance criterion will require perpetual and ubiquitous snooping in order to determine entitlements, we respond that the objection overlooks the meaning of culture. Human beings are inherently cultural creatures in two distinct but interrelated respects. We inherit a world made for us by our predecessors, and in the initial stage of our lives we are culture-dependent. But as human beings we are also under the perpetual necessity of living *into* the world, which means that when an individual exchanges dependence for autonomy he becomes a contributor to culture. I have remarked earlier* that culture thus provides the seemingly insubstantial virtue of generosity with an unshakable foundation—indeed, we may say that it wrings generosity from the most niggardly of men. Personal culture is the transformation of the world according to the meanings of the individual, and collective culture is the congregation of personal cultures, homogenized somewhat by the inertia of purely received culture that always remains. As the expression of personhood in the world, personal culture is performance, and its implication with respect to the "snooping" objection is that snooping cannot be called for by what is inherently and inevitably public in its manifestations.

Moreover, it deserves repeated emphasis that the justice to which this chapter is devoted—the justice of consequent sociality—is not to be conceived on the model of positive law. Even in a democracy, the intuitive meaning of positive law is that of a regulation imposed upon individuals by an authority external to themselves. (If I exceed the speed limit in my car, my apprehension is that I will be caught and punished by "the authorities"—a distinct "them" over and against me.) But the model upon which the justice of consequent sociality is properly conceived is not positive law but love, and its regulations are not externally imposed, but immanent within the individual, to be actualized by his self-love supported by the love of him by others. Self-love is the power of actualization of the innate excellence for which the individual is responsible, and justice in the individual is the discipline requisite to self-actualization. His entitlements are the requirements for actualization of his innate potential excellence, as illuminated by self-love, and were

---

* See Ch. 8, p. 252n2, where this is used against Sartre's conception of the thievery of "the look."

self-love perfect, no other authority would be possible, or needed, because each individual, in complete knowledge of what he needed to live a worthy life, would claim only these finite entitlements while willing comparable fulfillment to all persons. This willing of fulfillment to others is love of other persons, and the foundation of its universalization, as "fellow-feeling," or "caring," is the presupposition of the unique potential worth of all persons.

Public corroboration of entitled claims is necessary to consequent justice because self-love and the knowledge it confers are imperfect. But it is to be sought in the first instance from others who know and love the individual whose claims are in question, and only thereafter more widely. This does not imply snooping, but acquaintance, and the witness of acquaintance.

The present chapter opened with the proposition that justice begins with the presupposition of the unique potential worth of every human being. This presupposition *is* a presupposition for it is demonstrable only a posteriori, by acting upon it and assessing the consequences. But as a presupposition it is "no lose" and "fail safe," for a program based upon it is a priori certain to uncover and cultivate many more human excellences than are programs based upon the contradictory presupposition or upon contrary presuppositions. This being so, I see nothing to recommend our neutrality with respect to the presupposition of every person's unique potential worth. It is not to be presupposed, I think, in the manner of "entertaining a hypothesis," but rather as an ultimate commitment whose vindication is to be sought by every appropriate and intellectually honest stratagem. And while, as a presupposition, we cannot know its meaning fully or clearly until we act wholeheartedly upon it, nevertheless certain of its larger entailments can be foreseen. Paramount among these is the immediate need for education in the varieties of human value.

When the conception of "natural endowments" is released from the grip of the elitist presupposition and delivered to a presupposition by which it is universalized, it follows that we must be prepared to recognize and affirm the equivalence of an immense diversity of human excellences, including many already recognized but accorded an inferior place, and many others that have heretofore gone unrecognized. Under universalization it follows, for example, that there are excellences of carpentry, of cooking, of landscaping, of husbandry and agriculture, of seamanship, of shopkeeping, of craftsmanship, of caretaking—which are no whit inferior to such of the (for us) prestigious excellences associated with the practice of medicine, the law, industrial and corporate management, scientific research, statesmanship, (perhaps) scholarship and related "affairs of the mind," and (with strict qualification) the fine arts.*

That our parochialism with respect to varieties of value is enculturated is suggested (I carefully do not say "demonstrated") by our natural and spontaneous joy at the sight of a person working skillfully at what he loves. I take this response to be universal, though readily corruptible and often fleeting. As spontaneous it is unarmed, and succumbs to the subsequent reflection (for instance) that what we observe the person doing is after all menial. But in such cases it is our spontaneous response and not our reflection that is to be credited, for the work we observe is—presuming integrity—part of the larger work that is nothing less than the individual's life itself, and love of this larger work, of which the work we witness is an integral part, is the power that manifests the worth of that life.

We suppose that the work that is intrinsically worth do-

* I say "with strict qualification" because most of what passes for appreciation of excellence in the fine arts is no more than monument-worship, involving nothing in the way of powers of discernment. Were individuals' powers of discernment to be cultivated in any serious way, an assured consequence would be the release of the fine arts from the grip of "the Paris School," "the New York School," "the San Francisco School," and the like, in a wave of diversification. This wave, in turn, would greatly enlarge the audience of appreciators of works of the fine arts.

ing is but a minute proportion of the work that must be done, and this supposition has two crippling consequences. It constricts recognized natural endowments to those required by the privileged work, and in these attenuated terms "natural endowments" will be possessed by only a few persons. By conceiving most work to be intrinsically unrewarding the supposition serves to institutionalize this result, rather than striving to diminish it.

Per contra, the tenets of normative individualism afford opportunity for the recognition that the variety of kinds of work to be done is matched and overmatched by the qualitative variety of persons. It therefore can be supposed, and in the interest of value-maximization *must* be supposed, that for every kind of work that must be done, there are persons for whom that work holds intrinsic rewards, and by whom that work shall be skillfully and lovingly done. The point deserves to be put in the most concrete terms. No longer will you or I indulge our conceit that work we personally would be displeased to do is work that is intrinsically unrewarding (the obverse of the conceit that the work that is ours to do is divinely sanctioned), and no longer will we indulge this same conceit in others.

For illustration let us be likewise concrete. I have many times conducted an informal vocational-preference survey in my larger classes, where students (college undergraduates) in each case have numbered about one hundred. I begin by asking the students individually to indicate the work they would above all abhor. To this request they respond with immoderate zest, and in an hour I will have covered six or eight blackboards with their answers. Next we break ten minutes for coke or coffee. On return I ask them individually to indicate the work they prefer, the work each believes he would most dearly love to do. With only the rarest exceptions their answers do not require writing up, for they appear on the list of others' detestables.

The implication of this activity is that the enterprise of maximizing human value through universalization of meaningful work requires unprecedented emphasis on human diversity, together with systematic cultivation of the capacity of individuals to recognize varieties of value. The conceptual architecture of this enterprise is furnished by the tenets of normative individualism.

Justice is not handicapped aboriginally, as "common sense"—and Rawls—supposes, by the paucity of natural endowments among persons in the world, but by the myopia that obscures our recognition of these endowments. In short the fault is not metaphysical but epistemic, with this great difference, that as epistemic it is not relentless but tractable. To correct what he takes to be metaphysical injustice in the original distribution of potential worth at birth, Rawls constructs an "original position" that renders all persons (equally!) worthless. In diametric opposition, normative individualism institutes the presupposition of the equivalent potential worth of every person, and calls for a pattern of education designed to cultivate recognition of human worth in all its varieties. Far from seeking to eradicate qualitative individuation of persons, it endeavors to conserve and perfect such individuation, for it recognizes it to contain the criterion and principle of a distribution of material, social, and spiritual goods that is both just and voluntary.

As a justice of meaningful work, it is evident that the justice described requires a division of labor according to the natural diversity of innate human potentialities. Such a division has long been held to obtain for the minority of the privileged, but its democratization is obstructed by certain prejudices.

Foremost of the obstructing prejudices is the supposition that varieties of work constitute a hierarchy of relative worth, from statesman, scientist, doctor, lawyer, etc., down through marketing, sales, crafts, and farming, to child rearing, the manual labors, housekeeping, and refuse handling. Beneath the simple parochialism of such a hierarchy is the abstractionist fallacy of ascribing the value of a relation to but one of its terms. To be of value a vocation must be a life.

347

At the outset of this chapter we saw that persons cannot be conceived in independence of work, for the meaning of "person" lies in the fundamental work of self-actualization. Correspondingly work cannot be evaluated in independence of persons, and to judge certain occupations intrisically preferable or intrisically distasteful is to play at an axiology of pure phantoms. What can be evaluated is neither work nor person without the other, but strictly the conjunction of the two. Together, person and work constitute an actualizable value in the life in which they are commensurate. It is this value-concretion that is affirmed by our spontaneous joy at the sight of any person doing the work he or she loves and was "meant" to do.

Similarly the natural preferences of individuals harbor an immensely greater diversity than we acknowledge. The notion that everyone wants to be president of the United States, or Albert Einstein, or a brilliant surgeon, or a movie star is a wind-egg from the mechanical bowels of abstract, pre-individuated society. Doubtless individuals who lack self-knowledge are enticed by the culturally prestigious occupations, for they are without criteria by which to do their own choosing. But the individual who knows himself is impelled by an inner "I must." He wants the unrivaled satisfaction of knowing that he lives the life that is his own, and remains undistracted by rewards or prospects that properly belong to others.

Meaningless working is meaningless living, and its prevalence points, not to lack of universality or diversity in "natural endowments," but to our myopia in recognizing the infinite varieties of human value. This myopia is aggravated by the weighting-effect of unbalanced extrinsic rewards. Our economic practice of lavishly rewarding prestigious work is not merely redundant, but counterproductive. It is redundant on our supposition that the prestigious vocations are the intrinsically rewarding ones. And it is counterproductive because by its own exaggeration it all but extinguishes the spark of intrinsic reward as a function within culture.

We urgently and immediately need re-education in the intrinsic rewards of meaningful living through meaningful work. The starting-point of such re-education is the introduction of all persons to their right to meaningful work. From this principle arises the paramount aim of preparatory education as that of guiding each individual to the work innately his to do, his "vocation" in the original meaning of the term as a "calling." The immediate objection that individuated learning is incompatible with the obligation to educate *en masse* is annulled by the recognition that persons are unique individuals in the end, not in the beginning, and that beyond the conditions for its inception, individuation in its subsequent course is primarily the responsibility of the individual himself. In the beginning, and for purposes of primary and secondary education, meaningful differentiation will be confined to types of persons, and the requisite typology in the pattern of education is compatible with the requirement of educating *en masse*. Moreover, by the essential dependence of childhood* this differentiation has diminished emphasis in primary education, while priority is claimed by basic requirements of enculturation and enworldment that are alike for all.

Differentiated opportunities of learning assume priority in secondary education, where the paramount aim of education is to elicit innate potentialities to their first explicitness, affording self-discovery, and affirmation by others of each youth's distinctive personhood. Because self-discovery is necessarily a posteriori,† the requisite program of education takes the form of the exploration of alternatives. In the program, alternative vocational and life-styles must be carefully chosen to serve as archetypes of the full spectrum of possibilities, amid which students, with the fewest possible exceptions, can be expected to find themselves provisionally.

* See the section on childhood in Ch. 6.
† See the section on adolescence in Ch. 6, esp. pp. 180-181.

Exploration consists in enactment of alternatives, followed by evaluation by each youth himself, aided by teachers skilled in hermeneutics. Because knowledge is to be gained by the method we have termed "participatory enactment,"* the classroom is an inadequate arena, and education must enter the world by such means as work-study programs and apprenticeship structures. For it is an experimental *doing* that is to be analyzed for the evidence of innate potentiality it affords. Classroom study is no substitute for the required doing because it is its own distinctive sort of doing. Indeed, it is a highly constricted sort of doing, physically inert, focused upon books, and natively congenial to very few sorts of persons. Outside the classroom lies a vast world of quite different possibilities, and it is to these possibilities that youth must become related. Our mistake is to judge youth's relationship to the world's possibilities by the classroom experience, which in itself represents but one (or one type) of those possibilities, and with which many of our youth are inherently dysdaimonic.

Similar disparities currently permeate higher education, resulting from the popular belief that everyone—or everyone who shall count—requires college and graduate degrees. But four years of college studenthood is a hermetic endeavor, perambulating within the tight confines of classroom, library, and dormitory, involving endless sitting, great stretches of solitude, and uncanny quiet. Common sense should be enough to tell us that many natures are unsuited to it, nor should everyone be forced to endure academia any more than everyone should be a farmer or a mountaineer. We urgently need culturally endorsed alternatives to four years of college in the interest of talented youth for whom academia is purgatory.

"But in our day and age a college degree is the ticket to every good job!" I reply: true, but it need not and ought not to be. Bluntly put, a college degree is an impediment to fully seventy percent of the vocations for which the degree

* See Ch. 8, pp. 249-250 and *passim*.

is presently required; industry, commerce, and the professions implicitly and explicitly attest to the fact. They advise our colleges and universities that their graduates are of no use until they have been extensively retrained by the employer in each case. They regularly add that on the job, they teach more in six months than the college or university had managed to do in four years.

Just so, and with sound educational reasons. It is a well-established principle of pedagogy that students learn much faster and better when the need to know is viscerally felt by them as their own. Most learning in college, however, is directed to hypothetical needs. The student of civil engineering studies "Indeterminate Structures," not because he wants to ensure safe transport to people on a bridge of his design, but because the curriculum specifies the course. Likewise in the chemistry laboratory, the liquid "unknown" the student is asked to identify would be welcome to its anonymity, but for the course requirement.

Thus, the industry, business, or profession can train its practitioners much more effectively than can a university, and we have their word that they are required to do so in any case. Very well, why not let them do it? Let McDonnell-Douglas, in St. Louis, take a band of high school graduates who want to become aeronautical engineers and apprentice them to its own departments. There at the airport, amid the whine and bustle of its latest aircraft, in four years' time the company will produce twice the grade of engineer it now inherits from our universities. Let DuPont do similarly in Wilmington for its chemical engineers, and U.S. Steel in Pittsburgh for its metallurgists. Meanwhile the need for our universities will not diminish, but only be deferred and distributed, awaiting those points in the development of engineers when specific courses of study are required, for which leave shall be granted by employers.

Except for the small numbers whose true vocation is scholarship, the problem of general culture—the backbone of the liberal arts curriculum—may likewise profit by deferment and distribution. Presently we teachers in the humanities count ourselves fortunate if so many as ten percent of our students exhibit any of the signs of genuine love of learning, and where a student knows his own destiny to lie elsewhere, his impatience with us is palpable. To teach those courses colloquially known as, for example, "English for Engineers" is a demoralizing experience. Here again the recommendation is, let such students get on with what they themselves have the felt need to do. Let general culture wait. (Did not Plato advise postponement of the study of philosophy until the age of forty?) Later, when professional competence has in some measure been achieved, the need for general culture will be viscerally felt, and our professionals will prove themselves admirable students of it—the more so as it will not have previously been poisoned for them by premature force-feeding.

The supposition that academia is for everyone, and at the same age, is a product of antecedent, unindividuated sociality. By denying it, individualism must not be thought to deny that *education* is for everyone, for learning is growth and necessary as such to meaningful living. The aim in the above recommendations is not to minimize the importance of education, but rather to soften the imposed pattern of higher education, rendering it susceptible to the initiatives and needs of its students.

It is in the education of our adolescents that care and encouragement promise the greatest rewards. By exploration through participatory enactment, not only is the tender growth tip of individuation elicited, but internal knowledge is cultivated of alternative life-styles and their indigenous varieties of value. Once established, this recognition of varieties of human value can be limitlessly extended, enriched, and refined by imaginative and sympathetic means. It is the foundation for that love of diverse other individuals that is the concrete demonstration of the truth of Plato's principle of the "congeniality of excellences."

Love, as the Greeks taught, is aspiration to higher value,

352

and to found justice and division of labor in love is to render them immanent within human beings, and self-supporting. Where love and need are conceived to be unrelated, then ambition and desire lack internal regulation, and the constraints of justice and division of labor must be imposed from without. But the truth with which Socrates begins his contribution to the *Symposium* is that love and need are one. To love is to possess *in potentia* what one lacks in actuality and that which incomplete actuality requires for its completion and its worth. Normative individualism affirms this classical wisdom and universalizes it. The presupposition that every person contains an innate, irreplaceable, potential excellence is the presupposition that within every person is the regulatory principle of justice, to be manifested in that self-love that is the foundation of love of others.

Because human reality is genetic, the justice manifested by love is likewise genetic with the consequence that for a population at any given time the innate principles of justice will have achieved expression in only a minority of individual lives. In the rest, justice will subsist merely implicitly, and living justly will necessarily amount to living in accordance with a received pattern. But what makes all the difference is the character of the received pattern. By the tenets of normative individualism, the pattern must be such as to foster the growth of all persons to autonomy in the matter of justice, thereby presupposing the personhood of all persons, and adding to the number of those lives of integrity by which justice is expressed.

Unscholarly Epilogue

I do not much like philosophical treatises that endeavor to exhaust every implication of their theme, as if the reader were incapable of doing any thinking for himself. Despite the number of its pages, I have meant this study to be not exhaustive, but provocative to the minds and hearts of its individual readers. For in the end the only philosophy that profits a person is his own; and in the beginning he does well to adhere to his own intuition until (if such be the case) it proves untenable, and to furnish its replacement himself. Philosophies are not to be bought in the marketplace but cultivated in the ground, from seeds planted long before the philosopher plies his trade. But the tender first bud needs not only to look to the sun but also to know of the strong branch and trunk that support it.

The bud for which this study is meant to provide branch and trunk is the reader's intimation of his own unique, irreplaceable, potential worth. The book aims to fortify this intimation by summoning the philosophical tradition to which this same intimation long ago gave rise. This tradition charges each of us to trust his intimation, and at the same time to undertake the labor required to render it trustworthy. It explicates the intimation by uncovering its presuppositions and its entailments, thereby working to further self-knowledge in persons in whom the intimation has appeared. By this deployment of its tools, the philosophy reveals itself as a humanistic endeavor, given to the qualitative improvement of human life. Such a philosophical allegiance is just at present out of fashion, for recent Anglo-American philosophy disdains humanistic purpose and manages largely to ignore the questions of paramount importance to the conduct of life, leaving individuals in this respect to sink or swim. In virtue of the tentativity of the intimation of which we speak, however, and the harsh treatment that greets its first appearance in the world, to leave it unaided is very nearly to ensure its extinction.

By the argument of Chapter 10, the intimation is entitled to cultural sponsorship by means of institutions designed to afford it nurture and guidance. In the absence of such sponsorship (for today even the proximate institutions of the family and public education fulfill no such function) it is imperative that individuals have access to the quiet but resolute work over centuries that constitutes the tradition of eudaimonistic philosophy. There the individual may avail himself of the company of profound thinkers who have earlier trod his path, and who offer their services as guides on his way.

This book has sought to convert no one to a philosophy that is not his own, but only to afford help to native eudaimonists toward rendering their philosophy the fittest and best possible. Indeed, from the humanistic standpoint a philosophy that seeks converts is a contradiction in terms. The function of humanistic philosophy is not to impose invented forms upon human life, but to elicit and clarify the forms the lives of persons implicitly possess, thereby affording those lives a heightened measure of cogency. (By its explication of implications, it is true that philosophy will sometimes present an individual with features of his acts and principles that horrify him, producing in him an exchange of principles and patterns of behavior. But by so doing, philosophy only ministers to choice by rendering it knowledgeable.)

Preceding chapters have made clear, I trust, that eudaimonism does not purport to grant every human wish or gratify every desire. It is even sometimes criticized for being unsympathetic to certain hopes and desires that are both widespread and intense. It makes no promise to its adherents of supernatural immortality, nor of wealth, fame, or power, nor yet even of final "happiness." Instead it exacts what may at first sight appear to be an ascetic renunciation of certain persistent longings. It does so on the recognition that these longings contradict rather than complete human nature, with the consequence that their entertainment precludes recognition of the beauties, truths, and virtues that are proportionate to man. In the words of Montaigne, "We seek for other conditions because we understand not the use of ours, and go out of ourselves forasmuch as we know not what abiding there is."

To the Greeks the meaning of "Know Thyself" was inextricably implicated with *sophrosune*. Popularly, *sophrosune* meant moderation and self-control in the interest of prudence, but profoundly it meant proportion or measure, with express reference to human aspirations. Likewise Protagoras's "Man the measure"—when it is disentangled from Sophistic nominalism and linked to Hellas's humanism, where it belongs—means "Man the measure of man." The admonition is: Confine your aspirations to the possibilities of your own nature; to desire to be more than a human being is to become less, for extra-human aims betray humankind and produce blindness to the values human life affords. In this spirit Diotima, in the *Symposium*, advises Socrates to leave to the gods the kind of immortality that is appropriate only to their supernature, and to seek for himself that kind of immortality proportional to man—the immortality of "succession" afforded by the "pregnancy" of the human body and the human spirit.

Extra-human hopes and desires are not human necessities but rather impediments to the appreciation and participation in human worth. They are "compensatory dogmas" and "reactive concepts" formulated from the perspective for which life affords nothing worth having. To be itself worthy, this perspective must be earned, and it can be earned only by the exhaustion of human possibilities.

Human life in its essence is the actualization of possibilities by an aspiration that is unceasing but is aspiration to

357

human measure, and therefore humanly rewarding. Guiding it is finite, human perfection, serving as an ideal limit that, while it cannot be reached, can be actualized by degrees and is therefore available to be experienced by actual persons. But between extra-human ends and actual humanity the law of the excluded middle applies, precluding actualization by degree, and condemning human initiative to futility. By its formulation of such ends, humankind denies itself and looks to compensatory dogmas to be saved—from itself.

The historical outcome of the human experiment is unforeseeable, branding either condemnation or celebration premature. The present study has sought to demonstrate that the presence of human being is in itself the presence of possibilities of human betterment. The integral individual, I think, asks for no more. He who affirms the worth of human life does not embrace the idea of an afterlife that is the antithesis of the life he and all human beings live. The true individual does not hunger, Faustian-fashion, to be all things, nor something other than he is. He who loves another person for the individual that person is does not subsume that individuality in a desire for the All. He who knows power and concentration in himself does not seek power over others, but the discovery by others of their own power of personhood. To the integral individual the surplus connoted by "wealth" is a waste in which he will not participate, and "fame" is a gratuity with largely unattractive implications. Amid these distractions he is undiverted from the purpose that is inscribed in his existence—to become the person he potentially is and to cultivate the conditions by which others may do likewise.

Notes

CHAPTER I

1. Plato *Symposium* 175.

2. A flagrant instance is Schopenhauer's attempt to assign Socrates's daimon a place among premonitions, ghost-seeing, spiritualism, and other occult phenomena: See Arthur Schopenhauer, *The World as Will and Idea*, trans. R. B. Haldane and J. Kemp (New York: Charles Scribner's Sons, 1883), III, 98-99. Not dissimilar is Karl Jaspers, *The Great Philosophers*, ed. Hannah Arendt, trans. Ralph Manheim (New York: Harcourt, Brace & World, 1962), p. 20 and *passim*; and Søren Kierkegaard, *The Concept of Irony, with Constant Reference to Socrates*, trans. Lee M. Capel (Bloomington and London: Indiana University Press, 1968), Ch. 2, "The Daimon of Socrates." A brief but illuminating history of interpretations of the Socratic daimon is provided in Paul Friedländer, *Plato, An Introduction*, trans. Hans Meyerhoff (New York: Harper Torchbooks, 1964), Ch. 2, "Demon and Eros." But Friedländer himself narrowly skirts the "archaic irrationalism" pitfall. Against this we hold that Socrates's daimon was known by him to be no more and no less than his essential self.

3. Plato *Meno* 71.

4. *The Leibniz-Arnauld Correspondence*, ed. and trans. H. T. Mason, with intro. by G. H. R. Parkinson (Manchester and New York: Manchester University Press and Barnes & Noble, 1967), p. 15. Except that I have used Benson Mates's translation; see Benson Mates, "Leibniz on Possible Worlds," in Harry G. Frankfurt, ed., Leibniz, *A Collection of Critical Essays* (Garden City: Doubleday Anchor Books, 1972), p. 342.

5. Benedict de Spinoza, *Opera* (Heidelberg, 1925), IV, 240 (*Epistolae* L). See also the First Scholium to the Eighth Proposition, Part I of the *Ethics*.

6. G. W. Leibniz, *Principles of Nature and of Grace, Founded*

on Reason, in Robert Latta, ed. and trans., *Leibniz, The Monadology and Other Philosophical Writings* (Oxford: Oxford University Press, 1898), p. 416. On this page see also n. 44, by Latta.

7. George Santayana, *Scepticism and Animal Faith* (New York: Dover Publications, 1955), p. 129.

8. Largely through the literature of present humanistic psychology. See, e.g., Abraham H. Maslow, *Toward a Psychology of Being* (Princeton: D. Van Nostrand, 1962).

9. For a careful delineation of this change, see A. W. H. Adkins, *Merit and Responsibility: A Study in Greek Values* (Oxford: Clarendon Press, 1960).

10. Theodosius Dobzhansky, *Mankind Evolving, The Evolution of the Human Species* (New Haven and London: Yale University Press, 1962), p. 29. Likewise of interest is the following, from Hampton L. Carson, "Genetics, Human," *Encyclopaedia Britannica* (15th ed.), vol. 7, pp. 996-1010. "The number of possible hereditary combinations is hard to grasp intuitively. Even if a gross underestimate of only two differing gene pairs per chromosome were assumed, each potential human parent would be capable of producing more than 19,000,000,000,000 genetically different kinds of sperm (or eggs). It is extremely unlikely that even one of these trillions of gene combinations would exactly duplicate that of any ancestor" (citation from p. 998). In *Heredity and Human Life* (New York and London: Columbia University Press, 1963), Carson concludes, "Not only do you, the reader, represent an absolutely unique combination existing on earth at this present time in human history, but there has never existed before, and will never exist again, the same combination that you represent. This quality of uniqueness lends dignity to each human being" (p. 71).

I must add that while eudaimonism is entitled to cite the science of genetics in its behalf, the issues with which eudaimonism deals cannot be decided by such evidence, for it is possible to contend that genetic individuation is insignificant for social and moral purposes. Eudaimonism's individuation is *normative*, and thereby the responsibility for establishing its truth falls necessarily not to science, but to philosophy. But sound philosophy invites the counsel of science.

11. In a certain sense our common humanity is restricted by

"compossibility," but discussion of this principle would be premature here. It will be considered in Ch. 5.

12. Søren Kierkegaard, *Purity of Heart Is To Will One Thing*, trans. Douglas V. Steere (New York: Harper Torchbooks, 1956).

13. A. W. H. Adkins, *From the Many to the One* (Ithaca: Cornell University Press, 1970), p. 210.

14. For example, the annoyance of Callicles in the *Gorgias* 490-491.

15. Using the translation of Ernest Barker, *The Politics of Aristotle* (New York: Oxford University Press Galaxy Book, 1958), p. 36.

16. Aristotle *Politics* 1258b.11, in *The Basic Works of Aristotle*, ed. Richard McKeon (New York: Random House, 1941), p. 1141.

17. Aristotle *Politics* 1260a.11.

18. Barker, *Politics of Aristotle*, p. 35 n3.

19. Ibid., p. 13.

20. *Politics* 1330a.32.

21. I have here paraphrased a sentiment that was widespread among the Hellenes, centering in the idea of divine *phthonos* or "jealousy of the gods." For an example from Sophocles: "Pride, when puffed up, vainly, with many things / Unseasonable, unfitting, mounts the wall, / Only to hurry to that fatal fall" (*Oedipus Tyrannus*, trans. Sir George Young). Or Heroditus: "You may have observed how the thunderbolt of heaven chastises the insolence of the more enormous animals, whilst it passes over without injury the weak and insignificant: before these weapons of the gods you must have seen how the proudest palaces and the loftiest trees fall and perish" (*Polymnia* 8.10). For an extended discussion and fuller documentation, see S. Ranulf, *The Jealousy of the Gods and Criminal Law at Athens* (London: Williams & Norgate, 1933), pp. 63-84; and E. R. Dodds, *The Greeks and the Irrational* (Berkeley, Los Angeles, London: University of California Press, 1951), Ch. 2. A brief but keen analysis of the doctrine's social effects is to be found in Alvin W. Gouldner, *The Hellenic World, A Sociological Analysis* (New York: Harper Torchbooks, 1969), pp. 27-28.

22. Aeschylus *Agamemnon*, in *The Complete Greek Trag-

edies, ed. and trans. D. Grene and R. Lattimore (Chicago: University of Chicago Press, 1959), I, 46.

23. F. M. Cornford, *From Religion to Philosophy, A Study in the Origins of Western Speculation* (New York: Harper, 1957), p. III n.I.

24. Dodds, *The Greeks and the Irrational*, Ch. 2; Martin Persson Nilsson, *Greek Piety*, trans. Herbert Jennings Rose (Oxford at the Clarendon Press, 1948); Cornford, *From Religion to Philosophy*.

25. Gouldner, *Hellenic World*, pp. 116-118.

26. R. G. Collingwood, *An Essay on Metaphysics* (Oxford at the Clarendon Press, 1940), Ch. XXI.

27. Gouldner, *Hellenic World*, p. 126.

28. See *Ion* 533-535; *Phaedrus* 244-246; *Timaeus* 71-72.

29. *Timaeus* 71-72.

30. John Herman Randall, Jr., *Plato, Dramatist of the Life of Reason* (New York and London: Columbia University Press, 1970), p. 139.

31. *Lysis* 222. The apparently inconclusive ending of this dialogue is deceptive. Just after Socrates undertakes to look for a distinction between the congenial and the like, drunken roisterers appear and the inquiry is terminated. The note on which the inquiry ends is the following. "Suppose, then," says Socrates, "that we agree to distinguish between the congenial and the like—in the intoxication of argument, that may perhaps be allowed. And shall we further say that the good is congenial, and the evil uncongenial to every one? Or again that the evil is congenial to the evil, and the good to the good; and that which is neither good nor evil to that which is neither good nor evil? (Socrates's companions agree, mistakenly, to the second alternative.) Then, my boys, we have again fallen into the old discarded error; for the unjust will be the friend of the unjust, and the bad of the bad, as well as the good of the good. (Companions agree.) But again, if we say that the congenial is the same as the good, in that case the good and he only will be the friend of the good. (Companions agree.) But that too was a position of ours which, as you will remember, has been already refuted by ourselves." (Jowett translation.)

Apparent inconclusiveness here only reaffirms the fact that Plato-Socrates requires the reader to do a good deal of work for himself. The nature of friendship has been arrived at, but its description is tucked away in pieces throughout the text of the *Lysis*. Evil cannot be the friend of evil, for such is the nature of evil that it is unfriendly (uncongenial) even to itself. But good can be the friend of good, despite Socrates's proof that like cannot be the friend of like. This is for the reason that goods as they appear in the world are diversified with respect to kind. (This is exhibited with respect to the goodness of persons in Socrates's examination of Lysis, 207-211.) Where likeness is strict and unqualified, like cannot be the friend of like for neither of the likes can offer anything to the other which the other does not possess independently. But where goods are differentiated with respect to kind, likeness is not unqualified; it is likeness in the good, together with difference in kinds of good. The term for the relationship between two goods that differ with respect to kind is congeniality. It is not applicable to evils, for while these too are diversified with respect to kind, congeniality is itself a good, and evils that exhibit congeniality are demonstrating that they are mixed with goods, and are relating on the basis of the intermixed goods.

Explicitly the *Lysis* is devoted to friendship, but by no means can we regard it as attending to friendship to the exclusion of other affirmative human relationships. In the nature of friendship Socrates seeks the principle of human interrelationship per se, and finds it in the "congeniality of excellences." Our own consideration of this principle as the universal principle of human solidarity occupies Chs. 8, 9, and 10.

CHAPTER 2

1. E. Ehrhardt, "Individualism," in *Encyclopaedia of Religion and Ethics*, ed. James Hastings, asst. John A. Selbie and Louis H. Gray (New York: Charles Scribner's Sons, 1915), VII, 221.

2. R. H. Tawney, *Religion and the Rise of Capitalism, A Historical Study* (New York: Harcourt, Brace & Co., 1926), p. 176. Tawney here paraphrases the seventeenth-century political economist, Harrington, with whom he agrees.

3. Ibid., p. 180.

4. Ibid., p. 177.

5. F. H. Bradley, "My Station and Its Duties," in *Ethical Studies* (New York: The Liberal Arts Press, 1951), p. 100.

6. Bradley, "Why Should I Be Moral?," in *Ethical Studies*, p. 13.

7. Bradley, "My Station and Its Duties," in *Ethical Studies*, p. 104.

8. Ibid., p. 112.

9. Ibid., pp. 129-134.

10. F. H. Bradley, *Appearance and Reality, A Metaphysical Essay* (Oxford at the Clarendon Press, 1959), p. 120.

11. Ibid., pp. 321-322.

12. Ibid., e.g. p. 214.

13. Ibid., see e.g., Ch. xx for a summary of characteristics of the Absolute.

14. Bradley, "Concluding Remarks," in *Ethical Studies*, p. 147.

15. Bradley, *Appearance and Reality*, p. 215.

16. *Thomas Hill Green's Prolegomena to Ethics*, ed. A. C. Bradley (New York: Thomas Crowell Co., 1969), p. 199.

17. Ibid., pp. 74-75.

18. Ibid., Bk. 1, Chs. 1 and 2. These arguments are summarized on pp. 74-75.

19. Ibid., pp. 90-100.

20. Ibid., p. 237.

21. Ibid., pp. 201-202.

22. Ibid., pp. 92-93.

23. Henry Sidgwick, *The Ethics of T. H. Green, Herbert Spencer, and J. Martineau* (London and New York: Macmillan & Co., 1902), p. 64.

24. *Green's Prolegomena*, p. 197.

25. Ibid., p. 197.

26. Sidgwick, *Green, Spencer, Martineau*, p. 53.

27. Bernard Bosanquet, *The Principle of Individuality and Value* (London: Macmillan & Co., 1927), pp. 323-324.

28. Ibid., p. 335.

29. Ibid., p. 324n.

30. Ibid., p. 70.

31. Bernard Bosanquet, *The Value and Destiny of the Individual* (London: Macmillan & Co., 1923), p. 325.

32. Bosanquet, *Principle*, p. 334.

33. Bosanquet, *Value and Destiny*, p. xxi.

34. C. J. Gerhardt, ed., *Die philosophischen Schriften von G. W. Leibniz* (Berlin, 1875–1890), vol. 2, 240.

35. Bradley, *Appearance and Reality*, p. 75.

36. Ibid., p. 214.

37. Bradley offers a critique of monadism in *Appearance and Reality*, pp. 101-103, but it is hasty and inadequate, consisting merely in the reiteration of his principle that the real must be all-inclusive.

38. Max Scheler, *The Nature of Sympathy*, trans. Peter Heath (London: Routledge & Kegan Paul Ltd., 1970), pp. 234-237.

39. Rudolph Eucken, "Individuality," in *Encyclopaedia of Religion and Ethics*, VII, 222.

CHAPTER 3

1. *Kierkegaard's Concluding Unscientific Postscript*, trans. David F. Swenson and Walter Lowrie with introduction and notes by Walter Lowrie (Princeton: Princeton University Press, 1941), Part 2, Ch. II, e.g. 182.

2. Rene Descartes, *Meditations on First Philosophy*, Meditation II.

3. G. W. F. Hegel, *The Logic of Hegel*, trans. William Wallace (London: Oxford University Press, 1950), p. 48.

4. Søren Kierkegaard, *Purity of Heart Is To Will One Thing*, trans. Douglas V. Steere (New York: Harper Torchbooks, 1956), p. 140. The poet is Shakespeare, in *Henry V*, Act 2, Scene 4.

5. See Søren Kierkegaard, *Either/Or*, trans. David F. Swenson and Lillian Marvin Swenson with revisions and foreword by Howard A. Johnson (Garden City; Doubleday Anchor Books, 1959), "The Immediate Stages of the Erotic or the Musical Erotic," and "Diary of the Seducer."

6. Søren Kierkegaard, *Fear and Trembling and The Sickness Unto Death*, trans. Walter Lowrie (Garden City: Doubleday Anchor Books, n.d.), p. 178.

7. *The Diary of Søren Kierkegaard*, trans. Gerda M. Andersen, ed. Peter P. Rohde (New York: Philosophical Library, 1960), p. 200.

8. Kierkegaard, *Sickness Unto Death*, in *Fear and Sickness*, p. 205.

9. Ibid., p. 67.

10. Ibid., p. 66.

11. Søren Kierkegaard, *Works of Love*, trans. Howard and Edna Hong (New York: Harper Torchbooks, 1964), and *Purity of Heart*.

12. Kierkegaard, *Sickness Unto Death*, in *Fear and Sickness*, p. 201.

13. Ibid., p. 202.

14. Friedrich Nietzsche, *The Will to Power*, trans. Walter Kaufmann and R. J. Hollingdale, ed. with commentary by Walter Kaufmann (New York: Random House, 1967), p. 495.

15. Ibid., p. 510.

16. Friedrich Nietzsche, *Thus Spoke Zarathustra*, in *The Portable Nietzsche*, trans. Walter Kaufmann (New York: Viking Press, 1954), p. 189.

17. Friedrich Nietzsche, *The Dawn of Day*, in *The Complete Works of Friedrich Nietzsche*, ed. Oscar Levy (New York: Macmillan Co., 1909-1911), vol. 9, 330-331.

18. E.g. *Zarathustra*, in *Portable Nietzsche*, pp. 227-228; and *Will to Power*, Bk. 3.

19. Nietzsche, *Will to Power*, p. 353.

20. "Blond beasts" is Nietzsche's name for the barbarian conquerors of the Mediterranean basin, 900–700 B.C. Contrary to the common supposition, he does not hold them up as models for modern men, nor does the term refer to the *Übermenschen*. See *Beyond Good and Evil*, aphorism 257.

21. Nietzsche, *Zarathustra*, in *Portable Nietzsche*, p. 226.

22. This is Thomas Common's translation, which I have chosen in preference to Walter Kaufmann's "This ghost which runs after you." See Friedrich Nietzsche, *Thus Spake Zarathustra*, trans. Thomas Common, in *The Philosophy of Nietzsche* (New York: Random House Modern Library, 1954), p. 63.

23. Nietzsche, *Zarathustra*, in *Portable Nietzsche*, p. 206.

24. Ibid., p. 171.

25. Ibid., p. 174.

26. Nietzsche, *Will to Power*, p. 381.

27. Nietzsche, *Zarathustra*, in *Portable Nietzsche*, p. 148.

28. Friedrich Nietzsche, *Human, All-Too-Human*, Part II,

Preface, no. 4, trans. Paul V. Cohn, in Levy, ed., *Complete Works*, vol. 7.

29. Friedrich Nietzsche, *The Gay Science*, trans. with commentary by Walter Kaufmann (New York: Random House, 1974), p. 177.

30. Nietzsche, *Will to Power*, p. 275.

31. Nietzsche, *Zarathustra*, in *Portable Nietzsche*, p. 315.

32. Ibid., pp. 146-147.

33. Nietzsche, *Gay Science*, p. 219.

34. Friedrich Nietzsche, *On the Genealogy of Morals*, trans. Walter Kaufmann and R. J. Hollingdale, with *Ecce Homo*, trans. Walter Kaufmann (New York: Random House Vintage Books, 1967), p. 58.

35. Nietzsche, *Will to Power*, p. 485.

36. Nietzsche, *Zarathustra*, in *Portable Nietzsche*, p. 198.

37. Nietzsche, *Gay Science*, p. 219.

38. Ibid., pp. 270-271.

39. Letter to Peter Gast, Feb. 1, 1888. In *Selected Letters of Friedrich Nietzsche*, trans. Anthony M. Ludovici, ed. Oscar Levy (Garden City and Toronto: Doubleday, Page & Co., 1921), p. 215. For other expressions of the same idea, see, e.g. p. 166 (letter to Elizabeth Förster-Nietzsche), and p. 199 (letter to Malvida von Meysenbug).

40. Nietzsche, *Will to Power*, p. 434.

41. Ibid., p. 518.

42. *Wer das tiefste gedacht, liebt das Lebendigste.* "Sokrates und Alkibiades," stanza 2, line 1.

43. Nietzsche, *Will to Power*, p. 272.

44. Ibid., p. 288.

45. Ibid., p. 326.

46. Ibid., p. 326.

CHAPTER 4

1. Jean-Paul Sartre, *Being and Nothingness, An Essay on Phenomenological Ontology*, trans. with intro. by Hazel E. Barnes (New York: Philosophical Library, 1956), p. 619.

2. Ibid., p. 439.

3. Jean-Paul Sartre, "Existentialism is a Humanism," trans. Philip Mairet, in Nino Langiulli, ed., *The Existentialist Tradi-*

tion, Selected Writings (Garden City: Doubleday Anchor Books, 1971), p. 399.

4. Sartre, *Being and Nothingness*, p. 500.

5. Ibid., p. 482.

6. Jean-Paul Sartre, *The Emotions, Outline of a Theory*, trans. Bernard Frechtman (New York: Philosophical Library, 1948). This work is relied upon in *Being and Nothingness*, e.g. p. 445.

7. Sigmund Freud, *Totem and Taboo, Resemblances between The Psychic Lives of Savages and Neurotics*, trans. with intro. by A. A. Brill (New York: Random House Vintage Books, 1946), Ch. 3.

8. Sartre, *Being and Nothingness*, p. 552.

9. Ibid., p. 445.

10. Ibid., p. 445.

11. Sartre makes the point using writers as his examples; see "Existentialism is a Humanism," in Langiulli, ed., *Existentialist Tradition*, p. 405.

12. Sartre, *Being and Nothingness*, p. 52.

13. Ibid., p. 443.

14. For example, when he speaks of the "nothingness of what is not yet" (*Being and Nothingness*, p. 100), the "yet" is a qualification upon the "is not," hence the nothingness cannot be considered to be absolute in the sense of "unqualified." Or again, when he says, "The possible is an absence constitutive of consciousness in so far as consciousness makes itself" (ibid., p. 101)—for the possible is an absence (an "is not") strictly with respect to the actual. As possible, the possible *is*.

15. Sartre, *Being and Nothingness*, p. 67.

16. Ibid., p. 98.

17. Ibid., p. 445.

18. Ibid., p. 445.

19. Ibid., p. 451.

20. Ibid., p. 42.

21. Ibid., p. 42.

22. It is unclear whether Sartre is to be regarded as taking exception to this proposition. He seems to agree that autonomy presupposes a stage in which it is not to be expected when he says that prior to choice of his fundamental project the individual "is nothing. He will not be anything until later, and then

he will be what he makes of himself" ("Existentialism is a Humanism," in Langiulli, ed., *Existentialist Tradition*, p. 395). And the usually faithful Simone de Beauvoir speaks of childhood as the period in which an individual's freedom is "concealed from him," and says "It is adolescence which appears as the moment of moral choice. Freedom is then revealed and he must decide upon his attitude in the face of it" (*The Ethics of Ambiguity*, trans. Bernard Frechtman [New York: Philosophical Library, 1948], p. 40).

But in Sartre's biographical works, choice of fundamental project—which for Sartre is freedom and autonomy—is often ascribed by him to the childhood of his subjects. Baudelaire is represented by Sartre as having chosen his fundamental project at the time of his mother's remarriage, when he was seven years old; Genet's choice of himself as a thief is situated by Sartre in his childhood; and in *The Words*, Sartre represents himself as having made his fundamental choice to be a writer at the age of nine (Jean-Paul Sartre, *The Words*, trans. Bernard Frechtman [New York: George Braziller, 1964], p. 181).

Fundamental choice at the age of seven or nine is of course not irreconcilable with the requirement of a prior stage, but the latter does appear to be irreconcilable with Sartre's opposition to latencies and dispositional properties. Because human being is freedom, and freedom is absolute, the infant or child is identical to the mature man or woman with respect to freedom. "Man does not exist first in order to be free *subsequently*; there is no difference between the being of man and his *being-free*" (*Being and Nothingness*, p. 25). And if infants and children are free, this means they choose, for "freedom is choice" (*Being and Nothingness*, p. 495), and what they choose is their fundamental project, for such is the "original choice" (*Being and Nothingness*, p. 561), and all other choices are choice only by reference to it. But in this case, as Anthony Manser says, "It would seem that little remains of the freedom Sartre has been emphasizing . . . ; it is hard to see how an infant can be aware of what he is doing, and if not, then it is odd to call him responsible" (Anthony Manser, *Sartre, A Philosophic Study* [University of London, The Athlone Press, 1966], p. 122). I find Manser's somewhat tentative tone overly charitable. This piece of Sartrean reasoning flaunts the logic of the concept of "choice." Choice, to be meaningful, logically presupposes knowledge of alternatives, and this logical priority becomes temporal priority by the recognition that knowledge of alternatives must initially be obtained empirically. This means that choice and autonomy require a prior stage of life, and it is this prior stage that is termed "childhood."

Incidentally, the reader of *The Words* will have no lingering doubts about the true character of Sartre's nine-year-old "choice" of a life of letters. He grew to that age surrounded by books, was praised extravagantly for his interest in them, lived vicariously by means of them, and his "choice" was first pronounced, not by him, but by his grandfather, an author himself, and the person responsible for the household piety toward letters. As he writes in *The Words*, Sartre muses: "I sometimes wonder, when I am in a bad mood, whether I have not consumed so many days and nights, covered so many pages with ink, thrown on the market so many books that nobody wanted, solely in the mad hope of pleasing my grandfather" (*The Words*, p. 163). *Ipse dixit.*

Whatever Sartre's stance on the matter may be, we proceed with the analysis that follows this supernumeral in the text on the proposition that autonomy commences, not at birth, but necessarily "later," namely after the dependence of childhood, in adolescence.

23. Sartre, *Being and Nothingness*, p. 438.

24. Ibid., p. 21.

25. Ibid., p. 15.

26. Sartre, "Existentialism is a Humanism," in Langiulli, ed., *Existentialist Tradition*, p. 396.

27. ". . . for we are unable ever to choose the worse," ibid., p. 396. There is serious question whether Sartre can affirm this Socratic-Platonic psychological law without contradicting the conception of freedom in *Being and Nothingness*.

28. Sartre, *Being and Nothingness*, p. 550.

29. Ibid., p. 619.

30. Ibid., p. 551.

31. Sartre, "Existentialism is a Humanism," in Langiulli, ed., *Existentialist Tradition*, pp. 407-408.

32. Ibid., p. 397.

33. Sartre, *Being and Nothingness*, p. 376.

34. *Kierkegaard's Concluding Unscientific Postscript*, trans. David F. Swenson, intro and notes by Walter Lowrie (Princeton: Princeton University Press, 1941), p. 113.

35. Sartre, "Existentialism is a Humanism," in Langiulli, ed., *Existentialist Tradition*, p. 409.

36. George Santayana, *Scepticism and Animal Faith* (New York: Dover Publications, 1955), p. 279.

37. Sartre, *Being and Nothingness*, p. 615.

CHAPTER 5

1. The principle is so named by A. O. Lovejoy in his seminal study of it, *The Great Chain of Being* (Cambridge: Harvard University Press, 1936).

2. Demonstration that Aristotle's metaphysics exhibits the principle of plenitude appears in Jaakko Hintikka, "Necessity, Universality, and Time in Aristotle," *Ajatus*, 20 (1957), 65-90. See also Hintikka, "A. O. Lovejoy on Plenitude in Aristotle," *Ajatus*, 29 (1967), 5-11.

3. Etienne Gilson, *Being and Some Philosophers*, 2nd. ed. (Toronto: Pontifical Institute of Mediaeval Studies, 1952), pp. 49-50.

4. Discussions of compossibility-incompossibility in Leibniz are widely scattered. For a colligation, see G.H.R. Parkinson, *Logic and Reality in Leibniz's Metaphysics* (Oxford: The Clarendon Press, 1965), p. 104, n. 3.

5. E.g., *Discourse on Metaphysics*, XIII, XXXVI.

6. Bertrand Russell, *A Critical Exposition of the Philosophy of Leibniz* (London: George Allen & Unwin, Ltd., 1937) esp. Chs. I and XV (enunciating Russell's "two Leibnizes" theory). Also Louis Couturat, *La Logique de Leibniz* (Paris, 1901). And Parkinson, *Logic and Reality in Leibniz's Metaphysics*, Ch. IV. Likewise Strawson concerning instantiation under the Identity of Indiscernibles: P. F. Strawson, *Individuals* (Garden City: Doubleday Anchor Books, 1963), pp. 123-124.

7. See Parkinson, *Logic and Reality in Leibniz's Metaphysics*, pp. 105-106.

8. Ibid., pp. 88-89.

9. Thomas S. Kuhn, *The Structure of Scientific Revolutions* (Chicago and London: University of Chicago Press, 1964).

My comments apply to the first edition of *Structure*, in which Kuhn's thesis receives its most forceful expression. It has subsequently been much diluted by Kuhn himself.

10. The most thoroughgoing instance is Stephen Toulmin, *Human Understanding, Vol. I: The Collective Use and Evolution of Concepts* (Princeton: Princeton University Press, 1972).

11. Kuhn, *Structure*, p. 4.

12. Leibniz, *Monadology*, Par. 18.

13. George Santayana, *Scepticism and Animal Faith* (New York: Dover Publications, 1955), p. 278.

14. Instances are colligated in Parkinson, *Logic and Reality in Leibniz's Metaphysics*, p. 105, n. 2.

15. Louis Couturat, ed., *Opuscles et fragments inédits de Leibniz.* I have used Parkinson's translation, *Logic and Reality in Leibniz's Metaphysics*, p. 119.

16. See, e.g., Wilhelm Dilthey, *Pattern and Meaning in History, Thoughts on History and Society*, trans. and ed. H. P. Rickman (New York: Harper Torchbooks, 1962), esp. Ch. 1.

17. R. G. Collingwood, *The Idea of History* (New York: Oxford University Press Galaxy Book, 1956), Part v.

18. John Burnet, *Early Greek Philosophy* (Cleveland and New York: World Publishing Co., Meridan Books, 1957), p. 179.

19. *Metaphysics* 1. 6.

20. Quoted in William Chase Greene, *Moira: Fate, Good, and Evil in Greek Thought* (New York and Evanston: Harper Torchbooks, 1963), p. 70.

21. *Phaedrus* 252.

22. *Symposium* 210-211.

23. *Sophist* 252-260.

24. Santayana, *Scepticism and Animal Faith*, p. 78.

25. The words are André Gide's, but I no longer remember where they are to be found.

26. *Philebus* 30.

27. *Phaedrus* 249.

28. *Republic* 611.

29. *Metaphysics* 3. 4.

30. Extended discussion of this anti-individualistic doctrine of Aristotle's is to be found in Gilson, *Being and Some Philosophers*, pp. 47-51 and *passim*.

31. *Leibniz-Arnauld Correspondence*, trans. H. T. Mason (Manchester: Manchester University Press, 1967), p. 42.

32. See Montgomery Furth, "Monadology," in Harry G. Frankfurt, ed., *Leibniz, A Collection of Critical Essays* (Garden City: Doubleday Anchor Books, 1972), pp. 99-135, esp. Part 4. And Russell, *A Critical Exposition of the Philosophy of Leibniz*, pp. 146-147, p. 155, "The point of view, as we have seen, depends upon confused perception. . . ."

33. *Monadology*, Par. 42; and *Principles of Nature and of Grace, Founded on Reason*, Par. 9. The citation is from the latter.

34. Russell, *Leibniz*, pp. 177-178.

35. *Discourse on Metaphysics*, Par. xxx.

CHAPTER 6

1. Aristotle *Nichomachean Ethics* 1. 9. 1100a.

2. C. G. Jung, "The Stages of Life," in *The Collected Works of C. G. Jung*, ed. Sir Herbert Read, Michael Fordham, and Gerhard Adler (Princeton: Bollingen Series xx, Princeton University Press, 1960), vol. 8, p. 399.

3. C. G. Jung, "The Soul and Death," in *Collected Works*, vol. 8, p. 406.

4. Aristotle *Rhetoric* 2. 14. 1390b.

5. Friedrich Nietzsche, *Thus Spake Zarathustra*, trans. Thomas Common, Part 1, Ch. 21, "Voluntary Death," in *The Philosophy of Nietzsche* (New York: Modern Library, 1954), p. 76.

6. Jung, "Stages," in *Collected Works*, vol. 8, p. 399.

7. Aristotle *Nichomachean Ethics* 1. 9. 1100a.

8. E.g. *Politics* 1. 5. 1254a.

9. Jung, "Soul and Death," *Collected Works*, vol. 8, p. 401.

10. Jean Piaget, *The Moral Judgment of the Child*, trans. Marjorie Gabain (Glencoe: The Free Press, 1932), Ch. IV, "The Two Moralities of the Child, and Types of Social Relations."

11. Ibid., pp. 387-392.

12. I have developed this case in an unpublished manuscript, "Stages of Life: A Contribution to a Concept of Personhood."

13. Henri Bergson, *The Two Sources of Religion and*

Morality, trans. R. A. Audra and Cloudesley Brereton (Garden City: Doubleday Anchor Books, n.d.), p. 1.

14. See, e.g., Maria H. Nagy, "The Child's View of Death," in Herman Feifel, ed., *The Meaning of Death* (New York, London, Sydney, Toronto: McGraw-Hill, 1965), Ch. 6.

15. Erik H. Erikson, *Childhood and Society*, 2nd ed. (New York: W. W. Norton & Co., 1963), p. 251.

16. Aristotle *Rhetoric* 2. 12. 1389c.

17. Ch. 4, pp. 110-112.

18. Erikson, for example. See *Childhood and Society*, p. 263.

19. To the "immortal" adolescent, life is endless. What substitutes for the pressure of time is a native impatience—the correlate of vitality and exuberance—which has yet to be disciplined by the hard demands of an ultimate goal.

20. Aristotle *Rhetoric* 2. 12. 1389a.

21. Erikson, *Childhood and Society*, p. 266.

22. As does José Ortega y Gasset. See "The Sportive Origin of the State," published as Ch. 1 of *History as a System*, trans. Helene Weyl (New York: W. W. Norton & Co., 1961).

23. *The Sociology of Georg Simmel*, trans. & ed. Kurt H. Wolff (Glencoe: The Free Press, 1950), p. 351.

24. Ortega y Gasset, "The Sportive Origin of the State," in *History as a System*, p. 25.

25. Erikson, *Childhood and Society*, p. 262.

26. In conversations, 1963–1964.

27. Max Scheler, *Formalism in Ethics and Non-Formal Ethics of Values*, trans. Manfred S. Frings and Roger L. Funk (Evanston, Ill.: Northwestern University Press, 1973), p. 87.

28. Foremost is the ethics of Immanuel Kant. For Kant on promising, see e.g., *Foundations of the Metaphysics of Morals*, trans. Lewis White Beck (Indianapolis, New York, Kansas City: Bobbs-Merrill Library of Liberal Arts, 1959), pp. 18-19.

29. Friedrich Nietzsche, *Beyond Good and Evil*, trans. Helen Zimmern, in *The Philosophy of Nietzsche* (New York: Random House, 1954), p. 477.

30. *Leibniz, Discourse on Metaphysics*, trans. Peter G. Lucas and Leslie Grint (Manchester University Press, 1961), p. 23.

31. Jean-Paul Sartre, *Being and Nothingness*, trans. Hazel E. Barnes (New York: Philosophical Library, 1956), p. 568.

32. George Santayana, *The Life of Reason*, 5 vols. (New York: Charles Scribner's Sons, 1906), vol. 1, *Reason in Common Sense*, p. 13.

33. Arthur Schopenhauer, "The Ages of Life," in *Essays of Arthur Schopenhauer*, trans. T. Bailey Saunders (New York: A. L. Burt, n.d.), p. 187.

34. Ibid., p. 185.

35. F. H. Bradley, *Ethical Studies* (New York: Liberal Arts Press, 1951), p. 117.

36. Cited in Simone de Beauvoir, *The Coming of Age*, trans. Patrick O'Brian (New York: G. P. Putnam's Sons, 1972), p. 283.

37. Ibid., p. 290.

38. What I mean by sufficient reason as a "philosopher's principle" is explained in Ch. 2, p. 48.

39. Beauvoir, *Age*, p. 492.

40. Ibid., p. 378.

41. Jung, "Soul," in *Collected Works*, vol. 8, p. 411.

42. Aristotle *Rhetoric* 2. 13. 1390a.

43. Cited in Beauvoir, *Age*, p. 364.

44. George Santayana, *The Life of Reason*, one vol. ed. (New York: Charles Scribner's Sons, 1955), p. 258.

45. Plato *Timaeus* 37d.

46. Beauvoir, *Age*, p. 509.

47. The word "assigned" must not be supposed to convey that perspectival meanings are the unilateral product of the individual mind or person. Perspectival meanings are facets of meaning *in the object* that are actualized in correspondence with the perspectives of the persons to whom the objects are related by experience.

48. Max Scheler, *Ressentiment*, trans. William W. Holdheim, ed. Lewis A. Coser (New York: The Free Press of Glencoe, 1961), pp. 62-63.

49. The same is to be said of relativistic and subjectivistic systems. For relativism conceives the norm-generating *relation* to be unitary, while subjectivism either employs a unitary subjective principle such as need or interest (or a unitary hierarchy of such) or else it is devoid of any principle, in which case it is not a normative system.

CHAPTER 7

1. Aristotle *Nichomachean Ethics* 9. 4. 1166a.

2. The fact that eudaimonia is a genus of feeling permits us to describe the quality of integral living in general. Concerning the qualitative individuation of the feeling, see pp. 230-231.

3. See, e.g., Abraham H. Maslow, *Motivation and Personality* (New York: Harper & Row, 1954); *Toward a Psychology of Being* (Princeton and New York: D. Van Nostrand Co., 1962). Also significant are Maslow's articles in *The Journal of Humanistic Psychology*.

4. Especially the British Associationalists, e.g. John Gay, David Hartley, and Abraham Tucker. A useful survey of these origins is Ernest Albee, *A History of English Utilitarianism* (London: Swan Sonnenschein & Co., 1902). Kant is in accord when he defines happiness as "the sum of satisfaction of all inclinations": Immanuel Kant, *Foundations of the Metaphysics of Morals*, trans. Lewis White Beck (Indianapolis, New York, Kansas City: Bobbs-Merrill Library of Liberal Arts, 1959), p. 15.

5. Jeremy Bentham, *The Rationale of Reward* (London: Hunt, 1825), p. 206.

6. John Stuart Mill, *Utilitarianism*, ed. Oskar Piest (Indianapolis, New York: Bobbs-Merrill Library of Liberal Arts, 1957), p. 14.

7. Ibid., p. 12.

8. Ibid., p. 14.

9. Aristotle *Nichomachean Ethics* 5. 1. 1129b.

10. Strictly, dysdaimonia is but one of several terms used by the Greeks for the contrary of eudaimonia. *Kakodaimonia* is fairly common, but rare in Aristotle. The term used most frequently by Aristotle is *athlios*. For its symmetry we shall use dysdaimonia throughout.

11. G. W. Leibniz, *Discourse on Metaphysics*, trans. Peter G. Lucas and Leslie Grint (Manchester University Press, 1961), Part XVI, p. 27.

12. Lucretius, *On Nature*, trans. Russel M. Geer (Indianapolis, New York, Kansas City: Bobbs-Merrill, Library of Liberal Arts, 1965), p. 109.

13. Cited in Hiram Haydn, *The Counter-Renaissance* (New York: Grove Press, 1950), p. 206.

14. See pp. 194-195.

15. F. H. Bradley, *Ethical Studies* (New York: Liberal Arts Press, 1951), p. 117.

16. See pp. 152-153.

17. *Amor meus, pondus meum: illo feror, quocumque feror. Confessions,* XIII, 9, 10.

18. *Symposium* 199-200.

19. T. H. Green, *Prolegomena to Ethics,* ed. A. C. Bradley (New York: Thomas Y. Crowell, 1969), p. 166.

20. Ibid., p. 256.

21. Ibid., p. 166.

22. Ibid., p. 180.

23. Henry Sidgwick, *The Ethics of T. H. Green, Herbert Spencer, and J. Martineau* (London and New York: Macmillan & Co., 1902), p. 49.

24. See *Nichomachean Ethics* 1118b.

25. From *Anecdotes* of Joseph Spence (1699-1768). Quoted in Charles Singer, *A Short History of Scientific Ideas to 1900* (New York and London: Oxford University Press, 1959), p. 288.

26. Because unactualized possibilities are invisible to introspection. It follows that introspection is a mode of retrospection, utilizing materials furnished by prior enactments.

27. Kurt Baier, *The Moral Point of View* (Ithaca, New York: Cornell University Press, 1958), p. 293.

28. Moritz Schlick, *Problems of Ethics,* trans. David Rynin (New York: Prentice-Hall, Inc., 1939), p. 128.

29. Ibid., p. 129.

30. See Schlick's contortions, ibid. I have offered a rebuttal of his attempt to subsume noble suffering under psychological hedonism in my piece entitled " 'Eudaimonia' and the Pain-Displeasure Contingency Argument," *Ethics,* 82, no. 4 (July 1972), 314-320.

31. Abraham H. Maslow, "A Theory of Metamotivation: The Biological Rooting of the Value-Life," *Journal of Humanistic Psychology,* 7, no. 2 (Fall 1967), 97-98.

32. Plato *Laws* 7. 803.

33. Friedrich Nietzsche, *The Genealogy of Morals,* in *Basic*

377

Writings of Nietzsche, trans. and ed. Walter Kaufmann (New York: The Modern Library, 1968), p. 546.

34. Friedrich Nietzsche, *Ecce Homo*, in *Basic Writings*, p. 696.

35. Ibid., p. 708.

36. See, e.g., Bruno Bettelheim, *The Informed Heart* (New York: The Free Press of Glencoe, 1960), and Viktor E. Frankl, *From Death-Camp to Existentialism* (Boston: Beacon Press, 1959).

37. Friedrich Nietzsche, *Ecce Homo*, in *Basic Writings*, pp. 698, 711.

38. Bernard Bosanquet, *The Principle of Individuality and Value* (London: Macmillan & Co., 1927), p. 136.

39. I have used the citations in Jacques Choron, *Death and Modern Man* (New York: The Macmillan Co., Collier Books; 1972), p. 124.

40. See Immanuel Kant, *Critique of Practical Reason*, trans. Lewis White Beck (Chicago: University of Chicago Press, 1949), pp. 225-226.

41. See Josiah Royce, *The World and the Individual* (New York: The Macmillan Co., 1927-1929), vol. 2, 441-442.

42. Friedrich Nietzsche, *Beyond Good and Evil*, in *Basic Writings*, p. 291.

43. Søren Kierkegaard, *Purity of Heart Is To Will One Thing*, trans. Douglas V. Steere (New York: Harper Torchbooks, 1956), p. 124.

44. See Chapter 5, pp. 152-153.

45. "Abe Maslow, 1908-1970," in *Psychology Today*, 4, no. 3 (Aug. 1970), p. 16.

46. Sigmund Freud, *The Ego and the Id*, in James Strachey, gen. ed., *The Standard Edition of the Complete Psycho-Logical Works of Sigmund Freud* (London: Hogarth Press and the Institute of Psycho-Analysis, 1961), XIX, 47.

47. Jean-Paul Sartre, *Being and Nothingness*, trans. Hazel E. Barnes (New York: Philosophical Library, 1956), pp. 536, 543.

CHAPTER 8

1. George Santayana, *Reason in Common Sense* (New York: Charles Scribner's Sons, 1917), p. 149.

2. P. F. Strawson, *Individuals, An Essay in Descriptive Metaphysics* (Garden City: Doubleday Anchor Books, 1963), p. 97.

3. Max Scheler, *The Nature of Sympathy*, trans. Peter Heath (London: Routledge & Kegan Paul, Ltd., 1954), p. 10.

4. Sigmund Freud, "On the Universal Tendency to Degradation in Love," *The Standard Edition of the Complete Psychological Works of Sigmund Freud*, trans. under the general editorship of James Strachey (London: The Institute of Psycho-Analysis and Hogarth Press, Ltd., 1957), XI, 180-190.

5. Strawson, *Individuals*, pp. 97-98.

6. Ibid., p. 94.

7. Ibid., p. 95.

8. Ibid., p. 96.

9. See, e.g., Max Scheler, *Sympathy*, pp. 167-168; Wilhelm Dilthey, *Gesammelte Schriften*, 2nd ed. (Stuttgart & Göttingen: Teubner Verlag, 1957-1960), vol. VII, Part III, 232-238; R. G. Collingwood, *The Idea of History* (New York: Oxford University Press Galaxy Book, 1956), pp. 215-217, amplified throughout Part V.

10. G. W. Leibniz, e.g. *Discourse on Metaphysics*, trans. Peter G. Lucas and Leslie Grint (Manchester University Press, 1961), Part VIII.

11. The phrase appears as a refrain in Kierkegaard's "Two Notes About 'The Individual,'" first note. See Søren Kierkegaard, *The Point of View, Etc.*, trans. Walter Lowrie (London, New York, Toronto: Oxford University Press, 1939), pp. 111-122.

12. In "A Defence of Common Sense." After listing "truisms" of common sense, Moore first asserts that "with certainty" he holds each of them to be true, and then argues that this certitude with respect to these same propositions of common sense characterizes all other minds as well. The subtlety of Moore's position can be missed by supposing him to be arguing that, of a certainty, the truisms of common sense are true. Moore is only stating that he *holds* them to be certainly true, and that everyone else—the perversity of a few philosophers notwithstanding—does likewise. His thesis is directed to the psychology of belief (and is, I think, mistaken). Were Moore claiming that the truisms *are* "quite certainly true," he would be obliged to offer a demonstration, whose very offering would contra-

dict the purported certitude of belief. But he claims only that "*I hold* them [to be] quite certainly true" (emphasis added), and here no demonstration is required, for with respect to the manner in which Moore holds his beliefs, Moore's own testimony is privileged.

13. In cultural anthropology the very term "culture" represents the effort to formalize such patterned variation, as for example in Ruth Benedict's *Patterns of Culture*. In history, the explicit study of such patterned change is the province of "cultural history," foundational instances of which are Jacob Burckhardt's *The Civilization of the Renaissance in Italy*, and Johan Huizinga's *The Waning of the Middle Ages*.

14. See Mircea Eliade, *The Sacred and the Profane* (New York: Harper & Bros., 1961), and Abraham H. Maslow, *Religions, Values, and Peak-Experiences* (Columbus: Ohio State University Press, 1964).

15. Strawson, *Individuals*, p. 102.

16. Ibid., p. 95.

17. Ludwig Wittgenstein, *Philosophical Investigations*, trans. G.E.M. Anscombe (New York: The Macmillan Co., 1953), no. 243 *et seq.*

18. Ibid., no. 244.

19. Norman Malcolm, "Knowledge of Other Minds," in *Wittgenstein: The Philosophical Investigations* (Garden City: Doubleday Anchor Books, 1966), p. 382.

20. Friedrich Waismann, "Verifyability," in Antony Flew, ed., *Logic and Language* (*First and Second Series*) [Garden City: Doubleday Anchor Books, 1965] pp. 128, 129.

21. Ibid., p. 129.

22. Ibid., p. 142.

23. Max Scheler, *Sympathy*, p. 246.

24. José Ortega y Gasset, *On Love, Aspects of a Single Theme*, trans. Toby Talbot (Cleveland and New York: World Publishing Co. Meridian Books, 1957), p. 185.

25. For analyses of other familiar types of illuminations the reader is invited to see my piece, "On Teaching What Students Already Know," *The School Review*, 82, no. 1 (Nov. 1973), pp. 45-56.

26. See Martin Buber, *The Knowledge of Man: Selected Essays*, trans. Maurice Friedman and Ronald Gregor Smith,

ed. Maurice Friedman (New York: Harper & Row, 1965), pp. 72-81.

27. *The Sociology of Georg Simmel*, trans. & ed. Kurt H. Wolff (Glencoe, Illinois: The Free Press, 1950), "Discretion," pp. 320-324.

28. See John Stuart Mill, *A System of Logic*, 8th ed. (London, New York, Toronto: Longmans, Green & Co., 1941), Book VI, Ch. v, "Of Ethology, or the Science of the Formation of Character."

CHAPTER 9

1. Pitirim Sorokin, "Love: Its Aspects, Production, Transformation, and Accumulation," in Sorokin, ed., *Explorations in Altruistic Love and Behavior* (Boston: Beacon Press, 1950), p. 5.

2. Irving Singer, *The Nature of Love, Plato to Luther* (New York: Random House, 1966), p. 91.

3. Morris Ginsberg, "Psychoanalysis and Ethics," in Frederick C. Dommeyer, gen. ed., *In Quest of Value, Readings in Philosophy and Personal Values* (San Francisco: Chandler Publishing Co., 1963), p. 302.

4. Gordon W. Allport, "A Psychological Approach to the Study of Love and Hate," in Sorokin, ed., *Explorations*, p. 150.

5. John Stuart Mill, *Utilitarianism* (Indianapolis and New York: Bobbs-Merrill Library of Liberal Arts, 1957), p. 16.

6. Friedrich Nietzsche, *Ecce Homo*, trans. Walter Kaufmann, in Kaufmann, ed., *On the Genealogy of Morals* and *Ecce Homo* (New York: Random House Vintage Books, 1969), p. 224.

7. R. M. Hare, *Freedom and Reason* (Oxford: Oxford University Press, 1965), p. 107. Or "Suppose one claims to be an exception to some rule, or to be justified in some action, on the ground that he lives in a red house, with purple shutters and a green roof, situated on the corner of Cheshire Street and Kickaboo Lane"—Marcus George Singer, *Generalization in Ethics* (New York: Alfred A. Knopf, 1961), p. 23.

8. P. F. Strawson, *Individuals, An Essay in Descriptive Metaphysics* (Garden City: Doubleday Anchor Books, 1963). The argument appears in Ch. III. The citation is from a summary, p. 256.

9. Thomas Nagel, *The Possibility of Altruism* (Oxford at the Clarendon Press, 1970), esp. p. 103.

10. John Rawls, *A Theory of Justice* (Cambridge, Mass.: Belknap Press of Harvard University Press, 1971), p. 141.

11. C. I. Lewis, *An Analysis of Knowledge and Valuation* (La Salle, Ill.: Open Court Press, 1946); Roderick Firth, "Ethical Absolutism and the Ideal Observer," *Philosophy and Phenomenological Research*, 12 (1952), pp. 317–345; D. W. Haslett, *Moral Rightness* (The Hague: Martinus Nijhoff, 1975).

12. Ibid., pp. 63-64.

13. Hare, *Freedom and Reason*, pp. 139-140.

14. R. M. Hare, "Universalizability," in *Essays on the Moral Concepts* (Berkeley and Los Angeles: University of California Press, 1972), pp. 19-20.

15. P. F. Strawson, "Social Morality and Individual Ideal," *Philosophy*, 36, no. 136 (Jan. 1961), p. 3.

16. Ibid., p. 8.

17. Hare, *Freedom and Reason*, p. 152.

18. Strawson, "Social Morality and Individual Ideal," p. 5.

19. Ibid., p. 9.

20. Ibid., p. 14.

21. Ibid., p. 9.

22. Hare, *Freedom and Reason*, p. 147.

23. Hare, "Universalizability," in *Essays on the Moral Concepts*, p. 19.

24. Hare, *Freedom and Reason*, p. 71. On interests, pp. 157-158.

25. Concerning the term "inclination," Hare argues (against apriorism) that it cannot refer to structures antecedent to behavior, but only to patterns that appear in behavior. "No doubt we have the sort of principles we have because we are the sort of people that we are. The 'because' here is logical; it signifies an entailment in the strictest sense; but it is very important not to be mistaken about the nature of this entailment. It is not that we can deduce statements of the form 'I ought always to, etc.,' from statements describing what sort of person I am. This would be to offend against Hume's Law [that 'ought' cannot be derived from 'is']. It is rather that to have moral principles of a certain kind *is* to be a certain kind of person." Against the charge of a lurking arbitrariness with respect

to the choice of moral principles in this conception, Hare invokes the logic of moral concepts, and the test of consequences. Concerning the latter he says that the choice of a "first-order" moral principle is indeed arbitrary "in the sense that I accept it *libero arbitrio* . . . ; but not in the sense that it does not matter which principle I accept. . . ." No issue arises here, for we agree that moral principles are testable, in part, by the consequences of acting upon them. But it seems to me that Hare himself offends against Hume's Law in his regulative employment of the logic of moral concepts, for the source of this logic is ordinary usage, and by deriving correct usage from this source, is not an actual state of affairs being wielded normatively? For our part normativity is indeed grounded in the nature of the person, but we maintain that this does not offend against Hume's Law because included in this nature is not actuality alone, but also possibility. The possible also *is*, and if Hume's Law is interpreted to preclude necessary (logical) connection of the "ought" and the possible, then it is no law but a fallacy. Psychologically, Hare is entirely correct in contending that the individual cannot *set out* by asking what sort of person he is, and choosing his moral principles accordingly. But this is because mere potentiality is inaccessible to introspection. It has long been recognized by apriorists that self-discovery necessarily occurs, as Ortega y Gasset puts it, "*a posteriori.*" Here lies the need for a period (or periods) of exploration prior to the choice by the individual of the life which shall be his own.

26. Strawson, "Social Morality and Individual Ideal," p. 16.

27. George Santayana, *Reason in Society* (New York: Charles Scribner's Sons, 1905), p. 79.

28. Hare, *Freedom and Reason*, p. 172.

29. Ibid., p. 180.

30. Ibid., p. 176.

31. Max Scheler, *The Nature of Sympathy*, trans. Peter Heath (London: Routledge & Kegan Paul Ltd., 1954), p. 154 and *passim.*

32. Stendhal (Marie-Henri Beyle), *On Love*, trans. H. B. V. under the direction of C. K. Scott-Moncrieff (New York: Liveright Publishing Corp., 1947).

33. Why, then, did Stendhal celebrate "passion love" as love's

highest form, while insisting that it is blind? We must bear in mind that Stendhal is the quintessential artist, prizing the creative imagination, and ever in search of the blank page upon which to write, the empty canvas upon which to paint. The beloved is to him a blank page, inviting the work of creative imagination. Stendhal is quick to insist that while love sees nothing of the beloved, it is deeply revelatory of the lover. Moreover Stendhal is the quintessential aesthete, for whom the actual world is at bottom a poor affair, and actual persons are in themselves ugly twigs. Whatever of beauty is to appear is dependent upon those inventive processes that "crystalization" exemplifies.

34. Singer, *The Nature of Love*, p. 97.

35. *The Essays of Michel de Montaigne*, trans. Charles Cotton, ed. W. Carew Hazlitt (New York: A. L. Burt Co., n.d.), "Of Friendship," p. 188.

36. Plato *Phaedrus* 249d.

37. Ralph Waldo Emerson, "Love," in *Essays, First and Second Series* (Boston and New York: Houghton, Mifflin & Co., 1883), p. 169.

38. Arthur Schopenhauer, "The Metaphysics of the Love of the Sexes," in *The World as Will and Idea*, trans. R. B. Haldane and J. Kemp (New York: Charles Scribner's Sons, 1948), III, p. 339.

39. José Ortega y Gasset, *On Love, Aspects of a Single Theme*, trans. Toby Talbot (Cleveland and New York: World Publishing Co. Meridian Books, 1957), p. 47.

40. Simone de Beauvoir, *The Second Sex*, trans. H. M. Parshley (New York: Modern Library, 1968), p. 658.

41. Jean-Paul Sartre, *Being and Nothingness*, trans. Hazel E. Barnes (New York: Philosophical Library, 1956), Part III, Ch. 3, "Concrete Relations with Others."

42. Martin Buber, *The Knowledge of Man, Selected Essays*, ed. Maurice Friedman, trans. Maurice Friedman and Ronald Gregor Smith (New York: Harper & Row, 1965), p. 81.

43. Ibid., p. 80.

44. Plato *Lysis* 214-215, 221-222.

45. G. W. Leibniz, *Principles of Nature and of Grace, Founded on Reason*, in Robert Latta, ed. and trans., *The*

Monadology and Other Philosophical Writings (Oxford University Press, 1898), p. 416.

46. E.g. Friedrich Nietzsche, *On the Genealogy of Morals*, trans. Walter Kaufmann and R. J. Hollingdale, in Kaufmann, ed., *On the Genealogy of Morals* and *Ecce Homo* (New York: Random House Vintage Books, 1969), esp. Second Essay, no. 11, pp. 73-76. And Max Scheler, *Ressentiment*, ed. Lewis A. Coser, trans. William W. Holdheim (New York: The Free Press of Glencoe, 1961).

47. E. A. Burtt, ed., *The Teachings of the Compassionate Buddha* (New York: Mentor Books, 1955), pp. 49-50.

CHAPTER 10

1. Identified as a defining characteristic of self-actualizing individuals by Abraham Maslow. See his "A Theory of Metamotivation: The Biological Rooting of the Value-Life," *The Journal of Humanistic Psychology*, 7, no. 2 (Fall 1967), 93-125, esp. parts I-VII.

2. E.g., Norman Bowie, *Towards a New Theory of Distributive Justice* (University of Massachusetts Press, 1971), p. 5, "The need for distributive justice arises because men's wants and desires often exceed the means of fulfillment." Or Nicholas Rescher, *Distributive Justice* (New York: Bobbs-Merrill, 1966), p. 107 "In an economy of superabundance, where everyone has all that he needs and wants, the question of justice no longer arises." Or Andreas Esh, "Contractarianism and the Scope of Justice," *Ethics*, 85, no. 1 (Oct. 1974), 40: under "abundance . . . problems of distribution do not arise."

3. Robert Nozick, *Anarchy, State, and Utopia* (New York: Basic Books, 1974), e.g. p. 219.

4. John Rawls, *A Theory of Justice* (Cambridge, Mass.: The Belknap Press of Harvard University, 1971), p. 126.

5. Ibid., p. 11.

6. Ibid., p. 7.

7. Ibid., p. 7.

8. Ibid., p. 141.

9. Ibid., p. 137.

10. Ibid., p. 126.

11. Ibid., pp. 150-151.

12. Ibid., p. 151.

13. J. S. Mill, *On Liberty* (New York: Appleton-Century-Crofts, 1947), p. 65.

14. José Ortega y Gasset, *History as a System*, trans. Helene Weyl (New York: W. W. Norton & Co., 1961), pp. 21-22.

15. Nozick, *Anarchy, State, and Utopia*, pp. 160-174.

16. Ibid., p. 157.

17. Rawls, *Justice*, p. 76.

18. Ibid., p. 302.

19. Ibid., p. 75.

20. Ibid., p. 151.

21. Ibid., p. 127.

22. Ibid., p. 75 and *passim*.

23. Abraham H. Maslow, *Toward a Psychology of Being* (Princeton: D. Van Nostrand, 1962), p. 10.

24. George Santayana, *Realms of Being*, one-vol. ed. (New York: Charles Scribner's Sons, 1942), p. xiv.

25. Nozick, *Anarchy, State, and Utopia*, p. 227.

26. Ibid., p. 226n. Except that I have followed the slightly revised phrasing as it appears in Robert Nozick, "Distributive Justice," *Philosophy and Public Affairs*, 3, no. 1 (Fall 1973), 121n.

Index

Abbagnano, Nicola, 137n, 138n, 142n

Absolute, the (Bradley), 45, 50; normative impotence of, 66

Absolute Idealism, British, 42-63, 124; and eudaimonism, 59-62; and self-realization, 44, 44n; and traditional British individualism, 44, 62

acts, promissory character of, 19, 127, 140, 153, 192-93, 196

actuality: implicit, 129, 150; metaphysical, 128, 132, 137, 140; of personhood, 16

Adkins, A.W.H., 32, 360

adolescence, 197, 272, 292-93, 300, 369; and autonomy, 179-80; and choice, 181; clannishness of, 185-87; and comradeship, 185-87; discontinuous with childhood, 179; internal discovery of, 179-80; as exploration, 20, 180-88, 189, 287; extremism of, 182-84; fervor of, 179, 183-84; fickleness of, 178-79; hopefulness of, 184; "immortality" of, 181; impatience of, 374; insolence of, 183-85; and "migratory soul," 267; misunderstood, 179; moral stage of, 167, 178-88; Sartre's misconception of, 111-14; and shame, 187; solitude of, 187

Aeschylus, 35

Agassi, Joseph, 280n

age, developmental vs. chronological, 212

Albee, Ernest, 376

Allport, Gordon, 275-91

alternative world, and metaphysics, 141

altruism, 14

amor fati, 87

anachronism, fallacy of, 161, 168, 173, 212

analogical inference, 242, 273

Anaximander, 144

Anaximenes, 144

anger, as voluntary (Sartre), 102-103

Antisthenes, 30

Apollonian-Dionysian, 37-40

appearance-reality, in Plato's *Republic*, 27

Aragon, 201

arete (excellence), 16, 31

aristocracy, ancient Greek, 37

Aristophanes, 32

Aristotle, 5, 32-33, 107-108, 129-30, 142n, 145, 150n, 216, 219-20, 275; on adolescence, 178, 184; on childhood, 158, 165; his descriptivism, 38-39; on *dysdaimonia*, 220; elitism, 32; on God, 150-51, 150n; on individuation, 150-51; on justice, 326; nature of personhood in, 37; and Nietzsche, 81; on slavery, 34; on stages of life, 67n, 162-63; on old age, 205

artesans and tradesmen, ancient Greek conception of, 31-32

artist, the (Bosanquet), 57-58

asceticism, 29-30, 213-14, 232

Asheté, Andreas, 316n, 385

athlios, 376

Augustine, 226, 303

autarkia, 35; in slaves, 34; in women, 33

ment, 168, 241; accomplished by retrospection, 160n; in stages of life, 159, 212-14

contradiction, in self (Bradley), 45

Copernicus, 136

Cornford, F. M., 37

Couturat, Louis, 131

culture, personal, 343

daimon, 5, 16, 19, 21, 24; definition of, 14-15; and genius, ix; Greek hierarchy of, 35-36; and identity, 31; as "inner voice" vs. "conscience," 3, 4; as personal truth, 7-8; as principle, 26; Socrates's, 6-8, 359; source of, 24-25; as union of Apollonian-Dionysian, 38

daydreaming (reverie), 257

death, and childhood, 176-77; Hegel on, 101; Heidegger on, 101; and maturation, 188-89, 236-40; and old age, 204-205; Sartre on, 101

defects, birth, 310n, 333n

Democritus, 297

depersonalization, 30-31, 242, 291

deprivation, 314

Descartes, Rene, 65

desire, Green's theory of, 52

despair, Kierkegaard on, 68, 71, 72

destiny, 16, 19

determinisms, Sartre against, 97-107

development, as intelligible change, 128-30

developmental arrest, 136, 136n, 169n

Dewey, John, 143n2, 338

Dilthey, Wilhelm, 139, 249, 270

Diogenes, 219

Dionysian-Apollonian, 37-40

discontinuity, in personal development, 168; between stages of life, 202-203

distraction, 220, 232; temporal, 223-24; spatial, 223

diversity, of human excellences, recognition and appreciation of, 344-48

"divine madness," 39-40, 126

division of labor, 275, 281; founded in love, 352-53; Plato's, 148; principle of, 346-47

Dobzhansky, Theodosius, 25, 27n

Dodds, E. R., 38, 361

"double-mindedness," 29, 194

dreams, 257

duplicity, of human nature, 27-28

dysdaimonia, 191, 312-13, 376; Aristotle's description of, 220; signs of, 221-22

economy, in maturation, 199-200

education, and justice, 324; in meaningful living, 349-52; in varieties of human value, 344, 349-53

egalitarianism, 328, 329

egoism, 291-92, 294, 303-304, 308

Ehrhardt, E., 42

eimarmene, 16

Einstein, Albert, 136

Eliade, Mircea, 257

elitism, 31-32

Emerson, Ralph Waldo, 296

emotions, Sartre's theory of, 101-103

emulation, vs. imitation, 13

endowments, natural, 311, 333-34, 339-40

entitlement: actualization-of-potential-value criterion, 341-42; determinate, 316; differential, 311, 320-21, 328, 333; limited, 333, 333n; natural, 317; performance criterion of, 342-44; and scarcity, 319-20

environmentalism, vs. innatism, 21-22

envy, 10, 327

Epicurus, 299

Library of Congress Cataloging in Publication Data

Norton, David L
  Personal destinies.

  Includes index.
  1. Self-realization.   2. Social ethics.
I.   Title.
BJ1470.N68   170'.202   76-3011
ISBN 0-691-07215-9
ISBN 0-691-01975-4 (pbk.)